IMAGES THAT INJURE

IMAGES THAT INJURE

Pictorial Stereotypes in the Media

Third Edition

**Susan Dente Ross and
Paul Martin Lester, Editors**

AN IMPRINT OF ABC-CLIO, LLC
Santa Barbara, California • Denver, Colorado • Oxford, England

Library of Congress Cataloging-in-Publication Data

Images that injure : pictorial stereotypes in the media / Susan Dente
Ross and Paul Martin Lester, editors.—3rd ed.
    p. cm.
  Includes bibliographical references and index.
  ISBN 978-0-313-37892-8 (alk. paper) — ISBN 978-0-313-37893-5
(ebook) 1. Stereotypes (Social psychology) in mass media. I. Ross,
Susan Dente. II. Lester, Paul Martin.
  P96.S74I45   2011
  303.3'85—dc22   2010050951

ISBN: 978-0-313-37892-8
EISBN: 978-0-313-37893-5

15   14   13   12   3   4   5

This book is also available on the World Wide Web as an eBook.
Visit www.abc-clio.com for details.

Praeger
An Imprint of ABC-CLIO, LLC

ABC-CLIO, LLC
130 Cremona Drive, P.O. Box 1911
Santa Barbara, California 93116-1911

This book is printed on acid-free paper ∞

Manufactured in the United States of America

Contents

Preface

Everette E. Dennis

When Walter Lippmann transformed a common printing term—"stereotype"—into a concept now better known in its social and psychological form, he understood that those "pictures in our head" can simplify, distort, and even do injury to meaning (1922, 25). On the one hand, stereotypes are rather negatively defined as "a conventional, formulaic and oversimplified conception, opinion, or image" (American Heritage 2000), while on the other they communicate dramatically and without much subtlety or nuance. For visual communicators—whether they are web designers, photographers, videographers, filmmakers, graphic artists, or cartoonists—stereotypes are useful devices because they are easily understood and make a clear, if unfair, and, at times, even hurtful point. For cartoonists, such depiction is central to their job description, but for communicators charged with an accurate representation of news and information, entertainment, or advertising, they can be damaging and dangerous.

Visual messages can play a profound role in the construction of social memory, as a still photograph of the flag raising at Iwo Jima during World War II, the anguished cry of a young woman over the body of a slain student at Kent State University, video capturing the collapse of the World Trade Center towers, or a slur conveyed repetitively and forever on YouTube all attest. Some images that were once fresh and imaginative can become, when overused, hackneyed material that is eventually parodied because it is so predictable. Of far greater consequence, however, are what Paul Martin Lester, Susan Dente Ross, and the able contributors to this volume call "images that injure" in the form of pictorial and verbal stereotypes in the communication media. They grapple with various forms of prejudice or images that prejudge without reference to facts and reality.

These images are both dynamic and ephemeral, especially those involving individuals, groups, organizations, and institutions subject to negative portrayals. They differ from decade to decade. What is acceptable to a majority at one time—say, the disparagement of the Irish in America in the nineteenth century—gives way to other overt public prejudices against Jews, African Americans, gays and lesbians, immigrants, and others later on. Sometimes images that injure are projected with social approbation and apparent acceptance but are subsequently decried for their cruelty and prejudice. Thus the dismissive and insulting depictions of African Americans over the generations get a jolt in the face of the civil rights movement or the election of Barack Obama as the first African-American president in 2008. The dynamism of images that injure is underscored in the digital era when websites, social networks, and search technologies with all their evident benefits are also repositories of hatred, contempt, and ridicule played out with great redundancy.

Along the way, this gathering of gifted scholars, commentators, and analysts examines racial and ethnic stereotypes as well as those involving gender, age, physical disabilities, sexual preference, and other characteristics. They assess head-on the most overt and blatant representations as well as those that are subtler and, in some cases, even unintended. Always there is concern for the impact of an image on its collective audience in a social sense and on individuals as well. As it takes a serious look at the impact and consequences of these hurtful images, the book cuts new ground both in a theoretical sense and in offering a variety of measures—both quantitative and qualitative.

More than most books that critically examine the media, this one is open to different modes of analysis and thus of different ways of knowing. This has value for the scholarly literature as well as for individual readers of varying backgrounds and especially for students of media and media institutions. There is also much of value here for the professional communicator. At a time of sometimes reflective and politically correct assessment, most of these studies are anything but predictable and push the reader toward his or her own analysis and opinion. Always there is the question of what to do with such intelligence—whether to act on it and thus constrain ultimate freedom or to use it to engender understanding and tolerance. All that is a matter of judgment and taste, and the editors of this volume leave much of that to individual cogitation. Thus, this book connects richness of context and theoretical understanding with a focus on the visual cues and explications that foster ageism, racism, sexism, ethnocentrisms, homophobia, and a host of other distinct targets of concern. Those who strive to overcome these blots on the national consciousness can go only so far with written language without confronting visual evidence of prejudice. Awareness, acknowledgment, understanding, and the wherewithal to change are all enhanced by this book.

In a nation that prides itself on tolerance and equality, claiming both, these studies are a sobering account of how far we are from that illusive goal. Still, to the extent that the ideas offered here are followed by thoughtful action, we might just see a diminution of images that injure and thus give this work lasting and important impact.

Sources

Lippmann, Walter. 1922. *Public opinion.* New York: Harcourt Brace.
Stereotype. 2000. S.v. in *The American heritage dictionary of the English language,* 4th ed. New York: Houghton Mifflin.

Introduction

Susan Dente Ross

The term "convergence" has lost its cachet (and also a great deal of its accuracy) to capture the state of contemporary media, the fast and furious mergers, emergences, and acquisitions that characterized the transformation of media and computing as the twentieth century gave way to the twenty-first. Today, talk is of the death of newspapers, the supremacy of social network tools, and the ubiquity of cell phones. Yet these media and more are marked by a high degree of shared corporate ownership, shared professional norms and practices, shared content, and shared objectives. Although controlled competition or focus on the short-term bottom line spells financial danger for some traditional media, many media continue to flourish by focusing on delivering consumers to producers. The media remain a vital cog in the capitalist machine in the United States and around the world.

While it is true that websites such as Facebook and YouTube provide new opportunities for independent individuals to disseminate their personal images (for good or ill), each day these and other sites also offer viewers a recap of highlights of the previous day's top TV shows, trailers for the newest films, snippets of the gaffs that used to land on the cutting room floor, and overdubbed pontification by the talking heads of the week. To some degree, then, rather than expand the marketplace of ideas or the diversity of voices vying in the public sphere, media continue disproportionately to reproduce, redistribute, and magnify the powerful messages and images from the very few who control the purse strings of the major media conglomerates.

The euphoric promises of diverse content, resistance to stereotyping and profiling, expansion of access and participation, and engagement of a broader range of individuals and ideologies in and through the media have failed to materialize. While scholars, economists, and politicians continue to argue over whether the minutiae of regulations advance or impede free and independent and pluralistic media, massive media oligopolies continue to dominate public communications around the globe. Whether we speak of the content of news or advertising or public relations or political communications, study after study suggests a general conformity of content to mainstream views and perspectives. Most media tow the ideological line of the powers that be.

A major influence in research that linked the social sciences with technological concerns, Ithiel de Sola Pool wrote early and often about the multiple and conflicting effects of mass media in a democratic society, and his assessments were not sanguine (see, e.g., Pool 1983, 1990). Unlike so many others, he did not glibly believe in the corporate drive to serve the public interest, nor did he accept the oft-parroted notion that government regulation smoothes and rationalizes the marketplace. De Sola Pool was pessimistic about the influence of corporate greed (rent seeking) and government errors that imposed unwieldy and illogical obstacles to innovation, creativity, access, participation, and expansion. Yet he also believed in the power and drive of individuals to resist, to overcome these obstacles, to reclaim their place in the network of communications that drives society, and to communicate in ways that transcend both capitalist objectives and government prerogatives (1983, 226–51).

In the eloquent preface that precedes this comment, Everette E. Dennis notes that the signs and symbols, the photographs and drawings, the tabloids and posters, the stories and fables, and the films and web pages and cartoons that surround us every day "are both dynamic and ephemeral," always "open to different modes of analysis and thus of different ways of knowing." Yet, he cautions, despite their fluidity of meaning, and despite our personal and collective ability to "know" images differently, media images too often are stereotypical . . . because stereotypes are useful:

> For visual communicators—whether they are web designers, photographers, videographers, filmmakers, graphic artists, or cartoonists—stereotypes are useful devices because they are easily understood and make a clear, if unfair, and, at times, even hurtful point.

Stereotypes offer a blunt, effective tool for communicating—and, as with most blunt tools, their impact is most often overbroad and harmful.

This third edition of *Images That Injure* is written in the spirit of resistance to such harm; it is at once a work of careful observation, profound criticism, and social activism. By this, we do not mean to suggest that the volume as a whole or its individual contributors offers a rallying call; they do not. Rather, the contribution of this volume to the resistance of hegemony, stereotypes, and mind-numbing oversimplifications is to provide a richly informed point of departure for each and all of us to critically engage with the media images that surround us, flood our brains, and, sometimes, swamp and drown our independent thinking and original solutions.

In the following pages, you will find dynamic explorations of the intersections among images and history, memory, identity, marking, the discourse of Orientalism, and representations of race, religion, sexuality, age, social groups, the body, and gender. A quick review of the book will indicate that we have organized it loosely by *type* of images discussed. This structure was useful in allowing us to gather together various studies, perspectives, and commentaries on broader categories of social construction and resistance, such as gender and sexuality, race and ethnicity, religion, and nationality. At the start of each of these sections, you will find a brief introductory commentary by one of the editors. These comments are designed to facilitate linkages among the distinct chapters in the section, to highlight profound and important differences among them, and to draw your attention forward or back to other sections of the book where complementary essays can be found. Like the first section of the book, these commentaries also serve to outline the varied theoretical and methodological approaches employed by our authors.

In the end, this work offers a survey of a wide array of images. The following pages will present analyses of pictures found daily in most media forms and in most image genres. This volume presents discussions about the metaphorical illustrations that arise from vivid language and deeply acculturated narratives; the seeming verisimilitude of images presented through photography, film, video, television, and the web; the exaggerated, humorous, fantastic, and/or fantasy images of comic books, cartoons, and fairy tales; the power of fine art imagery; and the pictures conveyed through songs and accompanying graphics.

As a whole, the chapters also provide an array of theoretical foundations to permit the reader to employ a variety of methods and theories to deconstruct and understand the mediated images that engulf us. Within the arena of media criticism, fields as diverse as economics and sociology, law and political science, history and critical intercultural studies, art, aesthetics, ethics, cognitive sciences, design, rhetoric, persuasion, and more apply their scrutiny and develop their theories and conclusions. Some perceive these fields to be in conflict or prefer to attend to the several frictions that exist, for example, between narrative and social movements theories. Instead, we bring them together for you. From disparate theoretical points of view and in unique and varied ways, each author considers the ramifications of the use of particular images to persuade, to sell, to present "facts," to entertain, or to share tidbits interpersonally or among groups of friends.

The broad range of disciplines represented by our authors is intentional. We hope you will find that the diversity of images analyzed and the range of approaches adopted by the authors provide you with rich grounding upon which to develop your own style and strategy of media criticism. And we hope that this grounding will provide a springboard for your personal activism to resist and replace images that injure with images that heal.

Sources

Pool, Ithiel de Sola. 1983. *Technologies of freedom*. Cambridge, MA: Harvard University Press.
Pool, Ithiel de Sola. 1990. *Technologies without boundaries: On telecommunication in a global age*. Cambridge, MA: Harvard University Press.

PART I

Marking and Demarking: Images, Narratives, and Identities

Susan Dente Ross

Enter almost any conversation on media and society, global politics, the impediments to effective intercultural communication, or the social effects of increasingly mobile but electronically connected communities, and you quickly come face-to-face with the power and utility of images to inscribe concepts into the minds of readers and viewers. The notion of images embedding themselves almost automatically in the human mind and imagination was made commonplace in the 1960s when Marshall McLuhan (1964) penned his notorious aphorism that "the medium is the message" (or the "massage," depending upon the version you find more credible). Today, his discussion of cold (print) and hot (electronic) media seems dated and, well, rather simplistic, but the idea that images communicate more directly and forcefully than the printed word has been integrated into numerous theories and methods for analyzing and criticizing both the media and the media makers.

In the following part, a quintet of talented authors discusses the power of images, whether those images are presented graphically or through verbal descriptions, and how images shape the way we "see" and come to understand both our internal and our external realities. The following five chapters explore the significant ways that the abundant and highly varied images in which we swim each day commingle in our heads with our own often acute visual memories to help us construct what we call "reality." Many of these authors also discuss the responsibility associated with the power of images transmitted through the media to people around the globe.

As Everette Dennis noted in the preface, images are durable yet their meaning is fluid; they are subject to multiple interpretations, but they offer a shorthand to telegraph blunt, and often stereotypical, messages. As a consequence, images require producers and receivers alike to "grapple with various forms of prejudice" that can be transmitted so readily and powerfully. To open this part, both Deni Elliott and Willard Enteman provide rich resources to assist us—whether as working journalists, scholars who analyze the media, or citizens whose lives and understandings are shaped and molded by the media—in struggling with the images media disseminate far and wide.

Elliott focuses primarily on the responsibility of media makers, first and foremost, to do no unnecessary harm. Elliott ties the power of images to the nature of their production as well as to their transmission: to the techniques of image making, the choices of what is captured and what is excluded, the pathos of a moment cropped out of its context and frozen forever, the seeming truth and transparency of 9/11 victims jumping to their deaths, and the speed and potency with which a single image travels around the globe to be (mis)understood by so many people in such varied settings. Her chapter cogently reasons that those who create and distribute images that reasonably can be predicted to cause harm are responsible for the consequences of those images. Ethically speaking, the power to harm comes with the concomitant responsibility for the consequences of the acts arising from that power. In her conclusion, Elliott offers a four-point systematic ethical analysis that can be used by both creators and viewers of pictures to evaluate whether an image's harm can be justified.

Willard Enteman's point of departure is less the power and freedom of journalists to distribute the images and narratives of their own choosing and more the capitalist tethers that bind media producers and lead to the production of a partial and harmful media image of our world. In his discussion of the dual and often conflicting masters of journalism—the drive to maximize profits and the mission to communicate truth—Enteman suggests that the two should be reconciled through professional standards for journalists that place priority on public service over profit. He argues that professional licensing and review procedures in journalism can establish the moral and intellectual standards needed to encourage photojournalists to produce images that are free of stereotypes and stigma.

In the next two chapters in this part, Rick Busselle, Helena Bilandzic, Erin Steuter, and Deborah Wills shift the focus somewhat to examine the receivers of media messages and images. Busselle and Bilandzic explore audience members as active consumers of stories and therefore partners in the creation of meaning. To comprehend events and issues encountered through the media and to construct a broader network of meaning, audience members establish relationships among images, news narratives, and other bits and pieces of information. Media consumers build and borrow narratives both from single news reports and from multiple news and entertainment accounts received from different sources over different platforms and through time. Images play a central role in the mental processes involved in constructing a network of meaning. Images are key components of the narratives that drive "stories." They (re)present content in their own right independent of other information. They emphasize particular elements and so frame the stories they accompany. Images become iconic, holding entrenched meaning that can be transferred efficiently from one issue or event to another.

Steuter and Wills explore the role of images as metaphors (and metaphors as images) that "mark" groups and delineate those who belong from those who do not. Images of the racial, cultural, social, or political "other" as animals, insects, diseases, or subhuman or inhuman monsters perpetuate in-group/out-group boundaries and systematically stereotype and dehumanize those outside the mainstream. Dehumanizing media images and the verbal metaphors with which they are interwoven have grave and concrete real-world consequences, particularly because they become especially frequent and virulent in times of crisis, often dominating public discourse. The authors argue that the coherent body of these dehumanizing media images shapes a "reality" that invites prejudice, discrimination, random acts of violence, and genocide. Most saliently, they naturalize unthinkable acts, such as the torture of prisoners at Guantánamo Bay and Abu Ghraib by U.S. forces.

While each of the authors in this part offers insights and strategies for reducing or disrupting the injuries of violent or dehumanizing images, J. B. Colson's study of Dorothea Lange's photograph entitled *Migrant Mother* uncovers the varied uses of and responses to a single photograph to highlight the potential of one image that can both harm and heal. Colson suggests that good intentions, good images, and good understanding of our subjects are insufficient to assure that our images will heal. For the Lange photograph, good intentions go wrong—social documentary intended to improve the lives of the poor distanced them from the mainstream and distorted one woman's reality. To craft images that heal, those who produce images must recognize the different contexts in which these images will be consumed and must work rigorously to minimize the personal and social costs of objectifying another human being. To bolster his argument, Colson includes his own diagram that outlines the intentions of those who produce and those who consume images and shows how each constituency affects the message of the medium.

Sources

McLuhan, Marshall. 1964. *Understanding the media: The extensions of man.* New York: McGraw-Hill.

Chapter 1

Ethical Responsibilities and the Power of Pictures

Deni Elliott

Pictures are powerful. Strong images sell, both in print and in bringing eyeballs to advertisers on websites.

Pictures are almost always legal to make and publish, especially if they are photos taken in public, willingly distributed on the web, or originally created for product promotion.

Pictures often appeal to emotion or to our ideals of good composition. They are aesthetically pleasing.

But, none of these facts, nor all of them together, provides sufficiently good reason for publication if the picture can reasonably be predicted to cause harm.

This chapter is about ethics. Specifically, I describe the ethical responsibilities that follow when someone (or someone's news organization, advertising agency, public relations firm, or website) has the power to disseminate images to a general audience. Publishing images that injure is an ethically questionable act. Sometimes ethically questionable acts can be justified. Other times, they cannot. Publishing images that injure requires good ethical justification for the harms caused. Economic, legal, or aesthetic justifications will not suffice; personal ethical accountability is necessary.

While I argue elsewhere that correctly made ethical judgments apply universally and are not based simply on some individual's personal opinion or some culture's convention,[1] here the crucial ethical feature to be grappled with is the inequality of power between the person or organization publishing an image and the person or people who are potentially harmed by the publication. When someone has the power to harm another, that person has the accompanying responsibility to make sure that any harm caused is ethically justified.

Media and Power

Media institutions are powerful. According to a compilation from various credible websites (which are themselves examples of powerful media), children between the ages of 2 and 17 watch an average of 25 hours of television each week; adults are estimated to spend half of their leisure time watching television or consuming other media; more than 52 million copies of the more than 1,400 daily newspapers in the United States are sold each day; more than 25 billion books are sold each year; 86 percent of U.S. homes have cable TV, and 61.8 percent of them have computers (Infoplease.com 2007). The United States has the highest internet penetration rate in the world, with more than 72 percent of the population estimated to be users (World Bank 2009).

Our own awareness of the narrowness of any one person's experience tells us that only a small portion of what we believe that we know about the world is based on first-person sensory experience. Media provide vicarious experience for us. They provide sensory experience of events. They virtually connect us and provide access to a world of issues and differing opinions outside our personal sphere. Subtly, or explicitly, media presentations, both targeted and general, shape our perceptions of reality. How "evil" an influence this mediated reality might be is a point of contention among scholars (Starker 1989). But it is a given that media messages play a part in teaching us which lifestyles to value and what counts as appropriate behavior according to dominant society. This is true whether the literal media product is information, persuasion, personal opinion, or entertainment. From the choice of who or what counts as "newsworthy" to the decision about which body images are used to promote sales to the construction of contexts for situation comedies, media managers promote certain lifestyles and make it difficult for members of the audience to value others.

Media practitioners are responsible for the impact of their work, even if there is no intention on the part of the practitioner or on the part of the industry to cause harm. Individuals in the audience are necessarily vulnerable to the impact of the media in all of its social functions (Kovach and Rosensteil 2001).

The rapid and expanding involvement of individuals who are not affiliated with traditional media in the production of media content has not made individuals less vulnerable to the power of corporate messages. Instead, it has expanded the set of people who have power and who have special responsibilities that attach to having power over others. Bloggers, citizen-journalists, YouTube contributors, and others who provide messages to a mass audience have responsibilities that follow from those voluntary roles.

Role-Related Responsibilities and Basic Ethical Requirements

While ethics encompasses being the best people that we can be, the most basic minimal ethical requirement is stated in a negative way: Do not cause unjustified harm. Coupled with that requirement throughout the history of ethics is a second requirement: Do your duty. People have an ethical responsibility to do what others reasonably expect them to do. All legitimate adult roles in society have role-related responsibilities. If you can identify a role, such as college student, professor, parent, or journalist, you can also articulate the unique societal function that accompanies each role. Among mass communication practitioners, journalists have the job of gathering and providing information to citizens that is needed for self-governance; public relations practitioners have the job of promoting their client's message to identified constituencies; advertisers have the job of stimulating consumption from identified audiences; and entertainment media amuse us and disseminate culture. Practitioners should do their jobs, but, ethically speaking, they must also do their jobs without causing unjustified harm.

As an easy example, consider the parent's job of promoting the wellbeing of her children. She should do that to the best of her ability. But if her son needs a liver transplant, it is unjustified to intentionally have another child killed to supply her son with the needed organ. The fundamental ethical requirement—do not cause unjustified harm—defines an acceptable scope within which an individual can express her role-related responsibilities.

It is not surprising that these minimal ethical requirements to do your duty and not cause unjustified harm reflect basic human intuition. We are hardwired to understand ethics. Every competent rational adult human being wants to avoid being killed, caused pain, disabled, or deprived of freedom or pleasure unless there is some good reason for it.[2] All competent rational adult human beings also want this for the people they love. What's more, every competent rational adult human being knows that all other human beings have the same desire for how they and their loved ones should be treated. This human axiom—the understanding that all people want to avoid being caused these types of harms—is the foundation for both ethical and unethical behavior. As people assume that others want to avoid harms, they know how to avoid causing harm and they know how to intentionally cause harm as well. As an extreme example, terrorism and torture work only because the perpetrators know, without a doubt, how to inflict harm or the fear of harm on others. People are capable of calculated unethical behavior like this because of the universal understanding of what constitutes harm and the recognition that all of us want to avoid it for ourselves and those we love. Ultimately, what is irrational to want for oneself (e.g., being caused harm without good reason) is unethical to cause to others.

Most writing in historical and contemporary ethics takes the reader well beyond this minimal maxim to an examination of how humans should also promote good. Avoiding unethical activity is not enough to create a thriving relationship, family, or community. But most urgently, moral analysis starts with the recognition that someone has been harmed or that it is reasonable to predict that someone might be harmed. Sometimes harms happen with no one being at fault. If I trip over a tree branch while walking in the forest, I may suffer a broken leg, but it doesn't follow that another person is the cause of my harm. But suffering harm because of the publication of text or images is conceptually different from suffering an accidental harm. Someone has made choices regarding the publication. Whether those choices are made intentionally or only with awareness that the publication might cause harm, that person has committed an ethically questionable act. If the harm is caused through a neglect of duty, it is morally questionable even if the person did not know that harm could result.

Once harm or potential harm is established, the important questions focus on blameworthiness. Did someone do something that caused harm? Does that person have moral culpability for that harm? Is there anything that mitigates, explains, or justifies the harm caused? The questions of agency, culpability, and justification must be answered to determine whether an ethically questionable act, like publishing an image that injures, is ethically permitted or prohibited. For the purposes of this chapter, I am using "injure" (as in *Images That Injure*) as synonymous with the term "harm." Harm, as the word is used in a philosophically technical sense, includes both harms that are caused directly and those caused indirectly. Direct harms include being killed, being caused pain, being disabled, or being deprived of pleasure or opportunity. Indirect harms are those that can happen without the injured person even being aware that he or she was treated badly. Indirect harms are also those that cause injury of some sort to the community or to a group larger than a single individual. Indirect harms include promise breaking, cheating, deception, disobeying laws, and neglecting one's duty (Gert 2008).

Some philosophers have argued that causing offense is different from causing harm. Indeed, nineteenth-century philosopher John Stuart Mill would argue that it is important that we expose ourselves to ideas that we find offensive so that we can better know the truth. However, he also counsels that if a message that some people will find offensive needs to be presented, the message giver has an ethical (but not legal) responsibility to present that message in as civil and nonoffensive a way as possible (Mill 1991). The key element is in deciding what messages "need" to be presented. Those that need to be presented are those that fit most directly with the message giver's role-related responsibilities. And those messages should be presented in a way that is less likely to cause unjustified harm.

Indirect harms are often more difficult to identify than direct harms, but they are important when one considers the power of pictures. For example, if a news photo is altered to lead the viewer to believe falsely that a presidential candidate and a known activist were shoulder-to-shoulder at an antiwar rally, the viewers who see and believe the picture are harmed, even if they don't know they have been deceived. They are caused harm by forming opinions about the candidate based on false information. Deception causes direct harm to the reputation of the candidate and to the viewers by depriving them of the opportunity to grapple with truthful information and come to decisions about candidates based on accurate understandings. They are harmed in this way even if the truth is never known. However, if the truth does comes out, the previously deceived viewers suffer yet another indirect harm because they are likely to become less trusting of the authenticity of news photos and are likely to question useful, truthful depictions in the future. The media that distributed the deceptive picture are harmed directly by a loss of viewer credibility. News publications rely on viewers' belief in the accuracy of their text and pictures.

At a broader social level, the whole community has been indirectly harmed by the decrease in trust. Communities and relationships among people work only to the degree that trust is present. Deception is successful only because people expect the truth. Every act of deception always creates, at a minimum, an indirect harm by decreasing the collective trust upon which relationships and community are built. And this indirect harm occurs even if the only person who knows about the deception is the deceiver herself.

Images that injure can cause harm in both direct and indirect ways. For example, the images of women often found in advertisements cause harm to viewers. The subtle computer manipulation that elongates models' legs and narrows their hips to unattainable proportions causes viewers pain and cheats them as well. Young women who experience emotional pain based on the realization that they will never look like that idealized image are directly harmed. The presentations also cause indirect harm in that the idealized presentations suggest to the community as a whole that real women with proportional bodies do not match ideal standards but, rather, need enhancement. Images that create expectations that women cannot reasonably meet cause harm to relationships throughout society.

Ethical Questions Cannot Be Answered by Economics, Law, or Aesthetics

Scrutinizing injury within the scope of moral consideration is different from examining that injury from the perspective of economic, legal, or aesthetic concerns. Economics is important to the running of a media business, whether the focus of that business is entertainment, persuasion, or news. Mass communication industries, like other endeavors, require an economically stable base from which to operate, but the need for economic stability does not excuse unethical behavior. Physicians in private practice, for example, are financially dependent upon their patients, but we would not excuse a doctor's unethical activity by her need to make money. Doctors who take kickbacks from labs and specialists in exchange for patient referrals are quite rightly accused of having a conflict of interest. It is ethically wrong for a doctor to impose her own personal beliefs on what an adult patient should do. If a doctor believes that a patient will benefit from cosmetic surgery, it is not legitimate for the doctor to act without the patient's permission. The doctor's aesthetic choice is not justification for interfering with the patient's ability to withhold consent.

In this example, it is easy to see that a doctor's role-related responsibility is to her patient. Her recommendations for patient care should be made based on the clinical needs of the patient rather than on the opportunity for the doctor to receive additional income or because her choices reflect her own personal interest. In a similar way, corporations, including media organizations, have a role-related responsibility to provide the service they have promised to provide, but it doesn't follow that any means to that end is acceptable. The responsibility of all mass media image creators and managers is to recognize their power in creating viewer perception and to use that power judiciously by

1. presenting images accurately or clearly labeled as fiction, parody, or photo illustration; and
2. being responsible for the symbolic as well as the literal meaning of images.

Fulfilling that responsibility plays a fundamental role in explaining or justifying the publication of particular images. An image is more easily justifiable when its presentation relates directly to the media's role-related responsibility. It is more difficult to justify an injurious image when this direct connection does not exist. For example, news photos that cause audience members, the subjects, and the families of subjects harm but that relate directly to information that citizens need to know for self-governance, like pictures of dead and wounded soldiers in a war fought on our behalf, are strongly justified. Feature photos that show people in public in accidentally compromising positions are less easily justified. Whether a picture works in a marketing sense is ethically irrelevant.

If economic considerations do not justify the distribution of unethical images, neither are harmful images justified by an appeal to law. The law allows the publication of almost all texts and pictures. However, the fact that almost any image *may* be published does not suggest or determine that all such images *should* be published. Law sets the minimum expectation for how people should act; ethics sets the bar higher by examining potential harm to individuals rather than conformity with legal expectations. An everyday example is that people generally avoid lying to others, although very few instances of lying are against the law. Whether or not to publish harmful photos is rarely a question of law. For example, while it was legal to publish the pictures of people who were killed in the attacks of September 11, 2001, most news organizations refrained from showing identifiable corpses. They found insufficient justification to offset the harm caused to those viewing the pictures and the families of the deceased.

Aesthetics is often at the core of arguments to publish pictures that are ethically questionable. If a photo lacks aesthetic appeal, few will argue for its publication. In almost all cases, images likely to be published are

In this powerful news photograph, a man with a protective scarf walks along a street filled with ash and papers after terrorist attacks caused the Twin Towers of the World Trade Center in lower Manhattan to collapse on September 11, 2001. (Courtesy of the Library of Congress.)

compelling in an inviting or a disturbing way. However, the fact that an image is a "helluva picture" doesn't provide justification for publishing a picture that will cause someone to suffer harm. It is not likely that a picture will be published unless it is visually compelling. However, reasoning why it is acceptable to cause harm to a viewer or subject evokes a different set of considerations than viewer attraction.

Justification for Publishing Images That Injure

Justification is the process by which an ethically questionable act is determined to be ethically permissible. Sometimes the justification is weak; sometimes it is strong. Other times, publishing images that injure is not ethically justified. For example, publishing a freeze-frame from a security video in a newspaper or website when law enforcement is attempting to apprehend criminal suspects is strongly justified, even though it certainly causes harm to the suspects. If the suspects are members of a minority group that has been disproportionately presented as criminals, the publication may cause indirect harm by adding to stereotypical views. But the need to protect the community by apprehending the suspects makes the publication strongly justified. Some philosophers would argue that giving criminals their due by apprehending them and providing legal consequences for their action actually respects the criminals and their choices. Assuming that the law is being applied fairly and impartially, the criminals are being treated as competent, rational adults who knowingly and voluntarily chose to act in a nonpermitted way.

But now imagine the same news staff putting together a multipage photo essay as part of a year-end wrap-up. If the overwhelming number of pictures of African-American men that appear in that photo essay are those suspected or convicted of crimes, publishing the photos is not ethically justified. Historically, African-American men have been overrepresented in negative media depictions and Anglo-American men have been overrepresented in positive media coverage. The news staff cannot justify the harm caused by perpetuating the stereotype even if the photo essay accurately represents what appeared in news photos throughout the year. Indeed, if the news staff becomes aware that they are primarily publishing stereotypical photos of a particular racial group or gender, that should indicate to them that they need to be more conscious of the pictures they are selecting for inclusion in the paper throughout the year. Subtle racism and sexism can be found in the pattern of image choice in many news organizations.

Publishing news photos or illustrations in which race is important or evident is justified by the connection of the artwork to the news organization's responsibility to tell citizens information that is important for self-governance. The more direct that connection, the stronger the justification. However, the fact that there is a strong connection between the communicator's social function and the injurious image does not necessarily justify the act. If there are ways of fulfilling one's social function without including images that injure, that is always the better choice. To return to the presentation of photographs from the attacks on 9/11, the horror of that story could be told without close-up identifiable photos of those who jumped to their deaths from the upper floors of the World Trade Center buildings. To their credit, most news organizations avoided that choice.

Outside of news photography, the scale of presentation of racial minorities or people with disabilities as compared to the presentation of those from dominant society need not be demographically balanced. In fact, given that individuals who do not fit within the image norms of dominant society historically have been ignored, the tendency in more recent years has been to overrepresent such individuals in feature and public relations imagery. This ethically permissible approach to inclusion in positive visual depictions has been an implicit, but forceful, way of reminding the community of its diversity.

Systematic Ethical Analysis for Images That Injure

The following is a series of steps that may be used by individuals or media organizations to determine whether specific instances of images that injure are justified.

1. Identify the injury. Describe the different individuals and groups being hurt by the image directly or indirectly.
2. Ask whether it is reasonable to hold the image maker or distributor ethically blameworthy for the injury. Remember that infliction of injury does not have to be intentional. Those who publish are responsible to use their power judiciously. Not intending to cause harm does not decrease the publisher's ethical responsibility. The crucial ethical question is if it is reasonable to predict that the audience, subjects, or other vulnerable people will be directly or indirectly harmed by the image. What is the evidence for this prediction?
3. Describe the social function of the media and how this particular image connects to the duty of the image makers to do their jobs. The more tenuous and indirect the connection between the role-related responsibilities and the image, the less justified the image. If the role-related responsibility can be met without the use of an injurious image, or by using an injurious image in a less provocative way, publication is also less justified. Another way to examine the level of justification is to ask why people need to see this image.
4. To complete the analysis, consider how you would explain to everyone—subject, audience, your grandmother, children, and any other people affected by the image—why the publication is strongly, weakly, or not ethically justified. Provide alternatives if possible.

The easiest way to avoid taking responsibility for causing harm to others is to ignore one's accountability for the consequences of one's actions. Recognizing the implicit power that each of us has in communicating is the first step toward ethical action. The considerations above will help move each of us beyond mere recognition.

Notes

1. See, for example, Elliott (2008).
2. This is the starting point for common morality, as described in the works of Bernard Gert (2008).

Sources

Elliott, Deni. 2007. *Ethics in the first person.* Lanham, MD: Rowman & Littlefield.

Gert, Bernard. 2008. *Common morality.* New York: Oxford University Press.

Infoplease.com. 2007. *Conveniences.* http://www.infoplease.com/ipa/A0004941 .html (accessed January 31, 2010).

Kovach, Bill, and Tom Rosensteil. 2001. *The elements of journalism.* New York: Three Rivers Press.

Starker, Steven. 1989. *Evil influences: Crusades against the mass media.* New Brunswick, NJ: Transaction Media.

World Bank. 2009. *Internet users.* http://datafinder.worldbank.org/internet-users (accessed January 31, 2010).

Chapter 2

Stereotypes, the Media, and Photojournalism

Willard F. Enteman

Let us start with one of the central terms in this book.[1] While its origin is lost in the dim recesses of linguistic history, originally "stereotype" was most closely associated with journalism as a trade. The older print people among us may remember that a stereotype was a printing plate that facilitated typesetting by allowing the mechanical reproduction of the same material. Thus, a stereotype imposed a rigid mold on the subject and encouraged repeated use without revision. In this context, we might take note also of another term associated alliteratively and conceptually with stereotype: "stigmatize." In ancient Greece, a stigma was a brand used on slaves for identity purposes. Stereotypes are ultimately used to stigmatize.

We have taken both "stereotype" and "stigmatize" from their origins and developed them further through metaphorical application. Those who use metaphorical stereotypes substitute thoughtless reproductions for careful analysis. While we may be reluctant to accuse the old typesetters of laziness, that is a legitimate charge for the use of harmful stereotypes in modern media. In addition, even in its origin, stigmatizing was a form of laziness. It relieved the slave owner from treating the slave as a person.

Media

This is another central term for our book that warrants discussion. In this case, etymology will help, but a larger problem is that the term itself has been used so equivocally that it is in danger of losing all meaning. Those who wish to attack what they call "the media" typically suffer from a fallacy of ambiguous quantification. If what they mean by "the media" is all media, then, since media are so extensive and varied, the claims are false. On the other hand, if by the media they intend to refer to some media, then, for the same reasons, the claims are true but trivial. Ironically, as this chapter was being prepared, a radio personality declared that all the claims of the media are false. Since he is part of the media, it follows that his claim is false. If the purpose of such charges against the media is to provide a responsible reference to a quantitatively identifiable portion of media, then evidence should be provided. That would take work and probably not yield dramatic conclusions. We are back at laziness again.

The word *media* is a plural form of *medium*, which means what it suggests: something in between. Media include television, print, pictorial, radio, movies, commentary, advertising, public relations, blogs, webcasting, podcasting, message boards, video hosting, wikis, and so on. When Marshall McLuhan famously declared that the medium is the message (or massage, depending on your historical reading), he referred to the totality of that which stands between the subjects and objects. Media are, then, the means we use to inform, express, exchange, and persuade. That is the subject of media; the object is other people's beliefs, views, attitudes, and emotions.

In discussing media, we should take special note of journalism because when attacks are mounted against the media, often what is really intended is the journalistic portion. Bright lines are difficult to identify. The once nearly bright line between journalism and commentary is being dissolved as is a once-bright line between marketing and journalism. As we will develop in this chapter, this blurring has raised special issues for photojournalists, but first we should get some clarity about fundamentals of the media business.

The Media Business: Theory

Even though media are largely embedded in business, there seems to be little discussion of the media business by scholars. Nevertheless, we should be clear about the basic principles of business and the corporate structure.

Corporations are human artifacts. Legally they are referred to as artificial entities. They have only those privileges given them by law. Economists tell us the purpose of business corporations is to maximize profits. In the past, many discussions of business have been directed at the term "profit."

However, in the long run, every organization, whether or not a business, has to make a profit in the sense that its revenues must exceed its expenses or it will cease operations.

The term that should have caught our attention was "maximization." Maximization is a strict master, for whatever is to be maximized becomes the sole priority for the organization. As humans, we may have some difficulty thinking about this concept because we are not naturally maximizing creatures. The existentialists had it right: We invent ourselves as we order and reorder priorities in the process of making decisions.

A question may arise in the mind of readers as to whether corporate executives can make decisions that do not advance the maximization of profits for the business. In this context, it will be helpful to make a distinction between personal principles and organizational principles. It may be that an individual executive has such strong personal principles that she would not allow some activity to take place on behalf of the corporation even if it promised to contribute to the maximization of profits. Such executives do exist even at the highest management levels. If such decisions have a minor impact on the maximization of profits, the executive may get her way. However, if the decisions have a significant impact, and she orders them to be carried out, her management position may be in jeopardy. Even if her superiors do not reverse her personal decision, there are corporate raiders ready to take over what they identify as an underperforming corporation. Thus, while we may conclude there is a distinction to be drawn between personal and organizational principles, when the issue is significant for a business corporation, the profit maximization principle must dominate personal principles.

The Media Business: Applied

We are ready to apply what we have learned to our topic of stereotypes. Let us turn to the area of marketing in media. A marketing campaign that employs negative stereotypes will be pursued if it will contribute to the maximization of profits for the corporation. An example may help here: The advertisements I see for household cleaning products show females using the product in question.

(The only exception I can think of employs a male cartoon character!) It is likely that someone in a responsible management position believes such advertisements help the corporation maximize profits even though the exclusive use of women reinforces negative stereotypes. However, based

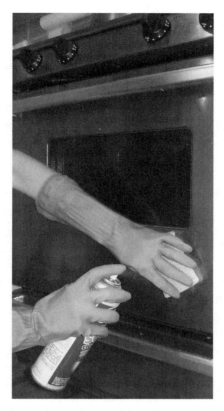

As they have done throughout the world and history, this woman performs the unpleasant task of cleaning the front of an oven. (Courtesy of Paul Martin Lester.)

on the analysis provided in the previous section, we may conclude that as long as those in charge believe the stereotyping maximizes profits, it will continue. We may also safely generalize from this conclusion: Irrespective of stereotyping, whenever a marketing campaign maximizes profits, it will be run. Thus, there is no sense in expecting corporate executives to follow a moral code related to the media (or anything else).

As individuals, we are not without some influence. Given, as said earlier, that we are not maximizing creatures, we can make personal decisions while considering moral issues. That may mean some sacrifice on our part, but it is not a barrier. We make many decisions in which one priority is placed higher than another. We can, then, through our personal decisions, react to corporations that allow negative stereotyping or any other activity we find offensive.

Journalism

A great deal of journalism takes place in corporate business settings. In earlier days, there were newspapers which, while businesses, were owned and controlled by individuals or families and may have been managed on the basis of personal principles. However, in keeping with what has been established thus far, such newspapers became attractive targets for takeover by profit maximizers. One result of this has been the conflation of journalism with entertainment to the downfall of the integrity of journalism. A particularly dramatic case occurred in June 2007, when television anchor Mika Brzezinski refused on air to follow a producer's instructions to lead a newscast with a story the sole merit of which was that it was entertaining because it would show a clip of a celebrity who is attractive to conventional adolescent male fantasies. Brzezinski argued—still on air—that a story about a major development in the war in Iraq should lead. Instead of giving her support, her two male colleagues treated her action in a sophomoric manner. Some of their sarcasm involved teasing her about her commitment to journalistic standards, even though they probably would like the audience to consider them journalists.[2] Along with the negative stereotyping of journalism, there was also negative stereotyping of women. Brzezinski's only acceptable means for dealing with the behavior of her male colleagues was to indulge them and play along with their weak attempts at humor. A good news part of this story is that the unexpected subsequent audience response supporting Brzezinski was dramatic.

We should now recognize a distinction between business and journalism. As said earlier, the goal of the former is to maximize profits. By way of contrast, the goal of the latter is to communicate the truth. That is what allows us to distinguish journalism from advertising, gossip, rumor, entertainment, and promotional material. While these goals are distinct, they are not necessarily in conflict. Journalism may be practiced in a context that seeks to maximize profits. However, if the controlling executives perceive a conflict between the two goals, as was pointed out in the discussion of advertising and stereotypes, except in economically trivial matters, executives must either obey the laws of economics or be replaced by people who will. Consequently, if the goal of journalism is to be followed in a business setting, there will have to be some means for constraining executive decisions.

Professional Journalism: Drawing a Bright Line

We should attempt now to develop a way in which journalism can be true to its mission while in a profit-maximizing culture. What I will soon describe as formal professions provide us with help in reaching that objective. The conclusion of this chapter is that some journalists should attempt to establish part of journalism as a formal profession. Before we turn directly to that, we will need to deal with ambiguities involved in the use of the word "profession."

Let us start with the concept of formal professions and some of the necessary characteristics: (1) a set of moral principles which have been developed by the professionals themselves, (2) a set of intellectual and skill requirements also developed by the professionals, and (3) an organizational means for the enforcement of these principles by professional peers. Thus, in formal professions, peers are ultimately responsible for maintaining professionalism.

With regard to informal professions, society seems to have adopted some variation on a sports metaphor in which amateurs are contrasted with professionals by virtue of the fact that the former are not paid for their services. Turning to journalism, while, presumably, people who report events using websites or blogs or newsletters are considered amateur journalists, people who earn money as reporters are currently informal professional journalists. None of this is precise, but it will do for our purposes here because our focus will be on the concept of formal professions.

Clergy, military, physicians, and lawyers are archetypal formal professionals. The clergy and the military are the oldest formal professions. By the middle of the twentieth century, medicine and law achieved standing as formal professions. In the late decades of the twentieth century, nursing, accounting, and engineering tried to become formal professions. Perhaps as a result of deep embedding in the profit-maximizing culture, engineering and accounting have not been successful yet. However, nursing seems to be moving steadily in that direction.

For the sake of convenience in this chapter, I will take an imperfect analogy from medicine and suggest we consider forming a Professional Journalism Board as an organization responsible for the formal professional journalistic membership requirements. Journalists who apply, are accepted, and abide by the principles will then be designated "Board-Certified Professional Journalists" (BCPJs). They would be what I have called formal professionals.

Following this suggestion, we will have drawn a bright line that will distinguish BCPJs from other journalists, from other employees in the corporation, and from other media people. We might, then, continue with our analogy to medicine. Nurses often find themselves employed in profit-maximizing corporations, whether hospitals or others. If they are to maintain their professional standing, they cannot violate their profession's standards no matter what their managerial superiors may command. A bright line is drawn between, for example, the nurse as a hospital employee and many other hospital employees. It is instructive to note that even though the professional nursing organization, the American Nurses Association (ANA), does not prohibit nurses from unionizing, its standards explicitly state that nurses may not endorse a bargaining agreement that causes them to act in ways that violate ANA standards.

The benefit to a media corporation of retaining BCPJs might be that, given the potential enforcement of the principles by peers, there should be increased confidence in the reliability of the reporting, which in turn may lead to maximizing profits. The disadvantage to a media corporation of retaining BCPJs would be that the corporation will be constrained in its control over such journalists even to the extent that on some occasions their work may cause harm to the corporate bottom line.

It has become increasingly difficult for consumers of the news to distinguish high-quality news sources from low-quality ones whether or not the journalists are compensated. People who seek a truthful and energetically pursued presentation of important events without commentary or personal bias are placed in a nearly impossible position because an almost limitless array of sources promises journalistic accounts with no clear way to assess trustworthiness. Drawing the kind of bright line suggested here would not guarantee resolution of this difficulty any more than the professionalism of nurses guarantees high-quality care. However, it gives us a higher degree of assurance than does the current system in which they are professionals only in the informal sense.

Another reason for suggesting we find a way to draw a bright line has to do with developments in the justice system over the past few years. As a citizen who is not a journalist, if I have relevant knowledge about a case being pursued by the authorities, I have an obligation to cooperate with them. There was a day in which the difference between citizens who were journalists and those who were not seemed reasonably clear and, in the context of the First Amendment, it may have made sense to grant journalists confidentiality privileges for sources even though there was no established formal profession of journalism. However, given current technology, we all have the ability to claim we are journalists, and, as a result, there is no effective distinction between journalists and other citizens. In far too many instances, the justice system could be ground to a halt by prospective witnesses claiming journalistic shielding rights and refusing to give information to authorities or testify at trial. Or, in contrast, excessive demands on journalists to provide confidential information on sources could undermine the ability of journalists to act as an independent check on government, including the judiciary. In this context, we should say that the citizen obligations of amateur and informal professional journalists trump any presumed obligations they may claim as journalists.

By way of contrast, in the case of acknowledged formal professions, socially accepted professional obligations should overcome the obligations of citizens who are not members of formal professions. For example, physicians and lawyers have an obligation to maintain the confidentiality of what they have been told in their formal professional role. The number of people who have such duties is severely restricted by virtue of the requirements for membership in the formal profession. In addition, such confidentiality obligations are not held without exception. For example, if a psychiatrist has good reason to believe a client is about to harm himself or someone else, the psychiatrist has an obligation to warn the authorities and the intended victim (Supreme Court of California 1976). In suggesting we should sustain an obligation of professional journalists to grant and maintain confidentiality of sources, I am not suggesting those obligations should be unlimited. Exceptions should be spelled out explicitly in the standards of the formal profession, and they should be explained to potential sources. They should also be supervised by the professional association, and it (not the media corporation at its discretion) should come to the defense of the professional journalist when legitimate obligations are attacked.

Fortunately, professional journalists would not have to start *de novo* in developing standards. There are some (unenforced) standards already in existence. For example, it might be wise to start with the standards of the Society for Professional Journalists (SPJ), those of the American Society of Newspaper Editors (ASNE), or the code of the National Press Photographers Association (NPPA).[3]

Photojournalism

Photojournalists are not merely photographers, and they are not primarily graphic artists. They should be first and foremost journalists. Their primary task is not to entertain or to develop works of art; it is to advance the consumers' understanding of the story. Thus, what has been said about journalists also applies to photojournalists.

However, let us recognize a special issue involving photojournalists. We may start by distinguishing between descriptive and metaphorical uses of language without suggesting a bright-line distinction. In general, there may be differences even where there may be no bright-line distinction. We might see this in the case of the earlier example of a difference between a journalist who is an amateur and one who is an informal professional. Following the sports example, it was suggested that payment might be used to indicate the difference, but the concept of payment is itself ambiguous. For example, presumably most students who are reporters for their college newspaper are amateurs. However, while students who receive academic credit for such reporting do not receive money, they are being paid in the coin of their realm and, thus, may have moved beyond mere amateur status. Ironically, similar comments could be made about a great deal of intercollegiate athletics. Thus, not all differences are distinctions with bright lines, but they still are differences. In this sense, there may be no bright-line distinction between the descriptive and the metaphorical use of language, but there is a difference.

For wordsmith journalists, descriptive language constitutes a large portion of what they produce, and they can depend upon the common use of the language to presume reasonably accurate communication between the journalist and the consumer. However, descriptive language is often insufficient for communicating thoroughly, and the wordsmith journalist may turn to metaphorical language.

When metaphors are used, their success depends not only on the cleverness of the speaker in selecting an appropriate metaphor but also on the hope that the receivers will understand the metaphor in the way the speaker intended. An example may help here. When I taught Ancient Greek Philosophy, I spent a great deal of time talking descriptively about differences between Plato and Aristotle. Toward the end of the semester, I made the course take a quite different turn. I showed a reproduction of Raphael's fresco called the *School of Athens*. This painting is like a metaphor that needs to be interpreted.[4]

In a sense, photojournalism operates almost entirely in the metaphorical domain. When I showed my students the *School of Athens*, I was there to listen to them discuss their understanding and interpretation of the painting. Photojournalists do not have the benefit of proximity to those who receive their work. However, it is not sufficient to ignore this issue. The photojournalist has an obligation to determine just what was communicated to recipients. That is not an impossible task to satisfy. There could be surveys of consumers of the photojournalism to determine whether they learned what the photojournalist intended.

This is an important task in the context of our topic, for a thorough investigation may also reveal that some people experience stigmatic stereotypes the photojournalist had no intention of transmitting. In the world of stereotypes, it is not sufficient to fall back on the weak but common response "I did not mean that" with its *sotto voce* "Thus, I should not be held responsible." If a negative stereotype has been received, we should be prepared to justify its transmission on professional journalistic grounds or apologize for our actions and change future behavior. Photojournalists may become board certified just as their wordsmith counterparts may. It would take extra effort, but it would also raise the standing of photojournalism and keep it out of the realm of mere entertainment.

By way of conclusion and summary, let us reflect briefly on the condition in which journalists find themselves currently. On the one hand, many journalists are employees in commercial corporations that exist under an economic imperative to maximize profits. Absent professionally enforced standards, even if individual journalists try to abide by personal standards, whenever there is a substantial conflict with the economic imperative, it will prevail. On the other hand, technology has created an opportunity for so-called citizen journalists who, also, operate with no professionally enforced standards, and the consumer is confronted with a host of sources that claim to present the news. A glance at a general news website such as Google News shows literally thousands of citations for a timely story. Thus, even the conscientious consumer is like a thirsty person trying to drink from a fire hose. There is no clear way to distinguish between reliable and unreliable accounts. In addition, postmodernism has so infected journalism that almost the only agreement among the ideologues is that there can be no impartial reporting of the day's news.

Image-related journalism has all these problems and more. As but one example, consider the NPR report on photojournalism, "Ruin Porno," which said photojournalists of respected publications reinforced stereotypes by producing pictures of run-down conditions in an urban neighborhood when more information or less tight shots would leave a quite different impression. We deal here only with the creation of the images. The technical ability to manipulate them subsequently compounds issues further.[5]

The partial solution suggested in this chapter is to form an organization of professional journalists that will establish and enforce professional standards. In that way, the conscientious consumer would have a means for distinguishing journalistic wheat from promotional chaff. In view of the extensive and increasing distrust of journalists and photojournalists, it is acknowledged that this solution is only partial. However, every journey must begin with one step, and this would be a step in the right direction.

Notes

1. This chapter is substantially changed from earlier editions of this volume. Some of those changes are due to intervening events and others are due to changes in the author's views. What is common is a conceptual analysis. Clarifying central terms is critically important because they arise from underlying concepts that might otherwise remain confused. Clarity does not necessarily yield truth. We can, after all, be clear but wrong. However, a lack of clarity often yields confusion that is neither true nor false.

2. Those who are interested may link to www.youtube.com/watch?v=6VdNcCcweL0.

3. Here are some links to journalism codes of ethics: SPJ, http://www.spj.org/ethicscode.asp; ASNE, http://asne.org/article_view/articleid/313/rtnda-code-of-ethics-and-professional-conduct-313.aspx; and NPPA, http://www.nppa.org/professional_development/business_practices/ethics.html.

4. Why, for example, does Plato's hand extend vertically and Aristotle's horizontally? For the interested, here is a link: http://en.wikipedia.org/wiki/The_School_of_Athens.

5. Those interested may find the radio story and transcript by linking to http://www.onthemedia.org/transcripts/2009/09/25/06.

Sources

Supreme Court of California. 1976. *Tarasoff v. the Regents of the University of California*. http://en.wikipedia.org/wiki/Tarasoff_v._Regents_of_the_University_of_California (accessed February 25, 2010).

Chapter 3

Images in Readers' Construction of News Narratives

Rick Busselle and Helena Bilandzic

When we think of images from the news—those we see in newspapers, on television, or on websites—we tend to think of well-known photographs that originated in famous or infamous events, such as passengers standing on the wings of a floating jetliner or hands on the bleeding chest of a dying Iranian protester. But there are also the images that are quickly forgotten. There are all the pictures of people waiting around another airport because of another malfunction or another storm; or pictures of another soldier leaving, coming home, or guarding some installation. While the stories these images accompany may be remembered, the individual images themselves are not. They do not become iconic symbols of a particular event. Rather, they serve as a source of information that audience members can incorporate into their understanding of the story immediately at hand or a larger narrative presented across days, weeks, or years of newscasts and news editions.

Thus, an image may be related to a narrative in a number of different ways. The image may serve as merely additional information available to the reader. It may contain most of the narrative so that relatively little else is required from accompanying text. Or it may become a symbol that represents the essence of the story through which we understand an event or issue.

We use narratives to make sense of and to construct our social world (Bruner 1991; Fisher 1984), and images play a number of different roles with respect to those narratives (Hariman and Lucaites 2003; Schwalbe 2008). This chapter will elaborate on the role of images in narratives and the relations between the words we read or hear, the images that accompany those words, and the narratives we construct to explain and recall events in our world.

Realization of Stories in the Minds of Readers

We approach this discussion of narratives and images from a cognitive-processing, narrative comprehension perspective. That is, our focus is on how readers, listeners, and viewers use texts that exist in public discourse, including the still and video images that accompany written and spoken words, to construct stories that exist within individuals' and sometimes the collective memory. To begin, we must distinguish between the text on the page and the realization of the story in the mind of the reader (e.g., Gerrig 1993; Oatley 2002). Distinguishing between these allows us to refer to that which exists outside the reader or viewer (the text) and the understanding that comes to exist within the mind of the reader (the story). This distinction is central to our subsequent discussions.

Any text representing an event or events—for example, a novel, a news report, a motion picture, or a photograph—can be considered a narrative (Abbott 2002; Ryan 2007). Narrative can be thought of as the "telling" of events and characters, real or fictional. Porter Abbott (2002) illustrates how a narrative can be as brief as a single sentence or a single image. The sentence "I fell down" explicitly communicates the occurrence of an event and suggests what preceded and followed the event. The speaker was standing and then, as a result of some mishap, found herself on the ground. Similarly, a black-and-white photograph of a ship wrecked on a rocky shore suggests to a viewer that the ship once sailed and that some event, possibly a storm, led to the ship's current state. The same argument can be made of images that less directly refer to events, such as war casualties, auto accidents, or victims of natural disasters. The image captures the outcome while also communicating the event that was not captured in its frame.

Although there are different conceptualizations and metaphors for stories, it is clear that we do not receive stories passively. Instead, readers, viewers, or listeners construct a story's sense in their own mind; the result is referred to as the "realization of the story" (Oatley 2002). Story realization is the audience member's cognitive and emotional understanding of the events based on both the words and images available in the text and their

Alfred R. Waud made this pencil sketch during the American Civil War of a ship wrecked in a storm with persons watching. (Courtesy of the Library of Congress.)

own preexisting, relevant knowledge related to the topic (Busselle and Bilandzic 2008; Graesser, Olde, and Klettke 2002). While the elements of the story exist in a text or texts, the realization of the story exists in the mind of the audience member as she or he experiences the narrative. David Bordwell (1985) describes a story as "the imaginary construct we create progressively and retroactively . . . the developing result of picking up narrative cues, applying schemata, and framing and testing hypotheses" (49; see also Zwaan, Langston, and Graesser 1995).

Mental Models and Narratives

A common way to conceptualize the realization of a story in the reader's or viewer's mind is to think of sense making as the construction of mental models of the narrative. Mental models are cognitive structures that represent aspects of the external world (Johnson-Laird 1983; van Dijk and Kintsch 1983). We have mental models for mechanical objects, such as levers or locks, and for abstract concepts, such as ownership, protests, or marriage. Mental models are similar to schemata or scripts. The important difference from a narrative-processing perspective is differing levels of specificity or generality; in narratives, mental models describe specific episodes or events with a temporal structure in specific locations. Mental models provide a theoretical explanation of the cognitive processes through which an audience member constructs meaning from a text, as well as the cognitive activity that facilitates this construction process.

Essentially, in comprehending a narrative, we construct mental representations—mental models—of settings, situations, and people, as well as the relations among them. To illustrate, consider the following brief narrative in three elements:

Element 1: *As the Ellis family ate their supper, they heard someone shouting.*
Element 2: *At the window, Nora Ellis strained to see into the darkness.*
Element 3: *She turned and looked at her husband. "It's John," she sighed. "It looks like he'll be staying on the couch again."*

From Element 1, we construct a mental model of the setting that is implied from the text (indoors, dinner table) as well as the situation (people who are related, seated facing each other, eating) and an event (unexpected noise).

Element 2 changes the situation slightly. We are told that Nora (a female) is looking outside. From this, we can infer that the sound must have come from outside. Also, supper and darkness indicate evening and possibly winter. Nora can see where the others cannot, and so the others likely look to her for more information.

From Element 3, we may detect weariness or inconvenience in Nora's sigh, suggesting that whatever situation has led John to their home, it is not the first time. Element 3 also suggests that Nora is the wife and probably mother of the family.

To further illustrate the story construction process, consider an alternative third element:

Nora put the wood beam across the door. Fear filled the room as more voices and the sound of horses could be heard. Anger and fear were mixed in the look Nora gave her eldest son. "I told you to stay away from them," she said.

From this new element, we construct very different mental models of the setting, characters, and situation. Nora is still the mother. Her son, probably not a child, appears to be the cause of the apparent danger, which takes the form of men on horses. (We assume men, don't we?) The setting is not modern given the horses and the barring, rather than locking, of the door.

All of this illustrates three important points. First, a story is not something we passively receive but rather something we actively and progressively construct from available text. Second, much of the story construction process is unconscious. In the example above, the reader is not consciously aware that the description of Nora peering out of the window communicates that the noise came from outside. However, had Nora looked toward the basement door, we would have unconsciously assumed the noise came from there. Third, much of the story we construct is based on information we bring to the text rather than information available in the text itself. Moreover, the information the reader provides takes many forms ranging from facts (e.g., that horses are no longer used for transportation) to stereotypes (e.g., preconceived notions about mothers, families, and men on horses).

News Reports and Images as Narrative

News reports can be considered as individual narratives about specific people and particular events. In this sense, news reporting is an act of storytelling (e.g., Friedman, Dunwoody, and Rogers 1999; see also Knobloch et al. 2004), and news stories are not fundamentally different from other narrative forms (Schokkenbroek 1999). There are types of news reports that may not take a narrative form, such as those that illuminate some state of affairs by reporting statistics on topics such as unemployment or crime rates (Zillmann 2002). However, news reports that are truly nonnarrative in their basic form and function likely are more the exception than the rule.

Images may serve as an additional narrative element available to the reader or viewer. Like words, images contain information that can be incorporated into the story that the reader or viewer constructs. Images are always linked to (either explicit or implicit) information not pictured (Mitchell 1994). This may include information ranging from background or cultural knowledge the viewer already possesses to a caption or accompanying news report graphically tied or merely adjacent to the image. Audience members use visual information contained in an image as well as their own preexisting knowledge and other available information to construct a mental model of the event. They draw inferences from the outcome shown in the picture to understand the event it illustrates. If text and picture are shown in conjunction, both visual and textual information are integrated into the mental model.

The amount of information contained in an image is considerable. For example, a single picture from the scene of a house fire may communicate time (darkness, and presence and attire of bystanders), weather conditions (snow, rain, and clothing), or affluence (houses, cars, and yard details). Images also may contain information that cannot be communicated quickly with words, such as information about the setting of an event; information that professional norms may preclude or discourage from being explicitly stated, such as race, ethnicity, and class; or emotion on the faces of victims or witnesses. Here images can add information to a narrative that generally is not or cannot be communicated any other way. A child clutching a soot-smudged teddy bear in front of a burned house provides information about the event and setting. But more importantly, it communicates emotional information that is unlikely to be spoken or written by a reporter. Similarly, the tear-lined face of a mother at a funeral provides emotional information that may be impossible to communicate in words, or at least in the relatively small number of words available to a reporter. In the following section, we will explore how this function of images relates to the plot-based definition of narrative we offered above.

Narrativization and Fictionalization of Events

A second way to consider news as narrative is by looking not at a single story or image but by considering the totality of information, both words and pictures, made available across time, news reports, and news platforms. Here we are not talking about "master narratives" (e.g., Schwalbe, Silcock, and Keith 2008; Slatterly and Garner 2007), which arise when similar narratives are imposed on different and potentially disparate events. Instead, we refer to the narrative of a particular event or issue as it is presented by many news professionals and organizations. For example, the narrative of Germany's reunification was available in countless reports about individuals, families, and institutions in the East and the West both before and after November 1989. It was also told through countless images of people's lives before and after reunification. Some of the most memorable and dramatic narrative elements were images of people from both sides celebrating by climbing on the wall and tearing it down with picks and hammers. Readers and viewers all over the world used these images to construct stories of celebration, triumph, and reunion, as well as more overarching stories about the Soviet Union and the Cold War. The manifold manifestations of these life courses and fates were also fictionalized by popular films such as *Goodbye Lenin!* (2003), *Herr Lehmann* (2003), and *The Lives of Others* (2006).[1]

From this broader perspective, images are often discussed in terms of framing, where it is argued that images construct meaning surrounding issues and events. Research indicates that images selected for inclusion in a publication can be biased in favor of one particular interpretation of an issue or event (Griffin 2004; Griffin and Lee 1995; Schwalbe 2006) and that those biases may be reflected in public opinion (Gilens 1996). From a narrative comprehension perspective, audiences use images to construct a story of an event. Carol Schwalbe (2006) demonstrated how, in the early days of the Iraq War, images of war machinery encouraged readers to construct stories of military superiority and discouraged the construction of stories of tragedy and suffering. The favored construction implied that the war would be won quickly and with relative ease. While images add to readers' mental models of a story by providing narrative information that is independent from the text, they also may serve as a frame for the text that influences the particular version of a story that is constructed.

Images as Symbols of a Narrative

An image may become an iconic symbol of an event or issue (Barnhurst, Vari, and Rodriquez 2004; Hariman and Lucaites 2003; Kampf 2006). In such cases, the image represents a narrative available through public discourse that has been constructed in individual and collective memories through observation and participation in that discourse. An image can activate a narrative in the mind of a viewer even when the image itself contains almost no information. The image serves as a cue that activates a narrative already known, a story already extant, in the mind of the viewer. Consider the image of the Space Shuttle *Challenger* explosion.

In the upwardly spiraling white plume, we may see the story of a teacher who died personifying science for schoolchildren. Of course, the image itself is little more than a uniquely shaped pattern of white smoke against a clear blue sky. It is the viewer who possesses these and other stories of the *Challenger*, its crew, and the NASA space program. The image serves merely as a cue to activate the story's retrieval from the viewer's memory.

Other images may contain more of a narrative. For example, with the proper historical context, the image of a sailor's V-J Day kiss in Times Square may represent the story of surviving the horrors of war to recapture the dreams of youth.[2] Without context—though it is hard to imagine the image without context—the photograph expresses a couple's joy and maybe reunion. The clothing, crowd, and confetti suggest a larger

On January 28, 1986, the space shuttle *Challenger* and her seven-member crew were lost when a ruptured O-ring in the right solid rocket booster caused an explosion soon after launch. (Courtesy of NASA.)

celebration in an earlier time. Here, as in Abbott's (2002) shipwreck photo, a narrative is in the image. But, without the context of the photo (celebrating the end of World War II), the narrative is somewhat limited to the individuals and setting contained within. Awareness of the V-J Day Parade as the setting gives the image a much more complete meaning or activates a more complete narrative.

In other images, most of the narrative can be found. The image of an African-American teenage girl, schoolbooks in hand, surrounded by uniformed men and angry, Anglo teens, tells the story of school desegregation in the United States. We really do not need to know that the girl is Elizabeth Eckford and the high school is in Little Rock, Arkansas. Most of the story is in that image.[3]

The point is that readers draw on information in the image as well as information from other sources to construct a story that explains what is before their eyes. In some cases, much of the necessary information exists within the image, and it can be interpreted with little background knowledge. In other cases, the story represented by the image depends to a great extent on the reader having previously learned the narrative from other sources.

Narrative, Emotion, and Images

While written stories certainly may convey emotion, they must do this through literary devices that describe a subject's emotional state. Images, on the other hand, can illustrate emotions on human faces and bodies. In this sense, pictures contain a different type of information than written words. A single photograph can, nearly instantaneously, convey an emotion or emotional state. We need no words to immediately interpret sorrow on the face of a young woman standing over a flag-draped coffin. We immediately understand the desperation and anguish on the Sudanese mother's face as she cradles her malnourished infant.

In our definition of narrative at the beginning of this chapter, we relied on a plot-based concept of story—a representation of events, possibly with a causal connection, is a story. Emotional pictures may serve this function and allow readers to make inferences about the underlying events. However, we argue that emotional pictures convey narrative information of a particular quality that goes beyond describing events.

A different definition of narrative, put forward by Monika Fludernik (1996), centers around the "experientiality" that stories highlight. Stories show the inner world of people and their emotions, intentions, and perceptions. In this conception, representation is not a distinctive feature of a narrative anymore; the stories presented in drama-laden images are a form of narrative as well. Carrying this notion further, we argue that images not only add to or define a narrative by referencing events, but also independently convey narratives by showing immediate expressions of experientiality.

Implications and Considerations

In this chapter, we have outlined what we see as four distinct but potentially related linkages between images and narratives. An image:

1. Can provide information, including emotional information that an audience member may use to construct the story that becomes his or her understanding of an issue or event.
2. May contain most of the narrative elements of a story, and thereby require little additional information from a caption or accompanying report. Sometimes the picture *is* the story.
3. Can frame a story by providing information that influences how an audience member interprets the story and, therefore, the underlying event or issue.

4. May come to symbolize an event. In these rare cases, an image—even one that within its borders contains little information—can bring back from memory the story that essentially is a viewer's understanding of an event.

Recognizing the different roles that images can play in a narrative has both heuristic and practical value. We hope that articulating these roles prompts deeper understanding of the impact of the images that injure which are discussed in this volume and offers useful suggestions for investigating the relations between the images and narratives that shape our world. We also hope this consideration of how audiences engage with and comprehend narratives (by news professionals and others) will provide a helpful framework for making choices about images, stories, and storytelling; for producing interesting, informative, and responsible news; and ultimately for critically deconstructing the news stories and images we receive daily.

Notes

1. We should note that there often is competition over the prominence of a particular narrative surrounding a person or issue, such as the war hero narratives that surrounded U.S. presidential candidates John Kerry and John McCain during their respective campaigns. The contestation of narratives in public discourse is beyond the scope of this chapter.

2. See http://images2.fanpop.com/images/photos/2700000/VJ-Day-Kiss-famous-kisses-2799413-600-897.jpg for a view of Alfred Eisenstaedt's famous V-J Day kiss at Times Square, New York City.

3. See http://extras.mnginteractive.com/live/media/site92/2007/1205/200712 05_055131_Eliz-Eckford%28famous%29-copy.jpg for a view of Elizabeth Eckford's ordeal photographed by Wil Counts, who later was a professor of one of the editors of this book while a student at Indiana University.

Sources

Abbott, H. Porter. 2002. *The Cambridge introduction to narrative*. Cambridge: University Press.

Barnhurst, Kevin, Michael Vari, and Igor Rodriquez. 2004. Mapping visual studies in communication. *Journal of Communication* 54: 616–634.

Bordwell, David. 1985. *Narration in the fiction film*. Madison: University of Wisconsin Press.

Bruner, Jerome. 1991. The narrative construction of reality," *Critical Inquiry* 18: 1–21.

Busselle, Rick, and Helena Bilandzic. 2008. Fictionality and perceived realism in experiencing stories: A model of narrative comprehension and engagement. *Communication Theory* 18: 255–280.

Fisher, Walter. 1984. Narration as a human-communication paradigm: The case of public moral argument. *Communication Monographs* 51: 1–22.

Fludernik, Monika. 1996. *Towards a natural narratology*. London: Routledge.

Friedman, Sharon, Sharon Dunwoody, and Carol Rogers. 1999. *Communicating uncertainty: Media coverage of new and controversial science*. Mahwah, NJ: Lawrence Erlbaum.

Gerrig, Richard. 1993. *Experiencing narrative worlds*. New Haven, CT: Yale University Press.

Gilens, Martin. 1996. Race and poverty in America: Public misperceptions and the American news media. *Public Opinion Quarterly* 60: 515–541.

Graesser, Aq.C., Brent Olde, and Bianca Klettke. 2002. How does the mind construct and represent stories? In *Narrative impact: Social and cognitive foundations*, ed. Melanie C. Green, Jeffrey J. Strange, and Timothy C. Brock. Mahwah, NJ: Lawrence Erlbaum.

Griffin, Michael. 2004. Picturing America's "war on terrorism" in Afghanistan and Iraq: Photographic motifs as news frames. *Journalism* 5: 381–402.

Griffin, Michael, and Jongsoo Lee. 1995. Picturing the Gulf War: Constructing images of war in *Time, Newsweek*, and *US News & World Report. Journalism and Mass Communication Quarterly* 72: 813–825.

Hariman, Robert, and John Louis Lucaites. 2003. Public identity and collective memory in U.S. iconic photography: The image of "Accidental Napalm." *Critical Studies in Mass Communication* 20: 35–56.

Johnson-Laird, Phillip. 1983. *Mental models*. Cambridge: Cambridge University Press.

Kampf, Zohar. 2006. Blood on their hands: The story of a photograph in the Israeli national discourse. *Semiotica* 162: 263–285.

Knobloch, Silvia, Grit Patzig, Anna-Maria Mende, and Matthias Hastall. 2004. Affective news: Effects of discourse structure in narratives on suspense, curiosity, and enjoyment while reading news and novels. *Communication Research* 31: 259–287.

Mitchell, W. J. Thomas. 1994. *Picture theory*. Chicago: University of Chicago.

Oatley, Keith. 2002. Emotions and the story worlds of fiction. In *Narrative impact: Social and cognitive foundations*, ed. Melanie C. Green, Jeffrey J. Strange, and Timothy C. Brock. Mahwah, NJ: Lawrence Erlbaum.

Ryan, Marie-Louise. 2007. Toward a definition of narrative. In *Cambridge companion to narrative*, ed. D. Herman. Cambridge: Cambridge University Press.

Schokkenbroek, Christina. 1999. News stories. *Time & Society* 8: 59–98.

Schwalbe, Carol. 2006. Remembering our shared past: Visually framing the Iraq War on U.S. news websites. *Journal of Computer-Mediated Communication* 12: 264–289.

Schwalbe, Carol, William Silcock, and Susan Keith. 2008. Visual framing of the early weeks of the U.S.-led invasion of Iraq: Applying the master war narrative to electronic and print images. *Journal of Broadcasting & Electronic Media* 52: 448–465.

Slattery, Karen & Garner, Ana. 2007. Mothers of soldiers in wartime: A national news narrative. *Critical Studies in Media Communication* 24: 429–445.

van Dijk, Teun A., and Walter Kintsch. 1983. *Strategies of discourse comprehension.* New York: Academic Press.

Zillmann, Dolf. 2002. Exemplification theory of media influence. In *Media effects: Advances in theory and research*, ed. Jennings Bryant and Dolf Zillmann. Mahwah, NJ: Lawrence Erlbaum.

Zwaan, Rolf, Mark Langston, and Arthur Graesser. 1995. The construction of situation models in narrative comprehension: An event-indexing model. *Psychological Science* 6: 292–297.

Chapter 4

The Dangers of Dehumanization: Diminishing Humanity in Image and Deed

Erin Steuter and Deborah Wills

As scholars from many disciplines have suggested, language, including the symbolic language of imagery, creates frames through which we see, interpret, and understand the world; what is reflected in this language is not reality but construct. The frames through which we view the world are often shaped by, even constructed by, the discourses that surround us: that is, by the visual and verbal languages that are circulated and ratified by media, including supposedly neutral media such as print journalism and news broadcasts. We often learn our ideas about other groups not from interaction with them but from media headlines, sound bites, pop culture artifacts, and other forms of truncated information.

The discursive processes by which, in wartime, we "make" enemies out of our demonized adversaries are at root the same processes by which, in times of peace, we dehumanize those we consider to be "Others"—our opposites, our antagonists, our inferiors. A central, persistent, and often systematic mechanism in achieving this construction of the Other, as this chapter will show, is the use of dehumanizing imagery: that consistent set of subhuman animal, insect, and disease images that circulates through media and popular culture to "mark" groups such as immigrants and racial or ethnic communities as less than human. These images are part of larger verbal and visual metaphoric systems linking the Other to objects or animals, dirt or germs, things that require managing, cleansing, or elimination. When the Other is depicted as inhuman, especially when metaphorically figured as toxic, invasive, insidious, and contaminating, it becomes a civic or moral duty to inhibit its pernicious spread. Dehumanizing metaphors in media that tell us persistent stories about the animal, diseased, or indistinguishably and threateningly conglomerate nature of our enemies ensure that we don't see them as fully human.

The visible distinctions of racial difference, in particular, offer a locus for enmity and Otherness. Our hostility to strangers, which Sam Keen (1991) identified as the central dynamic by which societies are organized, is reserved most particularly for those who look least like us. A society may construct an enemy of anyone when it perceives itself under threat; our varied campaigns against those of different sexual orientations, physical abilities, economic classes, and even ages demonstrate this. However, race and its potent visibilities of difference are fundamental to our most virulent processes of enemy construction.

Representing an enemy as subhuman based on racial characteristics offers us seductive ways of dealing with the threat. If they are beasts, for example, we have greater opportunities for control: we can "round them up," or "herd" or "ship them out," maintaining a pure space reserved for the humans who look like us. The "hostile imagination," fed by paranoid anxieties about an encroaching Other, creates a repertoire of images of the enemy (Keen 1991, 27). These images reflect and consolidate our sense of the enemy's fundamental difference. The expressions of the hostile imagination are often ingenious and compelling, which is part of their power. Dehumanization, however, goes beyond simple stereotype and stigma. It strips away humanity through the consistency of its metaphoric links with the bestial, the verminous, and the microscopic. Tropes of animal, insect, germ, and disease are so important to our contemporary construction of enemies and Others, and so linked to larger historical discourses of racism, that they require critical attention.

Historic Dehumanization

Historically, dehumanizing metaphors have provided justification for systems of enslavement under which humans are seen as, and often made to function as, animals. It is often theorized that the domestication of animals that began during the Neolithic Revolution provided the model for human slavery. Collars, chains, prods, whips, and branding irons were employed to domesticate and control animals; similar tactics were used to ensure that slaves remained docile, subservient, and unable to escape. In ancient Mesopotamia, slaves were branded like domestic animals (stigmatized) and priced according to their equivalent in cows, horses, pigs, and chickens. This laid the groundwork for later European and American racial theories that called for the exploitation of the "lower races," who continued to be regarded as animals and treated accordingly (Stannard 1993, 185). Thus, the first African slaves shipped to Lisbon in the mid-1400s were marketed like livestock and portrayed as possessing a "beastlike sexuality and brutish nature" (Wax 1980, 14). During the 1600s and 1700s, the growth of the slave trade reinforced this image.

Commodified, slaves became chattel that could be "bought, sold, traded, leased, mortgaged, bequeathed, presented as a gift, pledged for a debt, included in a dowry, or seized in bankruptcy" (Davis 2000, 170).

Bernarda Bryson Shahn created this lithograph of emaciated male and female slaves crowded onto the deck of a sailing ship. (Art © Estate of Bernarda Shahn/Licensed by VAGA, New York, NY.)

By the 1800s, Anglo-European scientists had developed theories promoting the superiority of the white race. American scientists confirmed this, proclaiming that African slaves could endure without undue suffering levels of brutality no "human" could sustain. Some doctors argued the bodies of black Africans possessed fewer pain receptors and therefore could be flogged without feeling it as a white body would (Schwartz 2006, 239). Both scientific and medical discourses were regularly employed to justify brutality to slaves, and their assertions informed the media of the period. In one widely distributed 1905 broadsheet, for example, a caption declares confidently, "Scientists Say Negro Still in Ape Stage" and "Races Positively Not Equal" ("Scientists Say Negro" 1905). In a quasi-scientific illustration designed to look like it was taken from a medical textbook, hand-drawn figures of "The Ape" and "The Negro" are juxtaposed in identical postures. To reinforce the clear visual message that "the Negro" is an ape masquerading as a man, elaborate anatomical labeling delineates, limb by limb, their identical features: Both have "big hands," "weak lower limbs," a "small brain," an "animal smell," the "ape groove" in the skull, and a "black ape color." As late as the 1970s, this pamphlet was distributed as white supremacist literature.

The trope of the ape as visual shorthand for the African-American resurfaced in the years immediately preceding and following Barack Obama's 2008 election. During the election campaign, T-shirts bearing a picture of a grinning, Curious George–like monkey over the slogan "Obama in '08" used the infantilized image to undermine the possibility of political power for a black man. Once he had gained that power, such images become more overtly malignant. In February 2009, a *New York Post* editorial cartoon by Sean Delonas depicted a dead chimpanzee, lying in a pool of blood, riddled by bullet holes and loomed over by armed policemen; one holds a still-smoking gun as the other verbally conflates the dead chimp with the president, saying, "They'll have to find someone else to write the next stimulus bill." The endurance of the simian trope confirms the resilience of the animal metaphor as a key mechanism in supporting racism.[1]

Such images are both potent and historically resonant. As researchers investigate the role of long-standing cognitive associations between "Othered" racial groups and animal images, they uncover the importance of such imagery to the process of dehumanization. Phillip Goff (2009) argues that the data produced by his seven years' worth of research into the relationship between media coverage, antiblack violence, and judicial inequities indicate that such images are influential in material and consequential ways: "Words and pictures, far from harmless, can be the very instruments of dehumanization necessary for collective violence—regardless of how innocently they are intended" (para. 11). Historically, producers of propaganda have mobilized such images to dehumanize a society's most feared and hated Others, those disenfranchised not only from citizenship but also from humanity itself.

A brief survey of dehumanizing practices illustrates their potency in provoking or justifying violence. The "lower" the form of animal employed, the greater the violence invoked; if the Other is so far down the evolutionary ladder that it is fundamentally without senses or thought, then normal checks to cruelty or aggression do not apply. One of the most striking historical examples comes from World War II, when the Japanese military performed medical experiments on human prisoners whom they called *maruta*—literally, "logs of wood" (Dower 1986, 338). Once identified as not only inhuman but also inanimate, the bodies of sentient beings could be brutalized without compunction and discarded in piles stacked like cord wood. In the same conflict, Western military and media applied similar strategies to dehumanize the Japanese, denigrating them in propaganda, news media, and other forms of public discourse as reptiles, insects, rats, cockroaches, vermin, and baboons.

While such images intensify in times of conflict, they are not solely the product of wartime propaganda. Indeed, they have been in place since the first intercultural encounters and are part of a rich symbolic world developed and relied upon by Europeans and Americans "over the ensuing centuries to put others in their place" (Dower 1986, 9). Historian John Dower notes that as early as the sixteenth century, traveling Spaniards characterized the Japanese as "wild beasts." One Spaniard wrote to his European audience that "[i]n wisdom, skill, virtue and humanity, these people are as inferior to the Spaniards as children are to adults. . . . [T]here is as great a difference between them as between monkeys and men" (Dower 1986, 145).

This simian image was remarkably persistent, showing up repeatedly in twentieth-century political cartoons along with the other dominant images of rats and bats; all three animals prominently featured pinched faces, squinty eyes, and protruding teeth. An American poster with the banner "Jap Trap," for example, shows a rat wearing a Japanese soldier's cap caught in a mousetrap; a U.S. Navy poster depicts a mousetrap ready to snap shut on a buck-toothed rat wearing a cap showing the Japanese insignia.

Another poster warning "Don't Talk. Rats Have Big Ears" shows a rabid-looking rat standing astride Japan, wearing a soldier's cap. The cover of the

"Jap Trap," a World War II propaganda poster, reveals a common racist representation of the Japanese people at the time. (Courtesy of the National Archives and Records Administration.)

popular *Colliers* magazine from December 12, 1942, shows another familiar image, the Japanese enemy as a vampire bat aloft over Pearl Harbor, with devilish-looking slit eyes, metallic-looking hooks at each wing tip, and giant fangs (Szyk 1942). This representation is particularly interesting in that the bat clutches both a traditional-looking, decorative sword and a modern-looking bomb in its prehensile, elongated, monkey-like fingers. A primitive with tools, an animal with access to modern weaponry, is clearly seen as a particularly horrific image.

European foes, in contrast, were not bestialized in the same way, largely because most Americans were of European descent. This difference is reflected in a comment made by a U.S. Marine to war correspondent John Hersey in 1942: "I wish we were fighting against Germans. They are human beings, like us—but the Japanese are like animals" (Hersey 1943, 56). American journalist Ernie Pyle wrote, "In Europe we felt that our enemies, horrible and deadly as they were, were still people. But . . . the Japanese were looked upon as something subhuman and repulsive; the way some people feel about cockroaches or mice" (Pyle, cited in Dower 1986, 78).

Our cultural lexicon of dehumanizing metaphors is remarkably enduring; it has permeated our public conversations about many denigrated or marginalized groups. The rat metaphor, in particular, has crept into many discourses of judgment. An article in *The 13th*, a conservative Catholic newspaper, claims, "Homosexuals, like rats, are crawling out of their holes, only to be fed lovingly by church people and politicians" (hatecrime.org n.d.). Vermin metaphors are also applied to immigrant groups, especially when increases in immigration are perceived as a threat. Media discourse on immigration frequently uses dehumanizing language. Animal images provide the dominant metaphor, with secondary metaphors of the hunt supporting and reinforcing it; illegal immigrants are described as being "hunted down," "baited," "lured," and "ferreted out" (Santa Ana 2002, 83). Otto Santa Ana and others argue that such metaphors produce and support negative public perceptions of the Latino community, portraying Latinos as invaders, outsiders, burdens, parasites, diseases, animals, and weeds.

Dehumanization's Incitement

Perhaps the most pressing reason to critique dehumanizing images is their key role in persecution and genocide. Gregory Stanton (1996) argues that dehumanization is a necessary precursor to genocide, initiating and inflaming its comprehensive violence. In the twentieth century's two most infamous examples of genocide, the incitement of dehumanizing metaphors is well documented, with images of lower-order animal life such as vermin and disease dominating not just official government or military propaganda but also mainstream media such as radio, film, and even children's books. In Nazi Germany, Hitler talked repeatedly of the "Jewish bacilli," a metaphor that conflated Jews with the instruments of contagious disease to "justify" or "rationalize" the Nazi project of extermination. Siegfried Bork's research shows that Nazi publications consistently described Jews as infection, poison, parasites, tumors, bacilli, vermin, leeches, bacteria, maggots, and malignant ulcers—intensifying the deliberate linking of Jews with the micro-organic or the verminous (cited in Ruud 2003, 50). According to Richard Grunberger (1971), the "incessant official demonization of the Jew gradually modified the consciousness even of naturally humane people" (465).

Andreas Musolff (2007) argues that the Nazis' anti-Semitic metaphor system provides a powerful demonstration of how stigmatization and dehumanization lead to genocide. He argues that

> the source imagery of Hitler's world-view consisted in the conceptualization of the German nation as a *human body* that had to be *shielded from disease* (or, in case of an outbreak, *cured*). Jewish people, . . . viewed as an *illness-spreading parasite*, represented the danger of *disease*. Deliverance from this threat to the nation's *life* would come from Hitler and his party as the only competent healers who were willing to fight the *illness*. (33, emphasis added)

The persistent metaphor of cleansing brings together this trope of the nation as a body that must be purified of infection with the trope of the enemy as a parasite that must be eliminated in the name of safety and hygiene. Since cleanliness is one of the binary opposites to both metaphors of infestation and metaphors of infection, the two notions of enemy as germ/disease and as rodent/plague are inextricably conflated. In the paranoid discourse of propaganda, bodily infection by disease, cultural invasion by the encroaching enemy, and national infestation by the corrupting enemy become one and the same thing, a single, resonant, three-sided narrative that demands the totalizing cure of elimination, eradication, and hygienic cleansing.

The same trope of purification, hygiene, and cleansing also supported the unfolding of the genocidal process in Rwanda. Like the Jews, the Tutsi were repeatedly publicly compared with insects and vermin. "A cockroach gives birth to another cockroach," said the Hutu newspaper *Kangura* in March 1993, just as the "evil of the Tutsis will reproduce itself for as long as Tutsis exist" (Belman 2004). Radio Television Libre des Milles Collines, a broadcaster, depicted Tutsis as snakes, animals, and, most insistently, cockroaches. Government leaders employed euphemisms for killing, telling citizens to "clear the bush," "get to work," or "clean around their houses" (Belman 2004). The resulting massacres and retaliatory killing, fueled by a public media discourse so toxic that its perpetrators were later indicted for war crimes (Wax 2003), resulted in the deaths of nearly a million people. Such tragedies warn us of "the horrific cost of misunderstanding metaphor as *mere rhetoric*" (Musolff 2007, 33, emphasis added).

Media Discourse

There is a crucial tripartite correlation between the dehumanizing image central to wartime propaganda and genocide, the echoing and reinforcement of such images in mainstream news media, and the performance or "acting out" of these metaphors when mobilized into action, as we see in the notorious photographs of prisoner abuse at Guantánamo Bay and Abu Ghraib. This abuse, recorded in images of leashed, caged, or crawling prisoners, literalizes the metaphor of enemy-as-beast, suggesting again how these images operate far beyond the realm of the rhetorical.

The persistence with which Al Qaeda, terrorism, and even Islam itself are internationally identified in mainstream news headlines with the viral, the microbial, and the cancerous recalls the dominance of the Jew-as-bacillus metaphor in 1930s Germany. These metaphors are invoked in headlines such as the following:

Al Qaeda Mutating like a Virus (*Toronto Star*, June 22, 2003)
Like Cancer Cells, Terrorist Organizations Are Proliferating (*Sudbury Star*, May 12, 2004)

Army reservist Private Lynndie England who served in the 372nd Military Police Company holds a leash attached to a prisoner the guards named Gus at the Abu Ghraib prison in Iraq. Pictures of prisoner torture taken by fellow soldiers were made public in early 2004. (Source: U.S. Military.)

Stop Sectarian "Cancer" in Iraq, Urges UN (*Toronto Star*, November 26, 2006)
The Terrorist Virus Is No Lightweight Matter: We Must Contain Its Spread (*Times* [London], November 11, 2006)
Al-Jazeera Notes Blair's Warning of "Virus of Islamic Extremism" (*BBC Monitoring International Reports*, January 4, 2004)
Headscarf Is a Cancer in Turkey (*Turkish Daily News*, November 21, 2003)
Root Out This Cancer of Evil (*News of the World* [UK], August 13, 2006)
Ridding Islam of the Cancer Within (*Irish Times*, October 4, 2005)
Al Qaeda Evil Is Spreading like a Virus (*News of the World* [UK], July 8, 2007)

When media speak of eradicating terrorists, they employ a word most commonly used when speaking of wiping out diseases or infestations. When the rhetoric of public discourse extends the eradication model to the war on terror, it fails to distinguish between those who harm us and those who seem indistinguishably like them. This historically charged metaphor of eradication has already slipped into public conversation on the war on terror, as illustrated in these headlines:

Cleansing of Foreign Evils a "Good Thing" (*Australian*, October 22, 2002)
Kuwait Vows to Exterminate Terrorists (UPI, January 20, 2005)
The Extermination of Saddam Hussein (*U.S. News and World Report*, April 14, 2003)
Exterminating the [Iraqi] Regime (*Providence Journal-Bulletin* [Rhode Island], April 16, 2003)
Iraqi PM Vows to "Annihilate" Terrorist Groups (*Hamilton Spectator* [Canada]), July 16, 2004)
Saudi King Vows to Annihilate Al-Qaeda (Agence France Presse—English, April 1, 2006.)
Iraq Premier Forms Security Service to "Annihilate" Terrorists (*The New York Times*, July 16, 2004)
Allies "Wipe out Iraqi Division" (Press Association [Central Command, Qatar], April 2, 2003)
US Bombs Failed to Eradicate Afghan Militia (*South China Morning Post*, April 25, 2007)
British Troops Wipe Out Key Taliban HQ (*The Express*, February 21, 2007)
Pakistani Forces Eradicate 4 Militant Centers (*Deseret Morning News* [Salt Lake City, Utah], June 30, 2008)

The language of annihilation, eradication, and extermination that circulates through mainstream news media echoes in unsettling ways the classically propagandistic language identified by scholars of genocide and the rhetoric that precedes it. The dehumanization of the enemy through a consistent metaphorical framing of animal, vermin, pest, and disease seems to find its corollary in the related metaphorical framing of extermination, a framing many mainstream media voices not only have failed to interrogate but also have often echoed and replicated. These words and their accompanying images, with their repeated and insistent linkages of the Other to the bestial, the verminous, and the diseased, constitute in themselves a kind of visual or verbal violence. These metaphors make us not more but significantly less safe by fostering the rage, misunderstanding, and alienation that create and foment conflict. It is unlikely that any community can break a cycle of physical violence by responding with a corresponding violence of image and imagination.

If there is power in these dehumanizing images, there can also be power in dismantling them. Although our cultural lexicon of dehumanizing metaphors has been remarkably enduring, it can also be subject to revisionary reframing. When, with critical awareness, we draw such images from the realm of the tacit into the realm of the visible, we take a first, necessary step toward that revision.

Note

1. See http://letustalk.files.wordpress.com/2009/02/curious-george-t-shirts.jpg and http://wwwimage.cbsnews.com/images/2009/02/18/image4809295.jpg.

Sources

Belman, Jonathan. 2004. A cockroach cannot give birth to a butterfly and other messages of hate propaganda. *Peace, war and human nature.* http://www .gse.harvard.edu/~t656_web/peace/Articles_Spring_2004/Belman_Jonathan _hate_propaganda.htm (accessed June 27, 2007).

Davis, David Brion. 2000. The problem of slavery. In *Slavery, secession and southern history*, ed. Robert Louis Paquette and Louis A. Ferleger. Virginia: University Press of Virginia.

Dower, John. 1986. *War without mercy: Race and power in the Pacific War.* New York: Pantheon.

Goff, Phillip Atiba. 2009. NY Post's racist ape cartoon is no small matter. Alternet.org, February 19, http://www.alternet.org/rights/127835/ny_post%27s_racist_ape _cartoon_is_no_small_matter/ (accessed August 25, 2009).

Grunberger, Richard. 1971. *Twelve-year reich: A social history of Nazi Germany.* New York: Holt, Rinehart & Winston.

hatecrime.org. N.d. Nazi anti-Jewish speech vs. religious right anti-gay speech. http://www.hatecrime.org/subpages/hitler/hitler.html (accessed July 25, 2007).

Hersey, John. 1943. *Into the valley: A skirmish of the marines.* New York: Knopf.

Keen, Sam. 1991. *Faces of the enemy: Reflections of the hostile imagination.* New York: Harper Collins.

Musolff, Andreas. 2007. What role do metaphors play in racial prejudice? The function of anti-Semitic imagery in Hitler's *Mein Kampf. Patterns of Prejudice* 41: 21–43.

Ruud, Kathryn. 2003. Liberal parasites and other creepers. In *At war with words,* ed. Mirjana Dedaic and Daniel Nelson. New York: Mouton de Gruter.

Santa Ana, Otto. 2002. *Brown tide rising.* Austin: University of Texas Press.

Schwartz, Marie Jenkins. 2006. *Birthing a slave: Motherhood and medicine in the antebellum South.* Cambridge, MA: Harvard University Press.

Scientists say Negro still in ape stage. n.d. Inventory of the Ku Klux Klan collection, University of Mississippi Libraries. http://www.olemiss.edu/depts/general _library/files/archives/collections/guides/latesthtml/MUM00254.html (accessed June 26, 2007).

Stannard, David. 1993. *American Holocaust: The conquest of the new world.* New York: Oxford University Press.

Stanton, Gregory H. 1996. The 8 stages of genocide. *Genocide Watch.* http://www .genocidewatch.org/8stages1996.htm (accessed June 26, 2007).

Szyk, Arthur. 1942. Pearl Harbor. *Colliers,* December 12.

Wax, Darold. 1980. A people of beastly living: Europe, Africa and the Atlantic slave trade. *Phylon* 41: 12–24.

Wax, Emily. 2003. Journalists sentenced in Rwanda genocide. Prosecutor said "hate media" urged killings. *Washington Post Foreign Service,* December 4.

Chapter 5

Images That Empower and Heal: Lessons from *Migrant Mother's* Migrant Meanings

J. B. Colson

One of the best-recognized images in the history of photography, Dorothea Lange's *Migrant Mother* illustrates with its varied uses and interpretations the difficulty in assuring fixed meaning to a particular image, much less assuring that the image has some positive psychological or social impact.

Lange's close-up framing of a destitute mother and her three children epitomized the devastation of so many by the Great Depression of the 1930s. It is also one of the best-known examples of documentary photography, a much-discussed photographic genre. At the time she took the photograph, Lange was part of a legendary group whose work helped define the documentary genre as they worked for a federal agency, the Farm Security Administration (FSA), that was a component of President Franklin D. Roosevelt's New Deal programs.

In his history of 1930s documentary photography, Jack Hurley (1972) credits a variety of workers and forces for contributing to our concept of the "modern documentary photograph," but he sees the 1930s as "a turning point" in which the FSA "played a key role in conditioning the aesthetic tastes of the nation to the documentary style" (vi–vii). Gretchen Garner's critical study of twentieth-century U.S. photography similarly notes, "The glory and high point of American documentary was the work of the

The original caption for Dorothea Lange's "The Migrant Mother" of Florence Thompson and three of her children read, "Destitute peapickers in California: a 32-year-old mother of seven children. February, 1936." (Courtesy of the Library of Congress.)

Historical Section—photographic, of the Resettlement Administration, later called the Farm Security Administration" (2003, 56).

Documentary, however, was not the only photographic genre in which *Migrant Mother* was used. The image was also presented in terms of photojournalism, personal records, promotional imagery, educational illustration, and fine art. Pierre Borhan summarizes its varied history, concluding that "*Migrant Mother* was not only widely published, but also manipulated, re-cropped and transformed for multiple purposes, notably advertising" (2002, 20). While the two basic image characteristics of content and style remained essentially constant and intact in all of these cases (discounting the occasional appropriation with manipulations), important shifts in meaning and responses occurred as the genres, functions, overall message design, and presentation context changed.

The following discussion considers the case history of *Migrant Mother* to illuminate how to better identify, predict, and produce images that empower and heal. Good intentions, even with good professional media skills, are not enough to ensure good outcomes because of the complexity of the process and the inability to know or control all of its aspects well into the future. The goal of this discussion is to provide an overview of the complexity involved and the issues at stake. The history and criticism of *Migrant Mother* as they appear in printed texts and increasingly on the web provide the basic material for this consideration, which is enhanced with some theory from the fields of communication, art and photography criticism, visual ethnography, and the philosophy of meaning. Diagramming the interactions involved helps identify and clarify their significance.

The Image Producers

Migrant Mother depended for its content and its original intentions on both Dorothea Lange, the photographer, and Roy Stryker, the director of the federal program for which she worked at the time she took the picture. There are many texts about each, and their history is known, at least in brief, to most of those interested in photography, documentary, and related subjects. (As an illustration of the breadth of interest in this topic, a search for "Dorothea Lange" on Google raises 555,000 citations.) The following discussion highlights some of the more relevant and significant facts related to the focus of this chapter and to appreciating the origins of the iconic image.

Dorothea Lange

Lange was born Dorothea Nutzhorn in 1895 to an educated, German American family. Polio at age seven left her with a damaged right leg and a limp. Biographies that detail Lange's life and work include *Dorothea Lange and the Documentary Tradition* (Ohrn 1980) and *Dorothea Lange: A Photographer's Life* (Meltzer 1978). Among well-considered discussions of her photographic career are *Daring to Look: Dorothea Lange's Photographs and Reports from the Field* (Spirn 2008), and *Dorothea Lange: The Heart and Mind of a Photographer* (Coleman and Stourdzé 2002). After her father abandoned the family when she was 12, she changed her birth name to her mother's maiden name. Her education in photography included working in the studio of Arnold Genthe, who held a Ph.D. in philology (literary or classical studies) from Germany and ran successful portrait studios in San Francisco and New York City. She also studied photography at Columbia

University with Clarence White, the most important photography educator in the early twentieth century in the United States. For about a dozen years, she operated a successful portrait studio in San Francisco, like Genthe, photographing mostly the elite. She married Maynard Dixon, a successful illustrator and fine art painter in 1920.

In the early 1930s, as her studio business diminished with the plummeting economy, Lange began to photograph the unemployed she saw in the streets around her. During these same years, Dixon was also documenting results of the Great Depression with drawing and painting noted for its social realism. After divorcing Dixon in 1935, Lange married the progressive agricultural economist Paul Taylor, who had earlier enlisted her to illustrate reports of his research. Both had long experienced troubled marriages before they connected professionally and then personally. Publications of their early work together led to Lange's appointment with Stryker on his staff of government photographers, and that income, coupled with Taylor's as a professor at the University of California, Berkeley, enabled her to devote herself fully to documentary photography. Her two marriages can be seen in different ways to have contributed to her ability to produce *Migrant Mother* and other noted documentary photography.

Lange's abilities, motivations, and circumstances demonstrate factors likely to produce images with positive impacts. Her early photographic training and experience were in portraiture, about which she said, "Good meant to me being useful, filling a need, really pleasing the people for whom I was working" (quoted in Ohrn 1980, 13). Portraiture and documentary photography share some traits; both involve direct interaction with individuals, usually strangers where both persona and social technique contribute to success. Not every would-be photographer has the necessary mix of confidence, assertiveness, charm, and verbal and nonverbal skills for success. The successful mix can take a variety of forms. Lange's colleague Russell Lee, for example, made up for his imposing stature with charisma and an unmistakable interest in his subjects. Lange, small and ever conscious of her own disability (her limp), was a different, quieter presence. Because of her work with Taylor, Lange, more than the other FSA photographers, also brought a social scientist's research point of view to her work. Like Lee and other FSA photographers, her devotion to the FSA project was supported by a disciplined work ethic. As Anne Whiston Spirn reported, "On assignment for the FSA, Lange usually photographed every day, from early morning into the evening. At night she wrote letters and prepared for the next day's work" (2008, 21).

Roy Stryker and the FSA

Stryker was born in 1893 to a Kansas farming family and grew up with an appreciation for the land and the people who worked it. After graduating with a degree in economics from Columbia in 1924, he stayed on to teach, using a personal collection of photographs to illustrate his classes. His academic mentor, Rexford Tugwell, joined the Roosevelt administration and enlisted Stryker in 1935 to head the Historical Section of an agency created to help farmers suffering from the Great Depression. The Resettlement Administration, later named the Farm Security Administration (FSA), became famous for its photographic documentation of the United States in the years 1935 to 1942. Not a photographer himself, Stryker hired and administered a small group of individuals who were, or would become, some of the best-known names in the medium's history, including Walker Evans, Russell Lee, Gordon Parks, and Dorothea Lange.

Stryker worked to inform his photographers of the economic and social history driving their assignments. He also worked to get the most from them, given the FSA's limited resources, and to get the most support possible from a reluctant government. Importantly he created a working file of photographic documents with captions in Washington, DC, and promoted its use by a variety of media, including newspapers, magazines, varied community centers, and museums.

The resulting work is staggering in its size and quality. Stating the number of photographs in the FSA file as it was finalized and still exists at the Library of Congress can be confusing because non-FSA work is sometimes included in the count and the numbers for negatives and prints differ. The most reliable figure comes from the government's statement that

> [t]he collection encompasses the approximately 77,000 images made by photographers working in Stryker's unit as it existed in a succession of government agencies: the Resettlement Administration (1935–'37), the Farm Security Administration (1937–'42) and the Office of War Information (1942–'44). (Library of Congress n.d.)

An explanation of why an accounting of the agency's work is confused is offered, at least in small part, by one episode in the history of the FSA. According to one source, in 1944, there was a

> transfer of approximately 270,000 negatives and 77,000 prints by the FSA photographers to the Library of Congress in Washington. A major portion

of the negatives contains punch holes, an editing or censorship measure on the part of Stryker. (University of Virginia n.d.)

That *Migrant Mother* or similar images would have existed without the FSA is probable. Lange was already doing such work in California before Stryker hired her. That it would have reached its distribution and fame without Stryker's agency and file is unlikely. Stryker singled out the image for his highest praise: "When Dorothea took that picture, that was the ultimate. She never surpassed it. To me, it was *the* picture of Farm Security. The others were marvelous but that was special" (quoted in Meltzer 1978, 133). The image was so special that eminent German professor of photography Klaus Honnef would write in his *Icons of Photography*, "This picture is among the most famous in the literature of photography" (Stepan 1999, 70).

Another factor contributing to the image's fame was its inexpensiveness and easy availability. Free photographs of quality have great appeal for mass media and anyone trying to illustrate their messages. Stryker's initial efforts to distribute FSA photography were followed by his employment at Standard Oil, Jones and Laughlin Steel, and the Carnegie Library of Pittsburgh, during all of which he created similar photographic files. Stryker's initiatives have been supplemented since by the Library of Congress, where the FSA (and other) photographs are made available to the public for modest service fees and without the use rights required to publish most professional imagery. Their availability has two profound effects: First, it has facilitated scholarship and critical writing about the images; and, second, it has encouraged their frequent use in a wide variety of presentations. Factors facilitating these effects upon images include the following:

1. Useful content supported by both significant documentary information and strong human interest
2. Inclusion in a large group of related images to choose from in one place
3. Accessibility facilitated by cataloguing and by availability on microfiche and digitized versions online
4. Negligible cost for copies and reproduction

While these factors aid most communication efforts, they offer a particularly useful set of lessons for producing images that heal.

Considering Genre

For critically considering photographic presentations, it helps to identify them in one of the broad but roughly definable photographic genres. This categorization is useful because the public viewing photographs has developed expectations for how to read, interpret, and respond to images, based on their perceived genre. An indication of these interpretive preconceptions is evident in how responses to images vary depending on their genre context—say, for example, when what was originally a news photograph (photojournalism) 50 years ago appears as an illustration in a history text (educational illustration), or, as another example, when an advertising photograph (promotional illustration) is displayed in a museum as artwork (fine art and photography). While the photographic genre categories listed below may, and do, overlap, genres are not to be confused with other possible categorical criteria such as content (portraiture, landscape, etc.), style (realistic, romantic, fantastic, etc.), or function (as information, persuasion, or entertainment). It is also noteworthy that these broad categories can be subdivided in a variety of ways depending on the analytical purpose or approach used.

Most photography intended for public viewing falls into one of the following eight genres:

1. *Personal records* are produced by both amateurs (snapshots of family, friends, travel and events, and so on) and professionals (such as studio portraits and documentation of births, weddings, and other family-oriented events).
2. *Photojournalism* produces photographs of current interest for timely distribution. News is the primary subcategory here, but less timely feature or human interest and other subcategories, such as sports (news rather than history), are traditional.
3. *Documentary* photography has greater scope and depth and less urgent timeliness than photojournalism. The distinction of documentary photography from photojournalism can be arguable because news media sometimes present material that better satisfies this definition than that of photojournalism. Also, both photojournalism and documentary are normally done in a straightforward, realistic style and often treat subject matter similarly.

As discussed here, documentary has two divergent subcategories: One emphasizes social information, and the other adds an argument for social change. In the first case, the goal is more basically analytical, exploring a social situation that we seek to understand better. Analytical documentary shares characteristics with the qualitative research practice of visual ethnography. A typical difference is that visual ethnography as practiced by social scientists tends to emphasize researched information, especially with associated text, with a lesser focus on the photography, which is often basic or even crude. In contrast, documentary as analysis and information tends to focus more on artistic and technically informed images with less research support. My decades of teaching photography have been devoted to bringing these two closer together and adding their influence to photojournalism. To some minds, documentary is inherently promotional, an effort to call attention to and help resolve social problems. Historically this has often been true. However, it is not essential to the definition or practice of a more neutral, analytical documentary that promotes no more than the interest and, possibly, significance of its subject. Examples of this form of documentary photography have been more widely seen recently, especially in new media such as the *New York Times* online series "One in 8 Million" (Cotton 2009).

4. *Promotional images* are most commonly seen in advertising, but public relations and propaganda (biased social and political persuasion) are other important subcategories of photography designed to market and persuade.
5. *Educational illustration* offers the images without which how-to instructions and informative textbooks would be much less effective.
6. *Fine art* is a difficult-to-define and often-elitist practice that depends principally on both tradition and the designation of those with the social power to do so (curators, critics, and so on). One typical aspect of fine art photography is that it is presented to the public to be appreciated directly for itself, for aesthetic pleasure, without (or with fewer or less central) other specific motives. However, there is also a tradition of fine art with a social message.

An important aspect of fine art is its role in creating a market of precious art objects, making art a marketable commodity. Until the 1970s, there was no significant art market for photography, but some icons of photographic history, including *Migrant Mother*, have been sold for hundreds of thousands of dollars.

Two other important genres of photography do not have as much public venue.

7. *Metaphotography* is devoted specifically to exploring aspects of the medium, such as the technical and visual testing that many photographers do to improve their work for the genres above.
8. *Scientific and technical photography* is used to develop, record, explore, and apply science and technology, such as the type of photography employed by astronomers and medical practitioners. Technical photography has major importance for production in the computer industry.

Postmodern and later theories mark a significant shift in the criticism of photography in general, seeing it as both a product and producer of the social systems and culture(s) involved. In his essay "On the Invention of Photographic Meaning," Allen Sekula suggests that "the meaning of a photograph . . . is inevitably subject to cultural definition" (1982, 84), and Victor Burgin concludes "Looking at Photographs" by noting that "photography is one signifying system among others in society which produces the ideological subject in the same movement in which they 'communicate' their ostensible 'contents'" (1982, 153). For Joel Eisinger, the dense and complex writings of postmodernism are summed up with the observation that "in place of a hermetic formalism, postmodernists have asserted the inescapably social nature of all art" (1999, 247). In this context, then, to hope for images that heal is to hope for a society in which the attitudes and motivations for producing and consuming them exist broadly.

Becoming Iconic

Five negatives from the shooting session that produced *Migrant Mother* are well known. (A sixth, not submitted to the government, is not in the FSA archive.) The first use of these negatives was as photojournalism by the *San Francisco News*. Lange had notified the editor that California pea pickers were starving, and the paper notified the United Press (a press agency that distributed news and images to its subscribers). As a result, on March 10, 1936, the *News* ran two photographs from the series, but not the famous one, with a report that the federal government was sending food to the migrants. Thus Lange's work as photojournalism, immediate news, had the positive effect of promoting food for starving farm workers (Meltzer 1978, 133).

The fame of *Migrant Mother* began with its appearance in *Survey Graphic* in the fall of 1936. A voice of the Progressive movement that believed in the possibility and need to improve the welfare of the disadvantaged, *Survey Graphic* is described by cultural writer Kay Davis (n.d.) as follows:

> Using documentary writing and photography, the editors, writers and artists of *Survey Graphic* presented a portrait of America that demonstrated their faith in social planning, their commitment to public education, and their interest in the human variety that made up the nation.

As presented in *Survey Graphic*, *Migrant Mother* was part of that documentary effort. The fall 1936 issue also ran five other Lange photographs, four with "a long article by Paul Taylor reporting what the [Resettlement Administration] was doing to meet the problems of rural people in the West" (Meltzer 1978). Four years later, *Migrant Mother* was first exhibited at the Museum of Modern Art (MoMA) in New York City from December 31, 1940, to January 13, 1941 (Lange 1966, 106).

Art principles and training have enhanced the work of many photographers working in many genres, and fine art considerations have been especially important to documentary photography and its criticism. Presentation as art in museums and the art market has increased the popularity of the genre and of specific works and workers. Edward Steichen, a major figure in twentieth-century photography, included Lange's photography in three large exhibitions while he was curator at MoMA. Her greatest representation there was the museum's retrospective exhibition of her life's work that opened just after she died of cancer in 1965. (She had spent her last months helping prepare the show, proud to be the first woman honored by MoMA with a "one-man" exhibit; Lange 1966.)

Migrant Mother has also had a strong showing in the art market. A print sold at Sotheby's auction house in 1998 for $244,500. In 2002, her personal print sold for $141,500, and in 2005 a set of vintage Lange prints including *Migrant Mother* sold for $296,000. A much higher price of $822,400 was paid for Lange's *White Angel Bread Line* in 2005 (*E-Photo Newsletter* 2005). This largess benefited neither Lange nor the real Migrant Mother, Florence Thompson, both of whom had died long before.

Migrant Meanings of the *Migrant Mother*

The varied meanings that viewers have taken from *Migrant Mother* depend on an interaction between reading a set of specific visual facts (frowning woman with three children, and so on) and its generalization among such conceptualizations as a news report of starving field hands; a symbol of 1930s rural poor or of the Great Depression; an artistic masterpiece of realistic portraiture; the epitome of Dorothea Lange's career, of FSA photography, or of documentary photography itself; propaganda for the New Deal; and, less often considered, a personal record of a time and situation in the lives of the family recorded.

From the time Lange shot *Migrant Mother* and for many years later, the principle subject was an abstraction and unknown. The original caption on the Library of Congress file print says simply, "Destitute pea pickers in California; a 32-year-old mother of seven children. February, 1936" (n.d.).

More than 40 years later, in 1978, a reporter for the *Modesto Bee* identified Florence Owens Thompson as the Migrant Mother. An Associated Press story went out with the heading "Woman Fighting Mad over Famous Depression Photo." In 2002, Geoffrey Dunn, in an essay entitled "Photographic License," described the Thompson family's reactions in detail for the *San Luis Obispo New Times*:

> "I wish she hadn't taken my picture," [Thompson] declared. "I can't get a penny out of it. [Lange] didn't ask my name. She said she wouldn't sell the pictures. She said she'd send me a copy. She never did." The photo had become yet another cross for Thompson to bear in a lifetime of hardships.

When Lange recalled the shooting session for *Migrant Mother*, she said she worked rapidly, shooting successively closer framings as she moved up to her subject. She obtained a brief statement from Thompson without getting her name and noted that Thompson asked her no questions (Lange 1966). Lange typically worked more like a social scientist than she did here, shooting pictures in groups as projects and gathering extended information from interviews and other research. In her carefully researched book *Daring to Look*, Anne Whiston Spirn (2008) describes Lange's methods in detail.

Thompson's version of the shooting, as reported later by her children, differs in some respects. They agreed that Lange never asked her questions and must have gotten her (mis)information from the children or others in the camp. For example, Lange reported that the family had sold the tires of their car to pay for food when that never happened. Another disagreement is from the forever frozen frown on Thompson's face. Dunn reported that one of Thompson's daughters later commented, "Mother was a woman who loved to enjoy life, who loved her children. . . . She loved music and she loved to dance. When I look at that photo of mother, it saddens me. That's not how I like to remember her" (2002).

Thompson's story, as researched by others, was quite complicated. She was a Native American born and raised on Indian Territory in Oklahoma. Her life included seven children, several husbands, and incredibly hard work. She was something of a migrant worker, but she had moved to California in 1926, years before the Great Depression, and was not one of the thousands migrating in desperation to California from other states. Lange took her pictures while two of Thompson's sons were in town getting their old Hudson repaired. The sons later finished the car repairs, and the family soon left the camp, too soon to benefit from the food sent to the camp as a result of Lange's first report.

The fact that photography records a thin slice of time is part of its strength and also its burden. What was true for a moment, a record that is fixed for convenient study and communication, is but a brief sample of its subject, and other, often contradictory truths may also describe what is at stake. This is just one explanation for why meaning migrates.

A happier relationship between the Thompson family and Lange's famous record of them occurred when the *San Jose Mercury News* published the story of Thompson's failing health and her need for expensive care as she was dying in 1983. The story spread nationally, and people responded with mostly small donations that added up to more than $35,000. After this generosity and about 2,000 letters, many indicating how Lange's photograph had moved them, one of her sons had a more positive response to their role in an icon:

> "None of us ever really understood how deeply Mama's photo affected people," said Owens. "I guess we had only looked at it from our perspective. For Mama and us, the photo had always been a bit of [a] curse. After all those letters came in, I think it gave us a sense of pride." (Dunn 2002)

Controversy and Conclusions

In a comprehensive critical appraisal of Lange's work, Anne Wilkes Tucker, curator of photography for the Houston Museum of Fine Arts, wrote,

> Both in her photography and in her terse informative captions, [Lange] was assiduously faithful to actuality, but always in terms of its human consequences. Her images, more than any others, have become icons of the rending social issues of thirties America. (1984, 54)

Pierre Borhan commented with finality that "'Migrant Mother' is, without doubt, a masterpiece, and was quickly and indelibly recognized as such" (2002, 58).

Yet, for all its fame and acclaim, *Migrant Mother* has also received considerable negative criticism as an image, as representative of the work of the FSA, and sometimes in terms of problems with the documentary process itself. The many people politically opposed to the New Deal and its programs categorically considered the FSA a prime example of government waste for biased political motives. Jack Hurley reported that "the agency was increasingly being criticized as a major waster of federal funds. By 1941, . . . the enemies of the FSA were massing their forces into a real attempt to have the entire agency done away with" (1972, 160). Hurley also noted that the FSA had to face "objections to the use of government-financed photographs" by established, and purportedly independent, newspapers and magazines. The images were viewed with "jealousy" as "propaganda" and as unfair "competition" because the work was "so obviously superior to the run-of-the mill" news photographs (123).

More broadly, social critics have seen *Migrant Mother* as a hopelessly one-note, negative image that has become a surrogate for lives inherently more complex than shown. They critique the acts of personification and objectification by which one individual comes to represent an entire and diverse group of people. Charles Shindo, for example, wrote, "As a character type and not an individual character, Thompson's specific concerns—as well as the particular concerns of the migrants as a group—were over-shadowed by the generalizing effect of symbolism" (1997, 54). Paul Martin Lester notes the obvious stage-managed manipulations that Lange performed to arrive at the famous portrait and the failure of Thompson to look directly into the camera's lens as possibly a way of telling the photographer to leave her alone (2011, 263–266).

Taken together, then, one main lesson from *Migrant Mother* is recognition that far more than the image itself is at stake if images are to heal. Lange's iconic image has been both helpful and hurtful. While it has been admired with high praise and great sums, it also has been critiqued as seriously flawed aesthetically and socially, and the costs of producing and distributing it have been decried as waste and malfeasance. Some of the factors involved are indicated in the diagram accompanying this chapter.

Without the space or perhaps the need to detail possibilities from the diagram, I leave it to you to imagine how the different aspects of analysis can be applied to the specifics of *Migrant Mother* and its shifting history as an example of how producers and consumers of photographs can move toward images that heal.

A focal point in this diagram is the need for those with the intention to produce images that empower and heal to understand clearly the knowledge and attitudes their viewers bring to a message. This is often an uncertain task. Many of the chapters in this book offer useful analysis for such considerations. Another important point is that few images have had the currency and appeal of *Migrant Mother*. As those working in advertising and public relations know, it is rare to get much response from a single

INTENTION

MESSAGE

PRODUCTION		VIEWING
Financing	**PRESENTATION**	Physical Setting
Photography	**MESSAGE**	Social Setting
Writing	**TEXT**	Previous Background
Design	**IMAGE**	with Content &
Editing	**WORDS**	Contexts
Media-Method	**DESIGN**	Attitudes Toward
Staff Roles	**DESIGN**	Content &
Technology		Contexts
		Psychology & Mood
		When Viewing

DISTRIBUTION MESSAGE

FEEDBACK or ACTION
IF ANY

A diagram of one theory about the visual process is a circular progression that involves intention, viewing, feedback, and production. (Courtesy of J.B. Colson.)

image or its one-time presentation; it takes a campaign and considerable repetition. Nevertheless, every image has its power to harm or to heal. Finally, a point too often neglected in discussions of communication is the responsibility of the viewer. Before expressing negative critique or rejecting a message, both its nature and apparent intent should be understood. All these aspects require attention and energy.

Despite all of the difficulties, however, to be of service with images that heal is a great and worthy challenge.

Sources

Borhan, Pierre. 2002. Destiny and determination and a photography in history. In *Dorothea Lange: The heart and mind of a photographer*, ed. Sam Stourdzé et al. New York: Bullfinch Press.

Burgin, Victor. 1982. Looking at photographs. In *Thinking photography*, ed. Victor Burgin. Hampshire, UK: Macmillan Education.

Coleman, Gibson, and Sam Stourdzé. 2002. *Dorothea Lange: The heart and mind of a photographer*. New York: Bullfinch Press.

Cotton, Joseph. 2009. One in eight million. *The New York Times*, December 24. http://www.nytimes.com/packages/html/nyregion/1-in-8-million/index

.html?scp=1&sq=One%20of%208%20Million&st=cse (accessed January 25, 2010).

Davis, Kay. N.d. Portrait of America: *Survey Graphic* in the thirties. University of Virginia, Department of American Studies. http://xroads.virginia.edu/~ma01/davis/survey/intro/introduction.html (accessed January 25, 2010).

Dunn, Geoffrey. 2002. Photographic license. http://web.archive.org/web/2002 0602103656/http://www.newtimes-slo.com/archives/cov_stories_2002/cov_01172002.html#top (accessed February 19, 2010).

Eisinger, Joel. 1999. *Trace and transformation: American criticism of photography in the modernist period.* Albuquerque: University of New Mexico Press.

E-Photo Newsletter. 2005. Issue 06. http://www.iphotocentral.com/news/issue _view.php/102/96 (accessed February 19, 2010).

Florence Owens Thompson. N.d. http://wapedia.mobi/en/Migrant_Mother (accessed February 19, 2010).

Garner, Gretchen. 2003. *Disappearing witness: Change in twentieth-century American photography.* Baltimore: Johns Hopkins University Press.

Hurley, F. Jack. 1972. *Portrait of a decade: Roy Stryker and the development of documentary photography in the thirties.* Baton Rouge: Louisiana State University Press.

Lange, Dorothea. 1966. *Dorothea Lange.* New York: Museum of Modern Art.

Lester, Paul Martin. 2011. *Visual communication: Images with messages*, 5th ed. Boston: Wadsworth Cengage.

Library of Congress. N.d. Farm Security Administration/Office of War Information Collection. Washington, DC: Library of Congress.

Meltzer, Milton. 1978. *Dorothea Lange: A photographer's life.* New York: Farrar, Straus and Giroux.

Ohrn, Karin Becker. 1980. *Dorothea Lange and the documentary tradition.* Baton Rouge: Louisiana State University Press.

Sekula, Alan. 1982. On the invention of photographic meaning. In *Thinking photography*, ed. Victor Burgin. Hampshire, UK: Macmillan Education.

Shindo, Charles. 1997. *Dust bowl migrants in the American imagination.* Lawrence: University Press of Kansas.

Spirn, Anne Whiston. 2008. *Daring to look: Dorothea Lange's photographs and reports from the field.* Chicago: University of Chicago Press.

Stepan, Peter, ed. 1999. *Icons of photography: The 20th century.* Munich: Prestel.

Tucker, Anne Wilkes. 1984. Photographic facts and thirties America. In *Observations: Essays on documentary photography*, ed. David Featherstone. New York: Friends of Photography.

University of Virginia. N.d. American studies, the 30s, documenting the 30s, chronology of the Farm Security Administration. http://xroads.virginia .edu/~ug97/FSA/fsabio.html (accessed January 25, 2010).

PART II

Images of Race and Ethnicity

Paul Martin Lester

As I write this introduction, March Madness, the annual NCAA Division I basketball tournament, is not quite so mad (if the games began and ended the month before, would we call them February Folly?). All that subdued craziness should change by this weekend when Four become Two, and then on Monday when the One is crowned. That's when members of the winning team get to set a ladder on the court, snip the net, and take a piece of it home, where they will no doubt await a call from an NBA executive who will promise them unimaginable riches to play a game. Madness.

Many social scientists, media critics, and reporters have studied cultural profiling related to the percentage of a given population (don't fret, I'll get back to the game soon enough). Typical is Callahan and Anderson's piece "The Roots of Racial Profiling," in which they write,

> Consider *Crises of the Anti-Drug Effort, 1999*, a report by Chad Thevenot of the Criminal Justice Policy Foundation, a group that monitors abuses of the American legal system. Thevenot writes: "76 percent of the motorists stopped along a 50-mile stretch of I-95 by Maryland's Special Traffic Interdiction Force (STIF) were black, according to an Associated Press computer analysis of car searches from January through September 1995. . . . Blacks constitute 25 percent of Maryland's population, and 20 percent of Marylanders with driver's licenses." As this story was being written, New Jersey was holding hearings on racial profiling, and one state police investigator testified that 94 percent of the motorists stopped in one town were minorities (2001).

If 20 percent of African Americans have driver's licenses in Maryland, the reasoning goes, then the same percentage should be stopped while driving. And yet, the percentage is 76. Lest you think profiling is an east coast phenomenon:

> In a study of 700,000 cases in which officers of the Los Angeles Police Department stopped pedestrians or drivers in 2003 and 2004, conducted by the Southern California branch of the American Civil Liberties Union (ACLU), it was found that African Americans were 127 percent more likely to be stopped than Anglos. (Lester, 2011)

Of course, inequities between a culture's population and its present situation abound. For example, although the Academy Awards made history in 2010 with a Best Director Oscar given to a woman for the first time—Katherine Bigelow for her anguished tale of U.S. bomb squad soldiers in Iraq in *The Hurt Locker* (2009)—Hollywood as a general rule has not been kind to the gender. With about 51 percent of the U.S. population, you would rightly assume that women should be represented with about that same percentage in the film industry. However, as reported in the *Los Angeles Times*, a study of 100 of the top-grossing movies made in 2007 revealed that only 21 percent are producers, 11 percent are writers, and an appalling 3 percent are directors (Abramowitz 2010).

Back to the madness in March. At my southern California university (you can see the peak of the Disneyland Matterhorn out some of the south-facing faculty windows), the number of African Americans who attend the school is about 3 percent. During the team's conference basketball tournament, my friends and I watched our team play. I counted 13 players on our team—12, or 92 percent, were African American. The other player was a Latino. To my knowledge, he never played.

Something is wrong when the percentages are so out of whack. Fortunately, the authors represented in this part know what is wrong and offer solutions.

In chapter 6, James W. Brown tells a moving and personal story of his awakening awareness of Native-American history and present cultural values. His chapter concentrates on the Lenape, also known as the Delaware tribe, who originally came from a land that Anglo immigrants now occupy along the eastern seaboard. But through a succession of forced moves that caused unspeakable horror and hardship, they are today left in relative peace in Oklahoma. Nevertheless, tribal leaders and others work to preserve their culture and educate those who are curious and care.

Continuing with Native-American stereotypes, in chapter 7 Lucy A. Ganje takes a more generalized viewpoint and discusses the commodification of the culture. She is particularly persuasive when she describes the ways in which sacred Native objects are used and misused by advertisers (e.g., Anheuser-Busch sold their beer with *Custer's Last Fight* imagery), state highway planners, and sports teams (an insidious and pervasive racism is all that can explain a country that uses the name "Redskins" for a team that represents its capital). She calls for all cultures to honor Native past and future.

In chapter 8, Paula M. Poindexter carefully studies African-American images as shown during news reports. Her results are the same as those often published elsewhere by many others concerned with media stereotypes. When shown in the media, African Americans are almost always "represented as poor, criminals, athletes and entertainers/celebrities." Despite the best efforts of social and media critics for more than 40 years, from press reports criticized by the Kerner Commission after the violence of 1968 to the most recent newspaper and televised accounts, that picture has not changed. Nevertheless, Poindexter is infectiously optimistic and offers five recommendations that would improve mainstream news coverage of African Americans "almost immediately." Her last point is perhaps the most useful for all of us: "Work at diversity every day."

In the interesting and highly readable chapter 9, the young, innovative academic Henry Puente details the fall and rise of a once-marginalized cultural group—individuals whose parents are of mixed races. Where once they were chastised as "the greatest cultural and social stigma in the United States," persons of mixed race, largely through a continuous line of motion picture and television successes, are no longer a taboo. In fact, they have reached a kind of Rawlsian "veil of ignorance" (Rawls 1971) status in which fans and other members of the public no longer care about their lineage. Such is the position that contributors to this edition would like to see bestowed on all of the cultural groups detailed here.

Finally, in chapter 10 by Paula Marie Seniors, Hollywood again is pivotal in branding media stereotypes, but not in a feel-good conclusion. For Seniors, the devil is in the marketing. Corporate decisions based on assumed consumer-based preferences dropped African-American Brandy Norwood as the lead role in a contemporary movie version of *Cinderella* and replaced her with an Anglo in other productions. When children fail to see themselves represented in the media, Seniors argues that their aspirations are constrained.

Sources

Abramowitz, Rachel. 2010. In Hollywood, female film directors are still the exception. *Los Angeles Times*, March 7. http://www.latimes.com/entertainment/news/la-et-women-directors7-2010mar07%2C0%2C4748720.story (accessed March 30, 2010).

Callahan, Gene, and Anderson, William. 2001. The roots of racial profiling: Why are police targeting minorities for traffic stops? *Reason Magazine*, August–September. http://reason.com/archives/2001/08/01/the-roots-of-racial-profiling (accessed March 30, 2010).

Lester, Paul Martin. 2011. *Visual communication, Images with messages*, 5th ed. Boston: Wadsworth.

Rawls, John. 1971. *A theory of justice*. Cambridge, MA: Belknap Press.

Chapter 6

The Lenape: Cultural Survival or Assimilation?

James W. Brown

People Are the Drum

Men in a circle
Singing and drumming
BOOM boom, BOOM boom
BOOM boom, BOOM boom
Rhythm of the drum
Heartbeat of the people
Sound connects
Present, past future—are all one
There is no beginning
There is no end
Dancers circle the drum
Drum encircles the dancers
BOOM boom, BOOM boom
BOOM boom, BOOM boom
The heartbeat of the one
Is the heartbeat of the many
Circle of the many
From the rhythm of each one[1]

Imagine that someone knocks on your door. When you answer, you are told to pack your belongings and move. Your homeland is needed for Euro-American expansion.[2]

This was essentially the experience of the Leni Lenape (len-NAH-pay), more commonly known as the Delaware Indians. The Lenape story is one of early contact with Europeans that gave little acknowledgment of the Lenape role in the making of the United States. Renamed "Delaware" by

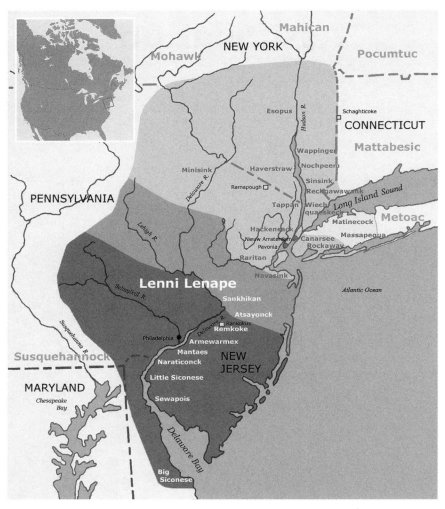

The original extent of the Leni Lenape or Delaware Native-American tribe. (Courtesy of Günter Strube.)

Anglo conquerors, the Lenape were forced from their ancestral homes along the Atlantic coast now known as parts of Connecticut, Delaware, Maryland, New Jersey, New York, and Pennsylvania. The encroaching Europeans accepted both the Lenape's hospitality and lucrative trade arrangements, and then forced them to leave their home (Brown and Kohn 2008b).

Giving up their land was a concept unknown to the Lenapes. A treaty with William Penn seemed to ensure permanent living, fishing, planting, gathering, and hunting in what is now western Pennsylvania. When that peace treaty was broken by Penn's sons, the Delaware, by then largely Christian, again moved westward to the Ohio Territory, where 28 men, 29 women, and 39 children were slaughtered in 1782 in what is known as the Gnadenhutten Massacre, six years after the Battle of Greasy Grass mentioned in chapter 7. It is acknowledged as one of the most senseless, heartrending examples of genocide known to humanity (Ohio Historical Society 2010).

After the massacre, the remaining members of the tribe moved to Indiana, a state named for the land of the Indians. But the Delaware, like all other Woodland Nations, were forced to sign treaties and again moved westward. Once more, the federal government's promises of protection from encroachment and a lasting home were broken. For a time the Lenape lived in Missouri, and then they were moved to Kansas. Their final move to Oklahoma after the American Civil War remains fraught with acrimony to this day.[3]

Stereotypes and Native Americans

Before reading the words of the Delawares, it is helpful to build some context, a context that includes an understanding of the prevalence of stereotypes disseminated by the media and among ourselves.[4] Stereotyping divides groups, nations, people, and ethnic minorities into "good" or "bad." Stereotyping distorts the mental representation of values through the idolization of some and the denial of positive characteristics of others (Hawkins 2005). Elizabeth Bird writes of stereotypes as the "legacy of a complex mesh of cultural elements, including formal history, literature, material artifacts, folklore, photography, cartoons, art, mass media and anthropological discourse" (1999, 62).

Stereotypes of Native Americans and their cultures are embodied in literature, movies, advertising, sporting events, and educational materials. In this edition, Lucy Ganje (see chapter 7) describes common Indian stereotypes—some idyllic and some harmful—that have been perpetuated. There are ample examples of how media perpetuate such stereotypes (Belanger 2002; Freng 2007; Miller and Ross 2004; Reinhardt 2005). Debra Merskin suggests that branding in advertising using Native-American images such as Land O'Lakes dairy products and Jeep Cherokee comprises contemporary examples of commodified racism (2007). Michael Green sees such advertisements as morally unacceptable (1993). Others note the problematic effect on personal identity caused by repeated stereotyping that erases distinctions among tribes. Such erasure of unique tribal cultures is evident in the work of noted film director John Ford, who often confused the Cheyenne, Comanche, and Navajo tribes (Lawson 2008).

Much has been published about the inappropriate use of Native-American imagery in sports, from the names of the teams—Braves, Indians, Redskins, Seminoles, and Fighting Illini—to the fans motioning the "tomahawk chop" or making scalping gestures (Black 2002; Bresnahan and Flowers 2008; Charles 1993; King 2000, 2004; Longwell-Grice and Longwell-Grice 2003). The use of Native tribal names in sports has been controversial for years. The National Collegiate Athletic Association (NCAA) policy on Native-American mascots does not require schools to change names of teams or mascots to non–Native-American names. Nor does the policy preclude players on such teams from playing in championship tournaments. The policy merely restricts players from "wearing uniforms or other paraphernalia that depict nicknames or images while competing in NCAA championship events" (NCAA 2008). The policy is a step in the right direction but is weak in eliminating the fan and cheerleader use of symbols such as eagle feathers, war bonnets, peace pipes, and the like that are revered or sacred among Native Americans (Pewewardy 2004).

The history of America is full of negative stereotypes of Native Americans. The common phrase "The only good Indian is a dead Indian" could not be more hateful. This statement is proverbially ascribed to General Philip Sheridan in an 1869 meeting with Old Toch-a-way, a Comanche chief who tried to impress the general by saying, "Me, Toch-a-way; me good Injun." General Sheridan denied having made such a response, but the sentiment was clearly his policy (Mieder 1993).

Regardless of whether Sheridan was the original source of the comment, the belief was widely held by Anglo society in the late 1800s. But how do such prejudices and stereotypes come to dominate a culture? Children are not born with knowledge of stereotypes; we learn stereotypes through repeated exposure. Media both create stereotypes and help perpetuate them. Media images that do not accurately portray the reality of our lives shape our pictures of others and ourselves. They are part of how others perceive us. Clark McKown and Rhona Weinstein (2003) showed that children become aware of stereotypes of others between the ages of 6 and 10. Children from stigmatized ethnic groups show this awareness at an earlier age.

One method of erasing false stereotypes is education, but education may also ingrain false images of others. A study of history classes in U.S. secondary schools in urban areas found remarkable distortions in the portrayal of Native Americans in seven textbooks (Hawkins 2005). The examined texts all portrayed Indians as living on reservations despite the reality that two thirds of Native Americans, such as the Delawares in this study, did not live on governmental reserved land. The secondary teachers who derive lesson plans from the books they use in their classrooms "appear to ignore the complex culture of Native Americans and refrain from teaching students about current issues and experiences," the study concluded (2005, 53). Given that secondary education is heavily directed by teachers, and that children become aware of stereotypes in the first through fourth grades (McKown and Weinstein 2003), deficiencies in the textbooks and the knowledge of teachers perpetuate stereotypes about Native Americans. It is within this environment of educationally and media-disseminated stereotypes that we consider how such portrayals may affect growing up as a member of a stereotyped class.

Attempts to Erase Delaware Culture

The parents and grandparents of present-day tribal elders experienced the stigma of the prevailing negative attitudes toward Native Americans. That stigma affected the way they taught or did not teach their children.

When the Delawares received their final eviction notice and moved to Oklahoma, they were not given their own distinctive space but were made to share the land with Cherokees. While there may be similarities across tribes, they also are distinctly different in language, clothing, and culture. We would hardly ask the French to be British, but the Delawares were asked to be Cherokees. As explained by Howard Barnes,

> Well, Delawares weren't only Delawares. When we went to Chilocco [school], we had to go under Cherokee. What happened in 1876 when that treaty was signed, Cherokees and Delawares would be known as Cherokees. But I always

said that I was Delaware 'cause you couldn't change your blood. (Quoted in Brown and Kohn 2008a, 131)

Today, Mike Pace speaks of the negative consequences of the Dawes Act of 1887 that allocated land to individuals rather than collectively to the tribe. The land allotted to tribal members was checkerboarded with Anglo lands, breaking up the tribal community. Pace's aunt, Anna Davis, had the allotment that was the site of the first productive oil well for Phillips 66, now Conoco-Phillips. Pace described his experience:

I did not experience those things that some people have gone through where they were raised in areas where there was a certain lack of pride in your history, your family that was brought on by the society at that time. It was a bad thing to be an Indian at that point. This probably really began at the turn of the twentieth century where there was a definite effort on the part of the government to acclimate tribes into mainstream society. Because of that, they tried to break down those structures within the tribes and to bust those tribes up. The allotment system was used to spread the tribes out so they couldn't commune together as a tribe. Spread them out all over the place so that they would lose that sense of tribal identity. In Oklahoma, the allotment system was used to break those things up [tribal identity]. The young were sent off to boarding schools and forced to give up their languages and their songs and any identity with the tribes. So, for a long period, it was not a healthful thing to even admit that you were an Indian. (Quoted in Brown and Kohn 2008a, 253)

In the early 1900s, many Delawares chose not to express their culture or to teach their children about Delaware ways. Annette Ketchum remembers her difficulty in speaking Delaware:

In our home, grandmother would not talk Delaware to us and mother wouldn't either. The thing was, they didn't want the kids to talk Indian. And we would ask them, "Tell us some Indian words." Sometimes we would get grandmother to say something in Delaware. My grandmother's last husband would teach us some Cherokee words. And we learned those words when we were kids. But grandmother did not want to talk about anything about Indians because she had very bad experiences, and my mother had worse experiences because she was mixed blood. It was like they were bitter and angry about things that happened in their lives. (Quoted in Brown and Kohn 2008a, 185)

Native boarding schools were another attempt to eliminate the perpetuation of culture. Anna Davis was Mike Pace's link to culture because she was educated at a Catholic school that allowed Indian language and culture. His mother was forced to attend a government boarding school and was traumatized by the experience. He described it in this way:

> My mother, who did not speak English until she was 14, was picked up one day by the county sheriff in Washington County, and two truant officers—who knew that she wasn't attending regular public school there, knew she was Delaware, knew she didn't speak English—picked her up and took her up 180 miles away and put her in a boarding school. The policy of the federal government was to try to acculturate tribes into the white man's space. So a lot of those young kids were taken to these boarding schools where their language and their traditions were just literally beaten out of them.
>
> So my mother was very traumatized even up 'til the very last of her life because when she did go to the schools they would not allow her to speak her language. If she did, punishments varied. Sometimes it was the old soap in the mouth. My mother told me the worst thing that happened to her was they would actually give her a bucket and a brush and she had to scrub floors all night long. Then the next day she was not permitted to eat and went right back to class, even though she was totally exhausted. Over time, it traumatized her so much she wouldn't even speak the language. Through her whole life, she would not speak the language.
>
> Any chance they had to sneak off into the woods, they would. They would sing and dance and still carry on their own languages. Unfortunately, for most of those kids in those schools, they were not from one tribe. But it would still allow them to learn each other's languages. Anytime those children escaped from the schools, the sheriff and the truant officers went after them to bring them right back. (Pace 2009)

Four Slaves and a Brave

Former Delaware Chief Dee Ketchum attended the University of Kansas (KU) from 1959 to 1961. He played point guard on the basketball team, first as a substitute in his sophomore year and then as a starter in his junior and senior years. He was co-captain of the 1961 Big Eight championship team his senior year. They traveled to Madison Square Garden to play St. John's University, ironically known as the "Redmen" at the time, since changed to "The Red Storm." A New York City newspaper led the story with the headline "Four Slaves and a Brave Invade Madison Square Garden." Ketchum was the brave, and his African-American team members were the slaves. Regrettably, such a racist headline passed for being catchy or humorous at the time. Even so, Ketchum says he did not feel as much prejudice as his teammates:

> We didn't think of it to tell you quite truthfully, but during that whole year and the time I was at Kansas, there was some prejudice, not so much toward American Indians I didn't feel, but there was some prejudice toward the black players. I remember when we went down to Texas and Kentucky, we had trouble and they had to have a highway patrol escort taking us on the campus of North Carolina. With the number of minorities we had on that team, we had to make special provisions wherever we went. I can remember very clearly when we went to North Carolina they told us we had to stay on campus because we couldn't stay in a hotel, obviously, and the coach told us don't go downtown. Bill Bridges was my roommate. He was a black player who went on and had a very successful NBA career, and we were co-captains together my senior year, so we roomed together. Bill and I said, "Let's go downtown Saturday morning." So we walked downtown and coaches didn't know about it. We walked into the restaurant and the welcome was not there, let's say that! The owner came over personally and said, "I think it'd be advisable for you two to leave." (Ketchum and Ketchum 2009)

For a semester, Ketchum roomed with Billy Mills, a Sioux from a reservation. Ketchum described an example of Native Americans stigmatizing another who had achieved success off the reservation:

> Billy Mills told me one time he had a problem going back on the reservation. I said, "Well, why? You're an Olympic gold medal winner, the only American that's ever won the 10,000 meters. You're a hero!" He says, "Well yeah," but he says, "When I go back there, they call me apple." I said, "Apple?" and he says, "Yeah, I'm dark on the outside and white on the inside." And I had never heard much about that, but obviously it's in the American Indian vocabulary, but he's the first who said that to me and I'll never forget that. (Ketchum and Ketchum 2009)

Annette Ketchum, now wife of Dee Ketchum, also remembers her years at KU. Growing up, she was made to feel good about being a Native American. As she began her college studies, she was surprised by the prejudices of others:

> It just seemed like when I grew up, they made us feel good because we were Indians; we were special 'cause we were Indians. And that's how my mother

and our aunts and people around us treated us—we were honored to be an Indian, you know? We were the best. So I didn't have an attitude about it.

My first experience was when we were at KU and I asked the girls at the dorm, "Do you ever go out to Haskell [Indian College in Lawrence, Kansas]?" They said, "No." And I said, "Well, I'd like to go out there, you know, I'm an Indian." And one of the girls, she just looked at me. I didn't know what she was, she was fairly dark; she may have been Jewish or something. She said, "Well you know you could pass." It was just like, "Don't tell anybody you're Indian 'cause you could pass." And I thought, "Well, why would I do that? Why would I want to pass for something else?" It was just very shocking to me. (Ketchum and Ketchum 2009)

Beverly McLaughlin lived on a Sioux reservation in North Dakota with her husband but now lives in Oklahoma after her divorce. She had to actively learn her Delaware heritage. She speaks of her frustration with stereotypes:

I don't feel all the bitterness and hurts that a lot of [Native] people do. But I've also lived on a reservation and know how it feels to be looked upon as a drunken, dirty Indian, too. It really does something to you when people put that expectation on you. And still today I cannot stand for any Indian to be looked down on just because of the way they're dressed, or alcohol on their breath or whatever. It's just a state of being for a time, hopefully. (Quoted in Brown and Kohn 2008a, 223)

The late Joanna Nichol was an activist and a journalist. If you asked her a question, you would take notes for an hour. When the federal government closed and then abandoned Alcatraz Island as a prison, Nichol was one of the protesters who took it over. Members of the American Indian Movement, an activist group founded in Minneapolis in 1968 to prevent police abuse, create job training, and fight stereotyping (American Indian Movement n.d.; Public Broadcasting System n.d.), supported the Alcatraz occupation in 1969. Eventually the federal government took back Alcatraz, and it is now a national park. Before her death, Nichol spoke about her activism and the prevailing sense among Native Americans of being subjugated:

[In the 1960s] I was really upset about what was happening because the Bureau of Indian Affairs was relocating everybody. They was offering everybody, making it sound like heaven, "Here's a one-way ticket. Go to San Francisco, Chicago, wherever you want to go and into the big cities. Here's some money and you can get yourself an apartment and you will really enjoy it." They didn't have a return ticket. They didn't know how to use a telephone. They didn't know how to find a restroom. They didn't even know how to order in a restaurant.

Because some of the tribes that we had at that time did not look at people in their eyes; they would look down and wouldn't speak until they were spoken to. I was working with the Indians all the time. In fact, I had a newspaper going. I had a newspaper going, and I occupied Alcatraz. I occupied their communication center, where the D-Q University is now. I was active all the time. And I had my own cell at Alcatraz. We all threw our gear in the cell, and that was our room, you know? I worked; I had a Title IV program for the whole county of San Mateo, which I worked on and started several good programs there for the Indians. We taught the teachers how to handle the Indian children because our children was not taught to try to be first or smartest. (Quoted in Brown and Kohn 2008a, 230–231)

Forty years ago, photographs of early Delaware powwows near Copan, Oklahoma, show regalia inappropriate for Delaware culture. Dancers wore headdresses that were Plains Indian culture, not the roach or otter turban worn by the Delaware Eastern Woodland culture. As a result of either federal government action to quash culture or parents' failure to teach and embody tribal culture, traditions were almost eliminated. When Dee Ketchum moved back to Bartlesville, Oklahoma, he remembered going to a Delaware gathering:

One of the ladies came up to me and said, "Dee, let's have a stomp dance." And I said, "Well, that's good, do we have any leaders?" And she said, "Why don't you lead, Dee?" and I said, "No, I don't know the songs." And so she made the announcement and asked if there were any leaders. And we didn't have one Delaware leader, and that was embarrassing to me because our history, the Delaware Tribe, we had wonderful leaders. We had some of the best stomp dance leaders in the country. And here we went through a generation where we didn't produce any. So I made a vow right at that point to learn the songs. I went down to the Creeks and learned from them as much as I could and learned from other elders around that I could and got as many tapes as I could. I started to learn how to lead those songs. (Quoted in Brown and Kohn 2008a, 205–206)

Recapturing Culture and Dispelling Stereotypes

From the earliest arrival of Europeans to North America until the twenty-first century, many forces combined to eliminate Native-American culture. Government actions intentionally sought to eradicate culture, and parents chose not to teach Native ways to their children. Media images contributed to prevalent negative stereotypes, and recognition that culture was disappearing prompted revival of Indian activism and attempts to reclaim and maintain Indian culture.

Fearing that their culture was slipping away, the Ketchums, Mike Pace, and many others in the tribe worked to regain their songs, dances, and distinctive Delaware clothing. Today, these ties to their ancestors are historically accurate. At the same time, they developed a successful program to dispel stereotypes about Native Americans. Each fall since 1992, the Delawares are guests at Conner Prairie, a living history museum in Fishers, Indiana. Separate programs designed to fit the attention span of fourth graders (the age when Indiana state history is introduced and stereotypes are learned or unlearned) cover clothing, the history of the Delawares, and traditional stories, language, and songs. About 2,500 students rotate in a round-robin fashion across various components of the daylong program over a week.

Mike Pace comments on the program and the need for it:

> The Indiana Indians program we do here for Conner Prairie has many different aspects to it. The program is especially for the children because of the

Mike Pace shows young visitors a Lenape (Delaware) water drum. Pace serves as the Delaware interpreter at the Conner Prairie Living History Museum. (Courtesy of James W. Brown.)

many, many stereotypes that exist about Native Americans, and even young people have ingrained stereotypes. They didn't really learn what they know from a Native American; they learned it from Hollywood and from watching television. They learned it from something their parents or their grandparents said; so there's that stereotype that we're savage, we're vicious people, we don't get along in white society—those images still exist.

We invited a lady from our church and her family to come over to our house one time. When they came, I offered a prayer, but I offered it in my own language and we kind of had a traditional Delaware meal. Everybody had a great time; they enjoyed that. Well a few weeks later, that family reciprocated. They asked us to come over to their house for a traditional meal at their home. But the interesting thing was that the young girl asked her mother a very strange question. What she said to her mother was, "Are the Paces coming over?" and she said, "Yes." And she said, "Well is Mike gonna cut my head off?" Because they knew I was an Indian, and that's what Indians do. And even though it was a strange question, she was only four years old, how did she get that impression? Those are the types of stereotypes we have to overcome. (Pace 2008)

The questions that the fourth graders ask the Delawares are often amusing but demonstrate their lack of understanding of Native culture. A common question is "How long have you been an Indian?" Mike Pace will jokingly answer, "Oh, the last 35 minutes." Pace says,

There used to be a time Indians were not popular, and it was not popular to be an Indian. But today, because of the new movies and because of the younger stories we get coming up, even though they may not be true or even close to the reality, the fact is now—it's great to be an Indian. So, even kids who have no Indian blood at all will claim that they have Indian blood. I remember one little girl that stood up and she said, "I'm half Indian." And I said, "Well what tribe are you?" and she said, "Well I'm not real sure. All I really know for sure is that I'm half Indian and half country." We all got a good kick out of that one.

So we have lots of those stories and even some of the questions the adults ask sometimes are kind of skewed with those prejudices and stereotypes that exist. So that's what we do, we try to dispel that; we want to give them a different attitude and a different look at Native Americans. But they are trying to learn, they're not stupid questions. They may be to us, they may be funny, but their intent—they really want to know about Indians. (Pace 2008)

There is a direct connection between these Delawares and the Conner Prairie museum. In the 1800s, William Conner developed a successful trading post just north of what is now Indianapolis. Conner married a Native named Mekinges, Lenape for "Dancing Feather." She was the daughter of Chief Kikthawenund, whose English name was William Anderson, after whom Anderson, Indiana, about 40 miles northeast of Indianapolis, was named. When the Delawares moved west of Indiana following a treaty that Conner helped negotiate, Conner abandoned Mekinges and their six children. He stayed in Indiana with his successful business and married an Anglo woman. The Delawares who developed this educational program for the Conner Prairie museum are direct descendants of either Chief Anderson or Mekinges.

Conclusion with an Eye toward the Future

Delawares are acculturated in Anglo society. In the past, there was time to learn the culture of the tribe from elders. Elders would wait to be asked before they would teach to ensure there was a desire to learn. Now younger tribal descendants are distracted by everyday activities including jobs that support their families. How will the youth of acculturated families carry on traditions or evolve them? And how can tribal culture reemerge in a society saturated with media that perpetuate racist stereotypes?

The Delawares' traditional dance, song, and culture were nearly lost because of the imposition of Anglo culture. Today, society celebrates diversity. But it wasn't always so, and despite societal changes, few non-Natives know a great deal about the tribal societies' laws and social systems before the invasion of European culture. The fabric of the United States is made stronger by preserving unique and dynamic cultures and learning from them. As the country becomes even more diverse, understanding of different cultures will become more important.

In moving forward, it will be a mistake to freeze Native culture within some romanticized past. Culture evolves in all societies, with parts of cultural symbols abandoned. For example, there are no more native Delaware speakers. That is not to say the language is gone or that no one can speak Delaware. The tribe has preserved the language from Native speakers and conducts language classes, but no one speaks Delaware as their primary language.

Stereotypes affect understanding, self-image, and social interactions, and can cause people to misperceive other cultures in ways that diminish us all. Appropriation of cultural symbols, most visible in sports, fails to honor Native Americans and should be unacceptable to Anglo society. We should understand how some symbols, however innocent in intent, are abhorrent to Native culture, and we should move forward to eliminate athletic symbols, images, and behaviors that injure. These stereotypes can be reversed if there is the will to do so.

Negative stereotypes are learned, but they also can be unlearned by a concerted effort to reexamine our own beliefs and attitudes. Today the Delawares are maintaining programs in their tribal center to proactively teach their culture without waiting to be asked. At the same time, more in-depth media coverage of Native issues could help address knowledge gaps, dispel lingering stereotypes, and help Anglos and others better understand the important Native contributions to U.S. history. Our educational system should correct incomplete information and unfair portrayals. It is imperative that history textbooks and lesson plans be revised to eliminate pejorative images of Native Americans. Journalists should go beyond the Anglo hot topics such as casinos or reservation life to report more fully on the complex nature of tribes. Accurate media information helps dispel stereotypes.

Elders have taken up the challenge to teach. The youth must also take up the challenge to learn. Progress, although slow, can be noted. Jake Sears, grandson of Dee and Annette Ketchum, whom I first photographed as a young teenager a decade ago, had the honor of being headman dancer at the 2010 Delaware Powwow at Copan, Oklahoma.

A thriving culture lives on, and media images should reflect its rich diversity.

Notes

1. By James W. Brown, © 2007.

2. The author wishes to express appreciation to Rita Kohn, coeditor of *Long Journey Home: Oral Histories of Contemporary Delaware Indians* (Brown and Kohn 2008a); Tracey Rector, who transcribed interviews and supported the research; Maggie Hillery, who helped edit the manuscript; and the Lenape People, who have held his attention and admiration for a long time.

3. A more detailed Delaware history may be found in Weslager (2000).

4. As a boy in the early 1950s playing cowboys and Indians with my Roy Rogers cap pistols, I was always a cowboy helping to tame the Wild West. My interest in being a cowboy resulted from the stereotype of Indians that was so prevalent and persists to this day. Some half-century later, my sympathies are with the Indians as a result of more than a decade of photographing and interviewing members of the Delaware Tribe of Indians of Eastern Oklahoma. That decade of work resulted in a book coedited with Rita Kohn, *Long Journey Home: Oral Histories of Contemporary*

Delaware Indians (Brown and Kohn 2008a). During that decade, many of the subjects of the book have become personal friends.

As a non-Indian, I struggle to put any words to paper that describe the Indian experience. After all, it was not my experience. Instead I rely on the words of the Lenape themselves. This chapter contains pieces of interviews from *Long Journey Home: Oral Histories of Contemporary Delaware Indians* (Brown and Kohn 2008a) as well as new interviews for this work. The quotes are the words of the Lenape people that Rita Kohn and I interviewed. Our method was to provide only minor editing to form logical sentences in transcriptions of recorded interviews. Each subject reviewed the transcription in response to our question "Is this what you meant to say?" All were given an opportunity to edit. Their responses ranged from no change to complete rewrites. The words in this chapter are not, therefore, the Brown–Kohn interpretation of the Delaware experience; they are the perspective of the Delawares themselves. Such oral histories are an important part of the fabric of history. They provide the context from the people who lived the history to other historic documents and news accounts. In this writing, the oral histories give voice to the Delawares.

Sources

American Indian Movement. N.d. AIM-GGC profile. http://www.aimovement .org/ggc/index.html. (accessed March 7, 2010).

Belanger, Yale. 2002. Journalistic opinion as free speech or promoting racial unrest? The case of Ric Dolphin and the Calgary Herald's editorial presentation of Native culture. *The American Indian Quarterly* 26, no. 3: 393–417.

Bird, S. Elizabeth. 1999. Gendered construction of the American Indian in popular media. *The Journal of Communication* 49, no. 3: 61–83.

Black, Jason Edward. 2002. The "mascotting" of Native America: Construction, commodity, and assimilation. *American Indian Quarterly* 26, no. 4: 605–622.

Bresnahan, Mary Jiang, and Kelly Flowers. 2008. The effects of involvement in sports on attitudes toward Native American sport mascots. *The Howard Journal of Communications* 19, no. 2: 165–181.

Brown, James W., and Rita T. Kohn, eds. 2008a. *Long journey home: Oral histories of contemporary Delaware Indians.* Bloomington: Indiana University Press.

Brown, James W., and Rita T. Kohn, eds. 2008b. The memory of place. From "Long journey home: Oral histories of contemporary Delaware Indians." *Traces of Indiana & Midwestern History* 20, no. 1: 18–23.

Charles, Jim. 1993. *Of mascots and tomahawk chops: Stereotypes of American Indians and the English teacher's response.* http://www.eric.ed.gov/ ERICWebPortal/custom/portlets/recordDetails/detailmini.jsp?_ nfpb=true&_&ERICExtSearch_SearchValue_0=ED355535&ERICExtSearc h_SearchType_0=no&accno=ED355535 (accessed March 13, 2010).

Freng, Adrienne. 2007. American Indians in the news: A media portrayal in crime articles. *American Indian Culture and Research Journal* 31, no. 1: 21–37.

Green, Michael K. 1993. Images of Native Americans in advertising: Some moral issues. *Journal of Business Ethics* 12, no. 4: 323–330.

Hawkins, Jeffrey. 2005. Smoke signals, sitting bulls, and slot machines: A new stereotype of Native Americans? *Multicultural Perspectives* 7, no. 3: 51–54.

Ketchum, Dee, and Annette Ketchum. 2009. Personal communication, July 31.

King, C. Richard. 2000. Fighting spirits: The racial politics of sports mascots. *Journal of Sport & Social Issues* 24, no. 3: 282–304.

King, C. Richard. 2004. This is not an Indian: Situating claims about Indianness in sporting worlds. *Journal of Sport & Social Issues* 28, no. 1: 3–10.

Lawson, Angelica. 2008. Native American Popular Culture and Race. In *Encyclopedia of race and racism*, ed. John Hartwell Moore, pp. 354–356. Detroit, MI: Macmillan Reference USA.

Longwell-Grice, Robert, and Hope Longwell-Grice. 2003. Chiefs, braves, and tomahawks: The use of American Indians as university mascots. *NASPA Journal* 40, no. 3: 1–12.

McKown, Clark, and Rhona S. Weinstein. 2003. The development and consequences of stereotype consciousness in middle childhood. *Child Development* 74, no. 2: 498–515.

Merskin, Debra. 2007. The princess and the SUV: Brand images of Native Americans as commodified racism. Paper presented at the annual conference for the International Communication Association, May 23, San Francisco.

Mieder, Wolfgang. 1993. "The only good Indian is a dead Indian": History and meaning of a proverbial stereotype. *Journal of American Folklore* 106: 38–60.

Miller, Autumn, and Susan Dente Ross. 2004. They are not us: Framing of American Indians by the Boston Globe. *The Howard Journal of Communications* 15, no. 4: 245–256.

National Collegiate Athletic Association (NCAA). 2008. Native American mascots. http://bit.ly/5CLkNP (accessed March 13, 2010).

Ohio Historical Society. 2010. Gnadenhutten massacre. http://www.ohiohistory central.org/entry.php?rec=499 (accessed March 13, 2010).

Pace, Mike. 2008. Personal communication.

Pace, Mike. 2009. Personal communication.

Pewewardy, Cornel D. 2004. Playing Indian at halftime: The controversy over American Indian mascots, logos, and nicknames in school-related events. *The Clearing House* 77, no. 5: 180–185.

Public Broadcasting System. N.d. Timeline of Indian activism. http://www.pbs .org/itvs/alcatrazisnotanisland/timeline.html (accessed March 13, 2010).

Reinhardt, Akim D. 2005. Defining the Native: Local print media coverage of the Nmai. *American Indian Quarterly* 29, nos. 3–4: 450–465.

Weslager, Clinton. A. 2000. *The Delaware Indians: A history*. New Brunswick, NJ: Rutgers University Press.

Chapter 7

Marketing the Sacred: Commodifying Native-American Cultural Images

Lucy A. Ganje

Ask just about anyone if they've contributed to the communication of American Indian stereotypes and identity theft, and you're likely to get an emphatic "NO." But ask them if they've ever spread a scone with Land O'Lakes butter or Sue Bee honey; made a toast with a Leinenkugel; worn a pair of Cherokee jeans; driven a Pontiac or vacationed in a Winnebago; eaten at a restaurant or bar where they were greeted by a "cigar-store" Indian statue; participated in—or were spectators at—games whose teams (primarily or completely non-Native) were identified through the use of images from Native cultures; or enjoyed watching the Disney movies *Peter Pan* or *Pocahontas*, and the answer might be different.

Products and businesses marketed with Native-American names and images have been around for a long time. But what makes these marketing and advertising devices so popular—so successful? And why have so many of these products' parent companies been asked by American Indian organizations to stop using them?[1]

As marketers who create and use them for this purpose know, images of American Native people, spirituality, places, and objects sell (Merskin 2001). And the most popular of these images is that of the Lakota warrior, known as the classic, archetypal Native American. Marsha C. Bol (1999), in

Since Native Americans introduced tobacco to European explorers and settlers, the use of cigar store Indians has been an advertisement symbol. (Courtesy of Paul Martin Lester.)

the book *Unpacking Culture: Art and Commodity in Colonial and Postcolonial Worlds*, quotes a perception of the Lakota by a German author:

> American Indians—who would not have in mind tall redskins, in feather headdresses galloping over the prairie with noble, aristocratic features, clothed in buffalo skins and deer hide; and who would not think of courageous and fearless hunts and battles? (215)

This chapter examines issues surrounding the persistence of this image and its use to brand or sell a concept or product. Branding is today considered a company's most valuable asset. On its website, the Brand Institute, a brand identity consulting agency, states that a properly developed brand can create "competitive advantages and maximize earnings" (www.brandinstitute .com). But equally important, branding is a way to promote and position your "message," to develop a memorable impression that ensures you will be noticed.

Commodification of "Indianness"

"Indianness" has become a branding device, a successful marketing strategy, because it allows people to claim a history and identity other than their own—to play Indian (see, e.g., Deloria 1998). To further understand this paradox, focus is placed on the Great Plains of North America, on North Dakota (a state located in the heart of "Indian Country"),[2] and on the means by which North Dakota and its "flagship" university came to appropriate a Native-American identity. In order to be adopted as an advertising tool, however, this "Indian brand" had to be transformed from a perceived negative (uncivilized) to a positive (valiant, but disappearing) image. The culture and image of the Lakota, Dakota, and Nakota (Sioux) people had to be converted into a desirable commodity.

"Culture" has become a branding device and an economic and ideological battleground (Wallerstein 1990). The meaning of the phrase "culture vulture" appears to typify a difference in approach to one's culture and heritage. "Culture vulture" in an Anglo-American context takes on a positive connotation. For example, *Webster's New Millennium Dictionary of English* defines a "culture vulture" as "a person who is extremely interested in and enthusiastic about the arts; a person who attends cultural events" (www.dictionary.com). The *American Heritage Dictionary of Idioms'* definition is: "An individual with a consuming or excessive interest in the arts. For example, a relentless culture vulture, she dragged her children to every museum in town" (Ammer 2003). The non-Indian community seems to have embraced the term, and an online search finds art galleries, art reviews, jewelry, and music under that name. But the online *Urban Dictionary* identifies the term as "someone who steals traits, language and/or fashion from another ethnic or social group in order to create their own identity" (www.urbandictionary.com). This definition is applied in a context closer to the understanding of those whose culture is being appropriated.

Writing in an article published in the *American Indian Quarterly*, Peter Kulchyski (1997) noted that culture can be characterized as "one of the most useful intellectual tools of the twentieth century—slowly coming to replace the nineteenth century concept of 'race.'" He argued that in the twenty-first century, cultural products including "images, 'authentic' artifacts, and perhaps even ceremonies and spiritual events, will likely be widely circulated commodities." And, he continued, cultural products deemed "authentic" and which serve to identify cultures other than the dominant one "will likely be among the most valuable commodities."

Identity is often used as a marketing tool in a commodity culture. Based on images manufactured by the media, artists, and scholars, popular culture provides ways of communicating who or what somebody is. Constructing new identities is also a popular pastime. Putting on a mask provides the wearers the opportunity to become that which they are not. One of the most widely used masks in the United States became that of the Native American. Indian "costumes" remain popular at Halloween, and "the Indian" constitutes a favorite costume party identity.

There are several cultural concepts of "Indian" that have been identified frequently, including the savage, the mystical environmentalist, and the exotic (see, e.g., Miller and Ross 2004). Historically, Anglo Americans have felt both revulsion and admiration for the original inhabitants of this land. On the one hand, Native people were admired for what was often termed their good and gentle nobility, and their "fine physiques." But they were also reviled for what was perceived as their savagery, heathenism, cunning, and warlike qualities (Deloria 1998, 3). Anglo-American or European people (and thus the marketplace) at one time or another have embraced most of these cultural identities, or images, of Native-American people.

Historical Stereotyping and Slaughter

These prevailing stereotypical images of Native people have been recorded since Indian–Anglo contact and continue to drive Anglo-American concepts of Indian identity today—and Anglo-American political conduct toward Native-American people and communities. This is particularly prevalent in the cultural imagery created as commodity art—art whose subject matter and style are tailored to appeal to the marketplace.

The Missouri brewing company Anheuser-Busch adopted the "savage" image when it distributed 150,000 copies of the lithograph *Custer's Last Fight* to help sell its beer. The image is described on the privately owned, nonprofit Custer Battlefield Museum's website as the most famous depiction ("seen by millions of people in the last 106 years") of the Battle of the Little Bighorn, "and the most famously inaccurate" (n.d.;

see www.custermuseum.org). This image is, according to American Indian social critic Elizabeth Cook-Lynn (2007), an example of what she terms "anti-Indianism" because of the false information it contains. Cook-Lynn argues that images like this insult and turn away thoughtful Indian readers.

The Anheuser-Busch Brewing Association began production of Budweiser beer in the United States the same year (1876) as the Battle of the Little Bighorn (six years before the Gnadenhutten Massacre mentioned in chapter 6). Cassilly Adams painted the first version of *Custer's Last Fight*, measuring 16 feet, 5 inches by 9 feet, 6 inches, on a wagon canvas for a traveling exhibit. Company founder Adolphus Busch came up with the concept of an advertising campaign based on the battle (during which 350 to 400 men were killed) and purchased Adams's painting. The Milwaukee Lithographic & Engraving Company in Milwaukee produced the prints, which were distributed to saloons all over the United States to promote Budweiser beer.

The image is a lurid depiction of the battle showing dead on both sides but focusing in the foreground on scalped, partially nude bodies of

Although the painting of Custer's Last Fight by Western genre painter Cassilly Adams was destroyed in a fire, a reproduction of it was used as an advertising tool by Anheuser Busch. (Courtesy of the Library of Congress.)

Anglo-American soldiers. Custer is portrayed with a flowing mane of blond hair (his hair was actually cut short), with a red scarf wrapped around his neck (he was not wearing a red scarf), and swinging a saber—all inventions of the artist. The dress of the Indian warriors is "fanciful," the Indian village in the background is shown on the wrong side of the Little Bighorn River, and some of the warriors appear to be carrying what have been described as "Zulu shields" (Kemmick 2002).

The painting contributes to erroneous notions of the battle and grossly misrepresents Indian experience, masking the colonialist extermination of the Lakota Sioux, who were fighting a battle initiated by Custer and the U.S. government. This particular battle (called the Battle of Greasy Grass by the Lakota) is especially significant because it was the culmination of 400 years of struggle. The National Park Service's website for the Little Bighorn Battlefield National Monument states that the battle rose beyond its military significance to the level of myth: "Thousands of books, magazine articles, performances in film and theater, paintings, and other artistic expressions have memorialized 'Custer's Last Stand'" (n.d.). The Battle of the Little Bighorn "epitomizes the clash of cultures—the Native American versus the Euro-American—that is so much a part [of] our heritage," according to the Midwest Archeological Center (n.d.).

News of this battle spread like a wildfire on the prairie. Newspapers covered the "massacre" (a descriptive still used today), taking their cue from the *Bismarck Tribune*, a Dakota Territory newspaper whose correspondent died at the battle. The *Tribune*, with no attempt at impartiality, described the Indians as "red devils" and "screeching fiends, dealing death and destruction" (Welch 2007, 192–193). The *Tribune*'s account, picked up by eastern newspapers and read by millions of people, outraged the country, contributed to Anglo-America's image of Native people, and helped reinforce an attitude toward them that was articulated as "The only good Indian is a dead Indian."

"The only good Indian is a dead Indian." This genocidal phrase, so often repeated in the history of Indian and Anglo relations and attributed to General Philip Sheridan in 1869 (Mieder 1993), actually was recorded as early as the seventeenth and eighteenth centuries, and was repeated on the floor of the U.S. House of Representatives by James Cavanaugh, congressman from Montana, during an 1868 debate on an "Indian Appropriation Bill." "I believe," he said, "in the policy that exterminates the Indians, drives them outside the boundaries of civilization, because you cannot civilize them" (Mieder 1993, 42).

L. Frank Baum (1890), author of *The Wonderful Wizard of Oz* (1900), wrote in an editorial published in his Dakota Territory newspaper responding to the 1890 Wounded Knee Massacre and the killing of Sitting Bull,

> The Whites, by law of conquest, by justice of civilization, are masters of the American continent, and the best safety of the frontier settlements will be secured by the total annihilation of the few remaining Indians. Why not annihilation? Their glory has fled, their spirit broken, their manhood effaced; better that they die than live the miserable wretches that they are.

And Theodore Roosevelt, in a January 1886 speech in New York, said,

> I suppose I should be ashamed to say that I take the Western view of Indians. I don't go so far as to think that the only good Indians are dead Indians, but I believe nine out of every 10 are, and I shouldn't like to inquire too closely into the case of the tenth. . . . Reckless, revengeful, fiendishly cruel, they rob and murder, not the cowboys who can take care of themselves, but the defenseless, lone settlers on the plains. (Quoted in Mieder 1993, 45–46)

This quote was also repeated in his book *The Winning of the West* (1889). Five years after making this statement, he became president of the United States.

University of California students in 1986 investigated the widespread use and acceptance of the phrase "The only good Indian is a dead Indian" for a course in folklore. A student collector recorded the following from a woman who grew up in North Dakota, illustrating a prevailing perspective of many North Dakotans (and Anglo Americans):

> My informant is a native of North Dakota where she tells me there were many Indian reservations. She learned this proverb (The only good Indian is a dead Indian) when she was a very young child [c. 1923]. She cannot remember any specific sources for the proverb; it was just something that you would hear at home or at school. People in North Dakota were extremely prejudiced against the Indians because they had the reputation of never working, always drinking. They were not very honest people and were believed by many to be murderers and looters. Indians were not respected by the white people at all. Thus, we can understand the reasoning behind the proverb. (Mieder 1993, 49–50)[3]

Although this sentiment against Native Americans was expressed throughout the United States, it was especially popular in the Great Plains.

Each of the above statements was voiced by people who lived and worked (however briefly) on the upper Plains: General Philip Sheridan, who played a decisive role in the U.S. Army's ruthless campaign against Native people on the Plains; Cavanaugh, who represented the state of Montana in Washington, D.C.; Baum, who was an editor of a "frontier" newspaper in Aberdeen, South Dakota; Theodore Roosevelt; and homesteaders who came to "settle" the Plains.

A Paradigm Shift?

Given the negative view of Native Americans shared by many Anglo-American people on the Great Plains, it might come as a surprise that, a little more than 40 years after Teddy Roosevelt called for their annihilation, North Dakota's flagship institution, the University of North Dakota, would name its sports team the Sioux and adopt an "Indian head" symbol to represent itself. What happened in those four decades that would create this paradigm shift? What caused this massive consciousness raising that carried people from calling for the extermination of a race of people to "honoring" them by taking on their name and visual identity for their sports teams, products, and educational institutions?

Native-American people were segregated onto reservations, and their children forced into boarding schools far away from their homes, where the U.S. government's strategy was to erase their culture. If American Indian people vanished, either literally or culturally, there would be no victims, and if in the end there is no victim—*there is no crime*. With Native people safely removed and out of sight, Anglo Americans could begin to reframe history, shaping and defining Native identity in their own likeness. "Playing Indian" is, according to Philip Deloria in his book by the same name, a tradition in American culture (1998). Deloria suggests there is a dual feeling about Indians in the U.S. national psyche, and two options often surfaced in the history of Indian–Anglo relations—extermination or assimilation. Both were aimed at making Native people disappear from the landscape (Deloria 1998).

The University of North Dakota (UND) was founded in 1883 in what was then known as Dakota Territory. This was only seven years after the Battle of the Little Bighorn (and in a region from which Custer and the 7th Calvary departed for the Montana Territory) and six years before North Dakota would become a state. This was also a time of increased government intervention into the lives of Native-American people with the aim of assimilation. Native people were prohibited from practicing their religion. Young people were removed from their homes and placed in boarding schools, where their hair was cut and speaking their language was forbidden. Reservation land was broken up into allotments, forcing the concept of individual ownership upon the people. There continued to be turmoil and great uncertainty within Native communities. While the university was celebrating the construction of its first building, American Indian Plains people were reeling from the massacre of friends and relatives at Wounded Knee and the murder of Sitting Bull at Fort Yates, North Dakota.

The visual messages formally chosen to represent the state and the university would signal the region's attitudes toward Native-American people. The territorial seal was approved in 1863 by the Legislative Assembly of the Territory of Dakota. Wording in North Dakota's Constitution describes one of the seal's symbols as "an Indian on horseback pursuing a buffalo toward the setting sun." A plow and anvil are in the foreground. This placement probably represents the disappearance (whether perceived as iconic or symbolic) of Indian people and their way of life. Although North Dakota's official website states that "research has failed to reveal the reasons the selected symbols were chosen" (State of North Dakota 2009), the social and geometrical perspective used by the artist (e.g., the Native man on horseback and the buffalo moving away from the viewer toward the setting sun) visually places these Native elements in the past. This seal was adopted as the Great Seal of North Dakota when North Dakota gained statehood in 1889.

North Dakota State Highway signs also celebrate the disappearance of Native culture and people. State highways began to be marked in 1923, at which time the chief highway engineer chose to use the image of a Native-American man named Marcellus Red Tomahawk (Tacanke Luta) as an emblem to mark the way through the state highway system (Standing Rock Sioux Tourism Website 2008). Red Tomahawk was a Standing Rock Sioux and sergeant of the Indian Police. He received notoriety as the man who had killed Sitting Bull in December 1890. This distinction earned him the label of "a good Indian" and therefore worthy of having the honor of becoming a logo and mascot. Red Tomahawk's profile also became the official symbol for the North Dakota State Highway Patrol in 1951 (Eriksmoen 2009).

After the university discarded its original sports team name and symbol (the Flickertail) in 1930, a new image was sought, and with little (if any) debate the university reemerged with a new face and name—the Fighting (a descriptive added later) Sioux with an Indian-head symbol. This

The seal of the state of North Dakota. (Source: State of North Dakota.)

identity was chosen, according to the student newspaper, for the following reasons:

1. Sioux are a good exterminating agent for the Bison [a rival team];
2. Sioux are warlike, of fine physique and bearing; and
3. The word Sioux is easily rhymed for yells and songs. (Annis 1999, 2)

The first images used to portray "the Sioux" were often big-nosed, cartoonish buffoons. In popular culture, according to University of Kansas Professor Cornel Pewewardy, "[U]sing a person for your clown has always been one of the major ways to assert your dominance over a person or a group of people" (n.d.).

These images changed over the years until the most recent incarnation. The UND Alumni Foundation in 2001, in the midst of considerable

A North Dakota highway sign. (Courtesy of Jordan McAlister.)

controversy, commissioned a Native-American artist to create another Indian-head symbol. The artist, a graduate of the University of North Dakota's Art Department, is an enrolled member of the Turtle Mountain Band of Chippewa. The symbol is of the head of an Indian male, with a stylized painted face and an eagle feather in his hair. The university claimed the symbol was commissioned and adopted to "honor" Indian people. The Alumni Foundation, dominated by Anglos, introduced this new symbol despite decades-long objections to the Fighting Sioux "tradition" by American Indian students, programs, faculty, and tribal organizations.

Historically, Anglo collectors and consumers of Lakota (Sioux) art had a definite notion of what comprised a "Sioux" identity. They were interested in art of the past, in objects that represented a Plains warrior lifestyle. Another pattern emerges regarding those who collect Lakota art, a gender pattern that differs from the collectors of Native art from other regions.

The symbol of the North Dakota Highway Patrol is a profile of Red Tomahawk, a Teton Dakotah (Sioux) who lived near the Cannonball River on the Standing Rock Indian Reservation near Mandan, North Dakota. (Source: North Dakota State Patrol.)

"By and large, the collectors of Lakota arts were (and are) men," according to Marsha Bol (1999, 215). She states that male collectors seem to find the artifacts of pre-reservation warrior society "particularly fascinating."

This pattern of consumption can be seen in the symbol chosen by the University of North Dakota as its signifier. The male figure, the painted face, and the eagle feather are all status signifiers. The university's choice of a mascot and symbol appears to coincide with certain characteristics of collectors of Plains Indian art and the criteria used to evaluate their acquisitions: Those who purchase the image are male; the image contains signifiers of status, including an eagle feather, considered sacred by Lakota (and other Native) people; and it places Indian people in the past. The

The University of North Dakota's "Fighting Sioux" mascot. (Courtesy of Lucy Ganje.)

mold of the Lakota Sioux, according to Bol, "was cast indelibly in nostalgia for the past; it is a tenacious image still accepted throughout the world and not easily extinguished" (1999, 215).

In 2010, after a four-year legal battle ending in a state supreme court ruling, UND agreed to "retire" its Fighting Sioux nickname and logo (Mador 2010).

Appropriation's Effects

Cultural identity is a complex and often deeply felt sense of connection and belonging. One can have the racial identity of "Indian," but a cultural identity is a different matter. A cultural identity as a Lakota (or, even more specifically, a particular band of Lakota such as Mnicoujou, Itazipco, Sihasapa, or Oohenumpa) means understanding or participating in ceremonies, understanding or speaking the language, following the social and cultural practices of the tribal community, and usually being able to trace one's ancestry or having family ties to one's home reservation or nation.

The Lakota culture is deeply rooted in a respect for the past, the ancestors, and a cosmology (sometimes represented by a medicine wheel) that suggests existence as a sacred hoop. Most Lakota, Dakota, and Nakota (Sioux) people take great pride in their identity and heritage, which are passed from one generation to another in a sacred manner.

Considering the depth of feeling regarding the importance of this type of identity, including the awareness of how their ancestors suffered to maintain their culture, it should come as no surprise that many Native people resent the appropriation of their images, stories, and history. Activist and author Winona LaDuke (2005), in her book *Recovering the Sacred: The Power of Naming and Claiming*, accuses the University of North Dakota of profiting from Indian culture. She calls the university's use of an Indian image a "strange and twisted tale" without any moral or ethical pretense. It is a tale, she says, in which Native people find themselves "at odds with a public institution pimping off their culture" (136).

When universities and/or corporations prey on cultures and cultural imagery to sell themselves or their products, the mass market will consume the culture. This does not mean the culture will spread to the masses, according to Hannah Arendt (1961/1993). The result will be that "culture is being destroyed in order to yield entertainment." She argues that the culture itself is not changed, but the "nature of culture is affected when these objects themselves are changed—rewritten, condensed, digested, reduced to kitsch in reproduction" (197). The result is "not disintegration but decay" (197).

When American Indian cultural imagery is reduced to stereotypes, mascots, and logos, we are all held captive, reduced to looking at American Indian people and cultures through a small window, unable to see or understand the entire picture. When our only understanding of a culture comes through marketing images and the mass media, when our only cultural encounter comes from wearing a piece of clothing with an "Indian-head" logo on it, and when Anglo-American people refer to themselves as "Sioux" without any sense of irony, we have become prisoners of our own stereotypes and contribute to the cultural violation of American Indian people.

Native Americans have transformed the political, social, and cultural practices of the Americas and the world. The world's food supply, medicines, architecture, agriculture, and systems of government have all been improved by their contributions (Weatherford 1988). The original inhabitants of North Dakota and North America are worthy of honor and respect. How can representatives of the "dominant" culture pay tribute to Native people?

Rather than appropriating historical images of Native-American people for our own gain, we can honor their sovereignty and treaty rights, support their efforts to revitalize tribal languages, respect and understand tribal economic and resource management, and assist in the repatriation of sacred objects. In this way, we honor their future as well as their past.

Notes

1. The National Congress of American Indians, National Indian Education Association, Native American Journalists Association, Minnesota Indian Education Association, North Dakota Indian Education Association, National Coalition on Racism in Sports and Media, Society of Indian Psychologists of the Americas, and others have made this request. See American Indian Sports Team Mascots (2009).

2. "Indian country" is a term used to describe land under tribal jurisdiction or areas with large populations of Native people.

3. Anne Artoux collected this text from Marge Donovan on November 28, 1986, in San Mateo, California (Folklore Archives at the University of California, Berkeley).

Sources

American Indian Sports Team Mascots. 2009. [Home page]. November 16. http://www.aistm.org/1indexpage.htm (accessed March 13, 2010).

Ammer, Christine, 2003. *American Heritage dictionary of idioms.* New York: Houghton Mifflin Harcourt.

Annis, Holly. 1999. Fighting the "Fighting Sioux" tradition. *Native Directions* 6, no. 2: 2–3.

Arendt, Hannah. [1961] 1993. *Between past and future: Eight exercises in political thought.* New York: Penguin.

Baum, Frank, L. 1890. [Editorial]. *Aberdeen Saturday Pioneer,* December 20.

Baum, Frank, L. 1900. *The wonderful Wizard of Oz.* Indianapolis, IN: Bobbs-Merrill.

Bol, Marsha C. 1999. Defining Lakota tourist art, 1880–1915. In *Unpacking culture: Art and commodity in colonial and postcolonial worlds,* ed. Ruth Phillips and Christopher Steiner, pp. 214–228. Berkeley: University of California Press.

Cook-Lynn, Elizabeth. 2007. *Anti-Indianism in modern America: A voice from Tatekeya's Earth.* Urbana: University of Illinois Press.

Custer Battlefield Museum. N.d. [Home page]. http://www.custermuseum.org (accessed December 15, 2010).

Deloria, Philip. 1998. *Playing Indian.* New Haven, CT: Yale University Press.

Eriksmoen, Curt. 2009. The man behind the Highway Patrol logo. *The Bismarck Tribune,* October 25.

Kemmick, Ed. 2002. "Custer's Last Fight" sales to benefit battle memorials, *Billings Gazette*, June 22.

Kulchyski, Peter. 1997. From appropriation to subversion: Aboriginal cultural production in the age of postmodernism," *American Indian Quarterly* 21, no. 4: 605–620.

LaDuke, Winona. 2005. *Recovering the sacred: The power of naming and claiming.* Cambridge, MA: South End Press.

Mador, Jessica. 2010. ND board: Fighting Sioux nickname is retired.Minnesota Public Radio, *MPR News Q Online*, April 8. http://minnesota.publicradio.org/display/web/2010/04/08/nd-board-fighting-sioux-nickname-is-retired/ (accessed April 10, 2010).

Merskin, Debra. 2001. Winnebagos, Cherokees, Apaches, and Dakotas: The persistence of stereotyping of American Indians in American advertising brands. *The Howard Journal of Communications* 12: 159–161.

Midwest Archeological Center. N.d. [Home page]. http://www.nps.gov/history/mwac/libi/index.html (accessed December 14, 2010).

Mieder, Wolfgang. 1993. "The only good Indian is a dead Indian": History and meaning of a proverbial stereotype. *The Journal of American Folklore* 106, no. 419: 38–60.

Miller, A., and S. D. Ross. 2004. They are not us: Framing of American Indians by the Boston Globe. *The Howard Journal of Communication* 15: 245–259.

National Park Service. N.d. Little Bighorn Battlefield National Monument. http://www.nps.gov/archive/libi/indmem.htm (accessed December 14, 2010).

Pewewardy, Cornel. N.d. Countering the assault of Indian mascots in school. *Educators' Resources.* http://www.aistm.org/cornel.countering.htm (accessed March 13, 2010).

Roosevelt, Theodore. 1889. *The winning of the West.* New York: Putnam.

Standing Rock Sioux Tourism Website. 2008. 1923—Marcellus Red Hawk. http://www.standingrocktourism.com/history/timeLineView.asp?timeSpan=6 (accessed March 13, 2010).

State of North Dakota. 2009. Great seal. November 24. http://www.nd.gov/content.htm?parentCatID=75&id=Great Seal (accessed March 13, 2010).

Wallerstein, Immanuel. 1990. Culture as the ideological battleground of the modern world-system, *Theory, Culture & Society* 7, no. 2: 31–55.

Weatherford, Jack. 1988. *Indian givers: How the Indians of the Americas transformed the world.* New York: Fawcett Columbine.

Welch, James, with Paul Stekler. 2007. *Killing Custer: The Battle of the Little Bighorn and the fate of the Plains Indians.* New York: W.W. Norton.

Chapter 8

African-American Images in the News: Understanding the Past to Improve Future Portrayals

Paula M. Poindexter

Prior to noon Eastern Standard Time, January 20, 2009, there had never been an African-American president of the United States. Would this historic swearing-in of Barack Obama as the 44th president change the image of African Americans in the news? Although it would take time to assess the impact on news coverage of an African-American president and family living in the White House, the history of news coverage of African Americans would suggest that without an awareness of past problems and a plan to remedy these defects going forward, future news coverage of African Americans would not differ significantly from news coverage of the past.

Four decades prior to the inauguration of the first African-American president, the Kerner Commission "reprimanded the press for its lack of diversity in both news coverage and newsroom employment" (Poindexter 2009, 434). In its report, the Kerner Commission emphasized that the news media had not communicated the difficulties and frustrations of being African American in the United States and had not shown understanding or appreciation of African-American culture, thought, or history. The exclusion of African Americans, the Kerner Commission pointed out, not only produced news that was distorted but also betrayed the public's trust and failed to live up to journalism's principles and responsibilities. It is the responsibility of the news media, the Kerner Commission emphasized, to tell the story of race relations in America with wisdom, sensitivity, and expertise (National Advisory Commission on Civil Disorders 1968).

No doubt, progress has been made since the Kerner Commission's national scolding of the press, but does inclusion of African Americans in the news automatically translate into fair and balanced representation? If the publication of the 1968 Kerner Commission Report is thought of as a defining moment that helped the news media move from excluding to including African Americans in the news, the "Diversity in News" chart in this chapter reveals that inclusion in news coverage has not necessarily been positive for the image of African Americans in the United States.

This "Diversity in News" chart is the result of a review and synthesis of the major results of approximately 45 articles, books, and conference papers that examined news coverage of race and ethnicity. Some of the categories in the chart, such as exclusion and stereotyping, are consistent with theories on news diversity by journalism scholars Clint Wilson and Felix Gutierrez (1985); other categories emerged after synthesizing results of various studies. In their theorizing, Wilson and Gutierrez (1985) proposed a five-stage evolution of mainstream news coverage of racial and ethnic groups: "(1) exclusionary, (2) threatening issue, (3) confrontation, (4) stereotypical selection and (5) integrated coverage" (135), which was later renamed "multiracial coverage" (Wilson and Gutierrez 1995, 52; Wilson, Gutierrez, and Chao 2003, 116).

Although five stages of mainstream news coverage were proposed, I have observed that Wilson and Gutierrez's stages are not exhaustive, and I have argued that the five stages actually reflect two dimensions of news coverage: exclusion and inclusion (Poindexter 2009). In addition to exclusion, the "Diversity in News" chart lists five broad categories of inclusion: minor inclusion, stereotypes, underrepresentation, segregation, and major inclusion. The last category primarily represents news coverage of Anglo Americans.

If the Kerner Commission Report is considered the first national documentation of the exclusion of African Americans from the news, minor inclusion was documented eight years later in the mid-1970s. For example, a study of network television news found that despite the fact that African Americans were included in almost one quarter of news stories, African

	Anglo Americans	African Americans	Latinos	Asian Americans	Native Americans
Exclusion:					
Historically Excluded	No	Yes	Yes	Yes	Yes
Inclusion:					
Minor Inclusion	No	Yes	Yes	Yes	Yes
Stereotypes:					
Outsiders	No	Yes	Yes	Yes	Yes
Historic & cultural relics	No	Yes	Yes	No	Yes
Exotic	No	No	No	No	Yes
Noble savages	No	No	No	No	Yes
Degraded	No	Yes	Yes	No	Yes
Bad & uncivilized	No	Yes	Yes	No	Yes
Vanishing race	No	No	No	No	Yes
Poor	No	Yes	Yes	No	Yes
Criminals	No	Yes	Yes	No	No
Threatening	No	Yes	No	No	Yes
Confrontational	No	Yes	No	No	Yes
Problems	No	Yes	Yes	No	Yes
Societal & gov't critics	No	Yes	No	No	No
Athletes	No	Yes	No	No	No
Entertainers/Celebrities	No	Yes	No	No	No
Gang members	No	Yes	Yes	Yes	No
Model minority	No	No	No	Yes	No
Emotional	Yes	Yes	Yes	Yes	*
Underrepresentation:					
As crime victims	No	Yes	Yes	*	*
In everyday activities	No	Yes	Yes	Yes	Yes
As achievers	No	Yes	Yes	Yes	Yes
Official & expert sources	No	Yes	Yes	Yes	Yes
Private citizen sources	No	Yes	Yes	Yes	Yes
Victims of race-related problems	No	Yes	Yes	Yes	Yes
Explains causes of problems	No	Yes	Yes	Yes	Yes
Solutions to problems	No	Yes	Yes	Yes	Yes
Segregation:					
Representation	Yes	Yes	Yes	Yes	Yes
Sources	Yes	Yes	*	*	*
Story assignments	Yes	Yes	*	Yes	*
Slice-of-life photographs	Yes	Yes	Yes	*	*
Major Inclusion	Yes	No	No	No	No

Limited research data

Diversity in News: Exclusion to Inclusion. (Courtesy of Paula Poindexter.)

Americans appeared to have been included as window dressing because they were seen and never heard in the network news reports (Roberts 1975). Perhaps the minor inclusion category represented a transition period for the news media as it moved from exclusion to inclusion of African Americans in the news. Once African Americans were included in the news, though, being unseen and unheard might have seemed less damaging to the image of African Americans than the stereotypes that became the core of mainstream news coverage.

If a stereotype is "a standardized mental picture that is held in common by members of a group and that represents an oversimplified opinion, prejudiced attitude, or uncritical judgment" (Merriam-Webster Online 2010), journalism has failed when covering racial and ethnic groups because according to the studies reviewed, news coverage on racial and ethnic groups has been saturated with stereotypes. Specifically, according to the chart, racial and ethnic groups have been covered using 18 different stereotypes, and the majority of these stereotypes have been used to report on African Americans. Four of these stereotypes have been particularly popular with the news media and potentially harmful to African Americans. African Americans have been portrayed in the news as poor, criminals, athletes, or entertainers or celebrities.

Stereotyping as Poor

Although African Americans represented less than one third of poor people in the United States, a political scientist found that visual messages used to illustrate newsmagazine or network news stories on poverty were most likely to be of African Americans. Furthermore, when the researcher distinguished between the underclass, which he called the "least sympathetic subgroup of the poor," and the elderly and working poor, which he described as the "most sympathetic subgroups of the poor," the face of the least sympathetic poor was also more likely to be African American (Gilens 1996).

Stereotyping as Criminals

In almost every decade from the time of the publication of the Kerner Commission Report through the first decade of the twenty-first century, studies have documented the prevalent stereotype of African Americans as criminal (Dixon and Linz 2000; Entman 1994; Free 2007; Gilliam and Iyengar 2000; Lester 1994; Lester and Smith 1990; Pease 1989; Poindexter, Smith, and Heider 2003; Roberts 1975). Beginning in the 1970s, the most frequently reported news story that included African Americans "concerned possible crime or past criminal activity on the part of blacks" (Roberts 1975, 52). The criminal stereotype of African Americans has been particularly salient in broadcast news, whether local or national. Images have not been of just any type of criminal but of violent and menacing criminals. Studies have found African Americans were significantly more likely than Anglo Americans to be shown in stories about violent crime (Entman 1992). African Americans were also more likely to be shown as suspects in murder stories despite the fact that "blacks do not account for the largest number of murders" (Gilliam and Iyengar 2000, 562). African Americans were also "more likely to be portrayed as perpetrators of crime even though arrest statistics do not support that representation" (Dixon and Linz 2000, 145). Finally, African Americans were "more likely to be portrayed as felons on television news than to be arrested for felonies (44 percent vs. 25 percent)" (Dixon and Linz 2000, 146).

Of seven network news topics—crime, politics, victims, human interest, statistics, government policies, and other—African Americans were most likely to be seen in crime stories (Entman 1994). Similarly, when researchers sorted reporter-delivered local TV news stories by their racial focus, "black-focused stories (69 percent) were almost two and a half times more likely than white-focused stories (28 percent) to be about crime" (Poindexter, Smith, and Heider 2003, 531).

Stereotyping as Athletes and Entertainers or Celebrities

When the African-American image in the news is not that of a criminal, the image is often that of an athlete, entertainer, or celebrity (Johnson 1987; Lester and Smith 1990). The African-American athlete image has been particularly dominant in the news. A comparison among photographs of African Americans in the *New York Times, Chicago Tribune, New Orleans Times-Picayune,* and *San Francisco Chronicle* during the pre–Civil Rights era, Civil Rights era, and modern era (defined as 1978 through 1990) found that sports dominated all photographic images of African Americans. In the modern era, sports-related images of African Americans in the four newspapers studied ranged from 30 percent to 52 percent of all images of African Americans (Lester 1994).

The overemphasis on the African-American male athlete even dominated newspaper coverage of the 2000 Olympics. An analysis of images from the 2000 Olympics published in five newspapers found "a dispropor-tionately high percentage of black athletes in comparison to the medal count" (Hardin et al. 2004, 221). When the same images were analyzed by race and gender, "Black males were overrepresented" (Hardin et al. 2004, 221). African-American males were represented in 21 percent of the images from the 2000 Olympic Games, but they won only 15 percent of the medals.

Underrepresentation

Although one might expect to find African Americans in the news as victims of crime, in everyday life and culture, and as news sources, that has not been the case. It has also not been the case that the problems and challenges uniquely faced by African Americans have been represented in the news. In local and network news, for example, African Americans were less likely than other groups of the population to be reported on as victims (Dixon, Azocar, and Casas 2003; Entman and Rojecki 2000). When network news stories of violent crimes were compared with federal statistics, the victim was African American in 48 percent of crime reports but only 30 percent of network news stories (Dixon, Azocar, and Casas 2003).

A comparison of coverage in the African-American press and mainstream press of two neighborhoods with large African-American populations documented African Americans' underrepresentation in everyday life. Negative stereotypes of African Americans were emphasized in 85 percent of the stories in the mainstream press, but in the African-American press, the majority of the stories "suggested a black community thirsty for educational advancement and entrepreneurial achievement, and eager to remedy poor living conditions made worse by bureaucratic neglect" (Johnson 1987, 50). The mainstream press also ignored stories about African-American achievements (Johnson 1987).

Similarly, an analysis of national newsmagazine photographic images for the decade from 1978 to 1988 found that photographs of everyday life of African Americans ranked seventh among eight categories of photographs coded (Lester and Smith 1990). African Americans were also underrepresented in stand-alone photographs that portrayed a slice of life (Poindexter, Coleman, and Shader 2010) and as sources for news stories in local TV news (Poindexter, Smith, and Heider 2003).

Problems, Causes, and Solutions Are Underrepresented

Despite the Kerner Commission's criticism of mainstream news media's failure in communicating the "difficulties and frustrations" of being African American in the United States (National Advisory Commission on Civil Disorders 1968, 383), issues, problems, and solutions directly related to race and ethnicity have also been underrepresented in mainstream news reports (Martindale 1990; Ziegler and White 1990; Poindexter, Smith, and Heider 2003). Discrimination, for example, as a local TV news story topic has been "rare" (Poindexter, Smith, and Heider 2003, 533), and race relations represented one of the least covered topics in network news (Ziegler and White 1990).

Segregation

Although segregation was outlawed with the passage of the 1964 Civil Rights Act, segregation has not disappeared from news coverage. For example, in a study of network news stories, there was evidence of segregation based on the race of expert sources (Entman 1994). African-American experts were more likely to appear in African-American–issue stories. When the reporter's race or ethnicity and the story's racial focus were analyzed to determine if local television news story assignments were segregated, researchers found that "African Americans were more than three times as likely as white reporters to report stories with a black focus" (Poindexter, Smith, and Heider 2003, 531). A similar pattern was found for newspapers (Pritchard and Stonbely 2007). Segregation has also been found in slice-of-life, stand-alone newspaper photographs (Poindexter, Coleman, and Shader forthcoming). Overall, newspapers published more segregated slice-of-life photographs than photographs that showed racial and ethnic diversity.

From the Kerner Commission's call for more African Americans in newsrooms and the efforts of the American Society of Newspaper Editors (ASNE), the Association for Education in Journalism and Mass Communication (AEJMC), and the National Association of Black Journalists (NABJ) to increase the number of African Americans and other people of color in journalism, the conventional wisdom has been that to achieve fair and balanced news coverage of African Americans and all racial and ethnic groups, newsroom employment should mirror the U.S. population.[1]

More than four decades after the first call for newsroom diversity, the goal of a fully diverse newsroom has yet to be achieved. Furthermore, with the downsizing of newsroom staffs and restructuring of the news industry in the wake of a web-transformed news media and advertising landscape, the possibility that newsrooms may never be as diverse as the U.S. population is not unthinkable. That's why achieving diversity in news coverage in the future must be guided by a different approach. These recommendations will produce news that is closer to what the 1947 Commission on the Freedom of the Press, also known as the Hutchins Commission, said a free society should expect from the press and, in turn, what the press should expect of itself: "the projection of a representative picture of the constituent groups in the society" (Commission on Freedom of the Press 1947). Whether conscious or unconscious, projecting an *unrepresentative* picture of African Americans is tantamount to committing journalistic malpractice. That's why the following recommendations have been developed to avoid this transgression.

Five Recommendations for Improving News Coverage of African Americans

Although the 1968 Kerner Commission Report has become the benchmark by which diversity progress has been measured, efforts to improve news coverage of African Americans date back to 1827, when the first African-American newspaper, *Freedom's Journal*, was founded (Poindexter 2009). Despite efforts by commissions, journalism associations, journalism educators, journalism foundations, journalism institutes, African-American journalists, and the election of an African-American president, the image of African Americans in the news still does not accurately represent the diversity and contributions of the African-American community. If the news media would commit to implementing the following five recommendations, the image of African Americans in mainstream news would improve almost immediately.

1. Embrace the Idea That Fair and Accurate News Coverage of African Americans Is the Responsibility of Every Journalist—Not Just African-American Journalists

In 1968, the Kerner Commission's call for the employment of African Americans in newsrooms was, perhaps, the first recognition that in order to achieve fair and accurate news coverage, African Americans needed to be present in the newsroom. Over the next few decades, individuals and groups, including ASNE, AEJMC, and NABJ, worked diligently to make the Kerner Commission's call a reality. Newsroom employment of African Americans increased, but news coverage continued to stereotype, under-represent, and segregate African Americans.

Why? Some say it is because there are still not enough African Americans in newsrooms; others say there are too few African Americans in decision-making positions; still others emphasize there is no commitment from the top. While too few African Americans in newsrooms, too few African Americans in decision-making positions, and too little commitment from the top can surely be contributing factors, it is believed that the source of the problem is that there is a failure among journalists to recognize and accept the fact that it is the responsibility of each and every journalist to ensure that news that is published, broadcast, or posted online provides a fair and accurate representation of African Americans in America. Only when every journalist embraces this responsibility will news coverage cease stereotyping, segregating, and underrepresenting African Americans.

2. Learn the Meaning of Diversity in News Coverage

Without a consensus definition, diversity in news coverage cannot be achieved. A careful reading of the following definition, which takes into account how people of color have been covered in the past and describes what diverse news coverage should be, makes it clear that diversity in news coverage is not inclusion alone. If, for example, African Americans are only included in the news as poor people, criminals, sports figures, and entertainers, diversity in news coverage has not been achieved.

Diversity in news coverage is therefore defined as

> the inclusion of as well as accurate and fair reporting about groups that historically have been excluded, stereotyped, or devalued because they were born with certain enduring and discernable attributes that differ from the dominant racial group. Diversity in news coverage requires that the definition of newsworthy be expanded to include issues, events, communities, and people who historically have been excluded from the news. It also means including sources, both experts and ordinary people, and experiences that represent people of color as well as angles that directly affect communities of color when reporting mainstream stories. (Poindexter 2009, 434–435)

3. Counteract Unconscious Racial Assumptions with Historical Context and Facts

This recommendation may be hard to achieve because journalists may resist the idea that they may harbor unconscious racial assumptions. Like unconscious gender assumptions, unconscious racial assumptions "are not visible; they are embedded, and women and men alike have been socialized with them since they were young children" (Poindexter, Meraz, and

Schmitz Weiss 2008, 320). These unconscious racial assumptions about African Americans can lead to news that stereotypes, underrepresents, and segregates African Americans, which is why it is imperative that these unconscious racial assumptions be understood, acknowledged, exposed, and counteracted with facts.

Sometimes, though, facts alone may be insufficient because facts may be interpreted to fit unconscious racial assumptions. For example, CNN's 2008 *Black in America* documentary reported a statistic that one in three African Americans is in the criminal justice system. Now if one third of African Americans are in the criminal justice system, that statistic also means that the majority, or a whopping two thirds of African Americans, are *not*, but that's not what was emphasized in the documentary.

Having been interviewed in the documentary, I saw this as a teachable moment for CNN and other news organizations, which is why I emailed the following to the producer in August 2008:

> [T]he statistic that one in three African Americans is in the criminal justice system could have been flipped to show that the majority (2/3) are not in the criminal justice system. If you reviewed the documentary, you'd think that at least two-thirds, if not all, African Americans are in the criminal justice system. Even two of the featured experts had a criminal past or someone in the family who was a criminal. You even managed to find a very successful black family, which looked more like my family and the families I know, to have a family member convicted of a crime.

How CNN used this crime statistic is a reminder that even when using facts to counteract unconscious racial assumptions, journalists must guard against using statistics to support unconscious assumptions that stereotype the image of African Americans.

4. Use the Definition of Diversity in News Coverage to Establish a Goal; Convert the "Diversity in News" Chart to a Codebook That Can Be Used to Conduct Regular News Audits to Assess Achievement of the Diversity Goal

By combining the diversity definition and the categories of news coverage in the "Diversity in News" chart, it will be possible to answer such questions as "Is news coverage stereotyping African Americans as criminals and athletes?" "Are African Americans underrepresented as news sources?" "Can African Americans be found in slice-of-life photographs and feature stories?" And "What is the image of African Americans in the news?" The answers to these questions should be discussed openly and honestly in newsrooms. Only then can progress be made in improving news coverage of African Americans.

5. Work at Diversity Every Day

This fifth and final recommendation is from R. B. Brenner, a Pulitzer Prize–winning editor at the *Washington Post* who was a journalist in residence at the University of Texas at Austin during the spring 2009 semester. After Brenner returned to the *Post*, I asked him his perspective on diversity in news coverage that I could share with high school journalism teachers attending the ASNE-sponsored workshop held at the University of Texas at Austin. In a July 29, 2009, email response to me, Brenner emphasized that diversity "can't be put up on a shelf and dusted off every now and then when there's a flashpoint," such as when an Anglo-American police officer arrested Harvard Professor Henry Louis Gates. Diversity, Brenner said, "needs to be a part of daily examination in the newsroom."

After the election of the first African-American president and more than four decades of effort to improve the image of African Americans in the news, a fair and accurate image of African Americans remains an unachieved goal. The harm that is caused by this failure to correct the inaccurate image of African Americans in the news is not limited to the African American community. The greater society and the journalism profession are harmed as well. African Americans are injured because their contributions are discounted and their potential is dismissed. U.S. society is harmed because its citizens are not portrayed equally, which diminishes the promise of the democratic ideals that this country represents. The journalism profession is damaged because its credibility as a truth teller of constituent groups regardless of status, color, or ethnicity is compromised.

Embracing the five diversity-in-news recommendations does not mean "weaknesses and vices" (Commission on the Freedom of the Press 1947) should be excluded, but it does mean that news that distorts, diminishes, and undermines the contributions and aspirations of African Americans as documented in the "Diversity in News" chart will become a thing of the past. Projecting an image that is accurate, fair, and balanced is essential for African Americans; critical for the public good; and mandatory for a free and responsible press in a democratic society.

Note

1. At least since the 1960s, individuals, organizations, foundations, and institutions have linked diversity in newsroom employment with diversity in news coverage. ASNE's mission statement as it relates to its commitment to diversity reflects this employment and news coverage connection: "To cover communities fully, to carry out their role in a democracy and to succeed in the marketplace, the nation's newsrooms must reflect the racial diversity of American society by 2025 or sooner" (ASNE 2010).

Sources

ASNE. 2010. More than three decades of commitment to diversity. http://asne.org/key_initiatives/diversity.aspx (accessed March 13, 2010).

Commission on Freedom of the Press. 1947. *A free and responsible press: A general report on mass communication: newspapers, radio, motion pictures, magazines, and books.* Chicago: University of Chicago Press.

Dixon, Travis L., and Daniel Linz. 2000. Overrepresentation and underrepresentation of African Americans and Latinos as lawbreakers on television news. *Journal of Communication* 50 (Summer): 131–154.

Dixon, Travis L., Cristina L. Azocar, and Michael Casas. 2003. The portrayal of race and crime on television network news. *Journal of Broadcasting & Electronic Media* 47: 498–523.

Entman, Robert M. 1992. Blacks in the news: Television, modern racism and cultural change. *Journalism Quarterly* 69 (2): 341–361.

Entman, Robert M. 1994. Representation and reality in the portrayal of Blacks on network television news. *Journalism Quarterly* 71 (3): 509–520.

Entman, Robert M., and Andrew Rojecki. 2000. *The Black image in the White mind: Media and race in America.* Chicago: University of Chicago Press.

Free, David. 2007. Diversity on-air: Racial/ethnic images in local television news. Paper presented at the annual meeting of the Association for Education in Journalism & Mass Communication, August, Washington, DC.

Gilens, Martin. 1996. Race and poverty in America: Public misperceptions and the American news media. *Public Opinion Quarterly* 60: 515–541.

Gilliam, Franklin D., Jr., and Shanto Iyengar. 2000. Prime suspects: The influence of local television news on the viewing public. *American Journal of Political Science* 44 (3): 560–573.

Hardin, Marie, Julie E. Dodd, Jean Chance, and Kristie Walsdorf. 2004. Sporting images in Black and White: Race in newspaper coverage of the 2000 Olympic games. *Howard Journal of Communications* 15 (4): 221.

Johnson, Kirk A. 1987. Black and White in Boston: A researcher documents disturbing biases in mainstream coverage of Blacks. *Columbia Journalism Review* (May–June): 50–52.

Lester, Paul Martin. 1994. African-American photo coverage in four U.S. newspapers, 1937–1990. *Journalism Quarterly* 71 (2): 380–394.

Lester, Paul, and Ron Smith. 1990. African-American photo coverage in *Life, Newsweek* and *Time,* 1937–1988. *Journalism Quarterly* 67 (1): 128–136.

Martindale, Carolyn. 1990. Coverage of Black Americans in four major newspapers, 1950–1989. *Newspaper Research Journal* 11 (3): 96–112.

Merriam-Webster Online. 2010. Stereotype. http://www.merriam-webster.com/dictionary/stereotype (accessed March 13, 2010).

National Advisory Commission on Civil Disorders. 1968. *Report of the National Advisory Commission on Civil Disorders.* New York: Bantam.

Pease, Edward C. 1989. Kerner plus 20: Minority news coverage in the *Columbus Dispatch. Newspaper Research Journal* 10 (3): 17–38.

Poindexter, Paula M. 2009. Diversity: Content. In *Encyclopedia of journalism,* ed. Christopher H. Sterling and D. Charles Whitney, pp. 434–439. Thousand Oaks, CA: Sage.

Poindexter, Renita Coleman, and Maggie Shader. 2010. Stand-alone News Photographs Portray Less Diverse, More Segregated Communities. *Newspaper Research Journal* 31: 83–88.

Poindexter, Paula, Sharon Meraz, and Amy Schmitz Weiss. 2008. Strengthening the news connection with women and cultivating the next generation. In *Women, men, and news: Divided and disconnected in the news media landscape,* ed. Paula Poindexter, Sharon Meraz, and Amy Schmitz Weiss, pp. 317–333. New York: Routledge.

Poindexter, Paula M., Laura Smith, and Don Heider. 2003. Race and ethnicity in local television news: Framing, story assignments, and source selections. *Journal of Broadcasting & Electronic Media* 47 (4): 524–536.

Pritchard, David, and Sarah Stonbely. 2007. Racial profiling in the newsroom. *Journalism & Mass Communication Quarterly* 84 (2): 231–248.

Roberts, Churchill. 1975. The presentation of Blacks in television network newscasts. *Journalism Quarterly* 52 (1): 50–55.

Wilson, Clint C., II, and Felix Gutierrez. 1985. *Minorities and media: Diversity and the end of mass communication.* Beverly Hills, CA: Sage.

Wilson, Clint C., II, and Felix Gutierrez. 1995. *Race, multiculturalism, and the media: From mass to class communication* (2nd ed.). Thousand Oaks, CA: Sage.

Wilson, Clint C., II, Felix Gutierrez, and Lena M. Chao. 2003. *Racism, sexism, and the media: The rise of class communication in multicultural America.* Thousand Oaks, CA: Sage.

Ziegler, Dhyana, and Alisa White. 1990. Women and minorities on network television news: An examination of correspondents and newsmakers. *Journal of Broadcasting & Electronic Media* 34 (2): 215–223.

Chapter 9

Racial Passing: Images of Mulattos, Mestizos, and Eurasians

Henry Puente

For the first time in its 210-year history, the 2000 U.S. Census allowed citizens of two or more races to check a unique category on the form. The 7 million Americans of mixed Anglo, African-American, Asian, Native-American, Pacific Islander, and Native-Alaskan races were finally given the option to escape their one-category pigeonhole and make a selection that more accurately reflected their family heritage (Navarro 2008).

The counting of mixed-race individuals by the U.S. government was a huge step in the right direction, especially when we consider that many administrations simply ignored the possibility that offspring of persons from two different races existed. No wonder advocates for those with complex personal histories are part of the so-called "Generation Mix" (Beltran and Fojas 2008, 1).

Part of our society's growing acceptance of mixed-race individuals is attributed to popular culture images that we consume on a daily basis as several prominent celebrities—Jessica Alba, Jennifer Beals, Halle Berry, Mariah Carey, Rosario Dawson, Vin Diesel, Mark-Paul Gosselaar, Dwayne "The Rock" Johnson, Keanu Reeves, and Tiger Woods—are mixed-raced personalities. In fact, it is unusual to *not* see a mixed-race person on a magazine cover, on the big screen, or featured in a television program. The emergence of so many popular mixed-race celebrities is a relatively recent U.S. media phenomenon. Focusing on this phenomenon, this chapter describes early stereotypical images of mixed-race persons in film and television. It then comments upon the careers of several racially ambiguous actors and actresses to illustrate how they have succeeded in part by passing primarily as Anglos in motion pictures or on television. The chapter lastly highlights the fact that our preconceived definition of what an Anglo person looks like may be expanding at the expense of depicting fewer clearly mixed-race people in film and television.

Historic Miscegenation

A miscegenation taboo dating from the colonial period (Sweet 2005) became crystallized under Hollywood's Production Code in the 1930s. Many African-American, Asian, and Latino actors were forced into stereotypical roles or had no work at all. However, if their physical features allowed them to pass as Anglos, individuals could hide their race or ethnicity by changing their names. While the Production Code slowly lost its power throughout the 1950s and 1960s, the concept of miscegenation became politically incorrect in the landmark U.S. Supreme Court case *Loving v. Virginia* (1967) that allowed interracial couples to marry legally. Six months later, the miscegenation taboo on screen was shattered with the debut of *Guess Who's Coming to Dinner* (1967), a drama about a young Anglo woman who brings her African-American fiancé home to meet her parents.[1]

A few decades later, Spike Lee, Wayne Wang, and Luis Valdez began to introduce multiculturalism to the nation's screens by telling stories from a non-Anglo perspective. This groundswell of multiculturalism and of accepting miscegenation as a normal part of society became more visible when *Time* magazine featured several mixed-race individuals on its cover in November 1993 (Park 2008, 184). The other watershed moment occurred when Tiger Woods appeared on the *Oprah Winfrey Show* and declared that he was "Cablinasian" (a mix of Anglo-African-Indian-Asian) (Nakashima 2001, 45). Woods's comfortable confession suddenly made being a mixed-race person fashionable. Jane Park refers to this new attitude as "Multiracial Chic" (2008, 184).

The emergence of mixed-race individuals who were traditionally hidden in the shadows of society into a more visible group should not come as a complete surprise. Michael Omi and Howard Winant (1994) noted that a society's definitions of race are in a constant state of flux (15). Over time, people deconstruct and reconstruct their definitions of ethnic and racial identity for both themselves and others. These racial meanings are affected by the economic, social, and political climates of a particular country and are limited to specific periods of time (Omi and Winant 1994, 15).

The Disappearing "Tragic Mulatto"

People of mixed African-American and Anglo racial heritage historically have experienced the greatest cultural and social stigma in the United States, with the combination traditionally considered African American. Marvin Harris (1964) refers to the practice of defining mixed Afro-Anglo individuals as African American as "hypo-descent" because the race of one parent subordinates the race of the other parent (56). In other words, the "African" component of the phrase exerts a hypo influence on offspring. Amid the societal stigmatization of the Afro-Anglo racial mix, the U.S. film industry crystallized the negative portrayal of mixed-race persons early in the twentieth century with the infamous Silas Lynch character in D. W. Griffith's racially flawed blockbuster *Birth of a Nation* (1915). Shortly afterward, director Oscar Micheaux featured this mixed-race image prominently in some films like *Body and Soul* (1925) (Benshoff and Griffin 2004, 79).

Donald Bogle (1973) refers to this mixed-race image as the tragic mulatto (9). Such a character is often a moral, likeable, light-skinned, African-American female who passes for an Anglo. With such stories, the protagonist's world appears to be on the road to happiness until her essence is revealed. The storyline is considered tragic because her race alone keeps her from achieving success (Bogle 1973). In this particular case, her happiness is solely determined by marrying an Anglo man of her dreams. Two early examples of the tragic mulatto were the characters Peola Johnson in *The Imitation of Life* (1934) and Patricia "Pinky" Johnson in *Pinky* (1949).[2] More recently, a notable tragic mulatto was Drew Purify in *Jungle Fever* (1991) directed by the African-American Spike Lee (Giles 1995, 75). Fortunately, the tragic mulatto image has vanished largely from recent films and television programs, with the mention of the term outside media studies discussions considered racist.

Although Vin Diesel would be called a mulatto in earlier eras, today he has been able to take advantage of his ethnically ambiguous physical features. Diesel's initial claim to fame was that he produced and acted in the short film *Multi-Facial* (1995).[3] This film highlighted his unique physical characteristics as well as critiques of the film industry for placing mixed-race actors in a kind of Hollywood limbo. He now illustrates a new heroic role being offered to mixed-race actors in film. For instance, Diesel is a mixed-race protagonist in action films like *The Fast and The Furious* (2001), *XXX* (2002), and *Fast and Furious* (2009). Despite his initial critical appraisal of the film industry, Diesel was wary of aligning himself with a specific race or ethnicity (Nakamura 2008, 67). Consequently, as Lisa Nakamura (2008) contends, Diesel promoted himself as a multiethnic everyman. She asserts that a moviegoer of any race or ethnicity readily could adopt him as a hero who represented them (Nakamura 2008, 67). Nakamura refers to the fluidity of Diesel's race as "ethnically ambiguous" (Nakamura 2008, 67). Diesel's features have made him a global star with significant revenues earned outside the U.S. borders, where the majority of moviegoers do not look like the traditional fair-skinned heroes featured in many earlier U.S. films.

Jennifer Beals is an African-American/Anglo actress who would have been the ideal mulatta in an earlier era. Like Diesel, she is ethnically ambiguous and has taken advantage of her lighter complexion. But unlike Diesel, she has not had the same level of success. After her major breakthrough role as an Anglo dancer in *Flashdance* (1983), Beals practically disappeared from the screen for the remainder of the 1980s. She continued her career as an actress throughout the 1990s, securing roles as an Anglo or some vague ethnic woman. Like Diesel, Beals did not appear either to be completely forthcoming or to deny her racial heritage. As a result, during her long film and television career that extends more than 25 years, Beals has played biracial characters only twice, once in *Devil in a Blue Dress* (1990) and more recently in the Showtime series *The L Word* (2004–2009). While her biracial background may not have been a secret in the African-American community (O'Neil-Parker 1999), Beals decided with *L Word* creator Ilene Chaiken to make her character, Bette Porter, a biracial character (Downie 2008). Beals' recent openness about her biracial heritage suggests that being a mixed-race person may no longer carry the social stigma that it had in the past.

The careers of Diesel and Beals demonstrate the shortage of mixed-race roles available to actors and actresses who are a black and white mix. While the tragic mulatta/o stereotype may not have the same social and cultural stigma that it had back in the days of D. W. Griffith, this particular mixed-race image has not really been redefined by producers of images. As a matter of fact, this image continues to be quite rare in motion pictures or television screens during a period when our society supposedly has grown more tolerant of this and other racial mixes. The dearth of mulatta/o images in contemporary media suggests that a taboo still remains in terms of writing and developing characters of this racial mix.

Shifting Latino Roles

U.S. Latinos hold a unique place in the racial and ethnic hierarchy in the United States due to the high degree of racial and ethnic mixing (*mestizaje*) throughout the Americas. Those who emerged from this *mestizaje* were referred to as *mestizos*. Consequently, Latinos have always had an advantage of being ethnically ambiguous, and actors who are partially Latino, such as Catherine Bach, Lynda Carter, and Jimmy Smits, could easily pass as Anglo. Carlos Cortes (1997) contends that Latino actors with light complexions who can pass as Anglo were often given more desirable roles than those with darker features (128). Unfortunately, these roles were often stereotypical.

Charles Ramirez-Berg (1997) classifies the various stereotypes played by *mestizos* as the half-breed harlot, the dark lady, the female clown, the Latin Lover, the male buffoon, and *el bandido* (113–115). The half-breed harlot is a lusty and hot-tempered female like Chihuahua in *High Noon* (1952) (Ramirez-Berg 1997, 113). She yearns for the Anglo male (Ramirez-Berg 2002, 71). The dark lady is an aloof and virginal woman like Belinnha de Rezende in *Flying Down to Rio* (1933) (Ramirez-Berg 1997, 115). The Latin Lover is a charming, lighter-skinned male who attracts women easily but is unsuccessful at sustaining relationships, exemplified by Roberto Santos in *Latin Lovers* (1953) (Ramirez-Berg 1997, 115; Benshoff and Griffin 2004, 138). The male buffoon is the comedic sidekick like Pedro De Pacas in *Up in Smoke* (1977). The *bandido* is the dangerous, dark-skinned villain prevalent in early Westerns like *Broncho Billy and Greaser* (1914) or urban gangsters or drug dealers like Felix Cortez in *Clear and Present Danger* (1994) (Ramirez-Berg 1997, 113; Ramirez-Berg 2002, 40). Regardless of the stereotype, these Latino characters rarely if ever had successful relationships with mainstream Anglo characters on the big screen. While these negative stereotypes persist today, successful Latino and Anglo relationships are seen occasionally in films like *Fools Rush In* (1997).

Nevertheless, at the start of the twenty-first century, Latina actresses still confront a studio system that provides them with few attractive roles. Many of them remain stuck playing the sexy female. Confronted with this dilemma, fair-skinned and ethnically ambiguous Latinas like Cameron Diaz and Jessica Alba have utilized their features and have opted to play

Anglo roles exclusively; neither has ever played a Latina character in the movies. The blonde Diaz fits Hollywood's traditional vision of beauty and easily passes as Anglo despite her Cuban background. She has been featured playing the Anglo leading lady in many films such as *Something About Mary* (1998), *Charlie's Angels* (2000), *Gangs of New York* (2002), and *My Sister's Keeper* (2009). In contrast, the more ethnically ambiguous Jessica Alba has been featured in more diverse roles. For example, Alba's first breakthrough role was in Fox's *Dark Angel* (2000–2002). She played an engineered and genetically enhanced character named Max (short for Maximum) Guevara, who has a Latina name (Beltran 2008, 254). But, actually, Max was multiracial in the television program (Beltran 2008, 256). Shortly afterward, she was featured as a biracial character in *Honey* (2003).

A damaged poster from the movie *Honey* that starred Jessica Alba on an Orlando, Florida, wall, 2003. (Courtesy of Paul Martin Lester.)

Following those two roles, Alba crossed over to more mainstream Anglo roles. She has starred in a wide variety of films like *Fantastic Four* (2005), *Into the Blue* (2006), and *Good Luck Chuck* (2007). While Diaz and Alba do not deny their racial backgrounds, both ethnically ambiguous actresses have been able to take advantage of their ability to pass as Anglo characters in a marketplace that does not provide many options for Latinas.

Freddie Prinze Jr. and Charlie Sheen are two fair-skinned and handsome Latino actors who fit the classic stereotype of the Latin lover. For the majority of Prinze's career, he has been able to take advantage of his racial ambiguity. For example, he was featured as an Anglo in horror films like *I Know What You Did Last Summer* (1997). He also played the romantic lead in teen films like *She's All That* (1999) and *Summer Catch* (2001). As with Diaz and Alba, Prinze has never played a Latino on the big screen, but he has played a Puerto Rican in the television series *Freddie* (2005–2006). Prinze contends that the program is based on his Puerto Rican roots (Diaz 2005). On the other hand, Charlie Sheen, a long-time film and television actor, has played a wide variety of roles in films. Early in his film career, he was featured in teenage dramas like *Lucas* (1984) and more adult-themed dramas like *Platoon* (1986) and *Wall Street* (1987). He slowly began to transition into comedies like *Major League* (1989) and *Hot Shots!* (1991). More recently, Sheen has become a fixture on popular television comedies like ABC's *Spin City* (2000–2002) and CBS's *Two and Half Men* (2003 to present). Throughout his long film and television career, Sheen has never played a Latino character. While Prinze has played a Latino recently on television, both Prinze and Sheen have been able to take advantage of their physical features to play either Anglo or ethnically ambiguous roles on the big screen. Their mixed-race backgrounds allow them to avoid being type-cast into a narrow niche. Like their Latina counterparts, these two actors do not deny their Latino heritage and easily navigate from one ethnicity to another in film and television.

To varying degrees, the Latino actors and actresses above have suppressed their ethnicity to secure roles that were once exclusively reserved for Anglos on film and television. While access to these roles is an enormous step in the right direction and illustrates that Latino talent has more opportunities for better roles, these actors rarely play a Latino in film and television, since these parts tend to be sporadic. When Latino images appear on television screens or motion pictures, they often crystallize preexisting stereotypes like the half-breed harlot even further. For example, the role of Gloria Delgado-Pritchett played by the Colombian-born actress Sofia Vergara in ABC's *Modern Family* (2009–present) and Gabrielle Solis played by Eva Longoria Parker, the daughter of Mexican-American parents, in ABC's *Desperate Housewives* (2004–present), are current half-breed harlot archetypes. Well-known Latino actors have little incentive to play the stereotypical or underdeveloped Latino characters who frequent current U.S. films or motion pictures. So despite the fact that Latino talent has more access to non-Latino roles, Latino images continue to remain static and rare.

The Invisible Eurasian

Asian-Anglo mixing was considered an American taboo in the nineteenth and early part of the twentieth centuries. This taboo manifested into the 1922 Cable Act that legislated that an Anglo-American woman could lose her citizenship if she married an Asian man (Nishime 2008, 302). Today, Asians and Anglos mix freely in the United States, and their offspring are referred to as Eurasians, *hapas* (Hawaiian for *half*), and even *mestizos* (Spanish and Filipino mix) (Beltran and Fojas 2008, 4). In popular culture, the Asian-European mix results in the tragic Eurasian, which originated in fiction during the "Yellow Peril" between 1850 and 1940 and often featured women (Nakashima 2001, 37). In this formulaic portrayal, the unsuccessful relationship results in the woman realizing that being Anglo is better than Asian and that the two races have "unassimilability" (Nakashima 2001, 37–38). Union between the two races always ended with the death of one (Nakashima 2001, 37). Over time, the stereotype shifted to focus on the male and became a bit more positive in the 1980s. Characters like Buckaroo Banzai exhibited positive characteristics stereotypically associated with both races in films like *The Adventures of Buckaroo Banzai: Across the Eighth Dimension* (1984) (Nakashima 2001, 40–41). A more recent example of a tragic female Eurasian trapped between the two racial worlds was Avik in the Australian film *Map of the Human Heart* (1993) (Williams 1995, 88).

Phoebe Cates and Kristen Kruek are two Asian-Anglo actresses who fit the tragic Eurasian typecast. Today, they are able to take advantage of their racial ambiguity in order to pass as Anglo. With a 25-year film and television career, Cates is most famous for appearing in teen films such as *Fast Times in Ridgemont High* (1982) and *Gremlins* (1985). She also has appeared in more adult roles in *Bright Lights, Big City* (1988); *Shag* (1989); and *Anniversary Party* (2001). She has never played a biracial person. However, she did play an Asian once when she was cast as Polynesian royalty in *Princess Caraboo* (1994). Kruek offers a more recent example of an Asian who consistently passes as Anglo. Her initial break occurred when she was featured as the lead in the nonanimated ABC version of *Snow White* (2001). She is best known as Lana Lang, a popular Anglo cheerleader and the girlfriend of Clark Kent, in the long-running series *Smallville* (2001–2009). In motion pictures, Kruek has played more diverse roles. For example, she was a Muslim in a short film entitled *Partition* (2007). More recently, she has starred as a U.S.-born Asian woman residing in Hong Kong in *Street Fighter: The Legend of Chun-Li* (2009). These two and their fellow Asian actresses have been able to use their racial ambiguity to secure primarily non-Asian roles.

Keanu Reeves and Mark-Paul Gosselaar are two Asian-Anglo males who have been cast primarily as Anglo characters in film and television. Reeves is a mixed-race star whose big break came when he appeared in the comedy hit *Bill and Ted's Excellent Adventure* (1989). Afterward, he used his ethnic ambiguity to appear in·a wide variety of roles that feature him as an Anglo protagonist in *Speed* (1994), *The Matrix* (1999), and *Constantine* (2003). The only time Reeves played an Asian role was as Siddhartha in *Little Buddha* (1993). The blond Mark-Paul Gosselaar initially became well known as a young television star when he played Zack Morris in the popular series *Saved by the Bell* (1989–1993). He successfully made the leap from children's television to more adult programming when he starred as Detective John Clark in *NYPD Blue* (2001–2005). In this role, he exemplified the best-of-both-worlds stereotype. More recently, he starred as another Anglo character in TNT's *Raising the Bar* (2008–2009). Similar to Latino and African-American actors with fair skin, Reeves and Gosselaar have taken advantage of their racially ambiguous features to secure and play Anglo characters in an era that does not provide many significant Asian roles.

Eurasian actors and actresses have had to deemphasize their Asian heritage in order to play Anglo roles on film and television. Like the mulatto, the Asian and Anglo mix is no longer viewed as a cultural or social taboo today. But, despite the end of the Yellow Peril era, U.S. producers of entertainment content never really changed the Eurasian stereotype. These producers failed to write and produce many Eurasian images. As a matter of fact, the Eurasian image continues to be one of the rarest visual representations in U.S. motion pictures or television programs. Thus, racially ambiguous Eurasian actors and actresses generally do not have any option but to pass as Anglo. The dearth of Eurasian images reflects the continuing failure of U.S. films and television producers to fully recognize and embrace roles for Anglo-Asians.

Conclusion

While a mixed-race heritage no longer embodies a taboo in our society, overtly mixed-race characters continue to be rare in contemporary U.S. film and television programs. As a matter of fact, several mixed-race actors such as Jennifer Beals or Mark-Paul Gosselaar continue to pass as Anglos in film and television. The lack of mixed-race images is a troubling trend for future generations, especially when we consider that the majority of mixed-race Americans are under the age of 18 (Navarro 2008) and that more than 20 percent of the U.S. population is expected to be of mixed race by 2050 (Jones 2004, 209). This scarcity of mixed-race roles and the resulting paucity of mixed-race images in the media need to change because an entire generation of mixed-race Americans is growing up without seeing its reflection on movie or television screens. Mixed-race actors are not being given an opportunity to play their mixed-race heritage and so cannot serve as role models for this growing demographic group.

One of the results of having racially ambiguous actors playing Anglos on small and large screens may be to expand our society's definition of whiteness at the expense of mixed-race images. Perhaps Cortes (1997) was correct when he asserted that one of the unintended consequences of eliminating stereotypes is that it may result in being left with no images at all (134). Even today, film and television writers develop few or no biracial images. Unfortunately, our early negative stereotypes of mixed-race individuals in film and literature, as well as cultural taboos about miscegenation, have not been eliminated entirely. In order to change the current situation, more biracial persons—from actors to everyday citizens—need to use the tactic employed by Jennifer Beals: We all need to ask those in the entertainment arts to produce shows that reflect biracial characters and their stories.

Notes

1. See http://www.youtube.com/watch?v=4a56FnhtuGI (accessed March 14, 2010).

2. See http://www.youtube.com/watch?v=dm09iOIjM1M (accessed March 14, 2010).

3. See http://www.youtube.com/watch?v=rBeuyjlbes8 (accessed March 14, 2010).

Sources

Beltran, Mary. 2008. Mixed race in Latinowood: Latino stardom and ethnic ambiguity in the era of Dark Angels. In *Mixed race Hollywood*, ed. M. Beltran and C. Fojas. New York: New York University Press.

Beltran, and Camilla Fojas, eds. 2008. *Mixed race Hollywood*. New York: New York University Press.

Benshoff, Harry, and Sean Griffin. 2004. *America on film: Representing race, class, gender, and sexuality at the movies*. Malden, MA: Blackwell.

Bogle, Donald. 1973. *Toms, coons, mulattoes, mammies, and bucks: An interpretive history of Blacks in American films*. New York: Viking Press.

Cortes, Carlos E. 1997. Chicanas in film: History of an image. In *Latin looks: Images of Latinas and Latinos in the U.S. media*, ed. Clara E. Rodriguez. Boulder, CO: Westview Press.

Deggans, Eric. 2005. Grading Hispanic gains on TV? Start with ABC. *St. Petersburg Times*, December 8, p. 1E.

Diaz, Johnny. 2005. Speaking volumes: Use of Spanish booms on network programs. *Boston Globe*, November 13, p. N1.

Downie, Stephen. 2008. Birds of a feather. *Daily Telegraph*, April 9, p. 46.

Giles, Freda Scott. 1995. From melodrama to the movies: The tragic mulatto as a type character. In *American mixed race: The culture of microdiversity*, ed. Naomi Zack. Lanham, MD: Rowman & Littlefield Publisher, Inc.

Harris, Marvin. 1964. *Patterns of race in the Americas*. New York: Norton.

Jones, Suzanne. 2004. *Race mixing: Southern fiction since the sixties*. Baltimore: John Hopkins University Press.

Nakamura, Lisa. 2008. Mixedfolks.com: "Ethnic ambiguity," celebrity outing, and the Internet. In *Mixed race Hollywood*, ed. Mary Beltran and Camilla Fojas. New York: New York University Press.

Nakashima, Cynthia L. 2001. Servants of culture: The symbolic role of mixed-race Asians in American discourse. In *The sum of our parts: Mixed-heritage Asian Americans*, ed. Teresa Williams-Leon and Cynthia L. Nakashima. Philadelphia: Temple University Press.

Navarro, Mireya. 2008. Who are we? New dialogue on mixed race. *New York Times*, March 31, p. A1.

Nishime, LeiLani. 2008. The *Matrix* trilogy, Keanu Reeves, and multiraciality at the end of time. In *Mixed race Hollywood*, ed. Mary Beltran and Camilla Fojas. New York City: New York University Press.

Omi, Michael, and Howard Winant. 1994. *Racial formation in the United States*. London: Routledge.

O'Neil-Parker, Lonnae. 1999. White girl? Cousin Kim is passing. But cousin Lonnae doesn't want to let her go. *Washington Post*, August 8, p. F1.

Park, Jane. 2008. Virtual race: The racially ambiguous action hero in *The Matrix* and *Pitch Black*. In *Mixed race Hollywood*, ed. Mary Beltran and Camilla Fojas. New York: New York University Press.

Ramirez-Berg, Charles. 1997. Stereotyping in films in general and of the Hispanic in particular. In *Latin looks: Images of Latinas and Latinos in the U.S. media*, ed. Clara E. Rodriguez. Boulder, CO: Westview Press.

Ramirez-Berg, Charles. 2002. *Latino images in film: Stereotypes, subversion, and resistance*. Austin: University of Texas Press.

Sweet, Frank W. 2005. The invention of the color line: 1691. http://backintyme.com/essays/?p=12 (accessed December 13, 2009).

Williams, Teresa Kay. 1995. The theater of identity: (Multi-)race and representation of Eurasians and Afroasians. In *American mixed race: The culture of microdiversity*, ed. Naomi Zack. Lanham, MD: Rowman & Littlefield.

Chapter 10

Exile and Erasure: The African-American Cinderella and the Asian-American Prince

Paula Marie Seniors

Through historical and film analysis, this chapter examines the marketing and images surrounding the stagings of the multiracial motion picture *Cinderella* to explore why African-American women and Asian-American men faced exile and erasure, and how this proved injurious. The story centers on Cinderella's need for love, her yearning to escape oppressive servitude to her stepfamily, and the Prince's desire for a romantic partnership. *Cinderella* resolves with the couple's wishes granted and her transformation into a beautiful princess in virginal white who marries the Prince in a fantastical wedding (Freedman, Rodgers, and Hammerstein 1997).

Cinderella, produced by the Walt Disney Company and Whitney Houston's Brownhouse Productions, offered a traditional rendering with the "white feminist" discourse of self-reliance, self-determination, and self-empowerment.[1] In contrast to the 1950 Anglo-American *Cinderella*, whose wishes are magically granted, the African-American *Cinderella*—like her twenty-first-century counterpart in *The Princess and the Frog* (2009)—must beg for her wishes and make them come true. She must exhibit self-reliance and self-sufficiency. Struggle remains the dominant factor for her; ready access to fulfilled dreams and womanhood exists for Anglo-American

An illustration from an 1865 edition of *Cinderella* created by the wood engraving brothers Edward and George Dalziel. (Source: George Routledge and Sons.)

women exclusively (Clements et al. 2009; Dargis 2009; Freedman, Rodgers, and Hammerstein 1997; James 1997; Lucas 2009; Sharkey 2009).

Disney and Brownhouse abandoned the Mammy, Pickaninny, and Jezebel clichés by casting Brandy, a dark-skinned girl with Afrocentric braids, to portray a conventional Cinderella embodying love, beauty, and desirability, tropes usually reserved for Anglo-American or light-skinned, African-American female characters. Filipino actor Paolo Montalban portrayed a customary prince imbued with chivalry, masculinity, and sensuality that opposed the stereotypes of the yellow peril, the sexualized brute, the asexual or homosexual, and the unrepentantly foreign or alien stereotypes of Asian-American men (as mentioned in chapter 9)[2] (Freedman, Rodgers, and Hammerstein 1997; see also Almaguer 1994; Bogle 1990; Dixon-Gottschild

2000; George-Graves 2000; Gray-White 1985; Lowe 1996; Okihiro 1994, 2001; Sison 1997; Spickard 1989; Tanner 1992; Woll 1989; Yu 2001).

Challenging stereotypes, rejecting victimization, and embracing empowerment are positive messages, but an African-American *Cinderella* inherently promotes racialized meanings. Consequently, the predominant message presented through the juxtaposition of the two *Cinderella*s is that Anglo-Americans' dreams will come true but African Americans need to accept unequal and unjust conditions.

Exile: Merchandising the Multiracial *Cinderella*

Many hoped that a radical shift in representation for African-American women and Asian-American men would follow from the casting of *Cinderella*. However, Cinderella products suggested otherwise. The cover for the 1999 Williamson Music Company's ("Rodgers and Hammerstein's *Cinderella*" 1999) sheet music featured Anglo-American dancers prominently displayed contrasted with indistinguishable African-American dancers attired in royal blue and purple in the background. The pink, green, and white staircase remained the focal point, with the African-American Cinderella and Asian-American Prince conspicuously absent. One must open the book to see beautiful multiracial photographs, an apparent marketing strategy to secure sales to those who might object.

Breaking with the tradition of creating merchandise in the likeness of their hero/ines, Disney abandoned this strategy and produced toys imaging the 1950 *Cinderella*.[3] Anglo-American, blonde, blue-eyed Cinderellas, and Anglo fairy godmothers and princes populated Disney Stores, superseding multiracial doppelgangers and communicating clearly that African-American women and Asian-American men remained unworthy of merchandise, romantic renderings, and womanhood and manhood rights. The omission of African-American products is confounding given that "[o]ne especially striking statistic" reported that "70 percent of girls under the age of 18" watched *Cinderella*, clearly suggesting that audiences readily accepted a multiracial Cinderella (Carter 1997). Disney Television President Charles Hirschhorn underscored this finding: "The success told us . . . that there is a huge family audience out there for quality programming" (Carter 1997).

Passionate portrayals of African-American women with Asian-American men proved a great financial commodity, signifying that consumers would buy multiracial *Cinderella* merchandise, especially given that African-American customers' purchasing power totaled $500 billion by 1998 and was estimated to reach $1.2 trillion by 2013. Asian-American buying power reached $427 billion by 2006 (*Charlotte Post* 2009; Elliott 2003; "Black Buying Power" 1998; O'Barr 2007; Williams 2003; see also "Asian Annual Buying Power" 2006). The incongruity of the marketing strategy of exclusion remains perplexing as it occurred at the height of Brandy, Houston, and Montalban's popularity.

The Influence of Erasure on Children

One must question how the erasure and elimination of multiracial messages and merchandise influences children of color because children's literature and the media play a role in identity formation by supplying imagery that provides them with cultural data about others, themselves, and "the relative status of group membership" (Spitz 1999, 427–440; see also Hurley 2005; Yeoman 1999). Children's intertextual knowledge of narratives and characters helps them understand their world and broadens or restricts their perspective.

Dorothy Hurley (2005) argues that fairy tales play a primary role in self-image and personality development and that children *must see themselves* in order to form positive self-images (221). When we expose children to disruptive narratives like the 1997 version of *Cinderella*, which "challenge" and move beyond the constraints of customary stories about race, gender, and class, children appear to cultivate more holistic viewpoints concerning these identity variables and ultimately themselves (Hurley 2005; Spitz 1999; Yeoman 1999). I would also suggest that toys influence children's self-image and induce them to learn their expected roles in society. Without seeing themselves on toy store shelves, children are forced to internalize a message of exclusion that makes them feel inadequate. Without the Cinderella merchandise, African- and Asian-American children could not *really* personify these cultural icons.

Elizabeth Yeoman (1999) discovered that her kindergarteners of color internalized fairy tales' Anglo-American beauty ideals to such an extent that they rejected their own uniqueness and beauty. Yeoman exposed the children to a dark-skinned heroine without revealing her color and asked them to draw her. Two brown girls sketched her as Anglo-Canadian and blonde and explained, "I imagine her dark, but I'm drawing her blonde," and "[S]he was good, so I wanted to make her pretty." This illustrates how children are injured and unconsciously assimilate the repetitive color symbolism and filmic signs that equate white to goodness such as the white, blue-eyed, female robot in *Wall-E* (2008) and the "blue-black" skin and "black" speech and movements of Ursula in *The Little Mermaid* (1989) as evil. Overexposure to stereotypical color symbolism proves toxic to children's psyche as it can lead to the rejection of dark skin as precious and beautiful (Hurley 2005). The oversaturation of corrosive color symbolism can lead children to believe that they personify negative attributes and helps explain why these girls depicted an Anglo-American heroine.

Reasons for the Marketing Strategy of Exclusion

One must ask why Disney adopted a marketing strategy of exclusion. Nancy Larrick's (1995) study of 1965 booksellers and *The Ethicist* offer some clues. Larrick argues that booksellers believed that Anglo-American mothers would not buy books featuring African Americans. As one representative sales manager asked, "Why jeopardize sales by putting one or two Negro faces in an illustration?" (6). In 2006, *The Ethicist* fielded a question from a theater-goer dismayed over seeing an African-American female snowflake dancing *The Nutcracker*. "The aesthetic incongruity was inconceivable. The entire ballet was spoiled. It is analogous to a one-legged midget playing Tarzan. Does this make me a racist?" (Cohen 2006). He counseled that *yes, indeed*, the questioner was racist and that "[a]s race-neutral casting becomes commonplace, I think you'll no longer see it as incongruous; you'll judge a dancer by her skill, not her race." Three years later, *The Ethicist* offered the case of a company that resisted publishing an African-American customer's photograph out of concern that it would deter Anglo Americans (Cohen 2009). Similarly, then, it is possible that Disney failed to create multiracial Cinderella products out of fear that Anglo-American reticence to multiracial renderings would undercut profits.

Black Enterprise might offer another reason for Disney's marketing strategy. The publication reported on an Amcast advertising sales staff memo directing staff to refrain from selling and buying ads on African-American radio to avoid losing "the more important" Anglo-American consumers. Amcast, a radio and television sales company, apparently believed they could, and should, avoid African-American media, eliminate advertisements for ethnics, and cull these customers from Anglo-American markets (Graves 1998). Perhaps Disney followed Amcast's strategy by not creating multiracial merchandise, counting on minorities to purchase "white" products and marketing toward Anglo Americans, whom they assumed would forgo purchasing multiracial hero/ines, although the film's viewership suggested the contrary. Disney's presumption of Anglo-American resistance to the

African-American feminine romantic aesthetic, subsequent loss of revenue, and advertisers' opposition might have led to a marketing strategy of exclusion.

Exile: "The Musical That Makes Dreams Come True"[4] . . . but Not for African-American Girls

The popularity of the multiracial *Cinderella* led to a national tour (2000) and productions at the New York City Opera (2004) and Paper Mill Playhouse in New Jersey (2005). Robert Freedman's teleplay inspired these shows, with Tom Briggs and Gabriel Barre adapting his script for the tour and Paper Mill. Anglo-American Cinderellas and Queens replaced African Americans. The tour featured the *Sopranos'* Jamie Lynn Sigler and pop singer Debbie Gibson as Cinderella, and Leslie Becker played a domineering Queen, with Ken Prymus as a subservient African-American King and African-American icon Eartha Kitt portraying the Fairy Godmother. Paper Mill cast Angela Gaylor as Cinderella, Joy Franz as the Queen, Anglo-American actor Larry Keith as the King, and African-American Suzanne Douglass as the Fairy Godmother[5] ("Eartha in Cinderella" 2000; *Cinderella* 2001; Fusco 2000; "NETworks" 2001; "Kitt-Gibson *Cinderella* Tour" 2000; Welsh 2001; see also Daniels 2005; "Rodgers & Hammerstein's Cinderella" 2004).

The resulting Anglo-American/African-American, female/male pairing followed casting trends in which Anglo Americans, Asian Americans, and Latinas replaced African-American women.[6] African-American actor Will Smith discussed this choice in casting for *Hitch* (2005):

> There's sort of an accepted myth that if you have two black actors, a male and a female, in the lead of a romantic comedy, that people around the world don't want to see it. . . . We spend $50-something million making this movie and the studio would think that was tough on their investment. So the idea of a black actor and a white actress comes up—that'll work around the world, but it's a problem in the U.S. (MSNBC.com 2005)

Anglo-Cuban Eva Mendes proved the solution "because apparently, the Black/Latina combination is not considered taboo" (MSNBC.com 2005).

The play *Cinderella* followed the casting trend and eliminated the African-American feminine romantic aesthetic while retaining the Asian-American Prince. The exile of the African-American romantic lead suggests that

African-American women are unsuitable for love and marriage. Stage shows of *Cinderella* cast an African-American Fairy Godmother, who like Mammy granted Anglo-American women's wishes, and evoked Mammy mothering their children and Jezebel "caring for" or more accurately facing ravishment by Anglo-American men. Ultimately, the Fairy Godmother remained fundamentally unrevolutionary and unimaginative ("Eartha in Cinderella" 2000; Fusco 2000; "NETworks" 2001).

The elimination of positive imagery alongside such negative portrayals damages African-American girls' sense of self-worth and shapes perceptions of what it means to be female and African American (Amber 2005; Collins 2004; Crouther et al. 2009; Seniors 2010; Sharpley-Whiting 2007; Steffans 2005, 2007).

An Altered Multiracial Narrative

The questions arise: What happened to the multiracial narrative that avowed that African-American girls could *see* themselves as Cinderella, and how did this exile and omission injure and affect them? Norma Manatu (2006) and Marcia Lieberman (1986) propose that Cinderella represents a "cultural mainstay" that teaches girls to want to incarnate Cinderella and all that she symbolizes, including *personifying* Anglo-American sublime models that dictate that she *must* be blonde and blue-eyed, *must* romance the Prince, and *must* participate in a fabulous wedding. Manatu suggests that African-American girls might experience indignation and bewilderment with the barrage of Anglo-American Cinderellas as society expects them to typify this Anglo-American exemplar (2006, 167). Given their erasure from Cinderella roles, African-American girls may suffer from feelings of inferiority and exclusion, internalize Anglo-American paragons, and reject the African-American feminine romantic aesthetic. Under this influence, young girls may try to fit into Anglo-American ideals of beauty, a practice they see modeled by African-American performers Vivica A. Fox, Gabrielle Union, Keri Washington, and rapper Lil' Kim.

The *Cinderella* stage productions included an obese, African-American, evil stepsister, advancing the malevolent Mammy mode. The inclusion of the malicious, portly, African-American stepsister and the exile of the African-American feminine romantic aesthetic reduced Anglo-American anxieties concerning African-American women. Andrea Elizabeth Shaw (2006) argues that hegemony dictates that we disdain the corpulent African-American female for her apparent refusal to thin down. Some

African Americans, like *Precious* (2009) director Lee Daniels, adopt this mind-set: "I thought they were dirty and not very smart" (Shaw 2006, 50; see also Hirschberg 2009). Shaw asserts that the porcine, African-American woman allays Anglo women's fears and disquietude of them as beautiful, sexually desirable, and amatory partners for Anglo males. In *Glee*, the mean, obese, African-American Mercedes, typified as nonsexual and no romantic foil to Anglo-American girls, exemplifies this model (Brennan, Falchuk, and Murphy 2009).

The regression to Anglo-dominated productions of *Cinderella* signified that no place existed for African-American women other than as the sub-servient Fairy Godmother or the unlovable stepsister, instructing us that Mammy, not the quixotic Cinderella or Queen, remains the only "ideal" to which they should aspire. These casting choices marked missed opportunities to continue to reshape conceptions of African-American females that are injurious, humiliating, and insulting to African-American girls. The musical remained complicit in imparting damaging lessons about African-American girls and left no space for them to envisage themselves in positive images other than the Fairy Godmother granting Anglo-American women their wishes while foregoing their own.

While African-American women faced exile from these shows, directors retained the Asian-American Prince. Paolo Montalban portrayed the Prince, but given European sexual conquest of people of color, this remains unsurprising and loaded with meaning. Asian-American manliness emerged in the movie *Cinderella* and contested Asian-American male clichés. An Asian-American Prince courting an African-American Cinderella illuminated their common labor histories of slavery and indentured servitude, and replicated real-life love relationships[7] (Almaguer 1994; Lowe 1996; Lowen 1971; Okihiro 1994, 2001; Quan 1982; Spickard 1989).

Reinscribing Asian-American Male Masculinity

While the casting brings conquest to the fore, we must consider what messages an Asian-American Prince conveyed to Asian-American boys. I assert that the norm for heterosexual masculinity remains that of the idealized Anglo-American Prince, which leads some to emulate this model. Such fairy tale renditions teach boys regressive patriarchal modes, instructing them that they will gain power, wealth, and property through marrying the most beautiful girl (Lieberman 1986). Allan Chinen (1993) argues that Anglo-American men needed fairy tales to reassert their masculinity, hierarchal authority, and heroic ideals, given people of color and feminists who "rise up against the patriarch" (1–9). Chinen claims that a single custom and belief system dominates—Eurocentric, with Anglo-American male authority at the axis.

Montalban's Prince complicated manliness exemplars and challenged the dominant model in which fairy tales symbolize regressive patriarchal modes.

The 1997 *Cinderella* reinscribed masculinity as Asian American, discarded color symbolism, and challenged Anglo-American male supremacy and stereotypes. It also portrayed the love match as an equal partnership and the Asian-American male as the embodiment of the quintessential romantic partner, thus jettisoning the love scene taboo and "apartheid-style racial codes" concerning romance[8] (Johnson 1930, 171; see also Bogle 1990; Shohat and Stam 1994; Spickard 1989). While the Asian-American Prince/Anglo-American Cinderella pairing illuminated conquest, the positive attributes of an Asian-American Prince allowed Asian-American boys to cultivate a holistic, affirming self-image and envision themselves within fairytales.

Conclusion

Subsequent to the multiracial *Cinderella*, African-American women and Asian-American men faced romantic exile. *Star Trek* (2009) offered the Asian-American Sulu as womanless. The African-American Uhuru and the Anglo-American Captain Kirk flirt, but in the end Spock romances her, teaching viewers that African-American women's *only* romantic opportunities are with aliens or *as* aliens, as in *Avatar* (2009). For example, the final scene in *Romeo Must Die* (2000) resolved with a hug instead of the traditional kiss between African-American singer Aaliyah and Asian-American action star Jet Li (Orci and Kurtzman 2009; see also Cameron 2009; Kapner, Bernt and Jarrell 2000). The media bombarded viewers with Mammies in *Chicago* (2002) and *Hairspray* (1988) and gold diggers and Jezebels in *Carmen: A Hip Hopera* (2001) and replaced the African-American feminine romantic aesthetic with non–African-American women (Condon, Fosse, and Ebb, 2002; Seniors 2010; Williams 2000). The news media joined in, assaulting First Lady Michelle Obama with racially malicious portrayals that depicted her as an ape and as an emasculating, Afro-wearing (i.e., radical), masculinized terrorist (Herbert 2009; see also Dowd 2009; *New Yorker* 2008).

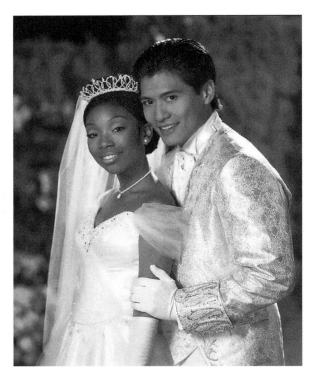

Brandy Norwood and Paolo Montalban pose in character for the Walt Disney television movie *Cinderella* that aired November 2, 1997. (Copyright Walt Disney Pictures. Courtesy of Walt Disney Pictures/ Photofest.)

Comparably, Asian-American male retrograde representations reappeared with the yellow peril mode wrapped in Cold War discourse of Korean males as a menace to the world and Anglo-American womanhood in portrayals such as Zao in *Die Another Day* (2002) and Kim Jong II in *Team America: World Police* (2004). *Lost* and Broadway's *Thoroughly Modern Millie* advanced Asian-American male stereotypes of unrepentantly foreign, romantically cold, and asexual men that were threatening to Anglo-American womanhood, gay, and un-American—so much so that they speak Korean and Chinese with English subtitles[9] (Fleming, Purvis, and Wade 2002; see also Horta 2006; "Kitt-Gibson *Cinderella* Tour" 2000; Le Espiritu 1997, 87–93; Parker, Stone, and Brady 2004; Scanlon and Morris 2000).

Tiny eruptions of change did occur with *Akira's Hip Hop Shop* (2007), in which the romance is between an Asian-American man and an

African-American woman, and *Up* (2009), an adventure with Russell, an Asian-American boy hero. *Annie* (1982), *Something New* (2006), and *Away We Go* (2009) highlighted African-American female/Anglo-American male love. The transformation of the African-American girl as Princess did not occur in Disney's *The Princess and the Frog*, for Tiana was a waitress and remained a frog for the majority of the movie. Reminiscent of African Americans who played amorous animals in *The Lion King* (1994) and *Song of the South* (1946), Disney rendered the African-American feminine romantic aesthetic animalistic while simultaneously reinscribing African-American female stereotypes (Doughrity 2007; see also Clements et al. 2009; Eggers and Vida 2009; Frost 2008; Mecchi and Meehan 1999; Peterson and Docter 2009; Turner 2006).

The multiracial *Cinderella* as a disruptive text worked to combat hegemony's nonaffirmation of people of color's beauty by presenting positive images and raging against the monopoly of children's intertextual knowledge held by Anglo-American, blonde, blue-eyed hero/ines. While the movie was progressive, it also offered an Anglo-American feminist-infused African-American Cinderella who had to beg for her wishes and demonstrate independence, which maintained hegemony's discourse of containing African-American aspirations and coercing African Americans to accept inequality. The success of *Cinderella* and the purchasing power of African Americans, Asian Americans, *and* Anglo Americans indicated that a lucrative market existed for multiracial Cinderella merchandise and romantic Asian-American male/African-American female portrayals. By failing to produce this merchandise, Disney and Brownhouse Productions signified that African-American women and Asian-American men remained unworthy of womanhood and manhood rights and could not *really* personify romantic fantasy icons.

If the movie and theatrical producers had challenged entrenched racism, this effort could have worked as a potent antidote to the clichéd African-American female and Asian-American male images that saturate twenty-first-century media. Sadly, it failed to mark a turning point of change.

Notes

1. The producers of *Cinderella* used colorblind casting, cross-marketing, and narrowcasting to revive the ABC television series *The Wonderful World of Disney* through *Cinderella*, their inaugural show, and to build the ABC network. In *Watching Race*, Herman Gray (1995, 68) defines "narrowcasting" as the targeting

of a particular audience, most specifically African Americans, to build television stations. Cross-marketing is the use of popular music on television, and the casting of African-American performers and (I would add) other ethnic and minority groups from the record, film, and Broadway industries (like Brandy, L.L. Cool J, and Will Smith) to attract large audiences and promote records, Broadway shows, and films. Fox television network successfully used narrowcasting and cross-marketing to build their network, and ABC, CBS, and NBC followed suit (Gray 1995, 57–60, 68).

2. For a comprehensive discussion of the African-American female stereotypes, see Seniors (2009). According to executive producer Craig Zadan, they made no attempt to turn the multiracial *Cinderella* into *The Wiz* (1978) but opted for a conventional rendering of the story (Purdum 1997, 35).

3. Power differentials abounded within Disney and Whitney Houston's Brownhouse Productions partnership, with Disney wielding far more power. As a consequence, when discussing marketing strategies, I speak exclusively of Disney.

4. Marshalls presents Rodgers and Hammerstein's "Cinderella." *San Diego Union Tribune*, May 28–June 3, 2001.

5. Jamie Lynn Sigler is an Anglo-Cuban. After auditioning an African American and an Anglo-American female for the role of *Cinderella*, the director chose the Anglo performer Angela Gaylor to play the lead for the Paper Mill Playhouse.

6. The news media reported during this time period that the Latino population was outpacing the African-American one, and this most certainly influenced this casting trend. The television show *Crash* (2009) followed this pattern by completely erasing African-American women as leading characters.

7. Having learned from their experiences with African Americans who reproduced and demanded citizenship, education, and land, the U.S. government sought to fully control the Asian-American worker by controlling their reproduction and their citizenship rights through laws that prohibited Asian-American female migration. In the 1870s, the Anglo-American planter class brought Chinese workers to Mississippi to work on the plantations as punishment for African Americans gaining their freedom and demanding rights. The Anglo-American planter class pitted the Chinese against African Americans. According to Ron Takaki (1990), by using the Chinese, the planters overthrew Reconstruction, and the Chinese eventually left the plantations and went into small business (95).

Because of laws that prevented Asian-American female migration, 20 to 30 percent of Mississippi Delta Chinese men found common bonds with the African-American community and married African-American women before 1940. After 1940, like the poor Anglo-American workers who aligned themselves with the planter class rather than the poor African-American worker with whom they shared a similar labor history, the new Chinese immigrants adopted Jim Crow racism in order to assimilate into Anglo-American culture and shunned Chinese males who married African-American women. Some in the Chinese community saw this behavior by the new Chinese immigrants as "selling out their cultural identity" in order to fit into Anglo-American society (Lowen 1971; Quan 1982; see also Okihiro 1994).

8. According to James Weldon Johnson (1930), the love scene taboo dictated that African-American men and women could not mate romantically on stage but must do so in a comedic or minstrel manner, while the taboo against Asian-American romance dictated that Anglo-American men in yellow face portray Asian-American men in romantic scenes with Asian-American women, in what Shohat and Stam (1994) define as "apartheid-style racial codes" concerning romance (189).

9. Alec Mapa's role as Suzuku St. Pierre on *Ugly Betty* is really a happily married straight man portraying a gay fashion commentator in order to gain entry into the fashion world.

Sources

Almaguer, Tomas. 1994. *Racial fault lines*. Berkeley: University of California Press.

Amber, Jeannine. 2005. Dirty dancing. *Essence*, March: 165–166.

Asian annual buying power has grown 59 percent. 2006. *Asian Reporter* 16 (39): 1, 2.

Black buying power tops $500 billion. 1998. *Los Angeles Sentinel*, August 27, A14.

Bogle, Donald. 1990. *Toms, coon, mulattos, mammies, & bucks*. New York: Continuum.

Brennan, Ian, Brad Falchuk, and Ryan Murphy. 2009. *Glee*. Los Angeles: Fox Television.

Cameron, James. 2009. *Avatar*. Los Angeles: 20th Century Fox.

Carter, Bill. 1997. TV notes: Happy ending for *Cinderella*. NYTimes.com, November 5.

Charlotte Post. 2009. May 14: 7A.

Chinen, Allan B. 1993. *Beyond the hero*. New York: Tarcher/Putnam.

Cinderella. 2001. *Playbill*, San Diego.

Clements, Ron, John, Musker, and Rob Edwards. 2009. *The princess and the frog*. Los Angeles: Walt Disney Animation Studios.

Cohen, Randy. 2006. Awkward dance. *New York Times Magazine*, December 17.

Cohen, Randy. 2009. The ethicist. *New York Times Magazine*, November 24.

Collins, Patricia Hill. 2004. *Black sexual politics*. New York: Routledge.

Crouther, Lance, Paul Marchand, Chris Rock, Chuck Sklar, and Jeff Stilson. 2009. *Good Hair*. New York: Chris Rock Productions and HBO Films.

Daniels, Robert L. 2005. Rodgers and Hammerstein's Cinderella (Paper Mill Playhouse, Millburn, N.J.) 1,200 seats: $68 top). *Variety*, October 24.

Dargis, Manohla. 2009. That old bayou magic: Kiss and ribbit (and sing). *New York Times*, November 25.

Dixon-Gottschild, Brenda. 2000. *Waltzing in the dark*. New York: St. Martin's.

Doughrity, Joseph. 2007. *Akira's hip hop shop*. Los Angeles: Light Speed Entertainment and Daydreamer Pictures.

Dowd, Maureen. 2009. Should Michelle cover up? *New York Times*, March 7.

Eartha in Cinderella. 2000. Broadway.com, 1–2.

Eggers, Dave, and Vendela Vida. 2009. *Away we go*. Los Angeles: Focus Features.

Elliott, Stuart. 2003. Procter & Gamble is giving a higher priority to developing campaigns aimed at Black consumers. *New York Times*, June 13.

Fleming, Ian, Neal Purvis, and Robert Wade. 2002. *Die another day*. Los Angeles: Eon Productions, MGM.

Freedman, Robert L., Richard Rodgers, and Oscar Hammerstein. *Cinderella*. 1997. Los Angeles: Walt Disney Television, Whitney Houston's Brownhouse Productions.

Frost, Jennifer. 2008. Hedda Hopper, Hollywood gossip, and the politics of racial representation. *Journal of African American History* 93 (1): 41.

Fusco, Elaina. 2000. Sneak peek at the new *Cinderella* tour with Gibson. *Theatre. com*, November 25, 1–6.

George-Graves, Nadine. 2000. *The royalty of vaudeville*. New York: St. Martins Press.

Graves, Earl G. 1998. Don't spend where you don't count. *Black Enterprise* 28, no. 12: 9, 1.

Gray, Herman. 1995. *Watching Race*. Minnesota: University of Minnesota Press, 57–60.

Gray, White, Deborah. 1985. *Ar'n't I a woman? Female slaves in the plantation south*. New York: Norton.

Herbert, Bob. 2009. The scourge persists. *New York Times*, September 18.

Hirschberg, Lynn. 2009. The audacity of Precious. *New York Times Magazine*, October, 22, 2.

Hurley, Dorothy L. 2005. Seeing White: children of color and the Disney fairy tale princess. *Journal of Negro Education* 74 (3): 221.

James, Caryn. 1997. The old glass slipper fits with a 90's conscience. *New York Times*, October 31.

Johnson, James Weldon. 1930. *Along this way*. New York: Viking Press.

Kapner, Mitchell, Eric Bernt, and John Jarrell. 2000. *Romeo Must Die*. Los Angeles: Warner Brothers.

Kitt-Gibson *Cinderella* tour launches Nov. 28 in Florida. 2000. *Theatre.com*, 1–2.

Larrick, Nancy. 1995. The all-White world of children's books. In *The all-White world of children's books and African American children's literature*, ed. Osayimwense Osa. Trenton, NJ: African World Press.

Le Espiritu, Yen. 1997. *Asian American women and men*. Thousand Oaks, CA: Sage.

Lieberman, Marcia K. 1986. "Some day my prince will come": Female acculturation through the fairy tale. In *Don't bet on the prince: Contemporary feminist fairy tales in North America and England*, ed. Jack Zipes. New York: Methuen.

Lowe, Lisa. 1996. *Immigrant acts: On Asian American culture politics.* Durham, NC: Duke University Press.

Lowen, James W. 1971. *Mississippi Chinese.* Cambridge, MA: Harvard University Press.

Lucas, Demetria. 2009. It ain't easy being green: "Princess and the frog." *Essence. com*, November 25.

Manatu, Norma. 2006. *African American women and sexuality in the cinema.* Jefferson, NC: McFarland.

MSNBC.com. 2005. Casting Will Smith's love interest in "Hitch" was not a simple black or white decision. February 24.

NETworks Presents Rodgers and Hammerstein's *Cinderella.* 2001. National Tour Program, 1.

New Yorker. 2008. July 21.

O'Barr, William M. 2007. Multiculturalism in the marketplace: Targeting Latinas, African American women and gay consumers. *Advertising and Society Review* 7, no. 4.

Okihiro, Gary Y. 1994. *Margins and mainstreams: Asians in American history and culture.* Seattle: University of Washington Press.

Okihiro, Gary Y. 2001. *The Columbia guide to Asian American history.* New York: Columbia University Press.

Orci, Roberto, and Alex Kurtzman. 2009. *Star trek.* Los Angeles: Bad Robot Productions, Paramount.

Parker, Trey, Matt Stone, and Pam Brady. 2004. *Team America: World police.* Los Angeles: Paramount Pictures.

Peterson, Bob, and Pete Docter. 2009. *Up.* Los Angeles: Pixar Animation Studios.

Purdum, Todd. 1997. The slipper still fits though the style is new. *New York Times*, November 2, 35.

Quan, Robert Seto. 1982. *Lotus among the magnolias: The Mississippi Chinese.* Jackson: University Press of Mississippi.

Rodgers & Hammerstein's Cinderella, The New York City Opera. 2004. Advertisement. *New York Times*, October 21, B9.

Rodgers and Hammerstein's *Cinderella* Part of the Magic of the Wonderful World of Disney. 1999. New York: Williamson Music, Rodgers and Hammerstein Company.

Scanlon, Dick, and Richard Morris. 2000. *Thoroughly modern Millie.* La Jolla, CA: La Jolla Playhouse.

Seniors, Paula Marie. 2009. *Beyond lift every voice and sing: The culture of uplift, identity, and politics in Black musical theater.* Columbus: Ohio State University Press.

Seniors, Paula Marie. 2010. Transforming the *Carmen* narrative: The case of *Carmen the Hip Hopera.* In *Message in the music: Hip hop, history, and pedagogy,* ed. Derrick P. Alridge and James B. Stewart. Los Angeles: Association for African American Life and History Press.

Sharkey, Betsy. 2009. The princess and the frog. November 25, LATimes.com.

Sharpley-Whiting, T. Denean. 2007. *Pimps up, ho's down: Hip hop's hold on young Black women*. New York: New York University Press.

Shaw, Andrea Elizabeth. 2006. *The embodiment of disobedience: Fat Black women's unruly political body*. Lanham, MD: Lexington.

Shohat, Ella, and Robert Stam. 1994. *Unthinking Eurocentrism*. New York: Routledge.

Sison, Marites. 1997. Actor Paolo Montalban. *Filipinas*, January.

Spickard, Paul. 1989. *Mixed blood*. Madison: University of Wisconsin Press.

Spitz, E. 1999. *Inside picture books*. New Haven, CT: Yale University Press.

Steffans, Karrine. 2005. *Confessions of a video vixen*. New York: Harper Collins.

Steffans, Karrine. 2007. *Vixen diaries*. New York: Grand Central.

Takaki, Ron. 1990. *Strangers from a different shore*. New York: Penguin.

Tanner, Jo Ann. 1992. *Dusky maidens: The odyssey of the early Black dramatic actress*. Westport: CT: Greenwood Press.

Turner, Kriss. 2006. *Something new*. Los Angeles: Focus Features.

Welsh, Anne Marie. 2001. Oddly enough *Cinderella* works onstage. *San Diego Union Tribune*, May 31, E1–E2.

Williams, Darrell. 2003. Hit discriminators where it hurts: African Americans must use their vast spending power to make change. November, *Black Enterprise Online*.

Williams, Sekani. 2000. *Carmen The Hip Hopera*. New York: MTV.

Woll, Allen. 1989. *Black musical theatre: From Coontown to Dreamgirls*. Baton Rouge: Louisiana State University Press.

Yeoman, E. 1999. How does it get into my imagination? Elementary school children's inter-textual knowledge and gendered storylines. *Gender and Education* 11, 427–440, 433.

Yu, Henry. 2001. *Thinking Orientals: Migration, contact, and exoticism in modern America*. New York: Oxford University Press.

PART III

Delimiting, Denying, and Selling Our Gender and Sexuality

Susan Dente Ross

Perhaps in no other aspect of human identity is the Western propensity for dualistic thinking more evident than in the area of gender and sexuality. Regardless of lived reality and abundant evidence that such mutually exclusive and fixed definitions of gender are socially constructed within the context of power and oppression (World Health Organization n.d.), Western language and tradition persist in prescribing gender as either male or female. Such thinking is grounded in religious tales of separation and immutable difference between man and woman that, in the words of Carol Christ and Judith Plaskow (1979), offer

> the model for domination because reality is divided into two levels, one superior, one inferior. . . . [Such] classical dualism also became the model for the oppression of women when the culture-creating males identified the positive side of the dualism with themselves and identified the negative side with the women over whom they claimed the right to rule (3, 15).

Two decades ago, Judith Butler (1990) convincingly argued in her classic book, *Gender Trouble*, that definitions of women (or men) based on assumptions of shared essentialist traits and interests distinct from the other "regulate" gender relations and create an oppositional, binary view of human sexuality that limits the range of possibility. Today, the following five chapters document how outmoded images of what constitutes the masculine or the feminine continue to injure. It is within the context of culture creation that the eight contributors to this part examine contemporary scripts of sexuality and gender. They investigate the graphics and texts of advertising, news, and entertainment media as well as the narratives inscribed in our psyches and written into our unconscious that hobble our human potential and corral our bodies and our minds into narrow, hierarchical, gendered boxes. They document how contemporary social practices of categorizing sex and gender perpetuate inequality and violate the fundamental concepts of dialogic ethics that Cliff Christians discusses in the conclusion to this book.

Rather than open us each and all to the myriad of alternatives to either/or visions of gender and sexuality and the resulting prolific opportunities for human relations, our imagined and public messages maintain models of ourselves and others that sometimes can enable and justify crimes of violence and hatred, foster obsessive concern with body and physical "beauty," fuel eating disorders and compulsive consumerism, and distance us from our true selves and the human community that nourishes our richest existence.

This part on gender and sexuality begins with a powerful exploration by Audra Diers and Katherine Hatfield-Edstrom of the mediated exploitation and commodification of the brutal death of Matthew Shepard. The authors argue that the powerful verbal image of the fence, onto which Shepard was tied and left to die, played a primary role in making his death iconic in shaping public discourse on hate and hate crimes. While the image of Shepard's murder helped push hate crimes onto the national agenda and propel federal anti–hate crime legislation, its recurrent evocation also inflicted pain on Shepard's family and friends as well as the broader national community. As a consequence, the imagined portrait of Shepard on the fence is an image that both heals and injures.

If Matthew Shepard's death helped "sell" the nation on the need for specific laws criminalizing hate crimes, explicit images of sexualized individuals routinely stimulate consumerism, objectify individuals, and sell us a constricted image of sex and what is sexy, according to Lisa Wade and Gwen Sharp. The idea that "sex sells" is so commonly accepted by advertisers and the public alike that we may overlook the fact that it is only a particularly narrow version of heterosexual sex, in which men are the active subjects and women the passive objects, that is proffered and normalized. Pervasive and recurrent images of only male-dominated heterosexual sex—often in the form of stylized, sexualized violence—limit rather than enhance our ideas of acceptable sexuality and mark our personal desires as unnatural regardless of our gender and sexual identity.

Turning specifically to the images and stories in leading U.S. newspapers, Lee Jolliffe next discusses the restricted, stereotypical portrayal of men and examines its implications for individuals, relationships, and society. Finding that news photographs are more likely to reinforce gender stereotypes of men as strong, violent, and tending to criminality than the texts they accompany, Jolliffe argues that the two, in tandem, stereotype men as disposable beings valuable only for their physical strength and the size of their paychecks. She calls for more inclusive photographs of men in expanded roles in the home, the family, and beyond.

The ways in which women are packaged and defined, shaped and presented, and commodified and marketed in the images and lyrics of country music and country music videos become Debra Merskin's focus. She offers a detailed analysis of the music video and lyrics of Gretchen Wilson's 2004 country song "Redneck Woman," a smash hit that stood atop the Hot Country Songs chart for five weeks. Wilson's song offers a number of seemingly contradictory messages about "redneck women" that simultaneously empower and demean country-music women. Merskin argues that the stereotypical sexualized images of Wilson counterbalanced with tough talk, hard play, and defiance sell the music and the musician and reshape what it means to be a woman, redneck or otherwise.

Julianne Newton and Rick Williams draw the part to a close with their careful analysis of the implications of media's misconstruction and misrepresentation of the fluid and multiple nature of gender archetypes with rigid, limiting, and immutable stereotypes. Based in Jungian analysis, they argue that media stereotypes that "mistranslate" profound human archetypes undermine honest communication and authentic representation of each person's unique self. These "mediatypes" injure profoundly because they create lasting archives deep inside our nonconscious minds that undermine how we see ourselves and relate to one another, and often lead to a solitary, counterfeit existence.

While the contributors to this part suggest strategies that can resist and replace the stereotypes of gender and sexuality they describe, none of the media images they study consistently (or, perhaps, ever) provides us with the resources of the imagination from which to create a reality of rich, diverse sexuality. Instead, the pictures of gay or straight, men or women in anthems of empowerment, reports of death, advertisements, or news bind us each and all to age-old and narrow-minded sexual conventions and prescriptions.

It is outside and against this media blizzard of images that we must exert our efforts and wage our struggle to open up the range of imagined, allowed, and pictured selves. It is within our personal ethics, through honest interaction with others and with "moral values . . . situated in the social context rather than anchored by theoretical abstractions," as Cliff Christians says, that we can and shall begin to reshape the images of our sex toward visions that can heal, help, and nourish.

Sources

Butler, Judith. 1990. *Gender trouble: Feminism and the subversion of identity.* London: Routledge.

Christ, Carol P., and Judith Plaskow. 1979. *Womanspirit rising: A feminist reader in religion.* San Francisco: Harper Collins.

World Health Organization. N.d. What do we mean by "sex" and "gender"? http://www.who.int/gender/whatisgender/en/index.html (accessed March 8, 2010).

Chapter 11

Shepard's Fence: An Iconic Image Examined

Audra R. Diers and Katherine L. Hatfield-Edstrom

It has been a little more than a decade since coauthor Audra Diers sat at her first meeting of the University of Wyoming Lesbian Gay Bisexual Trans-gendered Association (LGBTA) to observe the group in order to gather information for her master's project. Matthew Shepard attended that first meeting, but blended with the dozen who were present. Diers assumed she would get to know him later. But after an early morning phone call in October 1998, she knew she would never know Shepard. What followed his brutal murder propelled his name so prominently to the forefront of popular culture that President Barack Obama, in his 2009 address to the Human Rights Campaign, said,

> And there's no more poignant or painful reminder of how important it is that we [pass a new hate crimes law] than the loss experienced by Dennis and Judy Shepard, whose son Matthew was stolen in a terrible act of violence 11 years ago. In May, I met with Judy . . . in the Oval Office, and I promised her that we were going to pass an inclusive hate-crimes bill—a bill named for her son. (Obama 2009, para. 11)

That hate crimes bill bearing Matthew Shepard's name passed into law (Oliphant 2009, A20). But why did the president mention Shepard's name and not one of the 20-plus people murdered each year in the United States because they are homosexual (Stahnke et al. 2008, 3)? Why did he not mention Ryan Skipper, 25, found with 20 stab wounds and his throat slit and whose attackers drove his blood-soaked car around town and bragged about killing the "faggot" (Stahnke et al. 2008, 8)?

This chapter argues that the president's choice was made because the media have, for the past decade, consistently used a single image to refer to Shepard's death. This visual message made him in death an icon that captures the most frightening parts of the pervasive violence against lesbian, gay, bisexual, and transgendered (LGBT) people. An analysis of the construction and use of Matthew Shepard's fence image also helps explain how media images shape perceptions of the world. This chapter will study the critical image, discuss its implications in turning Shepard into an icon, and conclude with implications of what Matthew Shepard's death suggests for the future.

Constructing the Image That Injures

Before Matthew Shepard was murdered, Laramie, Wyoming, was a typical, small, college town: quiet and mostly anonymous. However, from the time he was found dead until the convictions of the two men responsible, no one in Laramie could escape the media's gaze. Despite the attention of a diverse international media presence, one description dominated the coverage—Shepard beaten, tied to a fence, and resembling a scarecrow ("Murder of Gay Student" 1998, 1011). References to him tied to the fence were so prevalent, it seemed as if the media followed a single script that continues to this day. For example, an article two years after his death reported, "On October 7, 1998, a mountain biker in the sagebrush hills east of Laramie, Wyoming, spotted what he thought was a scarecrow lashed to a buck-rail fence" (Black 2000, 93). And the 2009 *Urban Dictionary* entry for Shepard reads,

[A] young man who was murdered in Wyoming for being gay. On October 8, 1998, Matthew accepted a ride home from a bar. The two men pistol whipped him and tied him to a fence in freezing temperatures. He was found the next day by someone who originally thought he was a scarecrow because of his positioning on the fence. (Para. 1)

Discussion of hate crimes legislation in 2009 repeatedly commented that "Shepard, a 21-year-old University of Wyoming student, . . . was singled out by his attackers because he was gay, was tied to a fence, tortured and left in a coma to die" (e.g., "Matthew Shepard Act" 2009, para. 2).

Getting behind the Fence: What Is Seen and What Is Not

No photograph or film clip exists of Shepard's body tied to the fence. Instead, that picture of Shepard lives in our minds, where it is powerfully constructed from the verbal descriptions we have read and heard of the murder.

Charles Hill's (2004, 26) analysis of visual rhetoric as well as general research concerned with verbal and visual messages (Helmers and Hill 2004, 20) help explain the power and perseverance of the fence imagery and why it maintains its influence after a decade. Rhetorical presence, or the ability of a message producer to focus an audience's attention on specific elements that she feels will most serve the point (Hill 2004), is necessary if an image is to have an impact. A news story that opens, typically, by stating that Matthew Shepard, 21, was a gay student who was beaten, tied to a fence, and left in the cold to die may not be the most elegant of prose, but the media's repeated use of this single description has come both to represent the act of violence on Shepard and to galvanize it as iconic of violence toward all LGBT people.

What is powerful about the image is that its rhetorical presence is derived from both the surrounding conversation about Shepard's death *and* its representation of what it means to suffer from a "hate crime." This cognitive association means that the real visual referent (i.e., the actual fence or a photograph of Shepard from the crime scene) does not actually need to be seen for the description to have power. Instead, as Hill (2004) suggests,

> In many rhetorical situations, displaying the actual object, person or event under discussion—or a representational image of it—is not practical. When direct visual perception of the desired element is not feasible, then using concrete language to help the reader or listener construct a mental image can be quite effective for enhancing the presence of the favorable rhetorical element. (30)

Because of the human ability to convert concrete language into powerful mental pictures, images that injure or heal do not need to rely on a specific visual referent. In the case of Matthew Shepard's death, the absence of an actual visual artifact makes the visual message more powerful because the *language* of the description is vivid and clear. It allows each receiver to create a powerful,

The fence outside Laramie, Wyoming, where Matthew Shepard was left to die. (Courtesy of Jennifer Dunn.)

personal picture. In fact, Hill (2004) suggests that the mental work required to convert the rhetorical image into a personal picture likely strengthens the power of that image both because of the time invested in the topic itself and because the resulting image is the product of our own imaginations. Consequently, it is much more likely to be emotionally charged (30–33).

Certainly, the visual nature and impact of the account of Shepard's death rely substantially upon the rhetorical power of the image of him and the fence. The repeated rhetorical image of Matthew Shepard tied to a fence is powerful because it provides a visual referent for hate. However, independent of Shepard's death, fences hold symbolic power in U.S. culture that may have amplified his death's rhetorical presence in recent times. The fence and how he was tied are deeply rooted in acculturated images and narratives from religion and in their entrenched role to impose discrimination, oppression, and sanctified violence against the marginalized and those perceived as different.

Scholar Sandra Shannon (2003) argues that fences are important cultural symbols of demarcation that both protect and exclude (105). Her discussion of the themes of inhumanity and disenfranchisement connected to fence imagery is in the context of African-American experiences in the

United States. Nevertheless, her insights are applicable to any discriminated group, the LGBT included. The image of Shepard lashed to a fence also conjures Christian themes, for example, an innocent cast upon a cross for the sin of being gay (Loffreda 2000, 26–28). The fence is synonymous with crucifixion—a culturally significant word also associated with a powerful visual component.

The Emergence of the Icon

Images, whether described or actual, evoke emotional responses and enable audiences to feel engaged with a story in a way that is substantially more poignant than without them (Hill 2004, 30–33). Marshall McLuhan's notion of hot and cool media suggests that pictures embed themselves in the mind. The "hot" process sears the image (Hill 2004, 30–33) with all its cultural implications (Shannon 2003, 105) into the viewer's mind. Then the viewer participates with the image to give it meaning (McLuhan 2001, 22). And yet, that knowledge is not sufficient to explain why Matthew Shepard emerged as an icon. While the picture of a fence alone is powerful, it is a viewer's need to engage with the image persistently—through repeated, consistent media accounts—that gives it lasting impact.

Four months before Shepard's murder, James Byrd Jr., a young African-American man in Jasper, Texas, about 135 miles northeast of Houston, was dragged to death behind a truck by white supremacists. Byrd's gruesome death[1] was perhaps too extreme and too heavily freighted with the nation's complex struggle with racism to become a clear icon. Instead, Shepard's death, with its fence and its single focus on homophobia, became the emblematic representation of hate crimes.

Beyond the clearly visual nature of Shepard's death, his story, and not others, became iconic for several reasons. Part of the explanation lies in its central use of an everyday object to signify a horrible event. Shepard's fence is memorable because it bridges the literal—the fence itself—and the symbolic—the state of LGBT individuals in the United States. Other tragic stories, such as Ryan Skipper's senseless murder, evoked emotion but did not have a literal artifact on which to attach sentiment. Consequently, the power of the Skipper story was short-lived when only words were employed (Hill 2004, 36). In contrast, Shepard's story has become the dominant narrative in understanding violence against LGBT people because of the fence. The use of it resonates with viewers as it tends to inspire an automatic, unthinking response, or "affect transfer," with emotional responses that evolve and become much more effective over time (Hill 2004, 37; Lucaites and Hariman 2001, 25).

John Louis Lucaites and Robert Hariman's (2001, 37) analysis of iconic photographs in *No Caption Needed* (Lucaites and Hariman 2007) helps us to understand how powerful images become iconic. First, they are easily recognizable and accessible within public culture. Second, the image is widely recognized as a representation of a historically significant event. Third, the image represents a subject or an object that evokes a strong emotional response. And, finally, the image is reproduced repeatedly across a range of media, genres, and topics. For U.S. culture, think of the photographic icons of "the migrant mother," the flag raising on Iwo Jima during World War II, the death of a Kent State University student, and the collapse of the Twin Towers on 9/11. A decade ago, the media's pervasive use of the image of Matthew Shepard tied to an old wooden fence looking like a scarecrow met each of these criteria. The stage is set for his death to emerge as the central icon of hate-based violence.

Another reason that Shepard's death is particularly memorable is because visual rhetoric helps to simplify and cut through emotionally and culturally complex situations by appealing to core cultural values (Hill 2004, 34–35). Beth Loffreda (2000) argues that one of the functions of the repeatedly evoked combination of the fence, scarecrow, and Shepard's innocence is to help obscure the more socially challenging components of his death— the fact that he was a young, gay man and, as such, so easily murdered (26–28). He was gay in a society that continues to stigmatize gay, lesbian, bisexual, and transgendered people. The association between the image and the negative values it evokes helps to create an emotionally charged and durable response (Hill 2004, 34–35; Shannon 2003, 105–107).

Visual messages, particularly related to news events, are effective because journalists use them to symbolically evoke larger and/or more generalized issues (Bennett and Lawrence 1995, 25). In their analysis of news icons, Lance Bennett and Regina Lawrence (1995) argue that they are sustained through the symbolic meaning that journalists, their sources, and their audiences project onto them (23). These icons arise from what French photojournalist Henri Cartier-Bresson called "decisive moments," moments which "either celebrate or challenge cultural scripts, bringing societal tensions and contradictions into sharper focus" (Bennett and Lawrence 1995, 24; see also Lucaites and Hariman 2001; Ross and Bantimaroudis 2006).

In 2009, as the debate about federal hate crimes legislation heated up, Shepard's iconic status became a primary source of debate regarding the appropriateness of legislation, as U.S. Congress Representative Virginia Foxx (R-NC) stated on the floor of the U.S. House:

> The hate-crimes bill that's called the Matthew Shepard bill is named after a very unfortunate incident that happened where a young man was killed, but we know that that young man was killed in the commitment of robbery. It wasn't because he was gay. This—the bill—was named for him, the hate-crimes bill was named for him, but it's really a hoax that that continues to be used as an excuse for passing these bills (Luning 2009).

Representative Foxx, like others before her, tried to attack the need for hate crimes legislation by devaluing its emblematic personification. Ironically, she clearly demonstrated Shepard's status as an icon. Because Shepard's fence has been so commonly used and, as such, is so readily accessible to the public and to journalists, it is repeated without a need for a detailed verbal account (Bennett and Lawrence 1995, 26). The fence provides a symbolic shorthand reference to all hate crimes in the United States.

This case demonstrates that news icons become symbolic tools with the potential to shape public policy (Bennett and Lawrence 1995, 26). The emergence of the icon afforded the opportunity for shaping policy change, but, had it not been for sustained advocacy, it likely would not have translated into the hate crimes legislation (Bennett and Lawrence 1995, 37). Certainly, Judy Shepard's activism and the creation of the Matthew Shepard Foundation helped to influence the ultimate passage of the federal hate crimes bill, and their success was propelled by the powerful association between her son's murder and the image of the fence.

Ultimately, it is the power of the picture that explains why Matthew Shepard has been able to affect real public policy change. In many ways, this image that so deeply injured is also one that may help to heal. Indeed, a young man left to die on a fence is far too rich in associative imagery to be successfully branded with the ideological bias of either the proponents or opponents of change.

Implications for the Future

Following the passage of federal hate crimes legislation, the icon of the Shepard fence and his story have been connected with benefits for same-sex partners and the Defense of Marriage Act (DOMA) (Kaufman et al. 2008; Rothschild 2002, 3); cultural, legal, and political change for LGBT individuals (Robinson 2008); and the Equality and Youth-First Initiatives.[2] Clearly, Shepard's death is iconic with lasting implications.

However, the creation of an icon may not be entirely positive. In many ways, the strength of his iconic death means that Shepard has become *the* face for lesbian, gay, bisexual, and transgendered issues (Arana 2009). That role carries substantial risks to the public perception of the importance of civil rights issues and the need to address various forms of harassment. Connecting the violence of Shepard's death with issues like DOMA may confuse human rights and violence, ultimately undermining the real nature and implications of both (Weinstein 2008). For example, in his autobiography, the late Democratic Senator Paul Wellstone from Minnesota wrote,

> What troubles me is that I may not have cast the right vote on DOMA. . . . When Sheila and I attended a Minnesota memorial service for Matthew Shepard,

Matthew Shepard. From the photographer, "Matt had me do a series of portraits the last time I saw him, here he let me capture his splendor in front of my San Francisco windowpane. He later told me these photographs made him feel good about himself." (Courtesy of Gina van Hoof.)

I thought to myself, "Have I taken a position that contributed to a climate of hatred?" . . . I still wonder if I did the right thing. (Quoted in Weinstein 2008)

It has taken a decade for U.S. society to officially recognize, through the hate crimes bill, that violence based on a person's identity is unique and egregious. Although it is unclear how his death will be used in the future as the struggle for LGBT rights continues, it is vital to understand that Shepard's fence, as a symbol of advocacy, is both complex and important. As noted by Gabriel Arana,

In an objective sense, the "meaning" of Matthew is not to be found in the passage of legislation, candlelight vigils or passion plays. The real tragedy of Matthew Shepard's death is that it was senseless: He did not die for hate-crimes legislation or to become a martyr. The public can craft a narrative in which trauma finds redemption in politics, but ultimately the meaning we find in Shepard's death says more about society and the gay-rights movement than it does about Judy Shepard's son. (2009)

Notes

1. Byrd's head and arm were severed by a culvert as his body was dragged for miles behind the truck.
2. See http://MatthewShepard.org (accessed March 25, 2010).

Sources

Arana, Gabriel. 2009. The deification of Matthew Shepard. *The American Prospect.* http://prospect.org/cs/articles?article=the_deification_of_matthew_shepard (accessed March 25, 2010).

Bennett, W. Lance, and Regina G. Lawrence. 1995. News icons and the mainstreaming of social change. *Journal of Communication* 45: 20–39.

Black, Douglas. 2000. Straw men. *The American Scholar*, 93.

Helmers, Marguerite, and Charles A. Hill. 2004. Introduction. In *Defining visual rhetorics*, ed. Charles A. Hill and Marguerite H. Helmers, pp. 1–24. Mahwah, NJ: Lawrence Erlbaum.

Hill, Charles A. 2004. The psychology of rhetorical images. *Defining visual rhetorics*, ed. Charles A. Hill and Marguerite H. Helmers, pp. 25–41. Mahwah, NJ: Lawrence Erlbaum.

Kaufman, Moises, Leigh Fondakowski, Greg Pierotti, Stephen Belber, and Andy Paris. 2008. Has anything changed? *Newsweek.* http://www.newsweek.com/id/163027 (accessed March 25, 2010).

Loffreda, Beth. 2000. *Losing Matt Shepard: Life and politics in the aftermath of the anti-gay murder.* New York: Columbia University Press.

Luning, Ernest. 2009. Republican calls Matthew Shepard murder "a hoax" in hate-crimes debate. *The Colorado Independent.* http://coloradoindependent .com/27864/republican-calls-matthew-shepard-murder-a-hoax-in-hate-crimes-debate (accessed October 19, 2009).

Matthew Shepard Act. 2009. *New York Times,* May 6. http://www.nytimes. com/2009/05/06/opinion/06wed3.html (accessed September 6, 2009).

McLuhan, Marshall. 2001. *Understanding media: The extensions of man.* New York: Routledge.

Murder of gay student sparks outrage, debate. 1998. *The Christian Century.* http://findarticles.com/p/articles/mi_m1058/is_n29_v115/ai_21253080/ (accessed March 25, 2010).

Lucaites, John L., and Robert Hariman. 2001. Visual rhetoric, photojournalism, and democratic public culture. *Rhetoric Review* 20: 37–42.

Lucaites, John L., and Robert Hariman. 2007. *No caption needed: Iconic photographs, public culture, and liberal democracy.* Chicago: University of Chicago Press.

Obama, Barack. 2009. Address to the human rights campaign's 13th annual national dinner. *Huffington Post.* http://www.huffingtonpost.com/2009/10/11/ obamas-speech-text-transc_n_316844.html (accessed March 25, 2010).

Oliphant, James. 2009. Bill making violence against gays a hate crime passes congress. *Los Angeles Times,* October 23, A20.

Robinson, Rashad. 2008. The Matthew Shepard murder, 10 years later. *GlaadBlog.* http://glaadblog.org/2008/10/10/the-matthew-shepard-murder-10-years-later/ (accessed March 25, 2010).

Ross, Susan Dente, and Philemon Bantimaroudis. 2006. Frame shifts and catastrophic events: The attack of Sept. 11, 2001, and *New York Time*'s portrayals of Arafat and Sharon. *Mass Communication & Society* 9: 85–101.

Rothschild, Matthew. 2002. Movement liberal. *The Progressive,* 3.

Shannon, Sandra G. 2003. *August Wilson's fences: A reference guide.* Westport, CT: Greenwood Press.

Stahnke, Tad, Paul Legendre, Innokenty Grekov, Vanessa Petti, Michael Mcclintock, and Alexis Aronowitz. 2008. Violence based on sexual orientation and gender identity bias. 2008 Hate Crimes Survey: Human Rights First. http:// www.humanrightsfirst.org/pdf/fd/08/fd-080924-lgbt-web2.pdf (accessed March 25, 2010).

Urban Dictionary. 2009. Matthew Shepard. http://www.urbandictionary.com/ define.php?term=Matthew%20Shepard (accessed October 19, 2009).

Weinstein, Jeff. 2008. The legacy of Matthew Shepard. *Obit.* http://www.obit-mag .com/articles/the-legacy-of-matthew-shepard (accessed March 25, 2010).

Chapter 12

Selling Sex

Lisa Wade and Gwen Sharp

"Sex sells" is a common refrain used by scholars, marketers, and the general public alike to justify the use of sexualized images in advertising. Beyond the issue of whether sexy advertisements are actually an effective marketing strategy, the statement "Sex sells" begs another question: What kind of sex sells? Advertisements sell more than just products; they also sell us ideas about sex. That is, they present certain types of sex and sexual interactions as sexy, passionate, and desirable. What messages about sex and sexuality are advertisements selling?

Advertisers use a limited *version* of sex: a nearly uniformly heterosexual version that presents men as active sexual subjects and women as passive sexual objects who perform for the pleasure of the (implicitly male) viewer (Aulette, Wittner, and Blakely 2009; Eck 2007; Kilbourne 1999; Schutzman 1999). In truth, many advertisements use images that go beyond a simple active male/passive female dichotomy. They portray sexualized situations in which men are not just active but also aggressive and women are not just passive but also (potentially) victims of attack. Such representations are injurious to both men's and women's ability to develop healthy sexual selves.

In this chapter, recent advertising campaigns are employed to illustrate how advertisements reinforce and legitimize a sexual script in which men are taught to be active subjects of their own sexual pleasure, women are taught to be sexy objects of others' desires, and sexualized violence is presented as normal and even desirable. A discussion follows that details how the gender subject/object binary creates conditions that justify violent verbal and physical attacks against women in real life.[1]

Published in 1922, a poster for Akadama port wine is the first time a nude was used in an advertisement in Japan. (Source: Suntory Limited.)

Women as Sexual Objects

If sex sold on its own accord, there would be symmetry in how frequently men and women are presented as sexy objects alongside products. Instead, the sexual objectification of women is by far the most prevalent picture. To be sexually objectified is to be presented to the viewer as an object of desire without a discernible subjective desire of one's own. For example, a recent ad for Tango classes (1) features four frames of dancing in which the woman, but not the man, becomes increasingly undressed. In the final frame, she is naked and he is fully clothed. This ad is, indeed, using sex to sell Tango, but they are using female nudity to do it.

In some cases advertisements present an attractive woman, or part of a woman, alongside the product being sold. For instance, an ad for Cabana

Cachaça rum (2) includes the lower half of a woman's body. She lies on her back and is naked except for her high heels. Her legs are crossed, but there is a noticeable bikini tan line. On the floor alongside her, between her buttocks and her high heels, sits a bottle of rum. The ad associates Cabana Cachaça with access to conventionally attractive and sexually available women. The bottle is placed between her buttocks and her feet, within inches of her genitalia, drawing our attention to her exposed body.

In other cases, ads go further than simply associating attractive women's sexual availability with a product—they conflate a woman with the product itself. For example, a recent ad for St. Pauli Girl beer includes an image of a woman's silhouette that is filled with beer—her body has the yellow color and texture of light beer, and her hair appears to be made of foam (3). Here, the purchase and consumption of a St. Pauli Girl are, symbolically, the purchase and consumption of a woman. This is echoed in the name of the beer. When you order one, you order a "St. Pauli Girl." This merger of the woman and the beer suggests that she is a product like beer—buyable, consumable, disposable, and replaceable. In both ads, these women are not individuals with personalities, histories, and likes and dislikes. They are generic representations of sex. Their sex appeal is their only or primary characteristic. All of the other things that make women unique, imperfect, and interesting human beings are absent.

Another example is the recent advertising campaign for M&M's candy in which M&M's are anthropomorphized with each color a different personality. Notably, however, there is only one female, the green one. Unlike the male characters, which come in multiple colors, flavors, and shapes (plain, peanut, and almond), the female M&M is simply sexy. The ad campaign includes television commercials that feature a photo shoot with her as a model being ogled by the other M&M's candies (4) and print advertisements in the *Sports Illustrated* "Swimsuit Issue" in which she is taking off her green shell (5 and 6). By making all but one of the M&M's candies male and sexualizing the sole female, these ads reinforce the lesson that men's personalities and bodies vary, but women are primarily interchangeable sex objects. This is what it means to say that women are sexually objectified.

Objectification is problematic because making women into things erases their desires. Objects do not have feelings or preferences. Things do not have opinions, and they cannot disagree. If someone desires them, they can be had. If taken to its logical conclusion, two commercials for the convenience store AM/PM (7 and 8) present women as "good stuff" for heterosexual men to consume, while an advertisement for Redtape Shoes (9) shows a man who selects from several women enclosed in a vending machine. A commercial for the Mayflower moving company equates a woman with a precious "belonging" to be protected as one would a valuable, breakable object (10). In the latter, women are precious, while in the AM/PM and Redtape examples, women are cheap (like convenience store or vending machine items). But in both cases, they are objects and their value is determined by men.

Men as Sexual Subjects

The flipside of the sexual objectification of women is the affirmation of men's sexual subjectivity. When a woman is sexually objectified, she is made into an object *for* someone. Much of the time, that someone is a heterosexual man. For example, in the AM/PM commercials, it is men, specifically, who ogle the sexualized women; in the Mayflower commercial, we see a heterosexual couple in bride and groom costumes; and it is the green female M&M's candy that poses for male M&M's. In other contexts, a male viewer is not included but is implied by virtue of already gendered cultural rules. This is true in the M&M's advertising in *Sports Illustrated* and the one for St. Pauli Beer. Both beer and sports are typically associated with men. Combined with the invisibility of lesbians, the explicit or implicit inclusion of a male heterosexual viewer is frequent enough that a sexy woman is typically understood to be "for" a man unless advertisers go to significant effort to suggest otherwise.

In presenting a sexy woman for men's consumption, advertisers send messages that normalize and naturalize male (hetero)sexuality with men as sexual creatures with desire who respond to sexy women. This is an affirmation of a man's sense of himself as a sexual person (Connell 1987). To be positioned as a subject, then, is the opposite of being positioned as an object. A subject desires, looks, and owns. Subjectivity means that your desires are centrally important. An object has no desires, can only be viewed, and can be owned.

But, just as the objectification of women specifies one very narrow version of sexiness, men are taught that only one type of sexuality is acceptable. Gay men, for example, are excluded from this binary, and their sexuality is made invisible or derided. A commercial for Moosehead Light beer (11), for example, begins with two women in bikinis spreading suntan lotion on each other. Two men, leaning forward with interest, ask, "How come it works when they smudge stuff on each other?" the implication being "Why are two women together so sexy?" They consider, "What if we did it?" In their imaginations, experimentally, they visualize the scenario featuring the two of them. The music suddenly becomes silly, and the men sit back quickly and say, "It doesn't work." The message is that gay men are simply not sexy and that sexual attraction to men is not real.

Also excluded by advertisers is the sexuality of men who desire sexual relationships with women who do not fit norms of conventional attractiveness. A Slim Fast ad, for example (12), features the traditional bride and groom cake topper, but the bride is chubby (by some standard) and the groom is crossing his fingers so as to invalidate his vows. This suggests that no man would truly want to marry a chubby woman. Similarly, a series of Brazilian ads for Itambé Fit Light Yogurt (13, 14 and 15) features chubby women in famous poses (e.g., Mena Suvari in *American Beauty*, Marilyn Monroe in *The Seven Year Itch*, and Sharon Stone in *Basic Instinct*). The tagline is "Forget about it. Men's preferences will never change." The message for women is that men will never be attracted to chubby women, so they must change themselves. For men, it is that these women are not sexy and being attracted to them would be gross or ridiculous.

Finally, the subjectivity that men are granted alongside female sexual objectification is of a one-track mind. Men in ads want sex with any acceptable partner all the time and for any reason. This logic excludes men who desire sex only when other conditions, such as emotional intimacy, also hold.

In sum, when sex is used to sell, it usually involves the presentation of a conventionally attractive and sexually available woman as a sexy visual. Interchangeable and malleable, her own sexual desires and unique personality are irrelevant. This is sexual objectification. These ads simultaneously validate men's sexual subjectivity—the idea that men have sexual desires, wants, and needs is a central part of this narrative. However, the subjectivity accorded to men is rigidly prescribed. The narrative legitimates and indulges a particular, narrow version of male heterosexuality. At the same time that it objectifies women, then, advertising accords men sexual subjectivity but only insofar as they conform to the norm.

Object/Subject Relations

Thinking more specifically about women's sexual objectification and men's sexual subjectivity in mass media, it is useful to consider the terms "sexy" and "sexual" more carefully. To be *sexual* is to experience sexual feelings, while being *sexy* is to inspire those sexual feelings in others. In the United States, to be masculine means, in part, to be sexual. Men are taught to recognize their sexual desires and to sexually pursue women (Kimmel 2004; Quinn 2002). They learn to say, "I want." In contrast, femininity means, in part, being the thing that men want (Jhally 2000; Tolman 2001). Women are taught to emphasize, and conceive of themselves in terms of, their sexual attractiveness so that men choose to pursue them. Instead of learning to say, "I want," women learn to say, "I want to be wanted." When women and men break these rules of femininity and masculinity, they are likely to encounter social scorn. Men who do not pursue women sexually are "pussies" and "fags." Women who pursue men are "whores" or "sluts." Wanting to avoid these labels, many men and women attempt to mold themselves into the sexual roles sold to them.

Indeed, both men and women tend to accept men's sexual subjectivity and women's sexual objectification. That is why sexy women grace the covers and appear in ads for both men's (such as *Maxim*) and women's magazines (such as *Cosmopolitan*) (16). That women's object status and men's subjectivity are sold to women in magazines targeted to them in no way undermines the argument that men's sexual subjectivity is being sold. It's just that it is being sold to everyone.

The selling of sexual subjectivity for men and sexual objectification of women explains a ubiquitous meme in our society. In many television shows and movies, average-looking guys are matched up with gorgeous women. Consider the couples in *King of Queens* (17), *According to Jim* (18), *The Simpsons* (19), and two couples from the TV series *Ally McBeal*: Richard and Ling (20 and 21) and John and Nell (22 and 23). The gendered object/subject binary helps explains this. Since it is men's sexual desires that are made salient, her attractiveness to him is important. Therefore, she must be sexy. But since women are supposed to function as sexual objects, not subjects, her desire is invisible or irrelevant. Thus, his attractiveness is unimportant.

Sexualized Violence

We have discussed how marketers typically use sex to sell, and also sell sex by offering representations of men as sexual subjects and women as sexual objects. In ads, then, because only subjects have both desires and the ability to act on them, we should expect to see men actively pursuing women and women passively being acted upon.

In fact, women's passivity and men's active pursuit are, themselves, presented as sexy. Representations of men pushing a woman against a wall, throwing her onto a bed, or ripping off her clothes are *supposed to be* sexy, not scary. The women depicted in these situations often respond to this aggression with sexual arousal or with resistance that gives way to sexual arousal. Aggression, in this sense, works. We are told that it is what women want. In this way, both aggressive male sexuality and women's acquiescence to male aggression are normalized. Many movies, television shows, and video games include sex scenes that seem to represent a normal, mutually pleasurable sexual interaction but rely on male sexual aggression.

Images in the mass media repeatedly reinforce the idea that sexualized violence against women is both sexy and legitimate. Ads often present scenarios in which it is difficult to tell whether the image is simply another example of the passive female sex object or is supposed to represent (sexual) violence against women, and feature images in which it is unclear whether there is a seduction or an assault. Although a Dolce & Gabbana ad that featured what could be interpreted as a gang rape (24) is probably the most infamous, there are many other examples. In one for Unforgivable Woman (a perfume by the rapper Sean Combs), Combs presses a woman against a wall from behind (25). An ad for Isaia Napoli clothing shows a woman who leans away from a man who has her pushed against a wall (26). A Campari liquor ad (27) shows Salma Hayek looking worried as she is pulled into an elevator by three men.

Similarly, fashion designer Brian Atwood publicized one of his collections with two ads that showed Rene Russo in situations that blurred the line between pleasure and assault. In one, she is pushed against a glass wall by a man who grabs her from behind (28). In another, she is blindfolded in a shower, and pushed against one of two naked men who stand behind her (29). A third ad in the series shows a fully clothed woman (perhaps Russo) who lies face-down in a swimming pool, apparently drowned (30). Ads that feature beautiful sexualized dead women, such as those for Lanvin (31) and Missoni (32), further contribute to the glamorization of violence and actually turn women *into* inanimate objects.

Constant exposure to this model of sexuality (the female object/male subject binary) makes it seem natural to us. If it seems natural, we may play out these dynamics in our real lives or feel uncomfortable, even threatened, when people around us do not. For example, women's resistance to male desire—in effect, rejecting their own object status and prioritizing their own desires—may seem illegitimate. They are breaking the rules.

Resistance undermines men's power in two ways. First, male desire is dethroned. *His* desire no longer dictates what and who is sexy. Second, if the object/subject binary remains in place, men risk becoming objectified themselves. If a woman can want and feel sexual desire the same as men, then men can be attractive on women's terms. This turn-around strips men of the privileged spot in the gendered sexual hierarchy that is repeatedly affirmed by advertising in the United States. When privilege is threatened, members of privileged groups often react with violence, whether symbolic or real. Accordingly, women who step outside of their object role and express desire are often policed with name calling (Tanenbaum 1999). Sexual harassment and rape, too, can be understood as responses from men who see their claim to sexual subjectivity, and the accompanying ability to objectify others, threatened (Brownmiller 1975; Connell 1995; Kilbourne 1999; MacKinnon 1989).

On occasion, advertisements reverse gender roles. However, these images reaffirm, rather than challenge, the subject/object binary. It is not that men and women are shown as equals; rather, the power dynamic has simply been flipped so that women are aggressors and men aggressed upon. In ads for Patrick Cox shoes, Voodoo pantyhose, and Dolce & Gabbana (33, 34 and 35), women step on, restrain, and beat men. While the gender roles are reversed, the assumption that sexiness is based on dominant and submissive roles, that one partner is a subject while the other is an object, remains unchallenged.

Conclusion and Strategies

If men's desires are believed to be of primary importance, and women are sexual objects, then it shouldn't be a surprise to see violent imagery in advertising in which men use force to satisfy their desires. In fact, sexualized violence is the inevitable extreme of a view of sexuality based on male-subject/female-object relations. Objects, literally, cannot have feelings or desires. Their purpose is to satisfy the desires of the male subject. If a female sexual object expresses subjective desires of her own, she is breaking the rules by calling into question the entitlement of male subjects to use her, and other sexually objectified women, as they desire.

At the same time, the prescription of a narrowly defined role for men threatens to alienate them from their own sexuality. The wide range of men's sexual desires is invisible. Whereas women may find that they repress their sexual energy in order to conform to expectations that they be passive, men may channel their sexuality into one narrow model and actively pursue sex that they do not necessarily want because inaction is unmasculine.

The reversal of these power dynamics, when women take the subject position and men take the object role, only affirms the binary itself. Power, advertising asserts, is always part of sexuality—the only way in which women can avoid being sexual objects is to objectify someone else. What is missed by this view, and what all are denied by the subject/object binary, is a model of sexuality that emphasizes cooperation and interdependency.

What would sexuality look like if it were not about power, dominance, and submission? What would be sexy in a world where both aggression and passivity were seen as problematic ways to engage with one another?

In a world where sex and power are disentangled, a man's height and strength relative to a woman's might be less important. Beauty and thinness might be less central to a woman's attractiveness. Same-sex couples might be less perplexing. Being aggressively pursued might seem inappropriate rather than romantic. In a world in which sexual attractiveness is built on subjective preferences and experiences instead of a constant stream of carefully constructed and repetitive images, a wider range of characteristics could potentially be sexy. In this case, an individual would be free to construct a sexuality that reflects her own desires and preferences. Many under these conditions might choose more egalitarian relationships that do not depend on power dynamics and submissiveness.

Note

1. The images referred to in this chapter and referenced by the numbers in parentheses are presented at "Society Pages"; see http://thesocietypages.org/socimages/2007/07/21/images-that-injure/ (accessed March 25, 2010).

Sources

Aulette, Judy Root, Judith Wittner, and Kristin Blakely. 2009. *Gendered worlds*. New York: Oxford University Press.

Brownmiller, Susan. 1975. *Against our will: Men, women, and rape*. New York: Simon & Schuster.

Connell, R. W. 1987. *Gender & power*. Stanford, CA: Stanford University Press.

Connell, R. W. 1995. *Masculinities*. Berkeley: University of California Press.

Eck, Beth A. 2007. Men are much harder: Gendered viewing of nude images. In *Men's Lives*, ed. Michael S. Kimmel and Michael A. Messner, pp. 523–538. Boston: Pearson.

Jhally, Sut, dir. 1999. *Killing us softly 3: Advertising's image of women*. DVD. Northampton, MA: Media Education Foundation.

Kilbourne, Jean. 1999. *Can't buy my love: How advertising changes the way we think and feel*. New York: Simon and Schuster.

Kimmel, Michael S. 2004. *The gendered society*. New York: Oxford University Press.

MacKinnon, Catherine. 1989. Sexuality, pornography, and method: "Pleasure under patriarchy." *Ethics* 314: 314–346.

Quinn, Beth A. 2002. Sexual harassment and masculinity: The power and meaning of "girl watching." *Gender & Society* 16: 386–402.

Schutzman, Mady. 1999. *The real thing: Performance, hysteria, and advertising*. Hanover, NH: University Press of New England.

Scully, Diana. 1990. *Understanding sexual violence: A study of convicted rapists*. Boston: Beacon Press.

Scully, Diana, and Joseph Marolla. 1985. "Riding the bull at Gilley's": Convicted rapists describe the rewards of rape. *Social Problems* 32: 251–263.

Society Pages. n.d. Sociological images. http://thesocietypages.org/socimages/2007/07/21/images-that-injure/

Tanenbaum, Leora. 1999. *Slut! Growing up female with a bad reputation*. New York: Seven Stories Press.

Tolman, Deborah L. 2001. Doing desire: Adolescent girls' struggles for/with sexuality. In *Feminist frontiers*, ed. Laurel Richardson, Verta Taylor, and Nancy Whittier, pp. 375–385. Boston: McGraw Hill.

Chapter 13

Hard Targets: Men as a Disposable Sex

Lee Jolliffe

A popular and persistent media myth is that all Anglo men are part of a dominant group, with ready access to wealth and power.[1] Such a view is understandable given the fact that women since at least the 1950s have been portrayed as a combination of a sexy mannequin and a fertile incubator. Through marriage, men gained a household drudge, a baby maker, an on-site mistress, and free child care. But fueled by the politically active culture of the 1960s, radical feminists began to identify the harm done by the stereotypical treatment of women in which men are defined as the oppressors. As the radical feminist Redstockings wrote in their *Manifesto* (1969), "All men receive economic, sexual and psychological benefits from male supremacy. All men have oppressed women."

However, the stereotypical roles of men and women in mainstream U.S. society had costs and benefits for both genders. The feminist movement helped create changes in women's lives and some liberation from old stereotypes, but the men's movement did not gain as much traction in its efforts to normalize nontraditional roles for males in areas such as homemaking or childrearing, or in the freedom to express emotions beyond anger and lust. If men were dominant in the world of work, they were shut out of the home. A man without a paying job was a freeloader, as much to be scorned as a woman without a husband.

By the 1990s, the cost to men and the benefits to women of a man's stereotypical role in society started to become publicized. In marriage, women gained a wage slave, a protector, and, after the kids were in school, an endless vacation, while the men died young fighting in foreign countries or worked their way to heart attacks and an early death. In this chapter, common stereotypes of men and how they are made to seem natural through pictures in the media will be studied.

The Roles

Gender studies have consistently found that women do not have the same access as men to important roles in society (DeWall and Maner 2008; Duncan 1993; van Zoonen 1995). Within work and political circles, for example, men are seen as more authoritative, powerful, active, rational, intelligent, decisive, and qualified than women. As a consequence, men have more money and power.

Nevertheless, some researchers have noted a change in media portrayals of men and women (Beam 2010; Joliffe 1989; Thomas and Treiber 2000; Yunjuan and Xiaoming 2007). As early as the 1980s, the media began to show women as active and powerful in the workforce. They were seen as multifaceted people, but men were presented as anonymous workers with little individuality or complexity. Most significantly, portrayals of men's lives did not expand into the home as women moved into the workplace.

A study of newspapers of the 1880s found that more than a century ago men were occasionally referred to in terms of their family lives, personality, and appearance (Jolliffe and Bond 1985). One hundred years later, media coverage of men virtually ignored these aspects. The newspapers of the 1980s reduced men's importance as people by referring to them as their job titles, such as "Lawyer Jones" or "Bricklayer Smith" (Jolliffe 1989).

In today's newspaper headlines about ordinary men—not politicians and celebrities—men appear most often as victims of violence. As crime statistics affirm, men are far more often the victims of crime than women. However, printed photographs of men concentrate on them as strong and powerful. News editors seldom use a picture of a man as a victim. In contrast, they nearly always use a photograph when a woman has been a crime or accident victim (Jolliffe 1989).

In *Fire in the Belly*, Sam Keen (1992) writes powerfully of the damage done by society's stereotypes of men as warriors, workers, and stoics. He sees Marine boot camp as a quintessential example of U.S. society's depersonalization of men. At the Marine Corps Recruit Depot at Parris Island, South Carolina, a new recruit learns quickly that his opinions do not matter. During boot camp, he is not permitted to wear personal jewelry except his dog tags. He is given none of his letters from home. With a shaved head, identical uniform, and daily physical ordeals, he quickly loses his individuality, and learns to endure pain, kill other human beings, or die, if given such orders. Should he survive his initiation into warrior-hood, he will later reap the benefit and become a wage earner so he can provide for a wife and children and work long hours outside his home.

As with the military jarhead, most men are followers, not leaders. They will not become president of the United States or president of their own company. They are far more likely to dig ditches or stock grocery shelves. In addition, men are not expected to show emotion yet must somehow be the initiators of dating and the proposers of marriage. A man with close male friends might be suspected of being homosexual. If he sees a doctor about physical pain, he's a sissy. If he pushes a baby stroller, his wife must

Road construction in Durham, North Carolina, shows men at work, 2008. (Courtesy of Ildar Sagdejev.)

be sick at home. As seen in the media, men are sloppy, helpless at changing diapers, riveted to the television whenever sports programming is aired, and motivated by uncontrollable lust.

Men in the News

While few men have any opportunity to become Fortune 500 CEOs, Hollywood celebrities, or NBA All-Stars, newspaper photographs tell a different story. The news, business, and sports pages are filled with photographs of men who have achieved these heights. But what about the other men who make the news?

Gender researchers noticed in the 1970s that women were rarely pictured in the news media, an absence called "symbolic annihilation" (Tuchman 1978). In a 1985 research study of the *New York Times* (Jolliffe 1989), once politicians and celebrities were excluded from both groups, men appeared in news photographs 20 times more often than women. Since then, Shelly Rodgers and Esther Thorson (1999) found that men outnumbered women in print photos by two to one—a great improvement. Front-page stories from the top 10 U.S. newspapers[2] of 2010 were examined for this chapter, and the gap has narrowed yet again. Women and men appeared about equally.

Although newspaper editors appear to have made a conscious effort to be more inclusive, photographs reinforced gender stereotypes of men as strong, violent, and criminal. A comparison of the texts of news stories and pictures about men showed a stark contrast. In the texts, men were portrayed most often as workers valuable for their wage-earning capacity (Jolliffe 1989). Photographs more often reinforced stereotypes of men as strong, violent, and tending to criminality—or, as Pam Nilan (1995) put it, "hard, brave and victorious." Consequently, picture editing favored photographs that support gender roles, and those that contradict the stereotypes are included less often.

Nilan (1995) suggests that these representations constitute "how masculinity per se is defined and regulated." Robert Connell (1987) argues that this practice serves to "imply the subordination of women and 'lesser' men."

How News Pictures Distort Men's Reality

News pictures of men present them as violent, criminal, expendable, loners, and anonymous workers. When stories of male victims appeared, they were often printed on inside pages, an indication of their low priority.

Men as victims were not pictured in 1985 or 2010 studies. A story of a kidnapped U.S. Drug Enforcement Agency agent was buried on inside pages between two jewelry ads. Although the story noted that the U.S. Embassy offered a $50,000 reward for information and provided the victim's name and age, no photograph appeared. Other faceless male victims included a "Fort Worth Man Shot Dead by Gang" and an "Off-Duty Officer Shot 5 Times at Social Club." In one instance where a male kidnap victim was thrown from a ship, the photo with the story was a portrait of his wife. Pictures of male victims would run counter to our stereotype that men are strong, powerful, and violent.

Although male victims were slighted pictorially, most of the men suspected or convicted of crimes were photographed. News editors frequently selected pictures of convicted murderers on death row or white-collar criminals on courthouse steps. "Condemned Killer of 4 Electrocuted in Louisiana" and "Man Executed in Killing" merited photographic coverage. So did "Seven Indicted for Drugs Are Said to Sell to Players." In addition, headshots of bankers and CEOs accused of various shady dealings frequent the pages.

Despite this extensive use of photographs of men as criminals, few make the front page. Nonetheless, given the lack of pictures of murdered or injured men, a viewer might naturally think that men are mostly criminals and prone to violence. At the same time, photographs of women as victims support the stereotypes that women are helpless and weak. Women who committed crimes were not pictured. Headlines such as "Woman Is Shot after Taking Hostages on Jet," "Brink's Suspect Held without Bail," and "Nurses Suspended in Morphine Death" ran without photos (Jolliffe 1989). Women who committed misdemeanors remained anonymous. As a result, Martin Fiebert and Mark Meyer (1997) found that participants in their gender study produced "significantly more negative stereotypes for men than for women."

While men appear most often in headshot portraits, women are often depicted in three-quarter to full-length photographs (Jolliffe 1989; Petca, Graf, and Bivolaru 2009). The message of the headshot is that men's bodies are unimportant and therefore disposable. It communicates that society is uninterested in men's bodies or the physical pain they suffer. The use of full-body pictures of women reinforces society's view that women are sex objects (see related discussion in chapter 12). The scantily clad women in advertisements are hired for their physical attraction, but news photographs also present women in full-length photos, generally fully dressed.

However, the frequent use of headshots of men is as destructive a gender stereotype as half-dressed women in video games or advertisements.

Except for photographs of police officials with suspects in custody, most men pictured in the news are alone. Women, however, are often shown with other women. They are portrayed using affectionate gestures such as embraces and hand-holding. Men are thus, by contrast, shown as cold loners with few attachments to others.

Along with the detachment and loss of physical self in the classic headshots of men, there is a loss of the environment and surrounding activities. Nearly a third of men photographed in the news are portrayed in headshots that show minimal backgrounds. This omission creates a sense of sterility and removes place that adds to the alienation these photographs associate with men. Women were more often shown with an environment visible in the background. They enjoyed country gardens and pleasant home settings with pets, children, and friends. While feminists complain that these subjects relegate women to domestic life (Bridge 1997), this distinction in settings between the genders is important, given the significance of "home" in our society. Although women are shown at home—that is, secure, off-guard, and self-expressive—men are typically shown without environments, alienated, on guard, and carefully in control of themselves or others.

Men in news photographs tend to frown or are expressionless. They rarely look directly into the camera. Angry men look out from stories on Nicaragua, New Jersey campaigns, and radical South African religions. Police, convicted killers, a screenwriter, and a minister lacked emotion in their expressions in the 1989 news samples.

Shelly Rodgers and her colleagues (Rodgers, Kensicki, and Thorson 2003) found that "more females than males were depicted as happy, but more males than females were depicted as sad." Also, more men were shown as dominant. While feminists note that a woman's gaze into the camera suggests she is sexually available, men in news pictures are clearly not available for exchanges of emotion with others. Of 29 men in one sample of news photographs, only three were smiling—Reverend Jesse Jackson, the pope, and a philanthropist who visited toddlers in New York City's Central Park. While women hugged and affectionately touched one another in pictures, men touched others only twice—the philanthropist patting a toddler's head and a police officer arresting a suspect. The Reverend Jesse Jackson and the pope smiled but were turned away from each other. Thus, the predominant visual message of men in the news is of a stoic male, friendless, uncaring, serious, easily angered, and unable to share emotions.

Men appear in uniforms of one sort or another in most news pictures. "To wear a uniform is to give up your right to free speech in the language of clothes. . . . You become part of a mass of identical persons," says Alison Lurie in *The Language of Clothes* (1981, 20). About a third of the men photographed wore a suit and tie. As with the military garb on Parris Island, this uniformity of dress implies that most men are indistinguishable, in which one can readily be exchanged for another. Status is introduced by the price of the suit that can be judged from its fit and fabric. Such observations help viewers separate high-status men from their subservient counterparts (DeWall and Maner 2008). Other, more recognizable uniforms are depicted in news pictures of men that include the zip-up jumpsuit of the convict, police and paramedic clothing, corporate-labeled bill caps with work pants, and sports attire. Women's dress, conversely, is less constrained. They appear in tank tops, running shorts, full-skirted country tweeds, exotic evening gowns, and suits with ruffled shirts. No women wore classic uniforms in the 1989 and 2010 studies.

Uniformed or not, men appear most frequently as workers in news photographs. If a uniform is not evident, some other cue to a man's occupation is often part of the image. Even in tight close-ups, job cues are given to the viewer. One man wore a radio headset, another had a fragment of campaign signage visible behind him, and a third wore a clerical collar. In contrast, job cues are less often used in photographs of women. In general, news photographs rely on captions to depict women as workers, while men were shown more clearly in their work environments without a need for words.

Conclusions

News photographs present a skewed view of a man's reality—he works 24 hours a day, alone, and does not express emotions. Any man could be replaced by any other because they are indistinguishable, anonymous, and expendable. The deviant man—one who doesn't work—is a criminal.

How can these injurious images of men become examples that heal, that are more inclusive, and that offer a life of love, home, and friendship? Men should be freed from the constant coverage of work and instead be shown within their everyday lives. Photographic coverage of male victims should accompany stories that explain who they were before they were injured or mistreated. A man and his environment, not just his head, should be the subject of a news photograph.

The Berkeley Men's Center *Manifesto* sums up the new, nonstereotypical values that activist men hope to achieve:

> We, as men, want to take back our full humanity. We no longer want to strain to compete to live up to an impossible oppressive masculine image— strong, silent, cool, handsome, unemotional, successful, master of women, leader of men, wealthy, brilliant, athletic and "heavy." We want to relate to both women and men in more human ways—with warmth, sensitivity, emotion and honesty. We want to share our feelings with one another to break down the walls and grow closer. We want to be equal with women and end destructive competitive relationships between men (Doyle 2000).

Pictures about men and their relationships should be published just as with women. A man shown as a member of a helping profession who tenderly lifts a victim of war or watches over kindergarteners as they board a school bus would do much to end injurious stereotypes of men.

A father helps his sons discover the joy of reading. (Courtesy of Peter Merholz.)

Notes

1. The title for this chapter comes from a news release for a gallery exhibit that reads, "In Hard Targets, varied treatments of masculinity get a turn in the spotlight. Hard Targets seeks to revise and complicate our time-honored stereotypes of male athletes and athleticism (as aggressive, heterosexual, hypercompetitive, and remote) by presenting alternative, possibly more democratic, interpretations of subjects frequently revealed to us only in authorized and frankly commercial images. The artists in the show instead investigate sports and masculine identity through topics ranging from biology to business to celebrity, played out in locker rooms, stadiums, and advertising campaigns" (Bedford 2010).

2. The top 10 newspapers in the U.S. in terms of circulation are *USA Today*, the *Wall Street Journal*, the *New York Times*, the *Los Angeles Times*, the *Washington Post*, the *New York Daily News*, the *Chicago Tribune*, the *Long Island Newsday*, and the *Houston Chronicle*; see http://www.newspapers.com/top10.html (accessed November 19, 2009).

Sources

Beam, Randal A. and De Cicco, Damon T. 2010. When women run the newsroom: Management change, gender, and the news. *Journalism Quarterly*. 87 (2): 393–411.

Bedford, Christopher, curator. 2010. Hard targets: Sports and masculinity. Display. Wexner Center of the Arts, January 30–April 11. Columbus: Ohio State University. http://www.osu.edu/events/event403387 (accessed March 7, 2010).

Bridge, M. Junior. 1997. Slipping from the scene; News coverage of females drops. In *Facing difference: Race, gender, and mass media*, ed. Shirley Biagi and Marilyn Kern-Foxworth, pp. 102–112. Thousand Oaks, CA: Pine Forge Press.

Connell, Robert W. 1987. *Gender and power*. Sydney: Allen & Unwin.

DeWall, C. Nathan, and Jon K. Maner. 2008. High status men (but not women) capture the eye of the beholder, *Evolutionary Psychology* 6 (2): 328–341.

Doyle, Richard F. 2000. *The men's manifesto: A commonsense approach to gender issues, philosophy and politics of the legitimate men's movement*. Berkeley, CA: Men's Defense Association.

Duncan, Margaret Carlisle. 1993. Representation and the gun that points backwards. *Journal of Sport & Social Issues* 17 (1): 42–46.

Fiebert, Martin S., and Mark W. Meyer. 1997. Gender stereotypes: A bias against men. *Journal of Psychology* 131: 407–410.

Jolliffe, Lee. 1989. Comparing gender differentiation in *The New York Times*, 1885 and 1985. *Journalism Quarterly* 66 (3): 683–691.

Jolliffe, Lee, and Turner Bond. 1985. Sex-role stereotyping in two newspapers of 1885: The influence of the pioneer effort. Paper presented at the Association for Education in Journalism and Mass Communication annual conference, April 1, Memphis, TN.

Keen, Sam. 1992. *Fire in the belly: On being a man*. London: Piatkus.

Luebke, Barbara F. 1989. Out of focus: Images of women and men in newspaper photographs. *Sex Roles* 20: 121–132.

Lurie, Alison. 1981. *The language of clothes*. New York: Random House.

Nilan, Pam. 1995. Making up "men." *Gender & Education* 7 (2): 175–188.

Petca, Andra, Timo Graf, and Eliza Bivolaru. 2009. Gender stereotypes in Olympic online visuals: A cross-cultural panel study of Olympic online visuals from Brazil, Germany and the United States for the 2004 and 2008 Olympic Games. Paper presented at the International Communication Association annual meeting, April 20, Chicago.

Poole, Ross. 1990. Modernity, rationality and "the masculine." In *Feminine/masculine and representation*, ed. Terry Threadgold and Anne Cranny-Francis. Sydney: Allen & Unwin.

Redstockings. 1969. *Manifesto*. July 7. http://Jackiewhiting.net/Women/Power/Redstockings.htm (accessed March 8, 2010).

Rodgers, Shelly, and Esther Thorson. 1999. The visual representation of individuals of different genders, ages and ethnicities in the photographs of the *Los Angeles Times*. Paper presented to the Association for Education in Journalism and Mass Communication, August, New Orleans.

Rodgers, Shelly, Linda Kensicki, and Esther Thorson. 2003. Stereotypical portrayals of emotionality in news photographs. Paper presented at the International Communication Association annual meeting, San Diego, CA.

Thomas, Melvin E. and Treiber, Linda A. 2000. Race, gender, and status: A content analysis of print advertisements in four popular magazines. *Sociological Spectrum,* 20 (3): 357–371.

Tuchman, Gaye. 1978. Symbolic annihilation of women by the mass media. In *Hearth and home: Images of women in the mass media*, ed. Gaye Tuchman, James Benet, and Arlene Kaplan Daniels, introduction. New York: Oxford University Press.

van Zoonen, Liesbet. 1995. Gender, representation and the media. In *Questioning the media: A critical introduction*, ed. John D. H. Downing, Ali Mohammadi, and Annabelle Sreberny-Mohammadi, pp. 311–328. Thousand Oaks, CA: Sage.

Yunjuan, Luo and Xiaoming, Hao. 2007. Media portrayal of women and social change. *Feminist Media Studies,* 7 (3): 281–298.

Chapter 14

Ain't the Barbie Doll Type: Images in the Music Video "Redneck Woman"

Debra L. Merskin

Southern women are different. It's been said that they have "charm that disarms," can be "sweet as vinegar pie," might "spit in the devil's face even if it isn't nice manners," and have "beautifully camouflaged fiery determination and indefatigable spirit" (Rich 1999, 1, 127, 43, 165). Typical Southern women of myth run the gamut from the gracious Southern belle of Melanie Wilkes to the headstrong fireball Scarlett O'Hara, characters in *Gone with the Wind* (1939). At the same time, negative stereotypes plague poor Southern women. Their qualities of strength and resilience are often used stereotypically as indicators of belligerence and naïveté. Jim Goad (1997) observes that the poor Southern woman

> has seen too much brutality to retain any vestigial wisps of daintiness. But what she's lost in frilly femininity, she's gained in scrappy, cynical spirit that comes from having survived. Hard knocks make for hard women. . . . [T]hey're better hard-line feminists than many of the sheltered gals who so loudly espouse vagino-supremacy. (143)

Poor, Anglo, Southern women bear a triple handicap (Ripley Wolfe 1995, 8). From a history of war, deeply ingrained gender-specific roles in a patriarchal society, and, in some cases, painful lessons in which they had to learn to make do, poor, Southern, Anglo women have voices that are rarely heard, except through music.

Country music is the venue for voice and visibility that has drawn women performers and listeners for generations. Prompted by Robynn Stilwell's (2008) call for more research about country music, the focus of this chapter is the representation of social class and gender in the music video of country singer Gretchen Wilson's 2004 hit, "Redneck Woman" ("RW"). This analysis reveals the complex interrelationship among socially defined categories of gender, race, ethnicity, education, class, and consumption as they are articulated in the song. A feminist approach informs this chapter as it draws on interdisciplinary, philosophical, and theoretical perspectives in order to answer the question:

Is "Redneck Woman" for or against the redneck stereotype?

The Redneck Stigmatype

As a way to describe the class divide between those who work indoors at desk jobs and others who work outdoors as farmers, the term "redneck" was invented to refer to a person whose neck is burned from too much exposure to the sun. Over time, its meaning was expanded, and the term merged with other derogatory words and phrases such as "cracker," "hillbilly," and "white trash" or "trailer trash." A redneck is generally considered to be a poor, uneducated, Anglo from rural Southern regions such as the Appalachian and Ozark Mountains, Texas, Alabama, and Tennessee. During the Civil Rights movement of the 1960s, many poor, Anglo Southerners felt left out as the dominant, middle-class culture stereotyped them as "bigoted, conformist and stupid" (Bufwack and Oermann 2003, 270).

Redneck, as it evolved, is also an ambivalent and fluid concept that floats between urban and rural, Anglo and non-Anglo. "Redneck is emblematic of a much less clear contemporary historical moment, too, in which blue-collar workers and small town residents across the United States felt a profound sense of political disempowerment and economic and cultural insecurity" (Fox 2004, 25). Redneck is also "canonically bound up with a defensive articulation of whiteness—a particular class-positioned way of being 'white'" (Bufwack and Oermann 2003, 270).

The redneck identity includes a variety of class-based characteristics and attitudes that encompass "parochialism, nationalism, patriarchy,

Two self-confessed rednecks, Tony Viessman and Les Spencer, listen to Michelle Obama during the 2008 Democratic National Convention. (Courtesy of Michelle Uthoff-Campbell.)

inscrutability, a penchant for violence and an ingrained racism" (Fox 2004, 25). In *The Redneck Manifesto*, Jim Goad (1997) describes the stereotype based on repeated mass media representations:

> Gradually we come to believe that working-class whites are two-dimensional cartoons—rifle totin', booger-eatin', beer-bellied swine flesh. Skeeter-bitten, ball-tuggin', homo-hatin', pig fuckin', daughter-gropin' slugs. . . . Unwashed, uncomprehending kids with cavity-peppered teeth. The stereotypes aren't new, just more persistently cruel of late. (25)

Matt Wray refers to this designation as a *stigmatype*, a "stigmatizing boundary term that simultaneously denote[s] and enact[s] cultural and cognitive divides between in-groups and out-groups, between acceptable and unacceptable identities, between proper and improper behaviors" (Wray and Newitz 1997, 23).

During the 1960s and 1970s, popular television shows such as *The Beverly Hillbillies, Hee Haw,* and the *Dukes of Hazard* took advantage of redneck culture to create popular Southern characters. In recent years, the redneck has appeared in the comedy routines of Jeff Foxworthy, Ron White, Bill Engvall, Larry the Cable Guy, and Lee Roy Mercer, all popular with their "Blue Collar Comedy Tour." The Fox Network animated television show *King of the Hill*, created by Mike Judge (who also produced *Beavis and Butt-Head*), portrays a suburban family in Arlen, Texas, that is sometimes disparagingly called rednecks and hillbillies.

In many ways, "redneck" is a gender-based term, referencing the working-class Southern *man* rather than woman. A redneck *woman* carries different conceptual baggage. According to Michael Graham (2003, 170), there are two types of Southern women, in Northern eyes at least:

> If they're attractive and affluent, they're vapid, sorority-girl sellouts with big hair and bigger smiles, hanging off the arm of old money or nouveau riche manhood. If they're poor and pudgy, they're political prisoners of the trailer-park plantation, spending their days with Judge Judy and their nights with Miss Cleo. And either way, they're much too fond of Elvis.

A website ("You Might Be a Redneck If . . .") describes redneck women as

> most comfortable in tank tops and tight jeans - and they look good in them too! . . . [T]they also tend to have full make-up on at all times. Redneck women often are comfortable in bare feet, but they tend to love cowboy boots. Skin-tight jeans, tank tops and boots do have a certain appeal to them. Redneck women LOVE pick-up trucks. Who needs a wussy SUV when you can throw all the kids into the back of a truck and get on down the road?

But "redneck" can also be used as a title of pride. As a form of identity politics and as a performative act, self-labeling as a redneck emerged among Anglo, working-class Southerners who "found self-esteem and a defensive voice in country music" (Bufwack and Oermann 2003, 270).

Country Music

In his study of working-class Texans, Aaron Fox identified the importance of songs and music as forms of critical and playful talk and narrative as well as expressions of technical skill (Fox 2004). In country music, working-class people are able to "construct and preserve a self-consciously rustic, 'redneck,' ordinary and country ethos in their everyday life" (Fox 2004, 20). In *Don't Get above Your Raisin'*, Bill Malone (2002) says, "The bulk of the [country music's] major performers still come, overwhelmingly, from the South, and they exhibit their Southernness through their dialects, speech patterns and lifestyles and through the values and themes of the music that they perform" (15). Fox's (2004) study of a western Texas blue-collar community showed that country music is "an essential resource for the preservation of community and the expression of white (but not only white) working-class identity" (21). Thus, country music is more than an auditory experience; it is a constellation of stars and recordings that form and reify the musical genre as a form of identity and mass communication.

Picturing Country Women

Throughout the 1990s, women broke through barriers and appeared on the music scene, from pop to rock to country. In country music, female stars such as Mary Chapin Carpenter and Wynonna Judd led the call for women's liberation with success that resulted in sold-out concert tours and platinum records. Shania Twain's 1996 album, *The Woman in Me*, catapulted her to the rank of having the all-time top-selling female country album (CMAWorld.com). LeAnn Rimes followed closely with her hit single "Blue." Their success with nontraditional country arrangements and crossover hits into the pop music genre prompted critics to question their validity as real country singers. Steve Jones (2002) points out that the entire synergistic country music industry, comprised of theme parks, radio, records, tours, and fan groups, depends on the distinction between country and other musical genres. The industry asked, "Can good country music be commercially successful and creative or original, but also untraditional, at least in part, at least when done by women?" (Jones 2002, 191). The answer, for many, was a resounding "Yes."

At the end of the twentieth century, a new movement emerged among the women of country music. While loud and angry independent artists such as Fiona Apple, Alanis Morissette, and PJ Harvey voiced their opinions about female body image, men, and female sexuality, country music had a quieter revolution. According to Beverly Keel, "Although largely ignored by the mainstream music press, this movement has revolutionized the way women are portrayed in popular music's most conservative genre" (2004, 155).

If women performed in concerts and created financially successful hit songs, how did they appear in music videos? Just as MTV and VH1 market performers and their music by their videos, so too does Country Music Television and The Nashville Network. As powerful marketing tools, music videos also are "powerful, if playful, postmodern art. Their raw materials are aspects of commercial popular culture, their structures those of dreams, their premise the constant permutation of identity in a world without social relationships" (Aufderheide 1986, 77).

Motivated by the entertainment industry's declaration that 1997 was the "Year of the Woman," Julie Andsager and Kimberly Roe (1999) analyzed 285 country music television videos and found that they portrayed women more progressively than did men's music videos that included women. The findings revealed great similarity with other music genres—women were mostly absent. Despite the 1997 proclamation, in terms of both the number and the ratio of performers in videos, women were not on the same playing field as males. The ratio of male to female artists was four to one in other music genres, and three to one in country music videos. Men's videos were also played three times more often than were women's. Whether this is a form of symbolic annihilation is hard to tell, but certainly, in terms of numbers, the claim and the reality were different.

In addition, representations of women included two types of female artists: early-30s progressive women who were direct and assertive and who, while perhaps heartbroken, also spoke of emancipation. Mary Chapin Carpenter's "Tender When I Want to Be" is an example of this archetype. On the other hand, the opposite portrayal was also found—the scantily clad, sexually hungry, melancholic, objectified woman. They missed their men, even though they were sometimes mistreated. Faith Hill's "It Matters to Me" is an example of this representation. When women appeared in men's videos, they were often in stereotypical roles and completely dedicated to the man—often as brides and pregnant wives.

Female country music singers have had to navigate an industry in which sexism and double standards remain as strong as ever (Chandler and Chalfant 1985). Traditionally, country fans have been similarly conservative. Shania Twain was one of the first women to challenge the proscribed country music industry roles. "Frustrated by the fact that she faced constraints in the country genre," Twain told the *Hartford Courant*, "'I don't listen to the industry at all. I'm much more interested in what the fans think'" (Herzig 2003, 249). The fans loved her.

Country women had to ease feminist messages into their songs in a slower and more tempered way than their sister singers in other genres. But it worked, says Beverly Keel: "Today virtually every top female artist's songs reflect a feminist stance, and, if record sales are any indication, this new way of thinking has been received warmly by country record buyers" (2004, 156).

Shania Twain, Faith Hill, Martina McBride, Trisha Yearwood, Wynonna Judd, the Dixie Chicks, and Gretchen Wilson worked their way to the top of *Billboard*'s charts. In fact, more women than men have dominated the Top 10 charts in the last few years (countrywomen.com).

While songs of heartache remain, feminist political themes emerge. While Tammy Wynette selflessly stood by her man, today's country women haven't abandoned him. However, when asked if she is a feminist, Shania Twain answered,

> I guess you could say that I am, but I'm not an *angry* feminist, you know? I'm a very old-fashioned person, so I enjoy it when a man opens the door for me—I'm not offended by those things. I still believe in the theory of standing by your man. As long as the man is willing to stand by his woman! (Quoted in Herzig 2003, 249, italics in original)

Clearly the doormat days are gone. Not only have female country music performers crossed boundaries between genres, reaping immense financial reward, but also they are making their mark as performers, producers, and writers.

"Redneck Woman"

In 2004, Gretchen Wilson was among the country music women who boldly stepped forward and announced to the world that she had arrived. She also declared herself a redneck woman on the multiplatinum hit album, *Here for the Party*. The song "Redneck Woman" held the No. 1 spot on the Hot Country Songs chart for 5 weeks, and the album sold nearly 4 million copies (Stark 2005, 50). In a popular press story, Wilson is described as a "proud, beer-drinking, tobacco-chewing, jeans-wearing tomboy" who "had a "painful upbringing, including a life of poverty, her ogre of a stepfather and dropping out of school after the eighth grade" (Moody 2007).

In her autobiography, *Redneck Woman: Stories from My Life*, Wilson (2007) describes her one-stoplight hometown (Pocahontas, Illinois) as a place where "no one comes . . . that doesn't already live there" (2). According to Wilson, the town's credentials include "country music, stock car racing, pickup trucks and Jack Daniel's whiskey" (3). Although located in Illinois, Wilson defends Pocahontas as Southern (even though Illinois fought for the North during the Civil War) by describing how geographically and

"Redneck Woman" composer and performer Gretchen Wilson sings to a capacity crowd at the Little Creek Amphibious Base, Virginia Beach, Virginia, 2008. (Courtesy of U.S. Military/Mass Communication Specialist 2nd Class Oscar Espinoza.)

culturally close the community is to Kentucky and Tennessee. The fact that she makes a point of this history speaks to the importance of being Southern to the legitimacy of country music. In body, geography, and attitude, Gretchen Wilson wants everyone to know she is a *Southern* country girl and, even more importantly, a *redneck* country girl. She is curvy, is Southern born and raised, and can roughhouse with the best of them. However, does her song rally for or against the redneck stereotype?

Video Analysis

Carol Vernallis (2004) states that rap videos often take place in urban streets. Similarly, country videos have their own conventions, employing the visual iconography of country lyrics such as bars, small towns, traditional gender roles, rodeo cowboys, and the like (Fenster 1988, 291), and Wilson maintains these in "RW". Two important features of country music and its videos, "simplicity and ordinariness," are evident in the video—the viewer could be watching home movies (except perhaps for the scenes of her at home and undressing). Typical of early country videos, Wilson also performs in a bar. The song and the lyrics emphasize her accessibility and everydayness. It challenges listeners while the video invites viewers (particularly women) to take charge of their identity and to consider, "Who is a country woman singer?"

Mark Fenster (1988) argues that a goal of country music videos is to remain visually different from pop or rock yet maintain crossover potential should the song bridge genres. As noncountry outlets such as MTV and VH1 opened their doors to country crossovers, the videos became more sophisticated. Producers of country videos wanted to maintain the original audience and attract new members. They had to keep the aesthetic elements associated with country music but had to appeal to other groups as well. In such transitions, Vernallis (2004) argues, "Lyrics provide only one among many kinds of material to attend to" in music videos. Using Vernallis's method of a "chronological" description of the video, the lyrics are illustrated in the video with scenes of Wilson getting down and dirty with others on all-terrain vehicles (ATVs), looking sexy singing and playing her guitar in a bar, appearing in scenes with other redneck women in trailers and trucks, and finally displaying her unwillingness to be subservient to men (224).

The "Redneck Woman" video opens with Wilson and a group of men riding ATVs through the mud and across a rocky creek bed (Hogan 2004).[1] She is dressed in jeans, a sweater, sunglasses, and huge hoop earrings. She's also covered with mud. As she leans on an ATV, Wilson directly sings to the viewer about how she isn't the Barbie Doll type. (Full song lyrics are available online at http://www.hit-country-music-lyrics.com/redneck-woman-lyrics.html)

The scene switches to a bar/nightclub. Wilson wears (clean) jeans and a simple T-shirt, plays the guitar, her long hair loose, as she continues the song.

There are occasional cuts to a woman in a black negligee dancing in a cage of chains, sexing up the video, and flashes of the muddy ATV scene interspersed. The audience dances and sings along. When Wilson reaches the chorus, she asks women to join her in a rebel yell. Fashion model-pretty women raise beer bottles high and wear midriff baring tops and baseball caps. She sings:

> Victoria's Secret, well their stuff's real nice
> But I can buy the same damn thing
> on a Wal-Mart shelf half price

The camera turns again to the undulating, lingerie clad woman who dance on stage.

The scene changes to Wilson as she drives a truck, spins it in circles in the mud and is obviously not afraid to get dirty. The chorus repeats, but Tanya Tucker's name replaces Charlie Daniels in the lyrics. Back in the bar, she points out Tucker in the audience.

In the next scene, Wilson sings "Here's to all my sisters," as she drives to a trailer park where kids play, model-beautiful women sit in the back seats of cars, a camouflage-clad mom breaks up a children's fight and a pregnant woman in profile with only one side of her overalls secured shows her belly. Wilson pulls up to a rusted mobile home and sees motorcycles parked around it. Another scene of a graceful dancer is spliced in. She enters the trailer where Kid Rock and Hank Williams, Jr. sit in a living room with a big-screen television set. Beer bottles cover the coffee table. She kicks Rock's leg as she starts to clean the mess, walks to a sleeping Williams and plucks a cigar out of his hand, looks in the refrigerator, closes the door, goes to the laundry room and peels off her muddy clothes. She repeats the chorus but this time substitutes the Charlie Daniels and Tanya Tucker lyric with "Ol' Bocephus," a nickname for Williams. She then is shown in sexy underwear, removes her bra, and drops it into the washing machine. The video alternates between muddy bike rides and the bar for a final scene of women yelling "hell, yeah!"

Four themes emerged from this analysis of "Redneck Woman": (1) defiance and pride, (2) physical appearance, (3) consumption, and (4) legitimacy.

Defiance and Pride

During the song, the only people who look down on Wilson are those pictured in the posters on her wall. She is not about to be defined by or judged by the ubiquitous others.

Physical Appearance

The genesis of "RW" is important. According to Wilson's book, the idea came when she and fellow band members decided to write a new song. For inspiration, she watched three videos, one each by Shania Twain, Faith Hill, and Martina McBride. As she watched the elegantly attired women in the videos, she became aware of her appearance, dressed in "a wife-beater tank top, a pair of sweatpants and flip flops. I had no make-up on, and I had a cigarette in one hand and a bottle of beer in another" (Wilson 2007, 120).

"That's just not what I am," she said. "I guess I'm just a redneck woman!" Collaborator and band member John D. Rich replied, "You are not the Barbie Doll type!" (121). The song was born. The lyrics further embrace the pregnant and barefoot stereotype, as Wilson is proudly standing [barefoot] in [her] own front yard with a baby on her hip.

Consumption

Not only does Wilson sing about the literal consumption of beer over champagne, but also the song is in opposition to the Barbie Doll, Victoria's Secret, and Wal-Mart brands. According to the lyrics, Wilson doesn't lust for money but rather to be sexy for her man. In so doing, she reinforces the heteronormative subscript. As a discriminating shopper, she is not about to be taken in by the flash and glamour of Victoria's Secret.

Legitimacy

"RW" reinforces what Wilson is, as much as what she is not. Her choice of the culturally correct performers (Charlie Daniels, Lynyrd Skynyrd, Tanya Tucker, Kid Rock, and Hank Williams Jr.) secures her connection to a working-class community that substantiates her Southern musical roots. She demonstrates her membership in the Southern club when she swears and yells. In the end, she asks other country women to join her to preserve this attitude and the music by "keeping it country."

Conclusion

This chapter focuses on how "Redneck Woman" created meaning about being an Anglo Southern woman and the connection of that identity with consumption practices and brand choices. Drawing on Andrew Goodwin's (1992) analysis of rock music videos, it is important to highlight the importance of context within which videos are seen and heard. Audiences for music and television "[inhabit] a culture that has in common various discourses, attitudes and structures of feeling;" fans consume the product in particular times and places (Goodwin 1992, xix).

Theodor Adorno (1991) wrote that music serves a variety of functions, including its use by social movements. Music is universal. It spans time, people, and place in its ability to connect individuals to shared values and ideals and brings comfort, entertainment, humor, and catharsis. Music functions as a kind of social glue that affirms shared social ideologies (Eyerman and Jamieson 1998). Song lyrics facilitate group membership, emphasize sameness and difference, and provide information about characteristics of a person who belongs to a particular culture. The intertextuality among words, music, and images creates a discursive field ripe with meaning.

Mikhail Bakhtin's (1981, 281) term "dialogic" describes how a word in its symbolic form exists within a network of meaning. Thus "redneck" operates from a fully aware "background of understanding" in which the audience of the song experiences the music and lyrics with a primed openness to certain perspectives and within a particular social and cultural milieu, which Bakhtin calls "background" (1981, 281). It is within this background that audience members understand the meaning of the words. In this view, it is impossible to dislodge a culturally specific word, such as "redneck," from its context. "RW" used the term "redneck" as a bridge to a more contemporary encounter, and perhaps toward a reappropriation of the once hurtful term.

As an anomaly among mainstream country music, "Redneck Woman" is a worthwhile example of entertainment media worthy of analysis for what it says about the performative nature of not just gender but also class. In 2007, Wilson said of the song, "I think the girls, the blue-collar women in America, had just been waiting for ["RW"] for so long. It was just perfect timing" ("Blue-Collar" 2007, 20). Described as "anthemic," the song and video reclaim an otherwise derogatory word and reframe it to connect country to modern feminism. It thus demonstrates the mutability of language and meaning. The stereotypical characterizations of redneck women are thus confronted and reclaimed.

Is "Redneck Woman" a celebration or a condemnation of the redneck stereotype?

Yes.

Note

1. See "Redneck Woman," http://www.youtube.com/watch?v=82dDnv9zeLs (accessed March 26, 2010).

Sources

Adorno, Theodor W. 1991. *The culture industry: Selected essays on mass culture.* London: Routledge.

Andsager, Julie L., and Kimberly Roe. 1999. Country music video in country's year of the woman. *Journal of Communication* 49: 69–82.

Aufderheide, Patricia. 1986. Music videos: The look of the sound. *Journal of Communication* 36: 57–78.

Bakhtin, Mikhail. 1981. Discourse in the novel. In *The dialogic imagination*, ed. Michael Holquist, pp. 259–422. Austin: University of Texas Press.

Blue-collar downsizing. 2007. *Billboard*, April 14.

Bufwack, Mary A., and Robert K. Oermann. 2003. *Finding her voice: The saga of women in country music*. New York: Crow.

Chandler, C. R., and Paul Chalfant. 1985. The sexual double-standard in country music song lyrics. *Free Inquiry in Creative Sociology* 13: 1428–1433.

CMAWorld.com. 1999. Press release. http://www.cmaworld.com/news_publications/ pr_common/press_detail.asp?re=207&year=1999 (accessed March 26, 2010).

Countrywomen.com. n.d. http://countrywomen.com (accessed March 26, 2010).

Eyerman, Ron, and Andrew Jamieson. 1998. *Music and social movements: Mobilizing traditions in the twentieth century*. Cambridge: Cambridge University Press.

Fenster, Mark. 1988. Country music video. *Popular Music* 7 (3): 285–302.

Fox, Aaron A. 2004. *Real country: Music and language in working-class culture*. Durham, NC: Duke University Press.

Goad, Jim. 1997. *The Redneck manifesto: How hillbillies, hicks, and white trash became America's scapegoats*. New York: Simon & Schuster.

Goodwin, Andrew. 1992. *Dancing in the distraction factory: Music television and popular culture*. Minneapolis: University of Minnesota Press.

Graham, Michael. 2003. *Redneck nation: How the South really won the war*. New York: Time Warner.

Herzig, Jill. 2003. Shania the crusader. *Glamour*, October.

Hogan, D., dir. 2004. Redneck woman. Video. Nashville, TN: Epic.

Jones, Steve. 2002. *Pop music and the press*. Philadelphia: Temple University Press.

Keel, Beverly. 2004. Between riot GRRRl and quiet girl: The new women's movement in country music. In *A boy named Sue: Gender and country music*, ed. Kristine M. McCusker and Diane Pecknold, pp. 155–177. Jackson: University of Mississippi Press.

Malone, Bill C. 2002. *Don't get above your raisin': Country music and the Southern working class*. Chicago: University of Illinois Press.

Moody, Nekesa Mumi. 2007. Gretchen Wilson shows vulnerable side. *USA Today*, May 16. http://www.usatoday.com/life/music/2007-05-16-796705887_x .htm (accessed March 26, 2010).

Rich, Ronda. 1999. *What Southern women know (that every woman should)*. New York: Perigree.

Ripley Wolfe, Margaret. 1995. *Daughters of Canaan: A saga of Southern women*. Lexington: University Press of Kentucky.

Stark, Phyllis. 2005. Natural woman. *Billboard*, September 24.

Stilwell, Robynn. 2008. Review. *Women and Music: A Journal of Gender and Culture* 12, 104–110.

Vernallis, Carol. 2004. *Experiencing music video: Aesthetics and cultural context.* New York: Columbia University Press.

Wilson, Gretchen. 2007. *Redneck woman: Stories from my life.* New York: Grand Central Printing.

Wray, Matt, and AnnaLee Newitz, eds. 1997. *White trash: Race and class in America.* New York: Routledge.

You might be a redneck if . . . N.d. http://bsornot.whipnet.net/redneck/mightbea .html (accessed March 26, 2010).

Chapter 15

Archetypes: Transcending Stereotypes of Feminine and Masculine in the Theatre of Mediatypes

Julianne H. Newton and Rick Williams

At their most profound level, images that injure are stored deep within the archives of unconscious minds. These long-term memory deposits encourage behavior that undermines how an individual relates to the self, to others, and with society. Much media content misrepresents human complexity and offers simplistic but compellingly constructed story lines that model fantasies as reality to support consumer culture. These mediatypes, or media-perpetuated stereotypes, often are presented as the route to self-understanding, fulfillment, and relational motivation. When embedded as unconscious mental models, they distort our standard of reality, shape how we solve problems and make decisions, and support consumerism that masquerades as self-fulfillment.

This chapter argues that one antidote to the detrimental effects of unwitting consumption and assimilation of mediatypes is to understand and integrate deep patterns of human behavior that Carl Jung (1961, 1964) called "archetypes." Jung, a twentieth-century psychiatrist and theorist, maintained that individuals could find psychological health and wholeness by an awareness of unconscious archetypal models shared by all humans. An archetype is a pattern that emerges from conscious thoughts that help explain complex information whether from internal (mental) or external (media) sources. Although Jung (1964) considered archetypes primordial remnants of ancient humans maintained through our evolution into contemporary species, contemporary analytical psychologists argue that they are shaped from lived experience (Hogenson 2009; Merchant 2009).

Fortunately, resolution of the controversy over the origin of archetypes is not vital to help understand how persons respond to images of people. Archetypes tend to be broad patterns of ideal behaviors that can be integrated by individuals to help them understand and develop their sense of self. In Jungian psychology, the "self" is one of the primary archetypes that signifies a coherent whole, an integration of a person's conscious and unconscious components.

Neuroscience supports Jung's role of the unconscious as a factor in social behavior. The research of Antonio Damasio (1999) and Antoine Bechara (Bechara et al. 1997) indicates that unconscious biases and motivations direct much of a person's behavior. These studies suggest that an integration of rational and intuitive, and conscious and unconscious, mental processes can help solve challenges and serve the greater good.

And yet, opposed to this integrative mental process is mass media's fetish for oversimplification. The media's simple solutions are perpetuated through personal, cultural, and mediatypal constructs that impose simplistic ideas about groups with similar attributes in common. Built upon social stereotypes, mediatypes generate divisions in the collective culture as well as in individual personalities. They promote separation among the archetypal aspects of each individual personality. They create false dichotomies between cultural groups whether based on gender, sexual orientation, race, ethnicity, age, economic status, and so on. Most often, mediatypal messages suggest that a product's ownership or a personality model, with its accompanying cultural-specific behavior based on fantasy, is the source of self-fulfillment. In this way, mediatypal messages increase disharmony and encourage unstable personal and cultural models.

Repeated stereotypical images and recurrent media scripts that present fantasy as reality push aside or override personal memories and experiences as the basis of unconscious thoughts and behaviors. These false mediatypes encourage either/or thinking rather than the both/and concepts of archetypes.

Archetypes Are Not Stereotypes

For Carl Jung (1964), archetypes represented prototypical models of the highest levels of the human psyche and being. Archetypes shift, converge, turn, and interweave in the manner of a Möbius strip, emerging within and without the human psyche and body. Archetypes facilitate simultaneous, dynamic expression and development of varying human characteristics— both positive and negative.

Stereotypes are not archetypes. Stereotypes impose crude, reactive filters through which one human being can categorize another almost reflexively, without benefit of either conscious thought or interpersonal interaction. Stereotypes insist on either/or categories. In the case of masculine and feminine, stereotypes impose artificial boundaries for behavior and personality, including expression of sexuality and portrayal of sex roles. They exclude more than include, drawing limiting frames around human characteristics. They are a source of injury because they not only divide groups against each other but also disconnect individuals from the richly complex uniqueness of their own humanity. The term "mediatype" refers to a stereotype repeatedly constructed, enacted, and disseminated via media.

One way to distinguish archetypes from stereotypes is to understand that archetypes are inclusive rather than exclusive. They represent the unified ideal of an individual that embodies the power and grace of differences, such as feminine and masculine characteristics. Stereotypes, on the other hand, dichotomize and diminish the archetypal ideal of oneness.

A profound application of archetypal theory upon stereotypes addresses feminine and masculine characteristics of personality and culture. Many media messages designed largely to promote consumerism misrepresent the masculine and feminine archetypal principles as discrete, physical manifestations of male and female. Mediatypal images injure by misrepresenting the integrated character of the masculine and feminine archetypes, supporting a misguided determination to categorize one another by sex and sexual orientation. Media's persistent, simplistic portrayals of women as associated exclusively with the characteristics of the feminine archetypes—nurture, compassion, and interaction—and of men as uniquely aggressive, dispassionate, and independent corral the genders inside cultural fences that perpetuate stereotypical clichés that are more cartoon-like than human (see a discussion about the cultural meaning of fences in chapter 11). In this way, archetypes are reduced to mediatypes. After countless repetitions in various media, media stereotypes become unconsciously mistaken as archetypes. Consequently, they become models for behavior.

Rather than simplify feminine and masculine characteristics into convenient, consumable stereotypical images, clarity and integrity can be found in the expression of the unique energies comprised in every human being: female and male, transgender, transsexual, gay, lesbian, straight, bisexual, and queer. Feminine and masculine archetypes are attributes all people experience through genetic encoding, psychological manifestations, intrapersonal intelligences, the cultivation of personal traits, social interactions, dreams, myths, literature, the arts, and the media. These archetypes manifest through an infinite continuum of human expression, behavior, and personality. They are limited only by the imagination and creativity of the human psyche. Understanding feminine and masculine as archetypal characteristics within all human beings regardless of gender or sexual orientation frees people of culturally imposed, stereotypical boundaries that limit the capacity to feel, understand, express, empathize, and interact.

Expanding the Boundaries

What follows is a discussion of two media examples that push the boundaries of stereotypes. They help to remove the fences between cultural groups and to integrate archetypes. However, as these examples push boundaries, they can cause confusion, sometimes to the point of ineffectiveness in which they reinforce the stereotypes that they were meant to expose. They also can support the creation of new stereotypes.

The NBC show *The Biggest Loser,* a reality show in which participants compete to lose the greatest amount of weight, premiered in 2004 and challenges popular stereotypes of obese individuals.[1] The program reveals their humanity as it portrays them as complex humans who struggle with life experiences. *The Biggest Loser* teaches how important it is to know and care for a group of people and support their success. On the other hand, it exploits the contestants who are its heroic protagonists and uses their personal stories to make money through advertisements and product placements. Although the program can inspire viewers to improve their own lives, it asserts that the stereotyped obese people it seeks to humanize would be happier if they fit the mold of the mediatypal athlete—lean, muscular, and sexy. Although the show reinforces stereotypes by an emphasis on what is a culturally acceptable body weight, it also challenges them by the transforming obese individuals into socially acceptable heroes.

The Biggest Loser also merges feminine and masculine archetypes. For example, one of the trainers, Bob Harper expresses stereotypical feminine characteristics to nurture and empathize. The other trainer, Jillian Michaels, expresses stereotypically masculine characteristics of assertive, dominating forcefulness. As a result, internet gossips titillate with questions such as "Is Bob gay?" (Dehnart 2009) and "Is Jillian gay?" (AfterEllen 2009). Michaels also exploits her celebrity status and masculinity by marketing her own consumer products in television ads (Michaels 2010).

AMC's Mad Men, a multiple Emmy winner for "Outstanding Drama Series," explores the common stereotypes of male dominance and female submission that were post–World War II cultural norms until the rise of the feminist movement in the late 1960s.[2] Set in New York City's advertising hub on Madison Avenue, the show "depicts authentically the roles of men and women in this era while exploring the true human nature beneath the guise of 1960s traditional family values" (Mad Men 2010, para. 4). For instance, all of the executives are men. They make unselfconsciously sexual jokes at the expense of the female secretaries who, without complaint, fetch them coffee and make excuses for their indiscretions. Although the program concentrates on the advertising business, it also portrays the characters' life struggles through individuals who live and fight the stereotypes of their time.

Mad Men is popular because it presents a morality play with characters that battle mediatypes while they semiheroically seek archetypal authenticity. For example, this struggle is seen as Peggy Olson, played by Elizabeth Moss, evolves from her submissive role as an obedient secretary to an up-and-coming copywriter who directly confronts and successfully persuades her male bosses to address, at least partially, the inequity in position and pay when she does the same work as the men.

Television programs such as The Biggest Loser and Mad Men can be used in a prosocial format to encourage discussion of human complexity. As with life experiences, the use of mediatypes affects individuals differently. Because it is the intention of many advertising creators to persuade individuals to accept consumerist mediatypes as real in order to generate lifestyle acceptance and product use, the repetition of the messages facilitates the transformation from audience to consumer. In the same way, if it is the intention of the producers of *Loser* and *Mad* to advance equality among those who want to lose weight and people in the workplace, the repetitive successes of individuals either through scales or by sales can persuade viewers to support new mediatype concepts and integrate this model into their own behavior. The key is to understand and acknowledge stages and varieties of personal development and the integration of archetypes—in viewers, as well as actors and creators. This suggests the need for a high level of sophisticated media literacy in viewers. Development of that sophistication is part of the field of media and visual studies.

Although mediatypes may stimulate prosocial discussion, this is not the norm. Most mediatyping promotes the objectification of human beings to maintain cultural norms. Rigid norms established by mediatypes disintegrate and objectify the individual while characterizing difference as a threat to the norm[al].

Stereotypes are delivered in many ways, but mediatypes that are promoted visually are the most damaging—for several reasons. Visual stereotypes are most readily remembered (Graber 1990; Lang, Potter, and Bolls 1999; Madigan 1983; Paivio, Rogers, and Smythe 1968; Schultz 1993; Zillmann, Gibson, and Sargent 1999). Significantly, visual information takes a primary and separate route from rational thought through the brain (LeDoux 1986, 1996). It is stored as nonconscious, long-term memory in a prerational state to be used in future decision making as the standard of reality against which other information is judged (Bechara et al. 1997). When stereotypes are presented through visual mediatypes, their messages are stored uncritically to guide our subsequent behavior.

Long-Term Benefits of Integrating Archetypes

To examine how mediatypes help to explain human nature, it is necessary to return to the exploration of female/male mediatypes and feminine/masculine archetypes. As a point of departure, we ask whether it is possible that the expression of masculine and feminine characteristics, the archetypes of *anima* and *animus* that Jung believed all humans possess, have been misunderstood through time and incorrectly used to channel the tendencies of humans to be attracted to another person.

What if heterosexuality is largely a constructed concept with origins in ancient survival-based prescriptions? If the question is never considered, media consumers simply fall in line with conventional (and stereotypical) visual messages. Nature provides a clue for an answer.

The physiological differences between the genders are evident in a remarkable symbol system of feminine and masculine natural forms—avocados and asparagus, apples and bananas, and peaches and cucumbers.

There are also multisexual symbols—flowers with both stamen and pistils (consider the calla lily); watermelons with swollen, elongated bodies filled

In the arboretum on the campus of California State University, Fuller-ton, avocados hang from a tree. (Courtesy of Paul Martin Lester.)

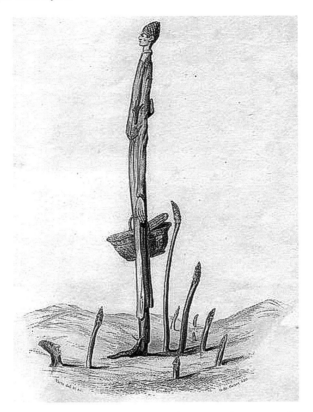

L'Asperge Native by the French printmaker Amédée Varin from Drôleries végétales. L'Empire des légumes, mémoires de Cucurbitus Ier by Eugène Nus and Antoine Méray, 1861. (Source: Gabriel de Gonet.)

with internal seeds; bell peppers that form into various shapes; and trees with long, rigid trunks and rounded, erupting, flowering greenery.

People may scoff at such references in comparison to human sexuality, but few would disagree with the ways that human beings have moved beyond imposed limits on their physicality and psychological expression. Among models in the fashion industry, for example, male and female androgyny is highly valued. Humans have moved beyond the relatively rare appearance of hermaphroditism through cross-dressing and surgery in order to match their physical appearance with their inner selves (Stone 1993, 1995).

Not only femininity and masculinity but also femaleness and maleness are now beyond either/or categories. The ancients expressed the integration

A close-up of a calla lily in the front yard of a home in Long Beach, California. (Courtesy of Paul Martin Lester.)

of masculine and feminine through such concepts as yin and yang, recognizing both were necessary for wholeness. Contemporary humans, however, have misunderstood the archetypes and assumed they are discrete and oppositional. At one time, it was supposed that the left side of the brain represented traditional masculine characteristics of linear, logical, and hierarchical thinking. The right side stereotypically represented traditional feminine characteristics that controlled visual, creative, and multidimensional thinking. The divided, stereotypically rational mind became the center of the understanding of human cognition.

What else has been misinterpreted? Consider an early Marshall McLuhan work, *The Mechanical Bride* (1951/2008). Long before such theories as social construction of reality (Berger and Luckmann 1966), symbolic interactionism (Blumer 1969), or brain hemisphere theory (Sperry 1973) were articulated,

McLuhan warned that the media constructed reality. He later asserted that the twentieth century's "global village" would need *both/and* thinking in order to prevent destructive conflict between Eastern and Western cultures (McLuhan and Powers 1989; McLuhan and Watson 1970).

Despite such forward-thinking theories, contemporary humans have lost their way. Women's bodies are prized if they are uncharacteristically tall, thin, and blemish free, while their character is desired if sexualized, frail, submissive, and infantile. Men's bodies are praised if muscular, tall, and ruddy. Their ideal character is athletic, aggressive, sexual, domineering, and powerful. These traits are the limited, counterfeit characters of the anti-archetype—stereotypes the media portray as normal.

Conclusion

Society influences through every external form imaginable. Through stereotypes, archetypes are confused and inappropriately merged into external forms called "mediatypes." Rather than draw upon ancient human archetypes to foster honest communication and authentic representation of the unique self, adherence to these media-reinforced and generated portrayals often leads to a lonely, counterfeit, and ultimately impossible search for fulfillment within a rigid structure of corrupted expressions of self in everyday life. This process that creates an inauthentic life includes educational models that marginalize primary visual components of learning, problem solving, and decision making, and values a rational bias over an integrated rational-intuitive model that has the potential to generate the highest levels of learning and sustainability.

To address the dilemma of the misrepresentation of archetypes through mediatyping, visual theorists have developed techniques to help understand and reformat images. Examples of creative new tools to help understand and reframe visual media include Paul Martin Lester's Six Perspectives for Analysis (2011), Rick Williams's Omniphasic Theory of Cognitive Balance (1999), Ann Marie Barry's *Visual Intelligence* (1997), and Julianne Newton's *Visual Ecology* (2001). In *Visual Communication: Integrating Media, Art and Science* (2007), Williams and Newton suggest a three-step plan for how an inclusive, nurturing, holistic media environment might be developed:

1. Focus on ways to enrich individual and mediated lives,
2. Take the initiative to develop a balanced self that chooses and practices activities that enrich all lives and culture, and

3. Support educational practices that empower personal growth through visual and media literacy and art processes.

With conscious effort, we can use these tools to move toward a clearer understanding of visual communication and toward applications of visual intelligence that integrate archetypal wholeness in the primordial spirit symbolized by the avocado, the asparagus, and the calla lily.

We can move beyond sexual mediatypes, the caricatures of human beings used to sell us deatharettes and deathahol and sexemup trucks and spend-all-your-money-on-them-'cause-then-you'll-look-sexy-and-like-you've-made-it.

Society is influenced by the creation of visual messages that demonstrate holistic integration. When bodies, psyches, and brains are merged, the evolution of the individual toward self-realization becomes an integrative experience for all of society. If not, media culture will continue to shape perceptions and guide behavior in limited ways to the detriment of the self and humanity.

Strip away the mediatypes and social stereotypes that constrict identity and present individual, interwoven expressions of archetypes. The goal should be psychic and physical freedom that leads to cultural sustainability.

Notes

1. See *The Biggest Loser*, http://www.youtube.com/watch?v=UD_8-I3gc_c (accessed March 27, 2010).

2. See *Mad Men*, http://www.youtube.com/watch?v=_2Lw7iS21rs (accessed March 27, 2010).

Sources

AfterEllen. 2009, http://www.afterellen.com (accessed March 27, 2010).

Barry, Ann Marie Seward. 1997. *Visual intelligence: Perception, image, and manipulation in visual communication*. New York: State University of New York Press.

Bechara, Antoine, Hanna Damasio, Daniel Tranel, and Antonio Damasio. 1997. Deciding advantageously before knowing the advantageous strategy. *Science* 275: 1293–1295.

Berger, Peter L., and Thomas Luckmann. 1966. *The social construction of reality: A treatise in the sociology of knowledge*. Garden City, NY: Doubleday.

Blumer, Herbert. 1969. *Symbolic interactionism: Perspective and method.* Englewood Cliffs, NJ: Prentice-Hall.

Damasio, Antonio. 1999. *The feeling of what happens: Body and emotion in the making of consciousness.* New York: Harcourt Brace.

Dehnart, Andy. 2009. Former contestants suggest Bob Harper is gay. realityblurred .com, January 27. http://www.realityblurred.com/realitytv/archives/the _biggest_loser_6/2009_Jan_27_bob_harper_gay (accessed March 9, 2010).

Graber, Doris A. 1990. Seeing is remembering: How visuals contribute to learning from television news. *Journal of Communication* 40 (3): 134–155.

Hogenson, George B. 2009. Archetypes as action patterns. *Journal of Analytical Psychology* 54 (3): 325–337.

Jung, Carl J. 1961. *Memories, dreams, reflections.* New York: Random House.

Jung, Carl J. 1964. *Man and his symbols.* Garden City, New York: Doubleday.

Lang, Annie, Robert F. Potter, and Paul D. Bolls. 1999. Something for nothing: Is visual encoding automatic? *Media Psychology* 1 (2): 145–163.

LeDoux, Joseph. 1986. Sensory systems and emotion. *Integrative Psychiatry* 4: 237–243.

LeDoux, Joseph. 1996. *The emotional brain.* New York: Simon & Schuster.

Lester, Paul M. 2011. *Visual communication: Images with messages.* Belmont, CA: Wadsworth.

Madigan, Stephen. 1983. Picture memory. In *Imagery, memory and cognition; Essays in honor of Allan Paivio,* ed. John C. Yuille, pp. 65–89. Hillsdale, NJ: Erlbaum.

Mad Men. 2010. About the show, *Mad Men.* http://www.amctv.com:80/originals/ madmen/about/ (accessed March 11, 2010).

McLuhan, Marshall. [1951] 2008. *The mechanical bride.* New York: Ginko Press.

McLuhan, Marshall, and Bruce R. Powers. 1989. *The global village, transformations in world life and media in the 21st century.* New York: Oxford University Press.

McLuhan, Marshall, with Wilfred Watson. 1970. *From cliché to archetype.* New York: Viking Press.

Merchant, John. 2009. A reappraisal of classical archetype theory and its implications for theory and practice, *Journal of Analytical Psychology* 54 (3): 339–358.

Michaels, Jillian. 2010. Jillian Michaels official online store. http://jillianmichaels .shop.sportstoday.com/ (accessed March 11, 2010).

Newton, Julianne H. 2001. *The burden of visual truth: The role of photojournalism in mediating reality.* Mahwah, NJ: Lawrence Erlbaum.

Paivio, Allan, T. B. Rogers, and P. C. Smythe. 1968. Why are pictures easier to recall than words? *Psychonomic Science* 11 (4): 137–138.

Schultz, Marilyn. 1993. *The effect of visual presentation, story complexity and story familiarity on recall and comprehension of television news.* Unpublished doctoral dissertation, Indiana University, Bloomington.

Sperry, Roger W. 1973. Lateral specialization of cerebral function in the surgically separated hemispheres. In *The psychophysiology of thinking: Studies of covert processes*, ed. Frank J. McGuigan and R. A. Schoonover, pp. 209–229. New York: Academic Press.

Stone, Allucquère Rosanne (Sandy). 1993. The "empire" strikes back: A posttranssexual manifesto. http://www.sandystone.com/empire-strikes-back (accessed March 27, 2010).

Stone, Allucquère Rosanne (Sandy). 1995. *The war of desire and technology at the close of the mechanical age*. Boston: MIT Press.

Williams, Rick. 1999. Beyond visual literacy: Omniphasism, a theory of cognitive balance, part I. *Journal of Visual Literacy* 19 (2): 159–178.

William, Rick and Julianne Newton. 2007. *Visual communication: Integrating media, art, and science*. Mahwah, NJ: Erlbaum.

Zillmann, Dolf, Rhonda Gibson, and Stephanie Sargent. 1999. Effects of photographs in news-magazine reports on issue perception. *Media Psychology* 1 (3): 207–228.

PART IV

Images of Age, Illness, and the Body

Paul Martin Lester

It is no coincidence that five days before President George W. Bush visited a Mississippi elementary school that was devastated by the fury of Hurricane Katrina's storm surge, a CBS News poll revealed that the former president's "overall job approval rating reached the lowest ever measured in this poll" (2005). Given the public relations disasters of the Iraq War, his premature "Mission Accomplished" speech aboard an aircraft carrier anchored outside San Diego, and his administration's ineffectual response to the travails of those in New Orleans and the Gulf Coast, it is perhaps not surprising that his handlers suggested a "feel good" photo opportunity with young children to give his poll ratings a boost.

Using children as smiling props by politicians is a common public relations ploy. Media critic and communications professor Dennis Dunleavy (2005) writes, "Children have been exploited by politicians to peddle agendas for a long time, and the press never ceases to pander to the powerful" (n.p.).

Children within a society have many special protections because they are the most vulnerable. Those of a certain age cannot find their own shelter, food, or safety from those who might cause them harm. As they are generally not in control or responsible for their own actions or cannot refuse a task demanded of them from others who are more powerful, children are not considered moral agents. They are stakeholders—affected by the actions of others—and as such can easily be subject to unfair use. Ethically, it should be a given that children in an enlightened society should never be objectified, commodified, or used in a cynical way by adults. And yet, those who are stereotyped in the media are often treated like children, unaware or powerless to stop their own commercial exploitation.

Although seemingly unrelated, the chapters in this part are concerned about the effect of commodification upon portrayals of individuals. Whether children who are stars adored by 'tweens, older adults who are the butt of easy jokes, those who enjoy their skin adorned with tattoos, women with breast cancer, or persons who use wheelchairs, their media stereotypes can be tied to marketable expediency.

Kathy Brittain Richardson in her chapter about children involved with the entertainment industry states that, far too often, young children are exploited to "sell programs, to sell program-related merchandise, to sell causes, and to sell sexuality." She then astutely concludes that such subjugation, even if desired by the young stars, results in "the commodification not only of the 'tween stars but also of their audiences." In other words, the industry's objectification of children lessens us all.

Following on the commercialization theme, Bonnie L. Drewniany looks closely at Super Bowl ads created for the flavored, sugar-water company Pepsi, with a focus on portrayals of older adults. She found a consistent and relentless series of commercials over the years that exploited differences in age, abilities, and interests between the mostly younger "Pepsi Generation" and older others. Like a seemingly benevolent "Cheshire Cat" with a smile that, upon close scrutiny, is obviously false, the Pepsi campaigns use humor to assuage the pain from the stinging stereotypical barbs of these advertisements. But when humor perpetuates negative stereotypes and is used solely for economic gain, it is, as Drewniany concludes, "No laughing matter."

Chema Salinas takes an opposite approach to the commodification theme of this part. He describes those persons who have chosen to adorn their bodies with physical modifications—through ink, scarring, and jewelry—as attempting to reject the cookie-cutter sameness of mainstream society. And yet, advocates of body modification too often are shown within mass media presentations as indistinguishable from one another; they are all criminals, sexually promiscuous, or freaks—outside traditional cultural norms. These stereotypes, Salinas points out, relegate "modified people to the margins of society," where many are denied full participation in the culture and its power circles.

In an extremely powerful chapter, Deni Elliott, with the help of Amanda Decker, notes how the social movement established to aid in fundraising for cancer research and treatments, readily identified through all things pink—ribbons, T-shirts, and products—has been co-opted by commercial interests more intent on promoting their brand sales than on serving those in greatest need of the generated funds. This chapter examines how the stereotypical media messages of "pink" campaigns transform those who must live with breast cancer into commercial artifacts and exploit their goodwill and trust in charitable organizations. In exploding the first of three myths about breast cancer detailed in the chapter, Elliott notes that simply because a corporate sponsor raises awareness with its "pink-branded products"; "fundraising walks, runs, climbs, [and] dances"; and mailings that "contain a line or two that encourages breast self-exams or annual mammograms" does not mean such campaigns can or should be considered philanthropic.

Jack A. Nelson, a longtime advocate of the fair representation in mass communications of those who use wheelchairs, concludes this part with examples throughout history of when individuals with disabilities were scorned, feared, or pitied because of media portrayals. Common stereotypes seen in print and screen media include the hero, the villain, the victim, and the burden. Unlike the other authors, Nelson finds amid these denigrating portraits both progress and hope for the future in recent images of those with disabilities in motion pictures, on television, and linked on the web. He observes that stereotypes are being reduced and eliminated through media portrayals that present a disability "as an inconvenience, not a disability that defined . . . character." Nelson suggests that in order to keep loyal viewers and gain new fans in this world of diversity, the physical condition of characters needs to be portrayed with respect and not exploited in typical commercialized fashion.

Sources

CBS News. 2005. Poll: Bush ratings hit new low. October 6. http://www.cbsnews.com/stories/2005/10/06/opinion/polls/main924485.shtml (accessed March 12, 2010).

Dunleavy, Dennis. 2005. Peddling propaganda and a pandering press: Rethinking the role of photojournalism in constructing social realities. May 6. http://ddunleavy.typepad.com/the_big_picture/2005/05/peddling_and_pa.html (accessed March 12, 2010).

Chapter 16

No Kidding: Using Mediated Images of Children to Sell Programs, Products, and Pleasure

Kathy Brittain Richardson

The attention of audiences the world over was captured early in October, 2009, by news coverage of a silver, flying saucer–shaped balloon floating through the Colorado sky while family members waited anxiously for news that their 6-year-old son, said to be in the balloon's basket, was safe. After the boy was discovered on the ground rather than aboard the balloon, authorities said they believed the incident was a hoax created by his parents, who were hoping to gain a position on a reality television program (CNN.com 2009). The news coverage of the "balloon boy" story provides an apt metaphor for ways in which images of children grab attention, motivate concern, and sometimes impose risks on the safety of children, as well as the roles that adults play in creating and perpetuating those pictures. All too often, images of children and 'tweens are used as a unique selling proposition: to sell programs, to sell program-related merchandise, to sell causes, and to sell sexuality. By so doing, the subjects of those images are being turned into objects for profitable use by adults.

Real Children and Reality Cameras

The fictional child popularized in the *Home Alone* movie franchise became the fodder of televised reality in 2007 in the CBS network reality show *Kid Nation* as 40 children ages 8 to 15 lived without their parents in a New Mexico ghost town for 40 days fending for their needs while rebuilding the town that had basically been abandoned (Hibberd 2007, 1). As the initial episode began, a group of racially diverse children were shown riding on a bus, the camera spanning across their faces: some smiling, and some looking a bit worried. Their first stop was not a hotel or even a school, however. Their first bus stop came in what appeared to be the middle of a desert, where the group was greeted by the adult host, who explained the "rules" of the adventure. Then the children were left to divide into small groups to pull large wagons loaded with supplies down an ill-kept trail into the deserted town. Individual interviews with some of the children on camera allowed viewers to hear their fears, their concerns, and their excitement and to see their homesick tears or serious faces.

The children were not completely alone. Along with the camera crews were medical professionals, nutritionists, and psychologists, CBS entertainment president Nina Tassler told the Associated Press (Elber 2007). Parents were not allowed to be present during the taping. The experience, which CBS said was like a "summer camp," brought questions about the work expected from the children and their personal safety. The show's story line called for the children to organize their town and to complete projects in teams. The children were divided into districts and elected a Town Council to help foster decision making. They were paid for completing their chores, money they could spend buying treats and supplies in the town. Outstanding leaders or workers were given gold stars by the Town Council members, which would later be converted into cash prizes.

Camera crews sometimes filmed more than 14 hours a day while the children worked, played, or talked. Each child received $5,000 to participate, which prompted some to raise questions about compensation and child labor issues. The *New York Times* reported that one child's face was burned by hot grease while she was cooking without supervision, and four children accidentally drank bleach (Wyatt 2007), although the children received prompt medical attention and were not seriously injured. Ratings for the show were mixed—but other "real" children are still featured for viewers to observe (Wiltz 2008).

"Glassworks. Midnight. Location: Indiana." Photographs of children laboring at glass and bottle factories in the United States were taken by Lewis W. Hine for the National Child Labor Committee, New York, 1908. (Courtesy of the Library of Congress.)

The eight children of Jon and Kate Gosselin, sextuplets and twins, have lived in front of TLC network cameras on *Jon & Kate Plus 8* for the five years since the sextuplets' birth. They attract almost 1 million viewers an episode (Hiltbrand and Kadaba 2009, E1). Cameras have filmed almost every event of the children's lives, from visits to the store to birthday parties to tantrums and illnesses. Images of the children on promotional merchandise are on sale through the TLC website.[1] The parents were active participants in this program, a marked difference from the plot theme used in *Kid Nation*. Kate has blogged about the children and about parenting on the show's website. The couple had spoken to groups about their parenting experiences and authored a book together.

The togetherness came to an end in summer, 2009, when the drama of their marital breakup became part of an episode that aired in June, attracting almost 1.7 million viewers (Selter 2009b, 1). It is rare that one gets to see the impact of a breakup on such a large group of children captured for prime-time viewing. Although the taping of episodes was suspended for a time after Jon requested that the children not be filmed anymore, TLC had announced it would continue the series as *Kate Plus 8*, but those plans were postponed (Selter 2009a).

TLC also offers other multiple-children families for viewing on reality shows, one being the conservative Christian Duggar family with its 19 children featured in *18 Kids and Counting* (Goff 2009, M17). The family is profiled on the show's website.[2] The Duggars home school their children while also working as real estate agents. Episodes frequently show the children at study or at play as older siblings assist a younger sibling with tasks or chores. Another program, *Table for 12*, features the family of police officer Eric Hayes and his wife with two sets of twins and sextuplets, one of whom has cerebral palsy. Episodes feature events such as trips to Hershey Park and family parties, along with the ordinary activities of a large family with a special-needs child.

Audiences seem captivated by the small and large dramas of family life and the interactions of so many people within the confines of one home (LaFayette 2009). The motivations for inviting cameras into one's home for hours, days, and weeks at a time surely vary from reality family to reality family, but in each, the children are not legally required to give assent or consent. Perhaps a 4- or 5-year-old may not mind his or her sadness or temper being captured on camera, but a 14- or 15-year-old certainly is more aware of how those viewing individual and family scenes may interpret or misinterpret their meaning. Just as ethicists have debated the impact on family members of politicians or entertainers involuntarily drawn into the public arena, the voluntary surrender of the private lives of one's children so they can be showcased on television and the internet deserves serious consideration as well. What is the impact on the children during the programs' life spans, and what happens when the programs are cancelled and the cameras are gone? How does such public living affect the quality of the family life? What is the impact of sharing these family images, and who bears responsibility?

Miley and Hannah Make the (Cash) Registers Sing

Walk through virtually any big-box retailer, and you'll see them on almost every category of merchandise: bedsheets and comforters; tooth-brushes and soap dishes; cups, bowls, and sandwich containers; T-shirts, jeans, and underwear; jewelry and purses; colognes and cameras; bike helmets and fishing poles; dolls, posters, and games; and DVDs and CDs.

But wait, there's more—bedroom furniture, entertainment consoles, hampers, and wastebaskets—all decorated with the smiling face and logo of the latest 'tween-age Disney star. The early days of marketing Davy Crockett coonskin hats have given way to a universe of brand logos representing personalities such as Lizzie McGuire, Hannah Montana, the Jonas Brothers, or Demi Lovato, and the images sell with great success in stores and through branded and retail websites. *People* magazine (Dagostino et al. 2008) estimates that the Hannah Montana merchandise alone, including video games, books, CDs, DVDs of the program, and now a self-titled film, has earned $1 billion.

The Disney Consumer Products website describes its strategy of converting viewers in more than 100 countries to image consumers: "Disney Consumer Products takes that enthusiasm to the next level with compelling 'tween merchandise, from fashion and home, toys and electronics, to stationery, books and much more." The strategy must work. Disney said sales of its licensed merchandise comprised about 40 percent of the U.S. and Canadian market in 2007 (Hunt 2008).

The success in marketing these products in some ways echoes the plot line of the Disney Channel leader, *Hannah Montana*, reported by Disney as the most-viewed television program by girls age 6 to 14 (Hunt 2008). In the program, Miley Stewart, played by Miley Cyrus, is a "normal" high school student living in California with her widowed father, a songwriter and musician himself, and one brother. But Miley has another life as well. By donning a long blonde wig and changing into glitzier clothing, she transforms into Hannah for her life as a fabulously successful rock star. With a simple change of costume, she enters an entirely new life of excitement and adulation. The savvy children and 'tween shoppers understand that message, which may help explain the appeals of the branded jeans, T-shirts, canopied bed, and, yes, wig: Change your look, change your life.[3]

The new Disney characters differ fundamentally from the animated images of the princesses that have become mythic icons. An animated film may become so familiar that every lyric and every line can be parroted, but children understand these are just stories. In contrast, the Hannah Montana character is a real young woman who is the actual daughter of the actor who plays her father on the program. Her concert tours as the Hannah character and Miley are real performances, filling huge concert venues, and her recordings are of Miley Cyrus singing as Hannah. The plot of the 2009 film, *Hannah Montana: The Movie*, ironically acknowledges Miley's struggle to remain a person of integrity, to retain her home-grown

Tennessee values rather than to adopt the self-centered lifestyle caricatured in the film by a fight in a shoe store with model Tyra Banks.

The struggle is not always a fairy tale. The controversy that resulted from an Annie Leibovitz photo spread of the young teenager draped in a sheet in the June, 2008, *Vanity Fair* focused on the appropriateness of the sexualization of the Disney star.[4] Who was being photographed—Hannah Montana or Miley Stewart or Miley Cyrus, and how might a 'tween audience member know the difference? The confusion in image represents, in an observable way, the commodification not only of the 'tween stars but also of their audiences, who may not be critically aware of the intense marketing involved in the basic plot choices and the merchandising of each element.

"Poverty Porn" or Consciousness Raising?

The 2009 recipient of the Oscar for Best Picture provided images of children a world away from Tennessee or California. *Slumdog Millionaire*, directed by Daniel Boyle and distributed by Fox Searchlight, offers a graphically violent, emotionally gripping, and cinematically beautiful account of two brothers and a girl they befriend, as children and then as young adults, as they struggle to survive as orphans in the slums of Mumbai, India. The child actors, two of whom actually came from poor backgrounds in India, portray characters shown in the film as victims of cruelty, violence, abuse, exploitation, and neglect who unite to protect each other. For example, one segment shows the captive children being trained to act as beggars, and, in one scene, the film shows a child's eyes being burned out to enhance his ability to gain the sympathy of tourists.

The award-winning film was lauded for the quality of its acting and direction but criticized by some for its depiction of poverty and pain. Alice Miles, writing in the *TimesOnline* (2009), called it "poverty porn." She writes, "When we are suckered into enjoying scenes of absolute horror among children in slums on the other side of the world, even dubbing them comedy, we ought to question where our moral compass is pointing" (2009, para. 16). The depictions did seem to nudge the moral compass toward compassion, at least in some viewers. The *Telegraph* reported a sharp upswing in the number of inquiries about adopting Indian children in the days immediately following the film's Oscar success, with requests rising from about 500 to as many as 1,400 ("*Slumdog Millionaire* Results" 2009, para. 2). Richard Turner, the fundraising director for the British ActionAid's fundraising activities, was quoted as saying, "We're calling it the Slumdog effect.

We haven't seen such a high level of interest in one country for a long time" ("*Slumdog Millionaire* Results" 2009, para. 2).

More overt attempts to use children to arouse a sympathetic level of interest are often found in the advertisements or public service announcements for international nonprofits (Dogra 2007). The advertisements almost always emphasize the images: large, dark eyes peering wistfully at the camera; ragged clothing; skinny limbs; swollen bellies; and skin of all hues. Rows of photos of children in need of medical attention. The smiling African or Asian girl, joyful in the midst of extreme poverty. The text or voice-over speaks of malnourishment, neglect, and war. These are the children of want, used as promotional devices for various charitable groups seeking to raise money for aid projects. Whether from South America, Africa, Southeast Asia, or Appalachia, they represent a vast horde of those not photographed who also stand in need. Susan Moeller (2002) explains the impact of these types of photos:

> There are few other obvious innocents in the world than children. . . . The American media feature images of Kosovo orphans, young Ethiopian famine victims, Sierra Leone amputee survivors, preadolescent Thai prostitutes or shantytown urchins in Brazil, for example, because the children seem, evidently, to be innocent victims of situations beyond their control. (49)

Yet relying on a single photo, grouped pictures, or video or film images may make it difficult to establish fully the social, economic, and political contexts of the child or children depicted. *Slumdog Millionaire* and its film images offer some truth, as do the more traditional fundraising iconic photos: Some children are victims. Yet the distortion occurs and the stereotype is created when only children are represented and when it is the only way and the only time children of some world regions are photographed and depicted. Repetition of uncontextualized images of children as victims of war or poverty enables audiences to ignore the problems represented because they have become desensitized to the horror of the image, so overwhelmed by the frequency of its appearance they no longer believe anything can change, or too emotionally aroused by the beauty of the image to fully take it seriously. Whichever reaction, we victimize the victims again.

Finding different, even jarring, ways to portray the truth visually may help overcome the problems of stereotyping, and audiences may be willing to respond to the new images with more active viewing, looking beyond the surface visuals to prevent the response of turning the page or flipping the channel to avoid dealing with the real issues. To mark the 10th anniversary of the adoption of the UN Convention on the Rights of the Child, the Norwegian government and UNICEF fostered the adoption of "The Oslo Challenge" in 1999 (Child Rights Information Network 2009) that called for media professionals to, among other areas of improvement, "work ethically and professionally according to sound media practices and to

Cameroon Armed Forces Navy Lt. Cmdr. Clement Fru Fon gives stuffed animals at the Save the Children Alliance Orphanage in Limbe, Cameroon, 2009. (Courtesy of Mass Communication Specialist 2nd Class David Holmes.)

develop and promote media codes of ethics in order to avoid sensationalism, stereotyping (including by gender) or undervaluing of children and their rights."[5]

Sexualizing Images of and for Children

Too often, the images of children and adolescents found in film, television, and advertising carry the explicit message that one's worth is proven only by one's beauty and sexuality. The 2006 film *Little Miss Sunshine*, winner of the 2007 Oscar for Best Screenplay and the Best Supporting Actor Oscar for Alan Arkin, challenges that message in a subversive way. Directed by Valerie Faris and Jonathan Dayton and distributed by Fox Searchlight, the film depicts a dysfunctional family on a road trip to a children's beauty pageant several states away (Puig 2006). Participating in the pageant is the dream of 9-year-old Olive, a plump girl with glasses, played by actress Abigail Breslin. In the emotional climax, Olive comes on stage at the pageant to perform a highly sexualized strip bar dance routine she's

Beauty pageant contestants at the National Rice Festival, Crowley, Louisiana, 1938, taken by Russell Lee of the Farm Security Administration. (Courtesy of the Library of Congress.)

learned from her porn- and heroin-addicted grandfather. The film satirizes the child-beauty-factory aspect of such pageants, evoking an ironic recall of the JonBenet Ramsey tragedy, through its selection of the cliché-busting actress, and yet it does so by including the sexual overlay of the dance—darkly funny and yet socially tragic.

Though media critics have questioned the use of children as sexual objects for years, and Congress and the U.S. Supreme Court continue to grapple with the legal limits that can be placed on extreme portrayals, the speed of internet downloads and the rise of digital imaging have made it easier than ever to exploit children through pornography. As new media proliferate, the ability to create crisper, faster, and more explicit images also grows—as does the danger to the children involved. The *New York Times* investigated the increasing number of websites that offer sexually explicit, nearly nude photos of children in requested specific poses (Eichenwald 2006). The paper argues these model websites are marketed to those interested in "original photographs of scantily clad under-age children" (para. 5). The endangerment of the children used in such photo sites is obvious and terrifying. The impact on other children who may become targets of sexual assault is certainly present, if not as direct, if these images do prompt sexual activities with children.

Perhaps viewers are less shocked by these explicit digital images because of the almost routine way in which girls are sexualized in mainstream media offerings, from advertising to films to television. Some indicators suggest sexual desirability may be critical for a child to be included on screen as a character. Stacy Smith and Crystal Cook (2008) analyzed more than 4,000 characters depicted in the best-selling 400 films rated G, PG, PG-13, and R released between 1990 and September 4, 2006. Though there were far fewer female than male characters, the female roles showed a distinct pattern: "Over half of the female characters children see in movie content are depicted in a nurturing and stereotypical manner. In stark contract, another significant proportion of the females in film are shown in a hyper-sexualized fashion" (14) through clothing and body shape. Even the G-rated films showed females, particularly animated characters, with an unrealistic body shape.

Analysis of 1,034 episodes of children's television programs from 12 different outlets found similar results (Smith and Cook 2008). There were twice as many male characters as females, but the females were four times as likely to be shown in sexy clothing, even on animated programs. Unexpected? Not among the plethora of advertisements, films, television programs, websites, and magazines that offer repeated images of children, 'tweens, and teens—particularly females—as beautiful, sexual, and available.

Children as Subjects, Not Objects

The creators of images have great power; they choose what is captured within the field of vision and frame it according to their viewpoint. Adult subjects can reasonably be expected to understand the opportunity, the benefits, and the risks involved through such exposure. Children, however, may not have such an understanding, and they may lack the power or the opportunity even to make the decision themselves to become the focus of mediated attention. Because of their age, their inexperience, and their dependence, children are largely subject to the choices of adults and the resulting rewards, issues, or injuries.

Objectifying children to sell a new reality program or so the children themselves become a merchandised brand turns them into an adult-created commodity. Decontextualizing children to represent causes may devalue the child, the image, and the organization. Sexualizing children for the amusement of adults is inherently harmful. Understanding that children are subjects, rather than objects, in imaging may help deflect some of the stereotypes noted above. Image gatherers—photographers, illustrators, directors, editors, or videographers—must remember that pervasive images portrayed in print and broadcast media create symbolic realities.

Audiences, too, must accept their responsibilities to discern and to question images they encounter. Viewers need to understand that each lens sees and defines reality differently; that each photo is, at best, one statement of what may be multiple truths; and that a photo may be an idealized vision held by the one with the lens. Adults may be taught to discount photos in advertisements, to look at different networks' video-tapes, and to look at how different photographers shot the same story. But children come to visual messages without learned skepticism. Consequently, media images of children geared primarily *for* children have a great deal of power to define reality. Certainly, media images of children have the ability to establish the *truth* for children as they see themselves in the images portraying children on screens, on packages, or on the page. Smallness in size or age should not provide an excuse for smallness in the representation of children and young people. Dignity and respect do not have age requirements.

Notes

1. See http://tlc.discovery.com/tv/jon-and-kate/jon-and-kate.html (accessed March 6, 2010).
2. See http://tlc.discovery.com/tv/18-kids-and-counting/duggar-family.html (accessed March 6, 2010).
3. See http://dcp.smugmug.com/gallery/2415763#499968961_QzUBL (accessed March 6, 2010). "The Hannah Montana/Miley Cyrus Singing Doll plays the song 'Hoedown' and is the first Miley Cyrus Singing Doll based on the movie in which Miley sings." Suggested retail price for the doll in 2009 was $21.99. Source: Disney Consumer Products.
4. See http://disembedded.wordpress.com/2008/04/30/annie-leibovitz-the-controversial-miley-cyrus-vanity-fair-photographs/ (accessed March 6, 2010).
5. A summary of the challenge is available at www.mediawise.org.uk/files/uploaded/Oslo%20Challenge.pdf (accessed March 6, 2010).

Sources

Child Rights Information Network. 2009. *Representations of children in news media: Revising the Oslo challenge conference report.* Institute of Education, London, and the Open University, April 22. http://www.crin.org/docs/oslo.pdf (accessed March 7, 2010).

CNN.com. 2009. Authorities: "Balloon Boy" incident was a hoax. October 18. http://www.cnn.com/2009/US/10/18/colorado.balloon.investigation/index.html (accessed March 7, 2010).

Dagostino, Mark, et al. 2008. Hollywood's richest kids. *People*, 69, 96–102.

Dogra, Nandita. 2007. "Reading NGOs visually": Implications of visual images for NGO management. *Journal of International Development* 19, 161–171.

Eichenwald, Kurt. 2006. With child sex sites on the run, nearly nude photos hit the web. *New York Times*, August 20. http://www.nytimes.com/2006/08/20/business/20model.html (accessed March 7, 2010).

Elber, Lynn. 2007. Producer defends reality shows that puts children alone in uninhabited New Mexico town. *Associated Press*, July 19.

Goff, Karen Goldberg. 2009. Reality TV gets religion: Christian families' faith co-stars on shows. *Washington Times*, March 22, M17.

Hibberd, James. 2007. The founding of 'Kid Nation': How CBS navigated legal, PR and logistical shoals to produce key show. *Television Week*, July 16, 1.

Hiltbrand, David, and Lini S. Kadaba. 2009. Jon & Kate minus love: Show on hiatus. *Philadelphia Inquirer*, June 24, E1.

Hunt, Aaron. 2008. Disney's 2007 holiday best sellers top consumer wish lists. *Business Wire News*, January 10.

Lafayette, Jon. 2009. TLC adds to its TV family; 'Table for 12' joins big-brood lineup. *Television Week*, March 9.

Miles, Alice. 2009. Shocked by Slumdog's poverty porn. TimesOnline, January 14. http://www.timesonline.co.uk/tol/comment/columnists/guest_contributors-article5511650.ece (accessed March 7, 2010).

Moeller, Susan D. 2002. A hierarchy of innocence: The media's use of children in the telling of international news. *Harvard International Journal of Press/Politics* 7, 36–56.

Puig, Claudia. 2006. 'Sunshine' beams, but darkly. *USA Today*, July 26. http://usatoday.com/life/movies/reviews/2006-07-25-little-miss-sunshine_x.htm (accessed March 7, 2010).

Selter, Brian. 2009a. A big crowd for 'Jon & Kate' finale. *New York Times*, November 24.

Selter, Brian. 2009b. Now it's Kate minus Jon minus 8? *New York Times*, October 7, C1.

Slumdog Millionaire results in increased charity help for Indian children. 2009. *Telegraph*, February 28. http://www.telegraph.co.uk/news/worldnews/asia/india/4864717/Slumdog-Millionaire-results-in-increased-charity-help-for-Indian-children.html (accessed March 7, 2010).

Smith, Stacy L., and Crystal Allene Cook. 2008. Gender stereotypes: An analysis of popular films and TV. http://www.thegeenadavisinstitute.org (accessed March 7, 2010).

Wiltz, Teresa. 2008. On reality TV, who's minding the kids? More shows raise issue of exploitation. *Washington Post*, July 26, A1.

Wyatt, Edward. 2007. 'Kid Nation' lesson: Be careful what you pitch. *New York Times*, August 25, B7.

Chapter 17

Pepsi's Generation Gap

Bonnie L. Drewniany

Youth has prevailed as a rallying cry in Pepsi commercials since 1961. Three weeks after President John F. Kennedy proclaimed, "The torch has been passed to a new generation of Americans," ad agency BBDO (Batten, Barton, Durstine, & Osborne) positioned Pepsi as the soft drink "For those who think young" (McDonough 2003). Four years later, the agency launched the now-ubiquitous "Pepsi Generation" slogan.

Youth continued to be a theme throughout the 48-year relationship between Pepsi and BBDO. In the process, Pepsi was propelled "from an off-price knockoff to a heroic cola warrior" (Garfield 2008), while BBDO won numerous accolades for creativity, including recognition for creating one of the top campaigns of the twentieth century by the industry bible, *Advertising Age* (Top 100 Advertising Campaigns 1999).

Ironically, baby boomers, those 76 million Americans born between 1946 and 1964, were targeted in the early commercials and later became the antithesis of Pepsi's youth movement. People over 30 are rarely seen in Pepsi commercials today. When they are shown, they are often the brunt of jokes that perpetuate ageist stereotypes.

This chapter explores age stereotypes that are portrayed in Pepsi[1] commercials that have aired during the ultimate advertising phenomenon, the Super Bowl, the American National Football League's championship. Sometimes dubbed "the Ad Bowl," the Super Bowl is the only media vehicle that allows advertisers to broadcast to about half the nation, the estimated viewing audience for the game, at the same time. While the Academy and

The Thunderbirds of the U.S. Air Force perform a flyover during the playing of the national anthem to start Super Bowl XLIII, February 1, 2009, in Tampa, Florida. (Courtesy of U.S. Military/Staff Sgt. Bradley Lail, USAF.)

Emmy awards, baseball's World Series, and the NCAA's college basketball title game have seen viewership decline over the past few decades, the Super Bowl has gained in popularity (Farhi 2007). The 2010 game attracted an average audience of 106.5 million U.S. viewers, making it the most-watched television program of all time (Nielsenwire 2010b).

Part of the attraction of the Super Bowl is the ads. Viewers welcome the commercials that run during the Super Bowl, which are often more entertaining than the game. In fact, a recent study found that 51 percent of viewers prefer the commercials to the game itself (Nielsenwire 2010a).

As a result, advertisers such as Pepsi view the Super Bowl as the premier advertising vehicle. Since the late 1980s, Pepsi has used the Super Bowl to launch new products, campaign slogans, and package designs. A company spokesperson explained the decision to run in the most expensive advertising medium:

We can't afford not to advertise in the Super Bowl. When you consider the millions of people who are watching it, and all of the discussion that goes on about the spots, the value is pretty good. It's one of the few opportunities we have to reach a multigenerational audience that is as focused on the spots as they are the game (Lemke 2009).

Pepsi became a popular mainstay of the Super Bowl and earned 25 "Top 10" spots in the coveted *USA Today* Ad Meter, including three number one spots (*USA Today* Ad Meter 1989). Their winning advertising formula includes humor, music, and celebrities. However, most of the laughs come at the expense of older people.

Why Age Stereotypes Matter

Society looks at visuals in advertising for cues on how various generations behave. If we believe that advertising has the ability to shape our values and our view of the world, then it is essential that advertisers become aware of how they portray different groups. Conversely, if we believe that advertising mirrors society, advertisers have a responsibility to ensure that what is portrayed is accurate and representative (Moriarty, Mitchell, and Wells 2009, 71).

Stereotypes in advertising and elsewhere are particularly damaging to children and others who haven't developed skepticism for and critical understanding of the media. "Media images have the ability to establish the *truth image* for children as they see themselves in the images portraying children" (McKee 2003, 159, emphasis in original). Negative images of older people have similar damaging effects. "They affect people's perceptions of the elderly, which can be life threatening; they affect the elderly's perception of their own mental and physical health, which can have a negative impact on that health" (Smythe 2003, 169). Stereotypes are also troublesome from an economic perspective. Findings indicate that "advertisers who continue to portray the elderly inaccurately in their advertisements may well suffer adverse consequences" (Festervand and Lumpkin 1989, 183).

Stereotypes of Older People

Older People Are Out of Touch

Although today's 50-plus consumers are more likely to switch brands than those in their 20s and 30s (Bouchez 2009), advertising portrays older people as rigid in their thinking (Smythe 2003). Pepsi's 1989 "Glasnost" commercial treats this stereotype as a universal truth. Set in the Soviet Union and spoken entirely in Russian with English subtitles, "Glasnost" opens on a teenage boy dancing to blasting rock music as his father reprimands him, "Noise! Noise! You call that music?" The commercial cuts to a street scene as teenagers skateboard past three older women who are wearing babushkas, drab coats, and sensible shoes: "Look! What is this craziness?" Cut back to the father–son scene: The boy is looking in a mirror, checking out his wardrobe of faded jeans and a leather jacket. The father sighs, "Look at you! Do you have to dress like that?" The mother, who is seen only briefly at the end of the commercial, is the only older person in the commercial who is in touch with the changes that are taking place. She tries to calm the father by giving him a Pepsi: "Yuri . . . come on, lighten up."[2]

Pepsi uses the out-of-touch imagery as a shortcut to depict rival Coca-Cola as old and boring. Pepsi is young and fun. A 1990 pre-game Super Bowl commercial shows deliverymen accidentally switching shipments of soft drinks. Pepsi is delivered to the Shady Acres retirement home and Coca-Cola is delivered to a fraternity house. "Coke? Pepsi? What's the difference?" asks one of the deliverymen. The camera cuts to older people skateboarding and dancing with boom boxes on their shoulders. "Rock 'n' roll is okay, but I prefer rap," says an older woman. Meanwhile, the fraternity brothers are about to nod off as they play a game of bingo accompanied by old-fashioned music in the background.[3]

Out of Touch? Then You Gotta Have It!

"Recognizing the spending potential of the aging baby-boom population" (Miller, Wright, and Shenitz 1992, 39), Pepsi launched a new slogan, "Gotta Have It," for the 1992 Super Bowl. A pregame spot set the stage for the new slogan as a farmer drives his pickup truck through an old Pepsi billboard. The "Choice of a New Generation" slogan, which Pepsi had been touting since 1984, lies scattered on the ground. A festival springs up around the collapsed billboard in Pepsi's opening spot of the game. A teenager wearing sunglasses and a hip-looking black leather jacket comments, "At first I was upset that all these old people started drinking it. And then I said, 'Hey. They're people, too.'" The commercial cuts to a group of elderly people as one exclaims, "It's just like Woodstock!"

Another spot during the Super Bowl featured celebrities who try to come up with a new slogan to replace "The Choice of a New Generation" catchphrase. New York Yankees catcher and manager Yogi Berra, famed for his malapropisms, offers the following gem: "Pepsi tastes great. But only if you drink it." In the end, it's neither a celebrity nor a wise adult who comes up with the perfect slogan but a little girl in pigtails: "If all these people gotta have it, why don't they just say, 'Pepsi. Gotta Have It'?" Berra has the last word: "I have two words for you: 'Gotta Have It.'"

The final spot features quick cuts of people of all ages enjoying Pepsi. The older generation looks a bit daft as they dance next to their youthful counterparts. An older woman, wearing a frumpy housedress, stands in front of her husband, who is doing cartwheels on the lawn: "Henry's only regret is that he started drinking Pepsi this late in life."[4]

The aim of the "Gotta Have It" campaign was "to turn the Pepsi Generation into an all-inclusive affair, in which Pepsi is the drink of choice for all generations, not just younger consumers," according to a BBDO spokesman (McCarthy 1992). The "Gotta Have It" campaign was criticized for trying to play to aging boomers. Marketing guru Jack Trout said, "'Gotta have it' was trying to be everything to everyone. They tried to be like Coke—it was a dramatic and wrong departure" (Winters 1993, 3).

While Pepsi may have been trying to go after everyone, the commercials portray older people as frumpy and dotty, which is a rather odd way to woo that generation. The next year, Pepsi dumped "Gotta have it" and went with a much more brash approach, "Be young, have fun, drink Pepsi."

Return to a Youth Focus: "Be Young, Have Fun, Drink Pepsi"

Pepsi launched its "Be Young" campaign in the 1993 Super Bowl. One spot showed two boys drinking a Pepsi when one asks the other what he wants to do. Thinking he's been asked what he wants to do for the rest of his life, the boy envisions his future. He finishes school, gets married, and has kids. As he continues to get older, his life gets more depressing. He "kisses butt" at the office, makes middle management, gives up Pepsi, and starts drinking prune juice. He finally gives it all up, retires to Miami, and buys some white shoes and pants that come up to his chest. The other boy interrupts him: "No man, what do you want to do *this afternoon*?" The commercial cuts to the beach and the boys going wild.[5]

A second spot in 1993 uses a similar setup. Here, a teenager describes how much of one's life is spent doing boring activities such as working

(13.5 years), sleeping (24.5 years), attending weddings (1.7 years), and listening to boring lectures (3.2 years). Old people are shown doing the boring activities, and scenes of young people drinking Pepsi and doing wild, crazy things are intercut throughout the commercial. The teenage narrator reminds us that we only have 5.1 months for pure, unadulterated, mindless fun.

Two other 1993 commercials poke fun at the boring lives of adults by spoofing public television shows on cooking and gardening (this is before cable channels made these topics cool). The commercials, which are excruciatingly slow-paced in the beginning, are abruptly interrupted with the message "Some day this will be interesting to you. But until that day comes. . . ." Cut to quick-moving images of teenagers enjoying life and drinking Pepsi.

The Woodstock Generation Adrift: Where Have All the Ideals Gone?

Woodstock is one of the iconic images that is "cemented into our cultural lore" (Groen 2009, R6). So what better setting in which to make a statement about the ideals of youth and the compromises of adults? Pepsi's 1994 "Summer of Love" commercial featured its version of Woodstock's 25th reunion. Canned Heat's "Going Up the Country" plays as Baby Boomers check their gas-guzzling BMWs with valets. The anti-establishment, flower children of the 1960s have grown up to be the pro-establishment, greedy consumers of the 1990s. These well-dressed bankers, golfers, and executives are glued to their cell phones and lament that the Bethel, New York, farm hasn't changed in 25 years.[6]

Boomer Bodies: They-Are-a-Changin'

Despite findings that today's older Americans are healthier, more affluent, and better educated than seniors in the past (Mitchell 1998), advertisers stereotype older people as feeble, foolish, and inept (Goldman 1993, B8). Pepsi uses these ageist stereotypes as a way to get some laughs. The years haven't been kind to the Woodstock generation in Pepsi's "Summer of Love." Members of Jefferson Airplane complain that they're on a low-sodium, low-fat diet and feel terrible. Country Joe McDonald, who played at the original festival, can't remember playing there. Children look on in disgust as their aging, out-of-shape boomer parents do the twist. "Think they'll go skinny dipping again?" asks one. "I hope not!" replies the other. The voiceover sums it all up: "Wouldn't it be nice if your youth was as easy to hold onto as an ice-cold Pepsi?"

If the image of adults skinny-dipping is tough for youth to imagine, the thought of older people having sex must be unthinkable. When Bob Dole appeared in a 2001 Super Bowl commercial and talked about his little blue friend that helped revitalize him, the audience was set for another commercial about sexual impotence since he had appeared in a commercial for Viagra. Set up to resemble a pharmaceutical ad, Dole walks along the beach with a golden retriever and talks directly into the camera about his "faithful little blue friend" that helps him "feel youthful, vigorous, and most importantly, vital again." Just as the audience is convinced this is a Viagra spot, Dole holds up a can of Pepsi. The commercial cuts to the interior of a convenience store and a clerk says, "Are the revitalizing effects of Pepsi-Cola right for you? Check with your local convenience store counter clerk." A warning appears on the screen: "Use only as directed." The commercial cuts back to Dole, who does a back flip on the beach and says, "I feel like a kid again." Unlike the medication, no warning is given if the youthful effect lasts longer than four hours.[7]

Stereotypes of Younger People

Generation Next: Brash, Cocky Know-It-Alls

It's not just older people who are stereotyped in Pepsi commercials. Young adults are often depicted as brash know-it-alls who treat adults with disrespect. Shaquille O'Neal and a little boy star in a 1994 send-up of one of Coca-Cola's classic commercials that featured the NFL star "Mean" Joe Greene.[8] After an intense basketball match, the boy grabs the last Pepsi from the cooler. He smiles and holds it up to the basketball legend. Thinking his young fan is about to share his ice-cold Pepsi, Shaq reaches out for the bottle. The little boy refuses, even after Shaq begs.[9]

Images of teens flash on the screen in the opening of a 2004 commercial. Superimposed over their images are the words "Incriminated," "Accused," "Busted," and "Charged." Fourteen-year-old Annie Leith says defiantly, "I'm one of the kids who was prosecuted for downloading music free off the Internet. And I'm here to announce in front of 100 million people that we're still going to download music free off of the Internet." As she says this, details about the Pepsi iTunes music giveaway are superimposed on the screen. She adds a final rebellious statement, "And there's not a thing anybody can do about it." Leith, who along with her sister and brother illegally downloaded 950 songs over three years, planned to use some of her undisclosed ad fee to help pay for the settlement with the Recording Industry Association of America (Howard 2004).[10]

Other kids also are depicted as know-it-alls in Pepsi's commercials. It's a little girl who bests the adults and comes up with the "Gotta Have It" slogan after several failed efforts by grownups. Despite being cast as know-it-alls, Pepsi gets a few laughs when it's clear that children don't always know what they're talking about. In the Woodstock reunion commercial, a boy says they're witnessing an important historic event: "Watergate."

Innocent Fun, or Something Much More Decadent?

Pepsi uses children to say and do things that would be inappropriate if done by adults. A 26-year-old Cindy Crawford, dressed in high-cut shorts and a low-cut top, slithers past two awestruck boys in a 1992 commercial. The sultry super model sips a Pepsi, and the Hollies' "Just One Look" plays throughout. As one of the boy's jaw drops almost to his knees, he utters the punch line, "Is that a great new Pepsi can or what?"[11]

The Cindy Crawford commercial gives viewers permission to ogle the supermodel through the eyes of innocent boys. Media critic Peter DeBenedittis (n.d.) found this commercial extremely unsettling:

> What's disturbing about this commercial is that the boys haven't reached puberty. Their plumbing isn't working yet. And Pepsi shows them being come onto sexually by Cindy Crawford. What kind of disconnect do you think happens to boys when their physical bodies are not yet able to perform, yet their mental and emotional bodies are being sexualized? What kinds of relationship do you think guys sexualized at age 10 are going to be capable of having when they're adults? At best this commercial is emotional incest. At worst, it's child abuse.

In a 1997 spot, Cindy Crawford and fellow supermodels Tyra Banks and Bridget Hall blow kisses at a newborn baby. The Flamingos' "I Only Have Eyes for You" plays as Cindy leans close into the camera and says, "I love you." The baby winks and blows back a smooch as the voiceover says, "Norman Phenny. Pepsi drinker for life."[12] Again, there were serious concerns:

> Think about the message we're taking in along with the laughter. Ask a psychiatrist what happens when a male infant is sexually abused. You'll find out that, in most cases, the baby will never be able to have a functional sex life. Those who overcome the physical dysfunctions, still have to deal with deep-seated fear whenever they are intimate with a woman. Have you wondered why so many guys are withdrawn or violent in their relationships? This generation of men has to cope with the psychological damage inflicted on them as children in order for Pepsi and other companies to sell products. (DeBenedittis n.d.)

The average viewer may not see the same level of debauchery in the Cindy Crawford commercials as DeBenedittis does. However, what would happen if a commercial replaced Crawford with a famous male model? Would it be OK for a man to be overtly sexual toward children? By using children, Pepsi has made these sexist acts seem like innocent fun.

A New Agency, a New Generation of Advertising?

Pepsi's 48-year relationship with BBDO ended late in 2008. The new agency of record, TBWA\Chiat\Day, continued the Super Bowl tradition in 2009 but with a twist: The young and older generations are united. Bob Dylan sings "Forever Young" as rapper Will.i.am chimes in. Footage from the 1970s is intercut with images from 2009. Concertgoers wave cigarette lighters in one century and cell phones in the other. The older generation has John Belushi, while the younger generation has Jack Black. Gumby is the favorite green animated character of the 1970s, while Shrek takes the spot in 2009.[13]

The commercial did well in the *USA Today* Ad Meter, making it into the top 10 (*USA Today* Ad Meter 2009). But some observers had their reservations, including an MTV news commentator:

> The point, as we are reminded at clip's end, is that 'every generation refreshes the world' and that we are supposed to feel hopeful, like keepers of the flame or makers of great art. But all it made me feel was *sad*. . . . There's no permanence in our generation. . . . Nothing is tangible. . . . If you stop and look around for a second, you'll notice that things are pretty lousy right now. They will probably get worse before they get better. So, you know, in

a cripplingly depressing aspect, Pepsi's commercial was a rousing success. (Montgomery 2009)

Perhaps intentionally to attract publicity, Pepsi and its new agency made headlines in 2010 by announcing they would not run a commercial in Super Bowl XLIV.

Discussion and Conclusions

Pepsi's portrayal of youth and older people is often unflattering. Despite this, their Super Bowl ads are frequently among the top-rated commercials of the game. Why would young people like commercials that portray them as brash know-it-alls? Why would older people like commercials that portray them as frumpy sellouts? The answer may be found in the use of humor and music, which put viewers in a positive mood.

Pepsi uses parodies to get a few laughs in several commercials. The 1993 parodies of cooking and gardening shows make us chuckle at how incredibly boring educational programming used to be. The humor makes us forgive Pepsi's jab at the boring lives of older people.

Bob Dole's 2001 spoof of a Viagra commercial is funny on several counts. The parody of prescription drug ads is dead-on, complete with a warning at the end of the message. The fact that Bob Dole agreed to pitch "his little blue friend" makes the commercial priceless. The self-deprecating humor makes Pepsi (and Bob Dole) seem approachable.

Likewise, Pepsi's 1994 send-up of Coca-Cola's classic Mean Joe Greene commercial catches viewers off-guard. We're expecting the boy to give his Pepsi to Shaq. The fact that he refuses makes us laugh. In a society that puts athletes and celebrities on pedestals, it's fun to see a superstar get put in his place.

Pepsi's ads also make us laugh because they contain human truths. Many of us know Boomers who have abandoned their 1960s ideals and have become greedy sellouts. Many of us have lamented the fact that "kids these days" don't have a respect for history. It's these human truths that make Pepsi's "Summer of Love" commercial funny.

Pepsi's ads sometimes show the opposite of what viewers know as human truths. Skateboarding, rap-loving senior citizens and bingo-playing fraternity brothers are totally unexpected in the 1990 pregame commercial. The commercial gets a few laughs by showing the opposite of viewers' personal knowledge and stereotypes of what goes on in fraternity houses and retirement homes. Pepsi doesn't say that older people don't enjoy rap. The viewers' own beliefs do.

Music is another device that helps make the Pepsi commercials so likeable. Pepsi frequently uses music from the Baby Boom generation to set a positive mood in its commercials. The music transports the older generation back to a happy time of peace, love, and rock and roll. The younger generation loves this music, too.

> The trend of youngsters craving oldies seems to be gaining momentum. Kids are snatching up Beatles and Led Zeppelin discs, flocking to ZZ Top and Steve Miller concerts, researching the troubled histories of Lynyrd Skynyrd and Black Sabbath, and scouring their parents' record collections for Jimi Hendrix licks and Allman Brothers Band jams (Gundersen 1994).

Canned Heat's "Going Up the Country" brings Boomers back to the ideals of Woodstock in Pepsi's 1994 "Summer of Love" commercial. Hank Williams' "Your Cheatin' Heart" helps narrate the 1996 spot in which a Coca-Cola employee sneaks (or at least tries to sneak) a can of Pepsi out

A woman on a sidewalk in Bijapur, India, under an advertisement for Pepsi. (Courtesy of Claude Renault.)

of a cooler. The Hollies' "Just One Look" has viewers singing along in the 1992 spot that shows two boys ogling Cindy Crawford. Green Day's remake of the Bobby Fuller Four's 1966 hit "I Fought the Law" adds a bit of social commentary to the 2004 spot that features a rebellious teen who insists she's going to continue downloading music for free. Bob Dylan's 2009 rendition of "Forever Young" helps Boomers remember the freedom they felt in the 1960s.

While Pepsi's ads often project ageist stereotypes, the use of humor and music puts the audience in a positive mood. The danger of this tactic is it makes the negative stereotypes easier to accept. It's like a trusted friend telling you that older people are sellouts, out of shape, and out of touch, and that young people are brash know-it-alls who really don't know much at all. Over time, you might just come to believe these stereotypes as truths. And that's no laughing matter.

Notes

1. This chapter analyzes commercials exclusively for the Pepsi brand. Soft drink brands Crystal Pepsi, Diet Pepsi, Diet Pepsi Max, Mountain Dew, Pepsi One, Pepsi Twist, and Sierra Mist, which Pepsico has also promoted in the Super Bowl, aren't analyzed due to space constraints.

2. See http://www.youtube.com/watch?v=pS6tYur34Nk (accessed March 7, 2010).

3. See http://www.youtube.com/watch?v=qCP-5xSisPA (accessed March 7, 2010).

4. See http://www.youtube.com/watch?v=xAseTDoo_w8 (accessed March 7, 2010).

5. See http://www.youtube.com/watch?v=tpIUV_EvXhM (accessed March 7, 2010).

6. See http://www.youtube.com/watch?v=wbXLY9anXt4 (accessed March 7, 2010).

7. See http://www.youtube.com/watch?v=i7oh1so-2M8 (accessed March 7, 2010).

8. See http://www.youtube.com/watch?v=xffOCZYX6F8 (accessed March 7, 2010).

9. See http://www.youtube.com/watch?v=7JZ8iQ9P9iI (accessed March 7, 2010).

10. See http://www.youtube.com/watch?v=N7-uknKhSuQ (accessed March 7, 2010).

11. See http://www.youtube.com/watch?v=AcroQsUN60s (accessed March 7, 2010).

12. See http://www.youtube.com/watch?v=rodU-UhK4qY (accessed March 7, 2010).

13. See http://www.youtube.com/watch?v=J35MV5-Dfkw (accessed March 7, 2010).

Sources

Bouchez, Brent. 2009. Your new sweet spot: The 50-plus consumer. Forbes.com, July 21. http://www.Forbes.com (accessed January 20, 2010).

DeBenedittis, Peter. N.d. Seduce me. http://www.medialiteracy.net (accessed January 20, 2010).

Farhi, Paul. 2007. The game's just the cherry on this Sunday; Super Bowl hoopla still pulls in viewers, advertisers & money. *Washington Post*, February 4, D1, D7.

Festervand, Troy, and James R. Lumpkin. 1989. Response of elderly consumers to their portrayal by advertisers. In *Advertising and society*, ed. Roxanne Hovland and Gary B. Wilcox, pp. 165–190. Lincolnwood, IL: NTC Business.

Garfield, Bob. 2008. BBDO made Pepsi what it is. November 24. http://adage.com/garfield/post/article_id=132790 (accessed January 20, 2010).

Goldman, Kevin. 1993. Seniors get little respect on Madison Avenue. *Wall Street Journal*, September 20, B8.

Groen, Rick. 2009. Amid the sex, drugs and rock 'n' roll, one guy's tepid tale. *Globe Review*, August 28, R6.

Gundersen, Edna. 1994. Kids are listening to their parents—their parents' music that is. *USA Today*, March 30, 1A, 2A.

Howard, Theresa. 2004. Pepsi ads wink at music downloading. *USA Today*, January 23, 1B.

Lemke, Tim. 2009. Coca-Cola, Pepsi in big Super ad battle. *Washington Times*, February 1, A01.

McCarthy, M., with C. Taylor, and G. Farrell. 1992. 'Gotta have it'; Pepsi's new theme and campaign to touch down on Super Bowl Sunday. *Adweek*, January 20.

McDonough, John. 2003. Pepsico, Inc. In *Encyclopedia of advertising*, pp. 1196–1201. New York: Taylor & Francis.

Miller, Annette, Lynda Wright, and Bruce Shenitz. 1992. Battle of the brown stuff. *Newsweek*, February 3, 39.

Mitchell, Susan. 1998. *American generations*. Ithaca, NY: New Strategist.

Montgomery, James. 2009. Pepsi's Bob Dylan/Will.i.am ad could have been worse. http://newsroom.mtv.com (accessed January 20, 2010).

Moriarty, Sandra, Nancy Mitchell, and William Wells. 2009. *Advertising principles and practice*. Upper Saddle River, NJ: Pearson Prentice Hall.

Nielsenwire. 2010a. Most Super Bowl viewers tune in for the commercials, Nielsen says. January 20. http://blog.nielsen.com/nielsenwire/consumer/

survey-most-super-bowl-viewers-tune-in-for-the-commercials/ (accessed January 20, 2010).

Nielsenwire. 2010b. Super Bowl XLIV most watched Super Bowl of all time. February 8. http://blog.nielsen.com/nielsenwire/media_entertainment/super-bowl-xliv-most-watched-super-bowl-of-all-time/ (accessed January 20, 2010).

Smythe, Ted Curtis. 2003. Growing old in commercials: Not always a laughing matter. In *Images that injure: Pictorial stereotypes in the media*, 2nd ed., ed. Paul Martin Lester and Susan Dente Ross, pp. 167–172. Santa Barbara, CA: Praeger.

Top 100 Advertising Campaigns. 1999. *Advertising Age* special issue: The advertising century. *Advertising Age* 70 (13): 24.

USA Today Ad Meter. 1989. The 49 Bowl ads. *USA Today*, January 23, 2B.

USA Today Ad Meter. 2009. Ad Meter 21 Super Bowl XLIII. *USA Today*, February 2, 4B.

Winters, Patricia. 1993. Pepsi harkens back to youth: "Gotta Have It" is all but gone in campaign saying, "Be Young, Have Fun." *Advertising Age*, January 25, 3.

Chapter 18

Tramp Stamps and Tribal Bands: Stereotypes of the Body Modified

Chema Salinas

For all his tattooings he was on the whole a clean, comely looking cannibal.

Herman Melville (*Moby Dick*, 1851/1926, 29)

What do you think when you see someone with a tattoo, a nontraditional piercing, or another type of body modification? Does that perception change if the person is male or female? Do you think tramp? Do you think criminal? Many people do. Yet, like everyone else, modified people are more than stereotypes. In recent years, tattooing has begun to gain a measure of acceptance in U.S. society, but large, obvious tattoos; stretched piercings; and even more extreme modifications like branding, scarification, and subdermal implants are often represented by media as indicators of sexual or criminal deviance.

This chapter suggests that media perpetuate stereotypes of people with body modifications through sexual and criminal imagery. To better understand and contextualize those stereotypes, the chapter begins with a brief history and review of body modification as it is practiced in modern U.S. society. Then common stereotypes will be highlighted, and their presence in contemporary media discussed. The analysis of the tight interweaving of the stereotypes with gender and socioeconomic class, as well as degree and type of modification, will rely upon popular depictions from television, film, and the web as touchstones for a discussion of the harm those stereotypes may cause. Concluding remarks suggest some means of addressing the harm caused by these depictions.

Tattoos, Primitivism, and Deviance

The roots of tattooing in modern Western society are commonly attributed to Captain James Cook's eighteenth-century voyage to Polynesia (DeMello 2000). But the practice runs far deeper and wider. In the oldest known example of tattooing, a 5,200-year-old frozen "ice-man" found high in the Italian Alps had numerous tattoos (Lineberry 2007). Cultures throughout the world developed unique body modification practices over time. Those practices generally carried ritual or religious significance. For instance, the Pre-Columbian culture in Mesoamerica used piercing, primarily of the ears, tongue, and genitalia, as a central element of religious life. The blood collected from these rituals was offered as a form of self-sacrifice to the gods (Joralemon 1974).

Generally, body modification in non-European cultures signified religious rituals, rites of passage, and social identification. In North America, various native tribes on the high Plains practiced the O-Kee-Pa, or Sun Dance, ritual. While underlying motivations varied by tribe and ceremony, the Sun Dance usually represented a form of rebirth. In this ritual, the chest or shoulders were pierced, and the participant was suspended over the ground from leather thongs until the flesh tore (Lawrence 1993). In Polynesia, the practice of "tatau" was used to denote members of different tribes as well as the status and social identity of individuals. The religious aspect of this form of tattooing was so integral to the culture that Christian missionaries considered it a threat to their dominance and demanded the practice cease (Utanga and Mangos 2006).

In European culture, the ancient Greeks were noted for having marked slaves and criminals with permanent visual indicators of their separation from the polis, or citizens of the communities (Fisher 2002). This forcible defilement offered a first glimpse into the Western stigmatization of body modification (see related discussion in chapter 2). Not only did the marking serve to confine people to the fringes of society, but also it gave rise to the perception of "marked" people as deviant and criminal.[1] Cook's

Taken by famed western photographer Edward S. Curtis in 1908, the image shows an Apsaroke man leaning back slightly with strips of leather attached to his chest and tethered to a pole secured by rocks, all part of the piercing ritual of the Sun Dance. (Courtesy of the Library of Congress.)

presentation of the Polynesian practice of marking the skin redoubled the dominant view of tattooing; its criminal nature became coupled with a savage, cannibalistic impression related to Eurocentric, Orientalist (Said 1979) perceptions of Polynesians and Pacific Islanders as primitive peoples.

Tattooing began gaining popularity in the United States during the Civil War. Patriotic images on soldiers and veterans served to initiate acceptance of tattoos in U.S. culture while keeping perceptions of the practice to

A woman with images tattooed or painted on her upper body, 1907. (Courtesy of the Library of Congress.)

marginalized people outside of mainstream, "civilized" society (Govenar 2000). Tattooing on soldiers and veterans remains common, and patriotic images like eagles, anchors, and flags form the basis of many traditional U.S. tattoo styles. Meanwhile, another stereotype of tattooed people became prevalent. The "circus freak," not originated but popularized by P. T. Barnum during the 1870s, became a common cultural image (Govenar 2000). Heavily tattooed people, almost entirely covered with ink, took their place alongside Native Americans, animals, and the physically deformed as sideshow attractions and subhuman objects for display. These associations, perpetuated by newspapers and magazines, helped cement tattooed people in the public consciousness as freakish, savage, and deformed.

Negative cultural implications of tattooing came to a head during the mid-twentieth century. Despite a small degree of acceptance in the higher strata of society, public sentiment led to attempts to ban tattooing altogether on the grounds that such overt markings undermined an image of professionalism (Govenar 2000). Ultimately unsuccessful, those efforts had the practical effect of relegating the actual practice of tattooing to working-class neighborhoods. As a result, tattooing remained a practice of marginalized people (Young 1990, 53). In the case of people with tattoos, marginalization was usually linked to criminality and sexual promiscuity.

Countercultural movements of the 1960s capitalized on these perceptions. One of the most prominent stereotypes of tattooed people to emerge during this period was the "biker." This embrace of tattooing within a criminal or deviant underclass reinforced the stereotype of deviance and criminality. A prominent and powerful media representation of body modification stereotypically associated modification with organized criminal groups.

Entering the "Modern"

The 1989 publication of *Modern Primitives* codified body modification and brought more extreme forms into the popular consciousness (Vale and Juno 1989). The most common forms of extreme modification are large piercings of nontraditional parts of the body like the septum, nipples, and genitals, as well as visible tattoos on the face, neck, or hands. Less common modifications include scarification (usually performed with a surgical scalpel), branding (typically with a hot or very cold iron), subdermal silicone implants that raise and texture skin (excluding breast implants), transdermal implants that project metal through the skin (such as a row of spikes on the scalp), and even more extreme surgical alterations like filed teeth, dental implants, or tongue and genitalia splitting. Indeed, the commitment level of modified people is often judged by the extremity of their engagement. Their physical alterations also serve to separate self-identified body modifiers from people who merely have tattoos or piercings. Those holding a greater sense of identification with the modification community tend to get relatively more extreme changes (Bell 2004).

Academically, body modification has been described as a rejection of mainstream society (Pitts 2003), as an attempt to deny the commodification inherent in capitalist culture (Braunberger 2000), and as a reclamation of the body as one's own (Kang and Jones 2007). Josh Adams (2009) offers one of the few direct engagements with media stereotypes, reporting that various forms of modification are framed differently. For instance, piercing is often depicted as having greater health risks and as an indication of greater social deviance than tattooing or elective cosmetic surgery. But Adams focuses on printed newspapers and magazines while ignoring the often more extreme and damaging depictions common in popular television, film, and web content. These media, which have much greater penetration and therefore greater impact than print, continually associate body modification with criminal and sexual deviance through their stereotypic depiction of characters. Media stereotypes work to reduce modified bodies to one-dimensional caricatures.

Body modification stereotypes also cause damage through explicit gender assignments. The sexualization of modified women serves to further subjugate them to common standards of beauty. While many women refer to their alterations as a rejection of mainstream values (Pitts 2003), media depictions can diminish or even negate this power. Some prominent and particularly damaging stereotypes of modified bodies are examined in the following sections using examples from the popular media.

Tramp Stamps: Promiscuity and Morbidity

The sensual and intimate nature of body modification, compounded by its association with the working class, contributes to stereotypes of modified women as overly and overtly sexualized. This stereotype even manifests itself in colloquial names given to particular tattoo styles. For instance, "tramp stamp" is a popular term for lower back tattoos on women. The sexualization implicit in that name is exemplified by two significant media depictions: a *Saturday Night Live* (SNL) sketch titled "Turlington's Lower Back Tattoo Remover," which aired in 2004, and the website SuicideGirls.com. The sketch depicts tattooing as a regrettable expression of youthful, sexual energy, while the website extends that focus into the "pornographization" of the female body.[2]

The SNL sketch is a mock advertisement for a rub-on (like deodorant) removal product for the "really cool lower back tattoo." The humor of the sketch obscures its underlying message: The youthful indiscretions that compel young women to get tramp stamps are intrinsically related to sexual promiscuity. The four women represented in the clip are all stigmatized by their lower back tattoos, which are presented in a number of absurd ways for comedic value. The first woman's tattoo, revealed as she reaches into a cupboard in the process of feeding breakfast to her children, exhibits three stereotypical images. The word "Juicy," an overt reference to sexuality, is written in cursive and bracketed by symmetrical roses and tribal blocks. The second woman's tattoo, revealed as she changes a light bulb, features a string of dancing skeletons reminiscent of the logo for the rock band Social Distortion. The third woman's tattoo, revealed as she hoists her child onto a school bus, pushes the limits of absurdity by depicting a NASCAR vehicle, the phrase "The Intimidator," and the face of the deceased NASCAR great Dale Earnhardt inexplicably wearing a fez.

The fourth woman suffers a more damaging depiction. The doctor states, "Look, here is a really cool lower back tattoo on an attractive 20-year-old girl." The image cuts away from the doctor and to the bare back of a young woman. The woman's tattoo has the phrase "Pretty Lady" bracketed by a Celtic-style design. The doctor continues, "Now watch what happens to that tattoo when that young girl becomes a 65-year-old woman." As the doctor speaks, video effects are used to age the woman's body and the tattoo. As her skin sags and wrinkles, the words "Pretty Lady" become the words "Pretty Sad." For each of the women depicted in this sketch, tattoos become a marker of promiscuity. This is reinforced by the fact that each of the first three women are shown with children.

In the final segment of the clip, Dr. Turlington touts his product as a remedy for the regrettable act of being tattooed: He states, "Soon enough, that silly mistake will be long gone. And that slight discoloration will be the only thing to remind you of that crazy weekend in Jamaica." As an African-American child enters the frame to hug his Anglo mother, the doctor continues, "Well, maybe not the only thing." The humor of the final part of this sketch derives from its message that the mother engaged in an interracial sexual fling and the tattoo is a symbolic marking of the stereotypical promiscuity of modified women. The tattoo and the inter-racial child are both given as odious indices of sexually "loose" women. There is a historical precedent for this type of stigmatization in Nathaniel Hawthorne's (1850) *The Scarlet Letter*. In that novel, women accused of adultery are forced to wear a red letter "A" on their clothing. The letter, like the "tramp stamp" tattoo, is presented and understood by society as an indicator of promiscuity.

Hypersexualized depictions of female body modifications are even more egregious on the popular website and cultural phenomenon

SuicideGirls.com. On its splash page, SuicideGirls claims to be "a community that celebrates alternative beauty and alternative culture from all over the world." But this celebration of diversity is represented solely by overtly sexualized images of "traditionally beautiful" women who simply happen to have tattoos and piercings. In reality, the site is little more than a minor reorganization of traditional soft-pornography sites to include modified women. The browser heading reads, "Beautiful naked girls with tattoos— punk rock girls, Goth girls, emo girls, tattoo girls—SuicideGirls." The site's popularity and size are staggering. According to the splash page, there are more than 2,000 different girls represented by more than 250,000 lurid photographs. The member count is not accessible, but there are almost 32 million members-only comments on those pictures. This count suggests that a large number of people have opted to pay the membership fee for access to the full content of the site.

There are a wide variety of images available on SuicideGirls, but most of them follow a predictable pattern of objectification while focusing on morbidity and sexual deviance. Many of the photographs depict women in homosexual acts, while others feature fully nude women in suggestive poses. One representative picture features a young woman standing in front of a neon sign with the word "DRUGS" in capital letters. Her bleached-blond hair is shaved into a short Mohawk. She has small dots tattooed over her eyebrows and a small inverted triangle, a signifier of homosexuality, above her nose. Her nose and lips are symmetrically pierced with large silver jewelry. She wears a tight black studded collar around her neck. She has a black "tribal band" tattooed below the collar and an inverted red and black nautical star that frames her cleavage. Her nipples are both vertically and horizontally pierced, and she is pushing her bare breasts together with her forearms. On her left wrist is a spiked bracelet, while her right forearm is completely tattooed, including the back of her hand. This tattoo is of a burning building, the smoke from which grows into a skull framed by three faces bearing expressions of fear.

There are strong indices of sexualization and deviance in this image from the background to the foreground. The neon sign clearly indicates an affinity for (illegal) drugs. The collar is a symbol of sadomasochistic domination. The inverted star is a loose reference to Satanism, which uses the symbol of the pentagram, or the inverted star, as its primary iconography. The spiked bracelet conveys a sense of danger and toughness. Meanwhile, the forearm tattoo clearly exhibits morbidity. Indeed, images of skulls and other morbid themes are commonplace throughout the SuicideGirls

A woman with a lower back tattoo. (Courtesy of Dennis Mojado.)

photographs. These sorts of images maintain and reinforce the tramp stamp stereotype.

SuicideGirls does little to enhance or celebrate alternative beauty. Instead, it offers a concentration of damaging, stereotypical images. By presenting those negative pictures and misleadingly calling the result a "celebration," the site's creators further reinforce dominant perceptions that modified women are sexualized and promiscuous. Furthermore, the title itself has implications for modified women. Using the moniker SuicideGirls implies that the featured women are self-destructive, morbidly fascinated, or both. The website employs this connotation as a revenue-generating device. It has capitalized, in the true monetary sense, on the false notion that modified women are self-destructive as well as sexually promiscuous tramps with low self-esteem.

Like other forms of pornography, SuicideGirls displays women for the gaze of others. That the featured women bear body modifications does not change their objectification and commodification. Rather, the objectification is amplified by their modifications. Representing modified women as a celebration of alternative forms of beauty does not ameliorate their treatment as sexual objects for consumption. In addition, the term "alternative" can also be interpreted as "deviant," further reinforcing impressions of promiscuity and morbidity.

Morbidity has also encroached into popular depictions of modified women in mainstream media. The CBS drama *NCIS* (Naval Criminal Investigative Service) offers one example. Abby Sciuto, the character played by actor Pauley Perette, has numerous piercings and tattoos that peek from beneath her white lab coat.[3] In the series, Sciuto is employed as a forensic coroner, a job that requires an interest in cadavers. Sciuto is effectively the televised transcription of a SuicideGirl. Sometimes wearing a spiked collar reminiscent of the spiked bracelet and collar worn by the SuicideGirl model, she is described on the CBS official *NCIS* website as "a talented scientist whose dark wit matches her Goth style and eclectic tastes." The term "Goth" is an abbreviation of "gothic," which is a direct reference to morbid fascination. This fascination is often manifested as a preoccupation with death, the occult, and other disturbing or unsettling things.

The character's gothic style is most clearly shown by her tattoos, which are usually hidden by the lab coat. However, one regularly visible tattoo is a spiderweb on her neck. The spiderweb carries a dual reference: First, it suggests an affinity for death; and, second, it ironically references a common prison tattoo. Beyond exhibiting morbidity, the character is also heavily sexualized. The CBS fan site for the show describes her "Signature look." According to the description, she "dresses Goth style; she has tattoos (especially the spider web on her neck), wears short skirts (they are certainly getting shorter) and tight pants, platform boots, and is fond of red and black and of course her white lab coat." Further playing into the stereotype, the fan site also states, "She adores gore."

Morbidity is further reinforced by Sciuto's employment, which highlights her morbid fascination while marginalizing the character, relegating her to behind-the-scenes work. Her visible tattoos make her unsuitable for employment in the public eye, and her sexuality is more overt than that of the other women on the show. Thus, even on television, modified bodies are marginalized, objectified, and sexualized.

Other television programs further reinforce the image of modified women as morbidly fascinated. The reality program titled *Tattoo Highway* on the Arts and Entertainment channel features a roving band of tattoo artists traveling the country in a bus that is also a mobile tattoo studio. In one episode, a woman in Sacramento named Heather gets a tattoo of a grim reaper on her chest. Meanwhile, her on-camera conversation revolves around dark fascinations, her experience working at a mortuary, and her collection of skulls and dead animals. Like a reality TV version of Abby Sciuto, Heather feeds the stereotype of morbidity associated with female body modification. Males, on the other hand, do not generally suffer from these kinds of sexual or morbid stigmatizations. Rather, they endure other stereotypes that more specifically reference their masculinity.

Tribal Bands: Violence and Criminality

Most male-oriented body modifications, particularly a style colloquially called the "tribal band," are stereotypically tied to concepts of masculinity. Tribal bands are usually black, blocky, geometric patterns or shapes that wrap around an arm or a leg. Stereotypes regarding this style either directly or indirectly reference the savage lineage of modern tattoo practices. Dominant images in the media represent male tattooing as inseparable from the extreme deviance and criminality associated with prison-style tattoos. Thus, the imagery of masculine body modification, like its feminine counterpart, is intrinsically class based. Where feminine stereotypes are often presented in reference to promiscuity and morbidity, masculine stereotypes are often presented in reference to criminality, violence, and aggression.

Media representations of the tattooed violent criminal stereotype abound, but a few stand out as especially noteworthy. Stereotypes of overt aggression being associated with tattooing are prevalent in broadcasts of professional, mixed martial arts (MMA) competitions, sometimes called "ultimate fighting." The images of participants in these fights commonly show tattoos. On television, a recent episode of the popular, prime-time cartoon *The Simpsons* focused on this kind of fighting and featured several tattooed combatants. The Oprah Winfrey interview with Mike Tyson, the boxer who bit off opponent Evander Holyfield's ear in the ring, offers another example.[4] While discussing his personal problems, time in prison, and well-documented domestic violence, the camera close-ups repeatedly emphasize the tribal tattoo that dominates the upper left side of Tyson's face. While body modifications themselves are rarely explicitly mentioned in such popular media, the recurrent linkage of tattooing with violence ultimately leads to the perception that tattooed people are inherently violent. This stereotype damages all modified people.

Criminality is one of the most enduring and damaging stereotypes of modified people. In one example, the FX network's *Sons of Anarchy* ties tattoos to the criminality of the biker stereotype. The show focuses on a motorcycle gang loosely reminiscent of the Hell's Angels and other organized criminal groups. The main business of the group is selling guns to other gangs, and virtually all of the unseemly characters in the show exhibit tattoos with various criminal themes. The show's introduction graphically relates leading characters to both criminality and tattoos. In the opening credits, video effects identify the actor behind each character by morphing individual tattoos into the names of the actors. The character's name is implied by his or her uniquely identifiable tattoos. Beyond the intimate association of tattooing and criminality, this visual montage also reflects the deep identification some people feel with their modifications. These tattoos are also racially charged. Each different ethnic gang, from African Americans to Anglo Americans to Latinos, exhibits different tattoo styles.

Race becomes a particularly important consideration when these stereotypical depictions move into the world of real-life criminals. Two examples of real-world criminality in tattoo stereotypes are the Fox Network's long-running *America's Most Wanted* and MSNBC's documentary program *Lockup*. Each show is based on criminal imagery and relies on depicting tattoos as an aspect of that criminality. *America's Most Wanted* regularly mentions the tattoos of dangerous criminals on the loose as a means of identification. Meanwhile, many of the people presented in *Lockup* have tattoos and spend significant time on the program discussing them. Among the most striking examples are white supremacist gang members. The image of the swastika is commonly paraded in front of the camera to enhance the sense of deviance and criminality that becomes associated with all modified people. An inmate named Curtis Allgier takes this imagery to the extreme. Frighteningly striking white supremacist tattoos completely cover Allgier's face and body and are the focus of much of the program.[5]

Modified people clearly are not all violent criminals. But like their feminine counterparts, masculine stereotypes in the media capitalize on false perceptions to draw viewership and advertising dollars. Even the future is not immune from these caricatures. The latest iteration of the *Star Trek* film franchise features a mining ship populated with murderous, working-class criminals bent on destruction of the human race (Abrams 2009). Like futuristic Mike Tysons, tribally inspired tattoos on the aliens' faces underscore a violent and criminal deviance.

The criminal depictions discussed here are particularly harmful to the body modification community. They prejudice nonmodified people against fair interaction with the modified and make all modified people appear to be criminals. And, as Adams's (2009) study of media representations of body modification clearly indicates, media choose to focus on the margins of modified people. In other words, creating the perception that modification is an act of criminals also creates the perception that modification is a criminal act. This kind of circular reasoning is intrinsic to most media stereotypes. It suggests that because criminals get tattooed, tattoos are a reflection of an already present or incipient criminality. For women, the process of sexualization is the same. In both cases, there is another underlying stereotype that magnifies the sense of intrinsic deviance: the freak.

Emergence of the Freak

The term "freak" most often has been associated with natural physical deformities. But the circus sideshows, or freak shows, of P. T. Barnum's day often included heavily tattooed people. Circus representations of the naturally deformed are no longer acceptable in society. As a result, the term "freak" has become increasingly associated with body modification and individuals who choose to violate social norms in altering their appearances. It is the aspect of choice and the violation of social norms that define the modern freak. For instance, breast implants are widely accepted in mainstream society. But move the placement and the shape of the same kind of implants to a different part of the body, and the freak emerges.

While the freak stereotype is not explicitly gender based, it tends to be more focused on masculine expressions of extreme modification. Due to its historical background in the circus sideshow, the freak stereotype also tends to be more of a live performance phenomenon than one regularly represented in broadcast media. Thus, media representations are more prevalent in online video-sharing websites. YouTube, for instance, offers an array of striking examples.

The most prominent example of the live freak show, the Jim Rose Sideshow Circus, has been regularly recorded and posted to YouTube. While the Circus has recently disbanded, Jim Rose himself still tours as an opening act for live bands. During its heyday, the Circus featured several performers engaged in live acts of what is most easily described as self-mutilation. This included walking on broken glass and acting as a human dartboard. Generally the performers are heavily tattooed, pierced, and otherwise modified. Perhaps the most famous performer from the Circus was an individual referred to as Mr. Lifto. Mr. Lifto's performance consisted of lifting heavy objects from his ear, tongue, nipple, and genital piercings and swinging them around like pendulums.[6]

Two individuals who make regular appearances in the YouTube videos dedicated to extreme modification are Lizardman and Cat Man. Lizardman, featured in a YouTube video series titled "World of Weird," has had numerous modifications to take on the semblance of a lizard.[7] His appearance has been completely transformed through filed teeth, a split tongue, subdermal implants, and full-body tattooing of scales, as well as the word "freak" across his chest. Even more notable is Cat Man, featured in a YouTube clip drawn from the *Guinness Book of World Records* television show. Winning the record for "Most permanent transformations to look like an animal," Cat Man has modifications similar to Lizardman but has taken on the appearance of a cat, including implanted feline teeth and whisker piercings.[8]

These performances are focused on the spectacle of body modification. The performers not only absorb the gaze cast upon them, but also thrive on it. On one level, this can have the effect of reempowering the disempowered. By turning the stereotype against itself, self-identified freaks force their recognition as members of society. On another level, by presenting themselves as objects for display, freaks reinforce perceptions that they are commodified objects and societal outcasts.

Depictions of such heavily modified people as freaks are more ambivalent than the explicitly negative frames of criminality and promiscuity. Lizard Man and Cat Man are generally celebrated in the YouTube videos for exercising the ultimate expressions of individuality. Indeed, Lizard Man's freak tattoo embraces his self-identification. But the word "freak" also carries the negative societal connotation of being weird or potentially dangerous that becomes associated with other people who have tattoos. Thus, the freak stereotype has the potential for both positive and negative readings. Unfortunately, being a freak is more often read in the negative light of deviance than it is in the positive light of self-empowerment and individuality.

In Praise of the Modified Body

Despite the negative nature of many body modification stereotypes, there is a slow movement toward acceptance of the practice. Positive images of modified people are becoming more frequent in the media. While they do not reduce the damage that stereotypes may continue to cause, positive images of celebrities, professional athletes, and popular musicians with tattoos and piercings show that body modification is not solely the province of the criminally or sexually deviant. Rather, body modification is an individual choice and can be a celebration of individuality and self-empowerment.

The documentary *Modify the Movie* (Gary and Abramson 2005) provides one example of a more realistic view of body modification than generally dominates the mass media. Featuring intelligent discussions with the heavily and uniquely modified, including Lizardman and Cat Man, the film offers an interesting insight into the motivations of modifiers without reducing them to caricatures or resorting to stereotypical depictions. It makes a point of reaching beyond typical conceptions of body modification. Plastic surgery, bodybuilding, surgical sex changes, and even makeup and cross-dressing are all covered in depth from a practitioner's perspective. Several of the interviewees mention less conspicuous forms of modification and describe their appearances as a logical extension of innocuous everyday practices like clipping fingernails, getting a haircut, or shaving.[9]

Exploring the motivations of modifiers as well as the tattoo artists, piercers, and physicians who actually do the modifying allows for a greater understanding of modification as an act of identity negotiation. Specific motivations range from simple aesthetic value to personal spirituality and even intentional appropriations of the ritual practices of indigenous cultures. Generally, the film presents modification as a means of self-empowerment. By reclaiming the body from dominant perceptions of normality, body modifiers also reclaim the right of self-determination. In the process, their bodies transcend objectification; they become an expression of individuality in an increasingly homogenized society.

As body modification has grown in U.S. society, so has the range of its media representations. Media should continue this trend by offering more positive characters. Only when media regularly represent modified people as human beings and not caricatures may those people begin to overcome the harm caused by stereotypes.

The negative accounts of media stereotypes of modified people described here are not comprehensive. They are meant as examples of where some of the more damaging and harmful images may be found. But there are steps that media outlets may take to lessen the harm these images cause. Media should stop sexualizing women with body modifications, and all women for that matter. By presenting these simplified accounts, media reinforce the perceptions that modified women are little more than self-destructive tramps. Media should also stop presenting modified women as morbidly fascinated and inherently attracted to gothic aesthetics or dark themes.

Furthermore, media must cease to focus on the criminal undertones of modification. While it is fair to identify wanted criminals by their tattoos, as in *America's Most Wanted*, it is the repeated and explicit focus on modification as an act of criminals, and thus as a criminal act, that causes harm. It may be obvious, but it remains worth mentioning that modified people are like everyone else. The personae they choose to wear on and through their skin are expressions of a complex process of identity creation and negotiation. Reducing modified people to stereotypes also hurts the nonmodified. Creating the impression that modification is a deviant practice restricts nonmodified people from meaningful, informed, and nonprejudiced interaction and limits the self-expressive options of all.

Stereotypes of body modification and modified people have moral undertones. Sexuality and criminality are both related to false perceptions of body modifiers as morally deviant. As a result, the continual presentation of those stereotypes relegates modified people to the margins of society. These unfair representations must be carefully considered by both those who produce and those who consume media. As with all stereotypes, producers need to consider the ultimate effects of their character representations. In turn, consumers must understand that the representations they are given are not indicative of an entire community. Even Herman Melville ultimately described Queequeg, the tattooed "cannibal" in *Moby Dick*, as an honorable and honest man. A century and a half later, modern media should learn from his example and do the same.

Notes

1. A similar practice was shown in the Quentin Tarantino–directed production of *Inglourious Basterds* (2009), in which the character played by Brad Pitt cut a swastika into the foreheads of German army prisoners.

2. See http://gprime.net/video.php/tattooremover (accessed March 8, 2010).

3. See http://www.youtube.com/watch?v=4wAgXoW17gw and other related videos (accessed March 8, 2010).

4. See http://www.oprah.com/dated/oprahshow/oprahshow-20090912-mike-tyson (accessed March 8, 2010).

5. See http://www.youtube.com/watch?v=eqKvGWtgbtc (accessed March 8, 2010).

6. See http://video.google.com/videoplay?docid=-3886894436886140518 (accessed March 8, 2010).

7. See http://www.youtube.com/watch?v=28SE_lWKnlE (accessed March 8, 2010).

8. See http://www.youtube.com/watch?v=FkKc6bsRmg8 (accessed March 8, 2010).

9. See http://www.youtube.com/watch?v=x_F7LQjYLFo (accessed March 8, 2010).

Sources

Abrams, J. J., dir. 2009. *Star trek*. Los Angeles: Paramount Pictures.

Adams, Josh. 2009. Bodies of change: A comparative analysis of media representations of body modification practices. *Sociological Perspectives* 52: 103–129.

Bell, Shannon. 2004. Tattooed: A participant observer's exploration of meaning. *Journal of American Culture* 22: 53–58.

Braunberger, Christine. 2000. Revolting bodies: The monster beauty of tattooed women. *National Women's Studies Association Journal* 12: 1–23.

DeMello, Margo. 2000. *Bodies of inscription*. Durham, NC: Duke University Press.

Fisher, Jill. 2002. Tattooing the body, marking culture. *Body and Society* 8: 91–107.

Gary, Jason, and Greg Abramson, dirs. 2005. *Modify the movie*. Los Angeles: Committed Films.

Govenar, Alan. 2000. The changing image of tattooing in American culture. In *Written on the body: The tattoo in European and American history*, ed. Jane Caplan, pp. 30–37. Princeton, NJ: Princeton University Press.

Hawthorne, Nathaniel. 1850. *The Scarlet Letter*. Boston: Ticknor and Fields.

Joralemon, David. 1974. Ritual blood sacrifice among the ancient Maya: Part 1. In *Primera mesa redonda de Palenque*, ed. Merle Green Robertson, pp. 59–76. Pebble Beach, CA: Robert Louis Stevenson School, Pre-Columbian Art Research.

Kang, Milann, and Katherine Jones. 2007. Why do people get tattoos? *Contexts* 6: 42–47.

Lawrence, Elizabeth Atwood. 1993. The symbolic role of animals in the plains Indian Sun Dance. *Society and Animals* 1: 17–37.

Lineberry, Cate. 2007. Tattoos: The ancient and mysterious history. Smithsonian.com, January, 1. http://www.smithsonianmag.com/history-archaeology/10023606.html (accessed December 17, 2010).

Melville, Herman. [1851] 1926. *Moby Dick or the white whale*. Boston: Simons.

Pitts, Victoria. 2003. *In the flesh: The cultural politics of body modification*. New York: Palgrave MacMillan.

Said, Edward. 1979. *Orientalism*. New York: Vintage.

Utanga, John and Therese Mangos. 2006. The lost connections: Tattoo revival in the Cook Islands. *Fashion Theory: The Journal of Dress, Body and Culture* 10: 315–331.

Vale, V., and Andrea Juno, eds. 1989. *Re/Search: Modern primitives.* San Francisco: Re/Search.

Young, Marion. 1990. *Justice and the politics of difference.* Princeton, NJ: Princeton University Press.

Chapter 19

Media Myths
and Breast Cancer

Deni Elliott with Amanda Decker

One morning several months into my breast cancer treatment, I drank my morning coffee and read the *Los Angeles Times* at a local Long Beach coffee shop. However, the normalcy of my routine was upset after I saw a half-page obituary about the brave struggle and activism of actress Wendie Jo Sperber, who had died from breast cancer the day before (McLellen 2005). It wasn't until much later that I realized why I had an extreme reaction to the story: How could she die? People don't die from breast cancer anymore, do they?

But breast cancer killed Wendie. She died in Los Angeles, my proverbial backyard, with at least the same access to world-renowned treatment that I had. This death stood in sharp contrast to the newspaper and magazine stories and websites that gave us the narratives and glowing images of young, attractive survivors who experienced epiphanies of one sort or another before resuming their normal lives, now cancer free. Breast cancer treatment was far from fun, but it hadn't occurred to me that it might still be fatal.

I had unconsciously swallowed one of the media myths of breast cancer, which was not surprising considering the circumstances. Despite the cheery stories and reassuring images that websites, other electronic media, and print media all supply, women[1] do die from breast cancer. And they continue to die a long time after diagnosis. Unlike some other forms of cancer, there is no "five-year cure" with breast cancer. Only about 11 percent of women diagnosed with invasive breast cancer die within five years of diagnosis; but approximately 40 percent are dead from the disease within 20 years (Breast Cancer Coalition Fund 2008).

Media myths of the disease are created through narratives that focus disproportionately on stories about young women who have femininity and fertility as their primary concerns. As noted by science writer Pamela Hogle,

> Motherhood, potential motherhood and the material role were strong themes in the narratives, mentioned in 17 out of 22 [magazine articles on breast cancer reviewed]. Many of the women, in fact, focused on their role as mothers and wives in their narratives, and nearly all of the women profiled have children or expressed a desire for children. A latent theme of "the women's role" is linked to the manifest themes of fear, uncertainty and the effect of the illness on a woman's fertility in many of the narratives. For example, a short article in *Cosmopolitan* featuring the story of a young woman with an unspecified cancer featured a screaming all-caps headline: "THE DRASTIC WAY I SAVED MY FERTILITY" with the dramatic sub-head stating, "When Lindsay Norh Beck, 31, was diagnosed with cancer, she fought for more than just her life," ranking fertility as more important than survival. (Beck 2007, quoted in Hogle 2010, 13, internal citation omitted)

The message? Fertility is more important than saving one's own life, and women get better because they do what the doctor says. The images portray all those with breast cancer as having access to all the treatment (and of the quality) that they need. And, the reader can presume that optimum treatment is provided with no consideration of the cost or of cumbersome and often difficult approval procedures, as financial burdens are excluded from the portrayal (Hogle 2010, 12).

Pictures also tell us a distorted story. In media presentations of breast cancer, the faces, physiques, and even breasts used to promote breast cancer "awareness" are youthful, powerful, robust, attractive, and feminine (Elliott and Alexander 2009). The presentation of breast cancer in text and images matters because of the "socializing" role played by media. According to communication scholar Kimberly Kline (2003),

> As important as the presentation of apparent facts about health issues, threats or behaviors is, it is also the case that people do not make health decisions based exclusively on evidence-based reasoning. Rather, people look to other individuals for clues about appropriate and/or desirable health practices. In other words, the informational value of a discourse may also be influenced

by the depiction of role models who provide "rules for living" or implicit instructions of how to do something (560).

When the presentation does not mirror reality, the stories affect perceptions of those included as well as those excluded, whether or not they have breast cancer:

> The narrative framework that drives these conventional stories illustrates both the exclusivity of particular survivors and the problem of ethics for those excluded audiences . . . [bringing] into question just who is being represented in such texts and thus how credible the speakers of these stories might appear to underrepresented readers. (Ryan 2004, 132)

Breast cancer is very much in the public eye. According to health education scholar Samantha King (2006),

> Over the past three decades, breast cancer has been transformed from a stigmatized affliction best dealt with privately and in isolation . . . to an enriching and affirming experience. . . . Sickness and death do not sell, but images of survivors who are uniformly youthful, ultra feminine, immaculately groomed and radiant with health do. (37)

These images have helped make breast cancer the most successful medical philanthropy of all time, with the top 20 charities devoted to fighting the disease bringing in more than $1 billion annually (Charity Navigator 2009).

Breast cancer brings in more charitable donations than any other medically related philanthropies, even though it is not the leading cause of death for women in the United States. Heart disease, causing nearly 350,000 deaths each year, is number one; cancer is second to heart disease in causing women's deaths, but lung cancer causes the highest number, killing more than 70,000 women each year. Breast cancer accounts for 40,000 deaths annually. Tens of thousands more U.S. women die each year from strokes, chronic obstructive pulmonary disease, and Alzheimer's disease than from breast cancer. The number of breast cancer deaths is comparable to those from diabetes and accidents, with pneumonia not far behind (Mayo Clinic 2007). Nevertheless, news and other informational media, public service announcements (PSAs) from corporate–charity partnerships, and websites have all embraced breast cancer "awareness" as a pet cause.

The images of breast cancer that help propel charity dollars in fact are dissonant with the reality of the disease. Despite the youthful images of those most often seen in "survivor" stories, in PSAs, and on websites, breast cancer is almost always an older woman's disease. The chances of someone in her 20s being diagnosed with breast cancer are about one in 2,000. Incidence in a woman's 30s rises to one in 233; in a woman's 40s, the chances that she'll get breast cancer are one in 69; in her 50s, one in 38; and in her 60s, one in 27 (Incidence by Age 2010). The disparity between this reality and the images results in confusion for those who confront breast cancer in themselves or loved ones. Media's inaccurate portrayal also deflects attention from research into the true causes and prevention of the disease by suggesting that victims are responsible for keeping themselves safe from breast cancer or, at least, catching the disease early if they fail at prevention. This misrepresentation places undeserved blame on victims of the disease, a well-known form of "Othering" that creates a "safe distance" for those without the disease and deprives all citizens of the opportunity to have a realistic view of the disease (Ryan 1976). The ability to make educated choices regarding public policy or philanthropy is diminished. Here we examine three pervasive media myths of breast cancer, contrasting them with some facts of the matter.

Myth 1: Buying "Pink" Products Helps Prevent (or Cure) Breast Cancer

Anyone who has walked into a U.S. grocery store during October's Breast Cancer Awareness Month (BCAM) knows that "baby girl" pink stands for breast cancer awareness and support. An array of products wear the pastel pink ribbon loop or are dressed entirely in pink, making it possible for consumers to caffeinate, sip soup, eat packaged foods, and even blow their noses "for the cure." In point of fact, the consumption of pink-branded products always contributes to corporate coffers, but often not much more than that.

Most corporate sponsors contribute a set amount to a charity in exchange for stamping the ribbon and affiliation on their product. However, they also pocket the healthy spike in profits that comes when consumers grab products bathed in pink. These additional profits generally more than offset the corporation's tax-deductible donation (Reisman 2007). *Advertising Age*, which calls itself the "leading global source . . . for marketing and media companies" (adage.com), wrote, "The potential payoff [of 'pink' marketing] is big for the company, even after donation" (Reisman 2007). The color triggers sales as consumers mistakenly believe that the pink product or pink ribbon loop signals that the corporation is helping to "cure breast cancer in our lifetime."[2]

For example, for the 2007 BCAM, Campbell's Soup changed its "trademark red and white label" on cans of chicken noodle and tomato soup to "limited edition" pink ribbon labels, and Campbell's donated $250,000 to benefit "breast cancer awareness initiatives across the country." Campbell's sales of cans of soup doubled that month from 35 million to 70 million at Kroger-owned stores alone—fulfilling the company's donation at a rate of 3.5 cents per can. Additional pink soup can sales equated to pure profit (less any marginal cost for the relabeling effort, which can be reused each year). Other corporations like Folgers, which sold its coffee in limited-edition pink canisters in October 2008 (Folgers Coffee 2008), apparently contribute nothing to any charity. A review of Folgers' website "awareness" campaign, which is no longer accessible, clarifies that their contribution amounted solely to the pink canister that helped encourage breast cancer "awareness" (Folgers Coffee 2008).

In addition, how the charities use these contributions is unclear, even with federal guidelines that require some reporting. Priority use of funds for many charities includes pay for professional fundraisers, fundraising walks, runs, climbs, dances, and every other imaginable activity that raises money for the purpose of raising more money. Charities send out direct-mail fundraising materials, such as address labels, that can be reported as educational programs (rather than fundraising) for the charity's cause because the mailings contain a line or two that encourage breast self-exams or annual mammograms. The fact that breast cancer awareness *looks* philanthropic does not make it so.

Pastel and Patronizing

What does pastel pink say to and about those living with breast cancer? To put it simply, it infantilizes them through direct associations with female babies whom we are acculturated to see swathed in pink, signaling that women living with breast cancer are passive, soft, and dependent on others. Breast cancer pink sends a different message from that evoked by the raging red emblem of HIV/AIDS. According to one scholar, "A red ribbon on a man is a shock, a demand that screams, 'I will not be silenced.' A pink ribbon on a woman is a plea that sighs, 'Please don't forget about me'" (Reifler 1997). In fact, the red symbol was born when angry young men took to

The closing ceremony of the three-day breast cancer walk in Atlanta, 2007. (Courtesy of Daniel Mayer.)

the streets, sporting blood-red banners, sashes, and ribbons to show their anger at the lack of governmental funding for HIV/AIDS research and treatment (Paulsen 1993). In contrast, the pink ribbons first appeared when AstraZeneca, a pharmaceutical company that profits from the drugs used in breast cancer treatment, first organized Breast Cancer Awareness Month in 1985. AstraZeneca is owned by Imperial Chemical Industries (I.C.I.), whose products include pesticides. Many pesticides are known carcinogens or have been linked to other diseases and environmental problems (Steingraber 1998). According to an investigative report conducted more than a decade ago by Monte Paulsen (1993) of *Detroit Metro Times*, I.C.I. "promotes theories that link breast cancer to heredity, lifestyle and diet— despite the fact that three out of four women who develop breast cancer have none of these risk factors."

More than a decade after the introduction of BCAM, at the annual Walk for the Cure, women in pink T-shirts wear SURVIVOR medallions hanging from pink ribbons on their prosthetic-covered chests. They sit passively on stage at the end of the "Walk," as other participants applaud them as heroes for having complied with the medical model of "slash, poison and burn."[3] They are waiting for others to bring the cure.

Myth 2: Sexual Exploitation of Women "for the Cause" Is Justified[4]

As is discussed in other chapters in this book (see, especially, Debra Merskin's contribution in chapter 14 and Lisa Wade and Gwen Sharp's chapter 12), using the female body, or parts of it, to sell products or promote messages is degrading toward women and has been documented to lead to self-image problems for vulnerable young girls. Dehumanizing women's bodies by including only provocative parts implies that the only important feature of a woman "lies between her neck and her knees" (Cortese 2004, 38). That these approaches are being used to promote breast cancer awareness is a new and ironic twist.

In Western society, the "sexual significance of the female breast rivals, if not exceeds, its biological significance," with breasts far more often portrayed as playthings for men than as biological essentials for babies (Ward, Merriweather, and Caruthers 2006, 705). "Cleavage between the breasts is perhaps the epicenter of display and stimulation of interest" (Cortese 2004, 28–29) in the female body as a sexual object. At the same time, media images of breast cancer build upon this sexualized female body within a

A Long Beach clothing store going out of business sells this mannequin for $1,000. (Courtesy of Paul Martin Lester.)

context of advancing women's health and wellbeing. Three examples of the sexuality used to promote breast cancer awareness will illustrate.

During 2009's Breast Cancer Awareness Month, Dillard's, a national department store chain, invited women to come to the store for a free bra fitting through a newspaper display ad. The ad featured a provocative young woman in lace lingerie. She gazes at the viewer over her boxing gloves and under the title "Help Knock Out Breast Cancer." The same month gave us the "Know Your Girls—The Yoplait Pledge." In this 50-second video PSA, the camera jumps through quick stills of the torsos of many women, clad in an array of clothes, some exhibiting cleavage and some not. Each woman cups her right hand on or under her left breast as a multivoice soft female chorus reads,

> I pledge allegiance to my girls, to my chi-chis, to my hooters, to my ta-tas, to my gonzangas and their normal state of being. I pledge to tell my doctor about any change I see or feel immediately. With specificity and tenderness for all.

Viewers were urged to go to Facebook and take the pledge, which resulted in slightly more than $3,000 raised by Yoplait during the pledge period (Great Ads 2009). The "pledge" manages to infantilize women and their bodies, makes women responsible for protecting "their girls" from breast cancer, and reinforces the myth that doctors can make everything all better in less than a minute. It is hard to imagine a similar video awareness piece that pictures men cupping their testicles and pledging to take care of their boys, their balls, their manhood.

In the summer of 2009, a Canadian-based charity, Rethink Breast Cancer, launched an awareness campaign that included a 1:04 minute PSA titled "Save the Boobs," which, as of the end of January 2010, had attracted more than 71,000 viewers (Boobyball 2009). The PSA features Canadian television host Aliya-Jasmine Sovina flaunting her large and active breasts as they roll about in her barely-there white bikini top.[5] Aside from a few establishment shots that show Sovina at a large, seemingly public, pool, the only part of Sovina's body seen through the camera's gaze is from her shoulders to her crotch, with most shots tight on her breasts. As Sovina walks on scene to a pool party, she is accompanied by bump-and-grind music and the jaw-dropping gazes of party guests, males and females alike. The camera darts away from her well-endowed assets only to focus on the suggestive body poses and reactions of others. The men and women shown, as well as the camera itself, are amazed, in awe, with gazes fixed to Sovina's breasts. Superimposed text (commonly known as a chiron) claims, "You know you like them. Now it's time to Save the Boobs." The final image presents Sovina in the pool, having switched the bikini top for a wet white T-shirt that allows a filtered view of her erect nipples. When she raises her shirt, the words "BoobyBall" appear in the form of rectangular black censor tape over her now bare breasts. The BoobyBall is an annual one-night cruise fundraiser that is marketed as a means to develop breast cancer awareness in women under 30 (Boobyball 2009).

This generation of breast cancer awareness PSAs suggests that the prevention and cure of breast cancer can be achieved through greater focus on what *Los Angeles Times* media critic Dan Neil (2009) appropriately called "awesome breasts." Neil argues that such [s]exploitation for the cause could only be objected to by someone who wants "to come off as somehow pro-breast cancer." However, exploiting another opportunity to dismember and objectify the female body neither promotes respect for women nor advances breast cancer prevention. "Breast cancer awareness" is, at best, a meaningless phrase. When it is used to justify further objectification of women, it crosses the line into unethical behavior.

Entwining sexuality with breast cancer reinforces other media messages that those with breast cancer should stay sexy and traditionally feminine, at all costs. A common piece of the breast cancer narrative includes shopping for a prosthetic breast to hide the amputation and/or shopping for

> a wig to hide chemotherapy-induced baldness. . . . Including such a scene in a breast cancer narrative suggests that a woman diagnosed with the disease will accept without question the standards for female beauty throughout her sickness experience, searching out sufficient substitutes for her treated body. (Ryan 2004, 132)

In fact, some women fear losing a breast more than other body parts:

> To lose a breast (or worse, both) in Western society often means that you lose a good part of your desirability as a person. . . . [S]urveys have shown that women consistently prefer other calamities, such as losing an eye, to befall them rather than to lose a breast to cancer. (Reisman 2007)

Focusing on one's appearance during active treatment for breast cancer may be more than many women can manage, financially, physically, or emotionally:

> Prostheses and wigs are expensive, not readily available to women of lower socioeconomic groups. Also, the individual breast cancer survivor must have

learned the importance of "keeping up appearances" to warrant the emotional and physical energy it takes to shop for such items while undergoing rigorous medical treatment for her disease. (Ryan 2004, 133)

Ironically, even though breast cancer has emerged as a favorite cause for public philanthropy and corporate sponsorship, women who are suffering the visible physical effects of active treatment are expected to hide those effects as best they can. Wigs and prostheses may be uncomfortable for the wearer, but they make it easier for individuals around her to deny her experience.[6]

Myth 3: Breast Cancer Is an Individual Challenge, Not an Index of Environmental Ills

More women are getting breast cancer than ever before. The chance that a U.S. woman will have breast cancer in her lifetime more than doubled from one in 20 in the mid-1960s to one in 11 in the mid-1970s to one in eight in 2008 (American Cancer Society 2008). The increased incidence suggests that factors unrelated to genetics or lifestyle, such as environmental factors in breast cancer, may deserve greater attention, funding, and study.

Dominant media images and messages of breast cancer play a role in shaping how the public, policy makers, and health workers respond to rising incidence of the disease. Yoplait's "pledge" exemplifies the prevalent message provided by breast cancer charity websites and their corporate sponsors: It is up to individual women to protect "their girls" from breast cancer. A study of the five wealthiest breast cancer charity websites (Elliott and Alexander 2009) showed that the texts and images on the home pages of these sites suggest that individuals have the power and responsibility to guarantee their survival through prevention, continual screening, and early detection.

The websites conflate ideas and collapse categories, such as prevention, screening, and diagnosis. Self-examination and mammography—screening techniques for cancer detection—are collapsed with the idea of prevention, although screening cannot prevent cancer. These techniques are also collapsed with diagnosis, although diagnosis involves costly and invasive biopsies and associated lab work to allow for a detailed analysis of suspicious cells. Regardless of the initial trigger for biopsy, one out of four diagnosed breast cancers has spread beyond the breast before a lump would be palpable, and one out of four would not be picked up by an annual mammogram.

Other misrepresentations abound on sites that tout themselves as educational and intended to reduce the incidence of breast cancer. The initially visible homepages of the breast cancer charity sites reduce the causes of breast cancer to one: genetics or heredity, which is known to cause only 10 percent of breast cancers. All promote individual responsibility through early detection and avoidance of risk evidenced by self-examination, exercise, and lifestyle choices. None of the charities mentions environmental causes on their initially visible websites or suggests environmental causes as a significant element of their research agendas.

On the other hand, the websites make it simple to donate, find corporate partners, purchase endorsed products, and take part in fundraising events with one or two clicks from eye-track-friendly positions on the home pages. Access to corporate sponsors, some of which make products with known carcinogens, are never more than two mouse clicks away from the home pages.

Despite all of the energy and money spent showing lifestyle choices as the antithesis of disease, more than 70 percent of people diagnosed with breast cancer have none of the "known risks." Little of the dominant media messaging on breast cancer addresses more than obliquely the fact that "non-industrialized countries have lower breast cancer rates than industrialized countries," despite the fact that one activist organization argues that "research into environmental links to disease should be a *priority*" (Breast Cancer Action 2007, emphasis added). Instead, the media message that we are in control of our own lives and health diverts our attention from questions of how the air we breathe, the water we drink, and the food we eat contribute to disease. Corporate sponsors that keep breast cancer charities wealthy include those that make significant profits from breast cancer screening, diagnosis, and treatment. Research into environmental causes for the disease is likely to speed prevention of breast cancer for future generations. Ultimately, making environmental research a priority contributes to the overall good of the community in a way far greater than creating and selling expensive designer drugs for the relatively few people living with breast cancer who can afford them.

This chapter is not intended to argue that media, whether exemplified by charity websites or heartwarming news stories about plucky survivors, intentionally create myths of breast cancer. Rather it offers an argument

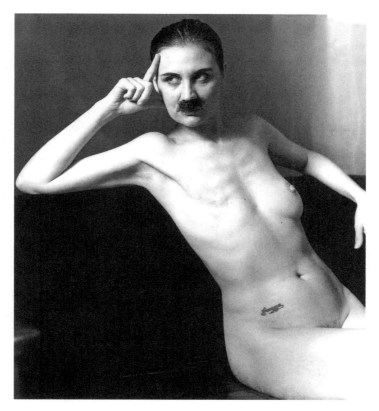

"I Am One Woman" (self-portrait as Chaplin) by the artist Matuschka. (Courtesy of Matuschka © 1994, www.matuschka.net.)

that media messengers have the responsibility to know the facts and to present them fairly. It offers an argument that those who claim or imply that they are giving a purportedly truthful message to a mass audience have a responsibility to do just that. Raising consciousness among viewers and consumers is an intent as well.

Acknowledgments

Research for this chapter was funded in part by a Page Legacy Scholar Grant for the Pennsylvania State University.

Notes

1. Men also get breast cancer, but as their incidence is less than 5 percent of that of women and inclusion of them in media narratives and portraits is even more rare, those who are living with breast cancer here are referred to with female pronouns and identification.

2. The Breast Cancer Research Foundation lists more than 75 corporate sponsors who assist the charity in their mission to cure breast cancer in our lifetime. See http://www.bcrfcure.org/part.html (accessed March 9, 2010).

3. This shorthand for the combination of therapies used most often in the treatment of invasive breast cancer—amputation, chemotherapy, and radiation therapy—is well enough understood among those living with breast cancer that alternative approaches to treatment are often compared to that combination; see, for example, Knopf-Newman (2004).

4. The following section on Myth 2 is from Decker (2009), used with permission of the author.

5. See http://www.youtube.com/watch?v=8tkB264wZZk (accessed March 9, 2010).

6. Women who are in treatment for breast cancer may access, free of charge, beauty consultation and cosmetics designed especially for them; see, for example, http://www.lookgoodfeelbetter.org/general/facts.htm (accessed March 9, 2010). Some cosmetics may contain chemicals that are possible carcinogens; see, for example, http://envirocancer.cornell.edu/research/endocrine/videos/makeup.cfm (accessed March 9, 2010).

Sources

American Cancer Society. 2008. *Incidence of cancer.* http://www.cancer.org/docroot/STT/stt_0_2008.asp?sitearea=STT&level=1 (accessed February 24, 2009).

Beck, L. N. 2007. The drastic way I saved my fertility. *Cosmopolitan*, December.

Boobyball. 2009. *Save the boobs.* http://boobyball.com (accessed September 16, 2009).

Breast Cancer Coalition Fund. 2008. *Facts and statistics about breast cancer in the United States.* http://stopcancer.org (accessed October 7, 2008).

Charity Navigator. 2009. *Charity Navigator ratings.* http://www.charitynavigator.org/index.cfm?bay=search.summary&orgid=4833 (accessed February 17, 2009).

Cortese, Anthony J. 2004. *Provacateur: Images of women and minorities in advertising.* Lanham, MD: Rowman & Littlefield.

Elliott, Deni, and Aimee Alexander. 2009. Clicking for the cure: A priorities and usability study of the wealthist breast cancer charity websites. Unpublished.

Folgers Coffee. n.d. Wake up call. *Folgers.com.* http://folgers.com/breast-health/ flash.shtml (accessed Feb. 20, 2009).

Great Ads. 2009. *Know your girls: The Yoplait pledge.* http://great-ads.blogspot. com/2009/09/know-your-girls-yolplait-pledge.html (accessed Sept. 16, 2009).

Hogle, Pamela S. 2010. Magazine-mediated disease: An analysis of illness narratives in women's magazines. Paper presented at the annual conference for the Association of Practical and Professional Ethics, March 6, Cincinnati, OH.

Incidence by Age. N.d. Imaginis: The women's health resource website. http:// www.imaginis.com/breasthealth/statistics.asp (accessed February 4, 2010).

King, Samantha. 2006. *Pink ribbons, Inc.* St. Paul: University of Minnesota Press.

Kline, Kimberly N. 2003. Popular media and health: Images, effects, and institutions. In *Handbook of health communication*, ed. Roxanne Parrot, Alicia Dorsey, Katherine Miller, and Theresa Thompson, pp. 557–581. Hillsdale, NJ: Lawrence Erlbaum.

Knopf-Newman, Marcy J. 2004. *Beyond slash, poison, and burn: Transforming breast cancer stories into action.* New Brunswick, NJ: Rutgers University Press.

Mayo Clinic. 2007. Women's Health Risks. *MayoClinic.com.* Feb. 9. http://www .mayoclinic.com/health/womenshealth (accessed Oct. 7, 2008).

McLellen, Dennis. 2005. Wendie Jo Sperber, 47: Actress drew on her battle with cancer to found support center for patients. *Los Angeles Times*, December, 2.

Neil, D. 2009. Breast cancer ads work by flaunting what's at stake. *Los Angeles Times*, September 22, p. B1.

Paulsen, Monte. 1993. BCAM scam. *The Nation*, November 15: 557.

Reifler, Ellen J. 1997. Why I hate pink ribbons. *Herizons*, July 1. http://www .herizons.ca/taxonomy/term/28 (accessed February 28, 2009).

Reisman, Suzanne. 2007. Breast cancer for fun and profit. *The panelist, social investing & culture*, January 22. http://thepanelist.com/index.php?option=com_ content&task=view&id=51&Itemid=10053 (accessed March 11, 2009).

Ryan, Cynthia. 2004. "Am I not a woman?" The rhetoric of breast cancer stories in African American women's popular periodicals. *Journal of Medical Humanities* 25 (2): 129–150.

Ryan, William. 1976. *Blaming the victim.* New York: Vintage.

Steingraber, Sandra. 1998. *Living downstream: A scientist's personal investigation of cancer and the environment.* New York: Vintage.

Ward, L. Monique, Ann Merriweather, and Allison Caruthers. 2006. Breasts are for men: Media, masculinity, ideologies, and men's beliefs about women's bodies. *Sex Roles* 55 (9–10): 703–714.

Chapter 20

Invisible No Longer: Images of Disability in the Media

Jack A. Nelson

Ten years into the twenty-first century, a monumental shift seems to be taking place in the portrayals of disability in the U.S. media. For centuries, those with disabilities have been portrayed in fairy tales, fiction, movies, and television in unfavorable or demeaning ways. Perhaps just as damaging was the lack of portrayal of any kind in films and on television. That is, those with disabilities simply didn't show up on the screen as they do in real life in any community. They were simply ignored as if they didn't exist—in a real sense they were "invisible," meaning unable to be seen. But as glacially slow as attitudes have been to change, by the end of the first decade of the new millennium, a remarkable face of the disabled seems to be showing up in the U.S. media.

The history of disability coverage in the media is not pretty. In decades past, any television viewer knew that when a maimed or hook-armed character showed up on the screen, it was a good bet that such a character would end up one of the bad guys. At least that's the way it often was portrayed in movies and on the small screen—with villains like Dr. Strangelove and Dr. No in their films named for them, each with disabled hands covered in black. In fact, such evil characters join a long line of media portrayals that show those with disabilities as someone to be feared or pitied—and avoided. It is heartening to note that, even though these stigmatizing stereotypes still are found in the media, on more fronts such portrayals are now coming to be questioned and replaced by more realistic and favorable representations.

Sociologists have long pondered the effects of such negative representation in feature films and on television programs (Mankiewicz and Swerdlow 1978). Yet it seems obvious that inappropriate and inaccurate presentations of persons with disabilities tend to stigmatize them in the public's mind. Often they are characterized as victims who possess undesirable social skills and personal qualities. In addition, three decades ago, a researcher found there was a conspicuous absence of persons with disabilities even in incidental roles on television, thus giving the impression that disability was not an important part of mainstream society (Donaldson 1981). Even when depictions of disability were present, they were usually accompanied by what Donaldson (1981) called "some sort of stress, trauma, overcompensation, character flaw or bizarre behavioral tendencies" (414).

Villainy has long been associated with abnormality. Fictional villains of the twentieth century were often marked by physical disfigurement, and we must remind ourselves that late in the twentieth century one of the most-watched television programs of all time was the final episode of *The Fugitive*. It was in this finale of the long-running series that the innocent Dr. Kimball, who had been hounded week after week as a suspect in the murder of his wife, was able to prove that the real murderer was a one-armed man he had been pursuing the whole time. More recently, Samuel L. Jackson's "Mr. Glass" character in *Unbreakable* (2000) has a rare disease that causes his bones to break easily. The portrayal is a more recent example of the disabled person as villain. Such stereotypes are burned deep into the public consciousness by centuries of portrayals of those with disabilities as tainted, with deformity of body usually associated with deformity of spirit.

When viewers are exposed to consistently stigmatizing stereotypes such as these, the results are indelible impressions that affect their reactions to those around them in the real world (Liebert 1975). In literature; in newspapers and magazines; and in movie, television, and web portrayals, until recently, persons with disabilities were generally shown in far more negative than positive roles.

The Roots of the Stigma

The roots of the problem go to the Dark Ages and beyond, into our fright-ridden dim past. In a time of ignorance and superstition, what

"The Witch No. 1," a lithograph by Joseph E. Baker that purports to show a scene from the Salem, Massachusetts, witch trials, 1692. (Courtesy of the Library of Congress.)

was not understood was feared and loathed. In the United States in 1692, Americans were hanged (not burned at the stake, as popularly assumed) after the Salem witch trials.

For centuries, the fairy tales of Europe often showed evil persons as afflicted in body as well as in spirit—the limping witch in *Hansel and Gretel*, for instance. Humpbacked evil witches are common in fairy tales. At the heart of the matter, of course, are ancient myths and beliefs that somehow the disabled were cursed or evil—as if those with obvious afflictions had in some way earned the wrath of God. In medieval times, the disabled often were shunned and sometimes stoned in the belief that they brought with them bad luck or a contagious curse. Shakespeare, for instance, gave Richard III— who in real life was not disabled—a twisted and deformed body to go along with his evil personality. One was seen as an extension of the other.

Even critically acclaimed children's literature is filled with characters whose evil ways are stereotyped as being accompanied by a physical disability. Robert Louis Stevenson in *Treasure Island* gave Long John Silver a wooden leg, innocuous at first, but later a symbol of evil as he thumps across the deck after his treachery becomes known.

A poster for a Federal Theatre Project presentation of "Hansel and Gretel" by German composer Engelbert Humperdinck in Los Angeles, California, that shows the children talking to a witch. (Courtesy of the Library of Congress.)

Patterning Stereotypes

The visual media are more powerful than written literature in shaping our views of others. The power of television to mold societal attitudes has been shown convincingly (Mankiewicz and Swerdlow 1978). Indeed, the pervasiveness and efficiency of television commercials are by themselves strong evidence that the medium is one of the most powerful institutions in our society today. At least until the twenty-first century, it was not comforting to recognize the power of movies and television, which, since their earliest productions, deluged the U.S. viewing public—and a world of viewers beyond—with a pattern of stigmatizing, stereotypical images of disability. These mostly fit one of five patterns: the hero, the threat, the victim, the misfit, or the burden.

The "Supercrip" Hero

Triumphing over great odds is the theme of one of the mainstays of all the media in portraying those with disabilities. The heartwarming story is common of someone who faces the trauma of a disability and, through courage and stamina, rises above it or succumbs heroically. Television especially thrives on this fare—which on its face seems favorable to anyone with a disability. The battles of these people seem heroic, such as *The Terry Fox Story*, which was the film account of a young Canadian who lost a leg to cancer and hopped on his other one across his country to raise money for cancer research.

In reaction to such coverage, one television actor who walks with a brace had this to say about the Fox story:

> Sure, Fox's story raised money for cancer, and, sure, it showed the human capacity for achievement, but a lot of ordinary disabled people are made to feel like failures if they haven't done something extraordinary. They may be bankers or factory workers—proof enough of their usefulness to society. Do we have to be 'supercrips' in order to be valid? (Kalter 1986)

As attitudes have changed in the new millennium, it seems that daring feats are triumphed in the media, with mixed effects. "Erik Weihenmayer had just become the first blind man to climb Mount Everest, putting him on the 'Today Show' and the cover of *Time* magazine. The sighted folks were inspired again," wrote Kathi Wolfe in the July 1, 2001, edition of the *Washington Post*. The writer had been blind for many years while working in the news media. With some sarcasm, she was pointing out the unfairness and the condescension of some media accounts of such heroic ventures that in a way make others with disabilities seem inadequate.

In the disabled community, such dramas are often regarded as "supercrip" stories that distract from and undermine effective work on real disability issues. By focusing public attention on the heroic (and often fictitious) struggles of a few, the "disability chic" approach diminishes the attention needed to address problems of access, transportation, jobs, and housing, and the movement to improve the status of all those with disabilities. Yet these stories of superachievement in overcoming great odds are popular, and some say that, in a sense, they give those with disabilities some hope of achieving something of importance—even if on a lesser scale.

The Disabled Threat

Conflict and suspense are central to most movies and television shows. Through the decades, this has meant that a portrayed disability usually meant a threatening, evil character whose very presence implied danger for the protagonist. Screen presentations have abounded in villains whose evil intent is exemplified by some obvious physical limitation: a limp, a hook for a hand, a twitch, a black patch over the eye, a hunchback. All of these play on subtle and deeply held fears and prejudices. It would be naïve to think that these attitudes, which have been nurtured through the years by Hollywood portrayals, do not carry over into attitudes toward others with similar limitations in real life.

In handling mental disabilities, the media have an even worse record. Interestingly, the disability that is portrayed most in dramatic television features is mental illness (Byrd and Elliot 1988, 146). Mental illness fits well into dramatizations where suspense and action are important to elicit audience anxiety. As a consequence, mental illness is almost invariably portrayed negatively. "Television programs tend to portray mental patients as dangerous, unpredictable and evil, and these portrayals may lead to unwarranted apprehension and ostracism of people who have such disorders," wrote sociologists Keith Byrd and Timothy Elliot (1988, 146). One often-cited example is that of the schizophrenic character played by Jack Nicholson in the memorable movie *The Shining*. In addition, patients in mental hospitals often spend a considerable part of each day watching television, and such depictions may affect their self-perceptions.

The Disabled Victim

One of the pervasive events on television has been the fundraising telethons that on a particular weekend may fill more than 50 hours of appeals for donations to benefit the "victims" of some disease or other.

These routinely feature tearful appeals from Hollywood stars, along with a mix of heartrending requests from those with the targeted disabling illness or condition. Most common are wide-eyed children asking for money to be given for further research of their particular disease or condition. (See chapter 16 for a related discussion on the more generalized use of children to sell products, programs, and pleasure.)

These telethons—such as Jerry Lewis's annual Labor Day Muscular Dystrophy Telethon—are popular, probably because of the star appeal. But disability activist groups have opposed them because they perpetuate the image of those with disabilities as objects of pity. Those featured are usually shown as childlike, incompetent, needing total care, nonproductive, and a drain on taxpayers.

It is rare that such telethons feature those who in spite of having the featured disease manage to live happy and productive lives. They rarely point out the accomplishments of such people. "Disabled people are not characterized [in telethons] as a social minority with civil rights but as victims of a tragic fate," writes sociologist Paul Longmore (1985, 32). It is worth noting that such presentations affect the attitudes not only of able-bodied viewers but also of those who may share some of the disabilities being featured. People have a way of living up to how they think others expect them to act.

The Disabled Misfit

In recent years, television programs have often featured the person with a disability who is maladjusted, unable to handle the trauma of his or her problem. Simply put—and the shows do put it simply—these people are bitter and full of self-pity because they have not yet learned to handle their disability.

Most of these shows feature a confrontational scene in which the protagonist—usually a friend or family member—sets the pitiable character straight. "Just buck up and take control of your life" is the usual message. There is no mention made of social prejudice contributing to or social programs helping to alleviate the problems of the disabled. In scenes modeled upon the now-classic "interventions" of family members with addicts, these images almost always present the able-bodied person as understanding, and being able to solve, the problem better than the one with the disability

Such messages imply that persons with disabilities don't really understand their own situations; such insights are provided by others. Therefore, says this myth, those with disabilities need guidance because they are unable to make sound judgments themselves.

The Disabled Burden

One consistent portrayal of those with disabilities is that of the frail person who needs to be taken care of, the burden on family and society.

Originally published in Elizabeth B. Brownell's 1901 book *Dream Children*, this child plays Tiny Tim for a production of Charles Dickins' *A Christmas Carole*. (Courtesy of the Library of Congress.)

Foremost is the view that care of the disabled is a duty that needs to be faced. At the same time, the implication is that a burden is difficult to bear and that one should attempt to avoid this. Thus the portrayal dehumanizes those with disabilities, transforming them from colleague, mentor, or loved one into a demanding task to be accomplished. As a dramatic device, this depiction is often used to show the nobleness and generosity of those who furnish the care, which objectifies the disabled person as little more than a prop rather than as a human being capable of interacting with others to the profit of both.

This is the portrayal offered in Johanna Spyri's 1881 novel *Heidi*, whose title character is hired as a companion to the "rich little cripple," Clara. Through the loving attention of Heidi, Clara gets well. In reality, Clara's role is as a prop to show the virtues of Heidi. Tiny Tim in Charles Dickens's *A Christmas Carol* serves the same function, adding poignancy and pathos to the tale of Scrooge's redemption. Such mythic distortions at times feed into the fear and unease some people feel when dealing with disabled individuals. For many, the sight of serious physical disability is also an unpleasant reminder of their own mortality and vulnerability.

A Different Visibility

It is apparent that the past two decades have been times of monumental social change in U.S. society. Yet even though the growing awareness of the rights of minority groups was one of the hallmarks of the twentieth century, societal attitudes are glacially slow to change. For of all the stereotypes about the disabled that have plagued the public, none is so insidious as the one that dwells inside the mind (Longmore 1990).

Still, the signals of disability such as a wheelchair, an unsteady gait, or a tremor elicit negative reactions that one might expect from unenlightened people. In preparing to star in the film *My Left Foot* (1989), Daniel Day-Lewis strove to get inside Christy Brown's head. To accomplish this, Day-Lewis used a wheelchair, was lifted in and out of cars, spoke with impaired speech, and had someone feed him in some of Dublin's best restaurants.

"It's strange what happens, even though everybody knew who I was and what I was doing," he explained later. "When people see someone in a wheelchair, their attitudes change. . . . They start treating you like a child." He found that people talked around him instead of to him; he had become one of the invisible disabled (Longmore 1990, 24).

To counteract such attitudes, significant media efforts in the twentieth century presented a different vision of those who used wheelchairs. For instance, in the early 1980s when Berk Breathed, the author of the popular cartoons *Bloom County* and later *Outland*, was looking for cartoon characters to portray, he deliberately sought a challenge. "I heard from black people and other minorities, but never from disabled people," he says in explaining how he came to feature a paraplegic Vietnam vet named Cutter John. It took a year for Breathed to convince his newspaper syndicate to accept Cutter John, but he became popular and somewhat controversial. No one else on America's comic pages had focused on having fun with a disabled character whose adventures didn't turn on the fact of his disability, who was "neither goody-goody nor an angry young man" (Randall 1989, 40). His girlfriend is most often seen riding on his wheelchair lap.

Cutter John blazed new trails, but the most important path he cut was modifying the stereotype of paraplegics in the readers' minds. He was charming, opinionated, and educated, someone who almost anyone would enjoy having a drink with—and in a wheelchair. Yet Breathed had calls from some people who worked with disabled people chastising him for "taking advantage of the handicapped." More importantly, though, he also received the Harry Sullivan Awareness Award from the Paralyzed Veterans of America (Randall 1989).

Different Language

One of the marks of the esteem in which any group is held is the language by which they are described. Until recently, the terms used most often in describing disability were "the handicapped," "the deaf," "the blind," and "the mentally retarded." In 2010 the Obama administration's White House Chief of Staff Rahm Emanuel learned quickly that calling someone "retarded" was the equivalent for some of calling an African-American "nigger" (Dwyer 2010). According to sociologist Paul Longmore (1985), "These labels rivet attention on what is usually the most visible or apparent characteristic of the person. They obscure all other characteristics behind that one and swallow up the social identity of the individual within that category" (32).

Such terms imply a social inadequacy that can settle deeply both into the attitudes of the able-bodied viewer and, perhaps more importantly, into the psyche of those who may share the disability being described. In short, such language stigmatizes by reinforcing the tendency to view persons only in terms of those disabilities.

However, as part of a newfound political correctness or, more properly, social correctness, such terms are becoming less commonplace. More accurate and acceptable terms have come into usage. For instance, for years the American Society of Newspaper Editors (ASNE) has focused on the language used to describe those with disabilities, recommending, for instance, that reporters write, "He uses a wheelchair," not "He is confined to a wheelchair," and "She has cerebral palsy," not "She suffers from cerebral palsy." The *ASNE Bulletin* (1990) affirms the role that it sees for newspaper editors in bringing to pass social change: "Our job as communicators must be to help surmount prejudice and uneasiness concerning disabilities" (13). In daily practice, however, by 2010 that advice was still often ignored in the columns of U.S. newspapers. Nevertheless, such emerging language may be a sign of a stigmatized minority's refusal to accept the role of marginalized human beings with marginalized civil rights.

Shifting Advertising

Advertising obviously has a strong potential to influence viewers, as evidenced by the huge sums spent by companies for a 30-second commercial during the Super Bowl. Since the early 1980s, ads featuring disabled people have appeared on television, and by the end of the twentieth century their roles were more frequent and more varied. Significantly, many of these ads show workers in high-profile places, such as law offices and newsrooms, carrying out routine tasks without fanfare like everyone else in those offices. In other words, the message is that those with disabilities have a place on the job like everyone else.

In advertising, the audience also seems to be showing a growing acceptance of those with disabilities. In an ad for Target, a photograph of a child in a wheelchair was included in a sales circular. This occurred at the suggestion of a vice president of marketing whose daughter was born without a left hand. He approved the ad with some trepidation, but the reaction of the public was enthusiastic. The company received more than 2,000 letters of praise (*New York Times*, September 23, 1991).

The Cusp of Change in the New Millennium

Despite the long history of mythic, stereotypical representations of those with disabilities, the past two decades have witnessed a major change in attitudes by those who produce the media. Inevitably, especially because of the power of the electronic media, it appears that a myriad of new, more realistic, and more positive portrayals will modify societal attitudes (Byrd and Pipes 1981, 51). One of the major influences in this change is the impact in the new century of the best sense of the term "political correctness" (PC). So-called PC values began to be ingrained in the public mind during the equal rights battles of the 1960s, when it became apparent to most people that demeaning stereotypes, especially racial stereotypes during those times, were a hindrance to a good society. Even though public attitudes are painfully slow to change, tremendous improvements have occurred partly because of mandates of the Americans with Disabilities Act of 1990.

Apart from the legal requirements, other social forces have been at work that are perhaps just as important. In the new millennium, even though the concept of PC often is used as a pejorative, it nevertheless has had a major effect on the treatment of those with disabilities in the media. Not only has the language of disability changed, but also disability advocates have become more vocal and aggressive. For example, in July, 2009, the Little People of America petitioned the Federal Communication Commission to ban the use of the word "midget" on broadcast television because it is demeaning. They reasoned that the word is just as offensive to that group as racial slurs are to others. The request was prompted by an April 2009 episode of *Celebrity Apprentice* in which the acid-tongued star, Joan Rivers, suggested bathing little people in a detergent and hanging them out to dry (Salt Lake City *Deseret News*, July 6, 2009).

During the 1990s, disability activist groups took note of the public relations activities of the gay community, with protests, marches, and publications asking for a fairer deal in U.S. society. For gays, the result was that there is now hardly a TV comedy show that doesn't feature a gay character. In a smaller way, since the year 2000, the disabled community has achieved almost unbelievable success in winning the battle for better portrayals in the media.

New Images on the Big Screen

In spite of its shortcomings, Hollywood has not been all bleak in representing disability. During the last half of the twentieth century, Hollywood occasionally turned from all the denigrating portrayals to produce a few fine films featuring a character with a disability, with one of the earliest milestones being the 1950 film *The Men*. In his screen debut a year before his breakout performance in *A Streetcar Named Desire*, Marlon Brando starred in the movie that was one of the first to offer an honest appraisal of paraplegia by telling the story of a soldier who is wounded in battle during World War II and faces life in a wheelchair.[1] The film's minor roles featured many of the soldiers in the veterans' hospital where the movie was shot who faced similar challenges. But that realistic depiction was offset by hundreds of other movies produced later that showed wheelchair users as helpless.

Hollywood actors have often looked at a major disability role as an easy way to win an Academy Award, as occurred in such leading roles as in *One Flew over the Cuckoo's Nest* (1975), *Rain Man* (1988), *My Left Foot* (1989), *Philadelphia* (1993), and *Forrest Gump* (1994). More recent motion pictures offer a fresh and growing maturity for both the large and small screens. Movies such as *Notting Hill* (1999) and *The Replacements* (2000) showed minor characters in wheelchairs, who were neither important to the plot nor received special attention but who were fully realized human beings. Deafness and sign language showed up in *Four Weddings and a Funeral* (1994) with a casualness new to the screen up until that time. Much as in real life, these characters were simply everyday people. Such representations are a major step forward in changing long-held societal attitudes.

After decades of denigrating portrayals (de Balcazar, Bradford, and Fawcett 1988), by 2010, it appears that Hollywood has turned a corner in gaining new sensibilities about those with disabilities. About time, disability activists say. After all, disability is one of the last stereotypes to remain commonplace in the public arena.

A recent example from the Disney/Pixar studios shows this evolution. Remember, it was Disney that brought the evil lion Scar in *The Lion King* (1994) and a host of other disfigured and malevolent characters into children's minds through the years. However, in *Finding Nemo* (2003) the title character (ironically named after Jules Verne's maniacal captain in *Twenty Thousand Leagues under the Sea*) is a clownfish who is born with one tiny fin that doesn't develop because a shark maimed it when Nemo was an egg. His father calls it Nemo's "lucky fin," and in school the other fish accept it as nothing special. As his father searches for Nemo, who has been captured by a dentist and put in his office tank, Nemo finds that most of the fish and shrimp with him have varying disabilities. Even the dentist's niece, Darla, has a cognitive disability. In short, almost all the characters have some sort of disability, but the disabilities seem unimportant. "It was the first movie that I discovered that was good on disability," wrote 10-year-old reviewer

Meecha Corbett, who herself deals with a disability. "They didn't say that disability is stupid. They were encouraging to bring disability into everyday lives" (Disability World 2004).

Another major step in the portrayal of those with mental disabilities was the more realistic approach that showed such persons as major characters whose situation was not presented as life dominating. For instance, in the Christmas 2009 Hallmark movie *A Dog Named Christmas*, the young protagonist, Todd, cajoles his reluctant father to participate in the "Take a Pet Home for Christmas" program from the local animal shelter, with the promise the dog would be returned following the holidays. Although obviously developmentally disabled, Todd is likeable, outgoing, and the kind of kid anyone wouldn't mind having around. Even though his father is adamant about the dog being a guest for just a few days, of course in the end he relents and the dog stays. Incidentally, the subplot dealt with another, less obvious disability, that of the psychological scars suffered by soldiers, post-traumatic stress syndrome. During the father's service during the Vietnam War, he loved the dog that saved his life. After both were wounded, he had to leave it behind on the battlefield. Of course, all ends relatively happily.

A more important film featuring disability was the visually stunning *Avatar*, released in 2009. In the most expensive and profitable motion picture in Hollywood history, a paraplegic former marine is featured. In James Cameron's futuristic 3D drama, Jake Sully is the marine who, through science, is given the body of a member of an alien race called the Na'vi from the distant planet Pandora. He initially infiltrates the Na'vi and reports back to the mining corporation trying to remove the natives from their jungle land in order to learn how to take the valuable mineral that can be found under their ground.

Back and forth, Jake goes from a new Na'vi who can barely contain himself at the thrill of once more being able to leap and run, to a paraplegic who has to swing his atrophied legs into the tube where he becomes his alter ego. Interestingly, he is promised that if he is successful in learning the Na'vi's secrets and reporting their vulnerabilities, he will be rewarded with the full use of his legs once more. A totally sympathetic character, Jake ultimately rebels and helps save the Na'vi. Moviegoers will almost certainly remember wheelchair user Jake Sully with fondness and respect as a person but also as a man who desperately longs for his body to be fully functional.

A documentary film that featured wheelchair users as strong, active, and satisfied with their lives was *Murderball* (2005), which followed the teammates of a quadriplegic wheelchair rugby team on their way to the 2004 Paralympic Games. The movie helped inspire public awareness of athletes who happen to use wheelchairs.[2]

Signs of Progress on the Small Screen

In the formation of societal attitudes, weekly television programs may be the biggest factor in changing long-held beliefs about disability (Liebert 1975). It is encouraging, therefore, that as the disability culture continues to mainstream, coverage is becoming more and more realistic. For instance, in the 2001 season of the popular series *The West Wing*, President Bartlett revealed to his aide that he was developing multiple sclerosis. Here was a real disability affecting the most powerful man in the United States, with his aide questioning whether he could continue to carry out his duties. Disability activists applauded the show for confronting head on such a debilitating condition, but they resented the aide's questioning his ability to function.

In the same vein, actor Michael J. Fox has made his struggle with Parkinson's disease a public battle, helping to bring a positive, realistic image of his disability. Similarly, on the popular television show *Medium*, the psychic lead character, Allison, had a major stroke in the 2009 season, which left her for months with her right arm mostly useless. The key to its power to challenge stereotypical portrayals is that it was shown as an inconvenience, not a disability that defined her character. She remained able to function normally with her family and to continue to assist the district attorney in solving crimes.

Another example is the popular medical show *E.R.* It featured several characters with disabilities. For instance, character Kerry Weaver had a mobility impairment, Robert Romano was missing a limb, Dr. Nathan had Parkinson's disease, Mark Green had brain cancer, and Gabriel Lawrence had Alzheimer's disease. Compare this array of characters to the popular medical shows during the 1970s: *Dr. Kildare, Ben Casey*, and *Marcus Welby, M.D.* There were no major characters with disabilities on those shows.

Even more dramatic, and more indicative of an emerging attitude, is the portrayal of the lead character in the award-winning *House*, which began on the Fox Network in 2004. It features Dr. Gregory House, played by Hugh Laurie as an unconventional, maverick, medical genius who not only is grouchy and largely friendless but also uses a cane and limps so badly that in earlier times he would have been called a "cripple." In developing the character, a central part of the show's premise was that the main character would be disabled. At first, the idea was to put him in a wheelchair, but the writers ultimately chose to give House a damaged leg that was caused by an incorrect diagnosis. The show was rated in the Top 10 in its second through fourth seasons, and it was still going strong by the end of the first decade of the twenty-first century. It appeared in 66 countries, and in 2008 it was the most-watched television program in the world (Fox Network 2009).

Just as important as TV shows that feature a disability is the growing trend to show incidental characters whose disability is no more than an inconvenience. For example, in the NBC show *Las Vegas*, one of the security guards who screens the gaming tables to watch for cheaters uses a wheelchair. Similarly, one of the characters in the award-winning Fox show *Glee* is Artie, played by able-bodied Kevin McHale, who not only sings with the high school group but also dances in his wheelchair with the rest of the cast on stage, and the character of the police officer Joe Swanson uses a wheelchair to fight crime and be with his buddies in the animated hit situation comedy *The Family Guy*.

This trend of showing real people doing real things in spite of some impairment appears likely to continue as producers discover that web-only productions, called "webisodes," can have a popular following. For example, the Discovery Health website features documentaries on the topics of conjoined twins and spinal cord accident victims.[3]

Conclusion

These dramatic changes in the portrayal of disabilities have been slow in coming, but they appear to have taken strong root in the media. In a world where the information highway is occupying a more and more central place in people's lives, public attitudes seem sure to follow. Ultimately, considering the powerful impact of the U.S. media abroad, that impact may have positive reverberations worldwide.

Perhaps most encouraging of all, those in the disabled community have emerged with stronger images of self-empowerment. As they view themselves as a significant part of society, the quality of their lives can improve vastly. After all, what most people with disabilities ask is that they be portrayed as real people with real problems that often are not connected to their disability. For some, the emergence of a stronger self-image could open the way to a whole new world.

A couple on deck of Carnival Cruise Line's *Splendor* ocean liner off the coast of Mexico enjoy the day, 2009. (Courtesy of Paul Martin Lester.)

Notes

1. See http://www.youtube.com/watch?v=b3QSF88grPE (accessed March 12, 2010).

2. See http://www.youtube.com/watch?v=_kaT5dDiISw (accessed March 12, 2010).

3. See http://health.discovery.com/videos/marathon-love-webisodes-marathon-love.html (accessed March 12, 2010).

Sources

Byrd, E. Keith, and Timothy R. Elliot. 1988. Disability in full-length feature films: Frequency and quality of films over an 11-year span. *International Journal of Rehabilitation Research* 11 (2): 146.

Byrd, E. Keith, and Randolph B. Pipes. 1981. Feature films and disability. *Journal of Rehabilitation* (January/February): 51–53, 80.

de Balcazar, Suarez Y., Barbara Bradford, and Stephen B. Fawcett. 1988. Common concerns of disabled Americans: Issues and options. *Social Policy* 19 (2): 29–35.

Disability World. 2004. 4 (22). http://www.disabilityworld.org (accessed December 16, 2010).

Donaldson, Joy. 1981. The visibility and image of handicapped people on television. *Exceptional Children*. 47 (March): 413–416.

Dwyer, Devin. 2010. Rahm Emanuel "retarded" comment puts offensiveness in spotlight. ABC News, February 3. http://abcnews.go.com/WN/rahm-emanuel-retarded-comment-puts-offensiveness-spotlight/story?id=9738134 (accessed March 12, 2010).

Elliot, Timothy R., and E. Keith Byrd. 1984. Attitude change toward disability through television: Portrayal of male college students. *International Journal of Rehabilitation Research* 7 (3): 320–322.

Fox Network. 2009. http://fox.com/house/showinfo/ (accessed December 28, 2009).

Kalter, Joanmarie. 1986. Good news: The disabled get more play on TV, bad news: There is still too much stereotyping. *TV Guide* (May 31), 41–42.

Liebert, Robert M. 1975. *Television and attitudes toward the handicapped.* New York: New York State Education Department.

Longmore, Paul K. 1985. Screening stereotypes: Images of disabled people, *Social Policy* (Summer): 32.

———. 1990. The glorious rage of Christy Brown. *Disability Studies Quarterly* 10 (Fall): 23–25.

Mankiewicz, Frank, and Joel Swerdlow. 1978. *Remote control: Television and the manipulation of American life.* New York: Ballantine.

Nelson, Jack A. 1994. Virtual reality: A brave new world for those with disabilities. In *The disabled, the media, and the information age*, ed. Jack A. Nelson. Westport, CT: Greenwood Press.

Randall, Megan. 1989. Out of the heartland: Cutter, Milo & the Penguin. *Disability Studies Quarterly* 6 (Summer): 39–41.

PART V

Images Shaping and Constraining Religions and Ethnicities

Susan Dente Ross

For the past couple of decades, increasingly raucous and diverse critics have accused journalism of being indifferent or even overtly hostile to religious ideas, concerns, and priorities (see, e.g., Marshall, Gilbert, and Green-Ahmanson 2008). Scholars, journalists, philosophers, and observers have commented upon the growing perception that the U.S. media ignore, distort, or fail to understand and communicate the religious side of events that are transforming our complex and pervasively nonsecular world. Some argue that rampant misreporting of religions and events in other locales with distinct ethno-religious-cultural histories feeds misunderstanding about faith and the world. As a consequence, "Americans have been educated to believe that democracy and secularization go hand in hand" and that rationality and religion are mutually exclusive (Marshall, Gilbert, and Green-Ahmanson 2008, 22).

Although some scholars have found that media typically present mainstream religious groups in neutral or favorable terms, new religious movements are consistently presented pejoratively (Hill, Hickman, and McLendon 2001). Such distancing and demonization are especially evident in media treatment of "fringe" religions, such as witchcraft. However, distorted images and misrepresentations about particular religions persist throughout media and propel ethno-religious profiling, typecasting, and stereotyping. For example, Miriam Cooke (2007) documents the sweeping overgeneralizations and reductionism of media representations since 9/11 that portray Muslims as the "Other." Cooke (2007) observed,

> Veiled Muslim women have become [Muslims'] visible representatives. Standing in for their communities, they have attracted international media attention. So intertwined are gender and religion that they have become one. I have coined the term the Muslimwoman to describe this erasure of diversity. (139)

At the same time, and in marked contrast, a consensus generally holds that religious resurgence in the United States has pushed religion more solidly and frequently onto the scholarly agenda and into news reports (Schmalzbauer 2002). Some studies describe generally positive and rising media coverage of holy wars, efforts to legislate morality, sexual and financial misbehavior by ministers, new spiritual movements, and other controversial religious phenomena (Silk 2008).

In the following part dealing with media coverage of ethnicities and religion, five scholars scrutinize a range of both topics to shed light on the interactions among religion, ethnicity, identity, and culture to increase understanding of the significant role that belief plays in shaping contemporary social, political, and economic realities (Smith 2008). The five contributors to this part reach far beyond newspaper coverage to examine the images of different religions and ethnic groups that populate television programming, comic books, political cartoons, news, cultural events, and marketing campaigns. Their analyses implicitly recognize that individuals ingest a diversity of media and work actively to reconcile the varied messages and portraits of different people they receive from news and entertainment programming, the printed word, and the moving image.

Their chapters also underscore the multiple subtle and overt personal and social implications of the observed patterns of mediated images of religions and ethnicities for people of all ages and identities. These images matter because, as Lynn Schofield Clark (2002) suggested,

> [S]tories from the entertainment media are either rejected or incorporated into what . . . people claim are their religious beliefs. . . . Entertainment media are one element of a culture that shapes and constrains religious identity construction . . . and an especially important one for those with few ties to formal religion (794).

To open this part, Dina Ibrahim and Michelle Wolf offer a qualitative study of the perceptions that young Jewish Americans have of television news images and stories about Jewish people. Focus group participants described the coverage as narrow, stereotypical, and hurtful and suggested that it had harmful effects on both themselves and others. They described feelings of anger and sorrow about the coverage as well as reluctance to overtly display their Jewish identity in public. They said they believed other people, especially heavy viewers of this coverage, develop distorted and negative images of Judaism and Jewish people.

In chapter 22, Ramón Chávez provides a historical perspective on the discrepancies between the lived realities and the mediated images of Latinos in the United States. Documenting the growing size and influence of the cultural group in the country and within media industries, Chávez argues that while new and more positive images of Mexican Americans are infiltrating the media, vestiges of historical stereotypes persist. He concludes that Latinos have yet to champion a strongly positive reimaging of themselves in the media as a resource for social action to improve the lives of this significant U.S. population that long has been marginalized and denigrated.

Shifting the focus to the perpetuation of injurious stereotypes, Erin Steuter and Deborah Wills analyze the dominant patterns of representation of Arabs as insects, vermin, or disease in editorial cartoons. They argue that the distilled messages of editorial cartoons are particularly powerful because they compress large quantities of information into quickly communicated and highly memorable visual codes. In cartoon portrayals of Arabs, visual codes emphasize distance and dehumanization, portraying Arabs as the enemy Other in consequential and potentially dangerous ways that call out for "cures" of eradication or extermination.

Nancy Beth Jackson presents a more hopeful look at shifting media images, detailing the emergence in the past half-century of Arab nomads from invisibility or stereotypes to self-branded media campaigns that emphasize their cultural wealth. Like Chávez, Jackson situates her chapter within the historical, lived realities of the Bedouins from the Arabian Gulf, whom media portrayals often romanticized as free-spirited, exotic desert dwellers. She suggests that following the discovery of rich oil and gas deposits in the region, a new stereotype of the Bedouins emerged as uncultured, overbearing "oil sheikhs," living lives of greed, decadence, and overt excess. More recently, and more positively, Gulf Arabs have begun to manage their own images through government-branding agencies that stress the nobility of their desert cultures.

Concluding the part in a similar vein, Marguerite Moritz examines a recent television show and a comic book as responses from Muslim voices to the historical dominance of Western media over the images and narratives of Islam. She argues that new and rapidly spreading communication technologies are providing spaces and occasions for once-excluded groups to build communities and shape their own image around the globe. As a telling example, Moritz outlines how Muslims today are using the media to critique dominant (negative) media portrayals of Islam and to distribute their own, more complex and positive images that provide new resources for imagining Islam and understanding the world.

Sources

Clark, Lynn Schofield. 2002. U.S. adolescent religious identity, the media, and the 'funky' side of religion. *Journal of Communication* 52 (4): 794.

Cooke, Miriam. 2007. The Muslimwoman. *Contemporary Islam* 1 (2): 139–154.

Hill, Harvey, John Hickman, and Joel McLendon. 2001. Cults and sects and doomsday groups, oh my: Media treatment of religion on the eve of the millennium. *Review of Religious Research* 43 (1): 24–38.

Marshall, Paul, Lela Gilbert, and Roberta Green-Ahmanson. 2008. *Blind spot: When journalists don't get religion.* New York: Oxford University Press.

Schmalzbauer, John. 2002. *People of faith: Religious conviction in American journalism and higher education.* Ithaca, NY: Cornell University Press.

Silk, Mark. 2008. *Unsecular media: Making news of religion in America.* Champaign: University of Illinois Press.

Smith, Christian. 2008. Future directions in the sociology of religion. *Social Forces* 86 (4): 1561–1589.

Chapter 21

Television News, Jewish Youth, and Self-Image

Dina Ibrahim and Michelle A. Wolf

For decades, media scholars and literacy advocates have argued that watching television is an active process in which viewers construct meaning from media texts (Crouteau and Hoynes 2003; Livingston 1998; Morley 1986; Thoman and Jolles 2008; Tyner 1998). When television news is considered, this research suggests that although journalists and other media professionals create the images and stories that populate the small screen, they do not control what their messages mean to individual viewers. Rather, it is the viewers themselves who determine the salience of images and stories that are a part of the news.

A group of Jewish Americans living in the San Francisco Bay area believe that understanding the impact of the images and stories of Jewish people on public and commercial television news should be grounded in the concept of an active audience. We do not suggest here that they think the meaning of television news is open and up for grabs; obviously, viewers often see the same messages repeated across and throughout the news media. We argue, rather, that the values and ideologies embedded in television news programming will be differently understood depending on a broad range of variables such as the cultural background of the viewers.

This research represents a departure from content analysis studies designed to illustrate the hurtful, stereotypical images that exist in electronic media. We offer a deeply textured analysis of personal understandings of news images and stories. To evaluate the *received* meaning of the news, we conducted a focus group to explore how Jews talk about their experiences watching broadcast television news, using cultivation theory (Gerbner et al. 1977) as a framework for understanding the cultural context in which religious identity and self-conception develop.

George Gerbner and his colleagues (1980) argue that television content plays a significant role in shaping viewers' social realities, a process defined as cultivation. Central to the cultivation perspective is the principle that dominant mass media serve as cultural levelers, bringing audiences into a common mainstream of thought. Television is seen as the "most common and constant learning environment" for individuals in our culture today (Morgan and Signorielli 1990, 13). As such, cultivation theory underscores the important role of television within the cultural context where religious identity and self-conception develop.

Researchers who examine relationships between television content and the formation of values and attitudes among viewers find a strong correlation between exposure to television messages and viewers' perceptions of reality (Greenwald 1968; Hawkins and Pingree 1980). James Potter and Ik Chang (1990) conclude that television has a substantial impact on attitude formation and construction of reality among middle school students, providing evidence that the influence of television on value formation begins in childhood.

Media scholars also use cultivation theory to explain some of the important relationships between television programming and self-conception (Wolf and Briley 2003; Wolf, Decelle, and Nichols 2009), making this theory particularly useful for this research. In addition to cultivation theory, the theory of the self-concept developed by John Kinch (1972, 247) is relevant to examining the self-conceptions of television audiences. "Self-concept" refers to how individuals perceive themselves, and Kinch (1972) argues that people's self-conception is the consequence of how others perceive them and their subjective perception of others' appraisals. Of course, independent self-identity evaluation factors into self-conception as well, particularly in terms of how people feel when they see images that fail to reflect their lived experience.

In this study, the participants spoke at length about news images of and stories about Jews, and they agreed that television news programming cultivates narrow and limited perceptions of Jewish people. Supporting Edwin Diamond's (1978) concept of third-person effect, they believed that this cultivated imagery shaped how other people thought about them and, as a result, how they felt about themselves. The participants discussed important relationships between television news images of Jewish people and their own Jewish identity and self-conception. Ultimately, they believed that these news images and stories contributed to their own feelings of inclusion in, and exclusion from, society. Television portrayals of Jews are particularly salient to the formation of Jewish American identity as the role of the Jewish community in the formation of Jewish identity declines. Without the strong, traditional Jewish community of the Old World, Jewish Americans learn about Jewish traditions, the Jewish community, and Jewish life from nontraditional sources such as television news.

To explore how Jewish Americans think and feel about the images and stories of Jewish people on television news, we conducted a focus group in San Francisco with 12 Jewish men and women between the ages of 18 and 35. Participants discussed common representations of Judaism on television news and evaluated how these depictions made them feel about themselves. We also asked the participants to think about how their views, experiences, perspectives, values, and beliefs are represented in and excluded from the news.

During the focus group, we asked participants to describe their television news usage patterns and preferences, to evaluate the news programming they consumed, and to examine their thoughts about the news sources they used. They also explored relationships between televised news images of their faith—representations of the individuals, the community, and the settings and situations in which "their people" live—and their own self-conception as members of these groups. As the discussion progressed, we asked them to explore how they thought these news representations contributed to their own self-conception, their sense of self-identity within their group, and how they felt as Jewish people. They contemplated the sources of these feelings by considering messages from media and from other people. Finally, we asked them to offer recommendations on how to improve news coverage of Jews and Judaism.

Representation of Judaism and Jews in Television News

Several patterns of predominantly negative images of Jews in the news emerged as points of discussion. Participants noted the lack of ethnic and secular diversity, the underrepresentation of Jewish women, stereotypes such as bargain-shopping shows associated with Jewish hosts, an over-emphasis of conflict as opposed to scientific and social advancement in Jewish communities, the paucity of news coverage of Jewish peace groups, the exclusion of Jewish empathy for Palestinians, and the marginalization of non-Israeli Jews.

Ethnic and gender diversity were frequently mentioned as missing from news images of Jews. For example, one participant was disturbed by a Fox News report on Israel's 2005 disengagement plan to dismantle settlements in the Gaza Strip and West Bank. The emotional scenes of Israeli settlers being evicted were widely covered in television news reports, but as the 23-year-old woman recalled, the coverage failed to convey the diversity of Jewish society:

> There were no women, only men. There weren't any ultra-orthodox; they were just like regular modern Orthodox. But they were still being pictured as religious, praying every day. I didn't see any Ethiopian Jews, or anything else. Just the typical European, not the diversity of Israel that is displayed. It's just the typical white, Jewish, Israeli men.

Ultra Orthodox Jews pray at the tomb of Joseph, a biblical figure from the book of Genesis, in the northern Palestinian West Bank city of Nablus, 2007. (Courtesy of MENAHEM KAHANA/AFP/Getty Images.)

A 23-year-old man agreed with this assessment, adding that the humanism of Israeli Jews was also absent from news. He was disturbed because this implied that Jews lack empathy for Palestinians:

> They portray the Israelis as all white, all male, and they just look very stoic, conservative, as if the deaths of the Palestinian people or their oppression does not factor into their value system as being relevant. I feel like it's casting an idea that all Israelis are these people that don't think these Palestinians are human, and we are heartless people.

The focus group participants agreed that news images and stories cultivate perceptions of Jews as right wing and orthodox. When asked to talk about how the news represented the experiences of Jewish people, several participants were critical of what they did not see. They agreed that the news decisions made by editors, producers, and reporters contribute to a predominant impression that is cultivated in the minds of audience members, including themselves. A 27-year-old woman was distressed by the recurring images of conflict in Israel and the paucity of narratives about Jewish peace

Members of the Jewish Voice for Peace contingent walk in an anti-war march near Judkins Park, Seattle, Washington, 2007. (Courtesy of Joe Mabel.)

groups. She wanted news organizations to diversify the non-Israeli Jewish experience:

> You don't see the peace groups in Israel, people who are trying to have a dialogue with the Palestinians, trying to change the situation. Like a tsunami, we have so many Jews and Israelis in cooperation with Jews all over the world, trying to get wonderful things all around the world and in Israel. You don't see it because the news [shows] are not interested in the nice parts, only the juicy parts. So [those alternate stories] will break the picture of Israeli as the bad guy, and Israeli culture, and many other nice Israeli aspects that you cannot usually see.

Participants regretted the choices made by news gatekeepers to frame the coverage. For example, a 23-year-old man took issue with the recurring images of mothers grieving over the loss of their family members designed to evoke sympathy among news viewers:

> You have this dichotomy between cultures where these Palestinians—there's the mothers who just lost their husbands and children—and the Israelis—men who are hard-working, or who are rough and tough, and they're just running around. Whereas on the Israeli side, there are mothers who are losing their children or husband, but they just don't show that. They show what they want to show, with the slant the network has.

According to a United Nations report, 4,228 Palestinians and 1,024 Israelis died in the seven years beginning in September 2000 as a result of the Palestinian-Israeli conflict (United Nations 2007).

Recognizing news conventions and the structural bias of emphasizing conflict and powerful images, the participants contextualized their analysis within a broader problem of misrepresentation that encompasses Christianity and Islam in addition to Judaism. A 25-year-old woman compared how Jews are depicted with stereotypical and disturbing television images of conservative Muslims and Christians:

> It's the same thing. We are talking about how Jewish people are portrayed, and how Muslim people are portrayed. The same typical beard, the little hat, they're praying five times a day, and they are all male. Mainly white, and that is how we see them. They just show whatever people picture in their minds, whether it's Jewish or Muslim people or Catholics. It's just how it works on television.

The lack of news images that fairly and diversely represent Jews who do not live in Israel is another theme that emerged during the discussion. As Jews living in the United States, these adults felt strongly that their own communities and Jewish communities in Europe were excluded from television news. As one 25-year-old woman complained,

> I don't see any representation of Jewish people who are not from Israel. There are Jewish people all over Europe. There is no news about them, no representation of how they are doing there, as far as discrimination, living conditions, nothing like that. You don't see it.

When the participants talked about images of Jews in the news, they agreed that the negative stereotyping on television, while sometimes benign, was all too common. A 23-year-old woman provided this example of how she felt about a San Francisco Bay area local news station that perpetuated the stereotype of the thrifty Jew:

> I think it's Channel 7. There is a guy, somebody Tennenbaum, and he does "Bay Area Bargains," and I'm always interested in what that is saying. If they chose him, it's like, 'Oh, he's this nerdy Jewish guy with a beard. . .' I just wonder who chose him. If that supports the stereotype in actuality, or if it fuels whatever the stereotype may be, positive or negative, it is there, and I'm conscious of it.

News Images and Sense of Self

Most of the participants expressed negative feelings when they talked about how Jews and Judaism are represented on television news. Sadness, anger, alienation, and shame were some of the common feelings these men and women expressed, and they conveyed their frustration and resentment toward the news. As one 25-year-old man explained,

> It has a very big impact on my perception of myself. I watch all this and read about it, and I'm very angry. It makes me angry because there is so much rhetoric and so much hatred just being spewed and there is no real answer to it.

These and related feelings led some participants to modify their behavior. They were reluctant to publicly display symbols of Judaism, like the Star of David or a *kippah,* or skullcap. A 22-year-old man described how news contributes to the ways he believes he is perceived by other people as a Jew, and how this perception caused him discomfort when he wore a symbol of his identity in public.

> When I keep seeing these stereotypes reinforced on the media, it just propagates the image of pushing Jewish and Israeli people further away from being accepted and integrated into society. It makes me sad because I'll walk down

the street and I'll have a Star of David on me and someone will automatically think that I hate Palestinian people or I think everyone should move to Israel and reclaim it as our land. They just have these ideas about me even though they don't know me, just by the fact that they know I'm Jewish. It's being reinforced by our stereotypes in the media and also how we are being portrayed in the international news.

This sentiment of sadness and alienation, contributed to by the cultivated imagery of television news, was echoed by several others in the group. The participants said the news branded them as having extreme views. As a result of these feelings, they kept a rather low public profile to avoid being judged by assumptions made as a result of how the news-viewing public perceives Jewish people. One 21-year-old man expressed his concerns about potential anti-Semitism provoked by images of Jews in the news media:

If someone here was wearing a kippah, I would definitely think twice about doing that, because you see Israel coverage, and you see these religious Jews. So if you're walking around with a kippah on your head, you are making that connection. So people could get that perception of me. I think we're not very much out there, only when we choose to be. It's like we're going to have a rally on campus. Well, OK, now suddenly we're all Jews because obviously we're here at this rally. But as soon as that rally is over and we're walking around going to classes, we're invisible again.

During the discussion, participants were asked to explain why they felt as they did and how these feelings shaped their self-perception. As they responded, they shared personal experiences that provoked their sense of outrage and alienation. A 23-year-old man described an incident on campus when other people made assumptions about his beliefs and identity based on the pro-Israeli T-shirt he wore:

There was a rally, and I was wearing my 'I love Israel, I love peace' shirt. It said 'I am a Zionist' on the back, and a guy was putting up a flyer that said, "Why you should support the Iraqi resistance." And I said, you are supporting terrorism; that is essentially what you are doing! He said I'm not supporting terrorism, these people are resistance fighters. He looks at my shirt, and goes, you must think all Muslims are terrorists, don't you! And I go, no, I think that is the most insane comment I've ever heard anyone say.

The participants felt these assumptions about Jews were hurtful and unfair. Some of the men and women did more than just publicly conceal their identity; they disassociated from it. When asked to share their feelings, some participants distanced themselves from the topic by focusing on other people's experiences rather than their own. In doing so, they provided support for Diamond's third-person effect hypothesis, which suggests that media audiences perceive messages to have a greater impact on other people than on themselves (1978). For example, one 22-year-old man speculated that news representations might be cultivating images of Judaism that impact the secularization of Jewish youth. He expressed his belief that news images inhibit young people from openly expressing their ties to Jewish culture and tradition, but instead of sharing a personal story to illustrate his point, he discussed his friend's experience of media effects:

> I have a friend from Santa Cruz, and he's a Jew from L.A., and maybe the media has affected him in such a way because when you are watching the media, the emphasis on tradition and that sort of thing is completely lost for him. He could care less, even though one of his parents is Israeli. He is, possibly from the media, but just popular culture tells him that to try to hold on to those values, his culture and tradition is not the most popular thing to do anymore. It's sort of looked down upon.

This story expresses a concern in the Jewish community that the widely cultivated realities presented in television news contribute significantly to the formation of Jewish American identity, an identity that is partially constructed from the messages and characters portrayed on fictional TV programs (Pearl and Pearl 1993). Media consumers interpret televised themes and characters relative to the social group from which they draw their identity (Cohen 1991; Liebes 1988; Liebes and Katz 1990). As members of the Jewish community and non-Jewish people are exposed to television images that are reinforced throughout the ever-expanding newer electronic media, the cumulative effect of these messages is to more powerfully influence Jewish identity and the feelings of exclusion from society expressed by these Jewish people. The result of this situation is that distorted media images create a situation whereby people who are unfairly represented struggle to find their own identity.

The Construction of Jewish Identity

Jewish identity reflects the complex fusion and balancing of religious and secular components, and the contending aspects of individual and group-based identity were evident in our research. The communication theory of identity, which argues that identity consists of four levels (personal, enacted, relational, and communal) is a useful framework for understanding the development and experience of Jewish American identity (Hecht, Collier, and Ribeau 1993).

The *personal* level of identity concerns the individuals' self-cognition and spiritual sense of wellbeing, while the *enactment* level focuses on how actual messages express identity. The *relational* level refers to how identity is formed through relationships with other people and is closely tied to reciprocal identities. Finally, the *communal* level explains how a community constructs and shares its identity. When images of communal identities are assumed to be the characteristics of individual group members, and when they are applied to individuals in fixed and rigid ways, they become stereotypes (Hecht 1998).

Jewish identity is dynamic and changes over time. Notably, modernism brought about a shift in religiosity that focused more strongly on meeting the needs of individuals rather than those of the community. The outcome of this is a dramatic variation that often emphasizes the secular aspects of identity (Liebman 1982). Michael Meyer (1990) describes this secularization process as a wearing down of Jewish identity that occurred as a result of increased exposure to non-Jewish ideas and symbols. Television is an important window into Jewish identity because audience members interpret the images and stories on television in the context of the community from which they derive their identity (Cohen 1991; Liebes 1988; Liebes and Katz 1990). According to Jonathan Pearl and Judith Pearl (1993), individuals construct their unique identities from messages and characters they see on television.

Participant Conclusion: A Plea for Fairness

The men and women in the focus group did not feel less Jewish, nor did they feel excluded from Jewish people as a cultural group. At the same time, they were aware of a gap between what they know about themselves and the cultivated imagery of television news stories about Jewish people, and about the impact of images that are consonant, cumulative, and ubiquitous throughout media culture. Researchers and media literacy educators and advocates are not alone in their call for news images and stories that are not injurious and harmful to viewers.. The focus group participants made a similar plea as they took the unfair and narrow TV news representations of Jewish ethnicity, gender, and national origin to task. So long as these images—and others such as the focus on Israel as a place of conflict—dominate the news, the cultivation process will perpetuate an unfair, narrowly defined, and damaging perception of Jewish people.

The cultural context in which religious identity and self-conception develop is particularly significant in terms of what is *excluded* from television news. The lack of images and stories that acknowledge the scientific advancements of Jews and that represent secular, successful Jews suggests a world that misses an important point. The rich, diverse culture of Jewish people, for example the significant efforts of Jewish peace groups, is lost to viewers who see the same stories repeatedly. The virtual absence of women and ethnically diverse Jewish people is not only injurious to Jewish people but also dangerous because it undermines the broader cultural efforts to celebrate diversity and include everyone in the public sphere. Other forms of popular electronic media such as radio and the web reinforce these ubiquitous messages as they re-create the relentless, repetitive, and cumulative message system that Gerbner and his colleagues so aptly described.

There are powerful outcomes of this type of media coverage. These participants believe that television news images and stories of Jewish people contribute significantly to their feelings of sadness, frustration, and alienation. They modify their behavior for fear of being ridiculed and criticized. These Jewish Americans are surely not alone as they reshape their identity and decide whether or not to express it publicly.

Recommendations for Television News

Many participants identified the profit structure of commercial television news and the blurred line between news and entertainment as factors that affect the quality of news and impact how audience members come to (mis) understand Jews. A 24-year-old man recommended that commercial news outlets focus less on tabloid journalism and more on in-depth current political and social affairs. A 23-year-old man suggested promoting critical news consumption and media literacy to help viewers deconstruct news about Jews.

Several participants wanted broadcast news organizations to carefully reexamine their representations of the Jewish faith and Jewish people, and to acknowledge what is missing from the visual images of Jews, particularly in Israel. As one 27-year-old woman exclaimed,

> Israel should be seen as a more diverse place. We have many problems, definitely, but many other aspects of peace and culture that we can bring.

Tel Aviv is such a modern city, and still people think Israelis ride camels. Israelis are [highly accomplished in] high tech and in medicines. So many areas. An Israeli won the Nobel prize this year [Ada E. Yonath, Chemistry, 2009]. These are the things we should see.

The other members of the focus group vigorously argued that the pattern of news stories of Jews engaging in conflict rather than promoting peace should stop because it can (and in their case did) lead to feelings of alienation and hesitancy to publicly express loyalty to the faith. They suggested alternatives to existing news representations, as in this comment by a 22-year-old woman:

I am more concerned about things on the news that aren't related to the Israeli-Palestinian conflict. When I think about Israel, there are major scientific advancements; those to me are more news than the conflict. It may be inevitable, but a lot of news just focuses on conflict.

When asked to think about what they would say to television stations to improve the Jewish image on the news, the participants offered four concrete suggestions:

1. Fund more in-depth features;
2. Provide more equitable, diverse images of the events in Israel;
3. Reduce the vast amount of sensational news; and
4. Diversify coverage of Jewish societies to include more women, non-Israeli Jews, and Jewish peace groups.

These Jewish Americans know firsthand how images can injure, and by the end of the focus group session it was easy for them to come up with suggestions for what news producers should do to begin to make up for a long history of programming that has failed them. Recommendations like theirs can be located in the long history of calls for more diverse and fair images suggested by media researchers and members of the global viewing public who have also cried out against news images that neglect ethnic, gender, and cultural diversity. The failure of the news media to reduce sensational content and to allocate more television time to in-depth news programming is an outcome of the business model of news organizations that Edward Herman and Noam Chomsky (1988) so aptly described more than 20 years ago as the propaganda model. As the calls for diverse news content continue, it should be asked: Why does change take so long?

Sources

Cohen, Jodi. 1991. The "relevance" of cultural identity in audience's interpretations of mass media. *Critical Studies in Mass Communication* 8: 442–454.

Crouteau, David, and William Hoynes. 2003. *Media/society: Industries, images, and audiences*, 3rd ed. Thousand Oaks, CA: Pine Forge Press.

Diamond, Edwin. 1978. *Good news, bad news*. Cambridge, MA: MIT Press.

Gerbner, George, Larry Gross, Michael Eleey, Marilyn Jackson-Beeck, Suzanne Jefferies-Fox, and Nancy Signorielli. 1977. Television profile no. 8: The highlights. *Journal of Communication* 27: 171–180.

Gerbner, George, Larry Gross, Michael Morgan, and Nancy Signorielli. 1980. The "mainstreaming" of America: Violence profile #11. *Journal of Communication* 30 (3): 10–29.

Greenwald, Anthony. 1968. *Cognitive learning: Psychological foundations of attitudes*. New York: Academic Press.

Hawkins, Robert P., and Suzanne Pingree. 1980. Some processes in the cultivation effect. *Communication Research* 7 (2): 193–226.

Hecht, Michael L. 1998. *Communicating prejudice*. Newbury Park, CA: Sage.

Hecht, Michael L., Mary Jane Collier, and Sidney Ribeau. 1993. *African-American communication: Ethnic identity and cultural interpretation*. Newbury Park, CA: Sage.

Herman, Edward, and Noam Chomsky. 1988. *Manufacturing consent: The political economy of the mass media*. New York: Pantheon.

Kinch, John W. 1972. A formalized theory of the self-concept. In *Symbolic interaction: A reader in social psychology*, ed. Jerome Manis and Bernard Meltzer, pp. 245–261. Boston: Allyn and Bacon.

Liebes, Tamar. 1988. Cultural differences in the retelling of television fiction. *Critical Studies in Mass Communication* 5: 277–292.

Liebes, Tamar, and Elihu Katz. 1990. *The export of meaning: Cross-cultural readings of Dallas*. New York: Oxford University Press.

Liebman, Charles. 1982. The religious life of American Jewry. In *Understanding American Jewry*, ed. Marshall Sklare, pp. 96–124. New Brunswick, NJ: Transaction.

Livingston, Sonia. 1998. *Making sense of television: The psychology of audience interpretation*, 2nd ed. London: Routledge.

Meyer, Michael. 1990. *Jewish identity in the modern world*. Seattle: University of Washington Press.

Morgan, Michael, and Nancy Signorielli. 1990. Cultivation analysis: Conceptualization and methodology. In *Cultivation analysis: New directions in media effects research*, ed. Nancy Signorielli and Michael Morgan, 13–34. Newbury Park, CA: Sage.

Morley, David. 1986. *Family television: Cultural power and domestic leisure.* London: Comedia.

Pearl, Jonathan, and Judith Pearl. 1993. All in the Jewish family: Understanding, utilizing and enhancing images of intermarriage and other Jewish family relationships on popular television. *Journal of Jewish Communal Service* 69: 24–39.

Potter, James W., and Ik Chang. 1990. Television exposure measures and the cultivation hypothesis. *Journal of Broadcasting & Electronic Media* 34: 313–333.

Thoman, Elizabeth, and Tesa Jolles. 2008. *Literacy for the 21st century.* Malibu, CA: Center for Media Literacy. http://www.medialit.org/reading_room/article540.html (accessed March 18, 2010).

Tyner, Kathleen. 1998. *Literacy in a digital world: Teaching and learning in the age of information.* Mahwah, NJ: Lawrence Erlbaum.

United Nations Office for the Coordination of Humanitarian Affairs. 2007. *Special Focus: Occupied Palestinian territory, Israeli-Palestinian Fatalities since 2000, Key Trends.* http://unispal.un.org/UNISPAL.NSF/0/BE07C80CDA4579 46 8525734800500272 (accessed Jan. 5, 2011).

Wolf, Michelle A., and Kelly Briley. 2007. Negotiating body image. In *Rethinking media education: Critical pedagogy and identity politics,* ed. Anita Nowakj, Sue Abel, and Karen Ross, pp. 131–148. Cresskill, NJ: Hampton Press.

Wolf, Michelle A., David Decelle, and Sandy Nichols. 2009. Body image, mass media, self-concept. In *Race/gender/media: Considering diversity across audiences, content and producers,* 2nd ed., ed. Rebecca A. Lind, pp. 36–44. Boston: Allyn & Bacon.

Chapter 22

Mass Media's Mexican Americans

Ramón Chávez

The dawn of the new millennium brought about a significant milestone in the demographics of the United States. The estimated Latino population of the United States reached 46.9 million in July 2008, making the cultural group the nation's largest ethnic minority. Latinos made up 15 percent of the nation's total population in 2000, according the U.S. Census Bureau (Bureau of the Census 2009).

With the growth of the Latino population in the United States came increasing visibility of Latinos in the media, owing in part to recognition of this group's market potential. Media attention to the growing purchasing power of them challenged historical negative portrayals of Hispanics in mainstream media and initiated more positive images. However, renewed debate over growing immigration from Mexico and Latin-American countries and its influence on U.S. demographics gave renewed life to outdated stereotypes. Consequently, the beginning of the new millennium offered a mixed bag of media images of Latinos.

Latino Sight(ing)s

Perhaps the biggest change in images of Latinos appeared in the entertainment industry. As prominent evidence, witness the rise of Mexican-American entertainers such as the young and vivacious Jessica Alba, who gained national fame with her starring role in the hit television series *Dark Angel* (2000–2002). The actress earned a Golden Globe nomination for her portrayal of an essentially non-ethnic character, despite the character's Latina name. She also became a staple of numerous magazine covers (e.g., "Jessica Alba" 2008).

Stand-up comedian George Lopez, whose initial appeal was to Mexican-American audiences, crossed over to garner wider network audiences, first with his eponymous television sitcom (2002–2007), then his late-night TBS talk show that debuted in 2009, the first hosted by a Latino. He joined veteran Cheech Marin, whose staying power with mainstream audiences since the 1970s blossomed into more diverse roles in movies and television.

In the same period, Eva Longoria Parker became a household name when she took on a starring role in the ensemble cast for the megahit *Desperate Housewives*. Acclaimed veteran actor Edward James Olmos landed on the revived and popular sci-fi classic *Battlestar Galactica*, and Mario Lopez emerged from his teen heartthrob role in the juvenile hit *Saved by the Bell* to become a star emcee on a variety of programs.

However, the personal success demonstrated by Alba, Olmos, and Lopez, among others, was qualified. Although they are recognized as Mexican-American actors, they did not play Mexican-American characters in the prominent roles mentioned above. The failure of such stars to portray overtly Latin characters raised concern about the relative absence of positive, credible Latino characters on television.

An Emmy and Golden Globe award-winning actor, Olmos had earlier played positive Latino roles in a number of acclaimed movies. In *Selena* (1997), Olmos played the supportive but hard-driving father who managed the career of his daughter, Selena, the ill-fated Tex-Mex music star. In *Stand and Deliver* (1988), Olmos portrayed the dedicated, real-life math teacher Jaime Escalante, who pushed his minority students toward academic excellence despite a tough environment. In *American Family* (2002), audiences encountered the realistic trials and tribulations of a Latino family in East Los Angeles, headed by their conservative patriarch Jess Gonzalez, played by Olmos (Cengage n.d.).

Yet such fully realized, complex Latino characters—as with actors and directors of color—remain scarce. For example, a 2001 study by the Screen Actors Guild found that only 22 percent of all roles went to performers of color (HearUsNow.org n.d.). Of the 826 episodes of the top 40 drama and comedy series on the air in 2000–2001, Latinos directed only 2 percent. The lack of Latino role models is also hard-felt in children's programming. The Children Now organization found the family hour on television to be the least ethnically diverse on the air (HearUsNow.org n.d.). Yet given the rising political power of Latinos, their increasing number, and their growing economic impact, Children Now argues that a show targeted to Latino children likely would be a success. When Nickelodeon tested the waters, their show *Dora, the Explorer* became a huge hit not only in Latino households but also with all viewers.

Absentee Latinos in the U.S. Media

Historically, progress for Latinos in the U.S. media, as in most social situations, has been painfully slow. Media portrayals of them in general, be they in popular culture, such as television or movies, or in mainstream press depictions in newspapers and magazines, often have been stilted at best and racist at worst (Berg 2002, 25).

In the 1950s, television's *The Cisco Kid* offered a positive, if unrealistic, western hero of Latino origin, a rarity.[1] The "Kid" rode through the desert Southwest dressed in a fancy Charro outfit more typical of Mexican troubadours, or *mariachis*, and hardly the appropriate outfit for a *vaquero*, or cowboy. His get-up was akin to wearing a business suit while gardening. Pancho, his dim-witted sidekick, fulfilled the stereotypical "dumb Mexican" role. Nonetheless, the series' actors Duncan Renaldo, a Spaniard, and Leo Carrillo, a Mexican American, were the first regularly appearing Latino television stars. A year after the series production began in 1949, Desi Arnaz, a Cuban American, made his debut with his wife, Lucille Ball, in *I Love Lucy*. His largely positive portrayal as a crooner was marred by his tirades in Spanish about Lucy's antics, which became part of the skewed image of the hotheaded Latin.

Other characters emerged, many not positive. Comedian Bill Dana's alter ego, Jose Jimenez, had a heavy accent and none-too-bright demeanor.[2] His classic self-introduction, "My name, Hosay Hee-men-ess," did not go over well with Latinos in his audience, who mounted a grassroots protest (Wilson, Gutierrez, and Chao 2003, 103–104). After 10 years of performances, Dana, who was of Hungarian descent, gave in to the pressure and announced in 1970 that he would no longer play the character. Other secondary characters of the period were primarily domestics or laborers.

Progress toward more positive images often has been measured in small victories, not in sweeping trends. For example, the popular television series *Zorro* brought a heroic Latino character to the forefront in a widely popular program. However, the lead role was played by Guy Williams, an Anglo.[3]

Many of the more important and recent changes have come about as a result of the hard work of Mexican Americans and other Latinos themselves who have risen through the ranks of the media professions into positions as writers, directors, and producers. Among the most notable of these have been filmmakers such as Luis Valdez (*La Bamba* [1987] and *Zoot Suit* [1981]), Gregory Nava (*Selena* and *El Norte* [1983]), and Moctezuma Esparza (*The Milagro Beanfield War* [1988]). These directors brought a more realistic and complete picture of Mexican-American life to the screen that has been recognized by the industry and appreciated by Latino communities. Much, however, remains to be done by these and other professionals, who continue their efforts to become part of the image-making power structure.

Shifting Portrayals on the Screen

Prior to *The Magnificent Seven* in 1960, a movie whose plot was borrowed from a classic Japanese tale, *The Seven Samurai* (1954), a number of westerns portrayed the Mexican stereotype that included the helpless *campesinos*. These village peasants could not fend for themselves and had to rely on the Anglo hired guns to save them. More recently, the stereotype was repeated in the less than amusing *¡Three Amigos!* (1986). The other extreme was occupied by the Mexican *banditos* who terrorized a village. These outlaws, preying upon their own people, became the generic bad guys whenever the script called for a change from the customary villains in westerns, Native Americans.

Rarely was a hero of Latino descent. Even when the script called for a Spaniard or a Latino, Anglos frequently played the character and Latino actors were not called upon. For example, Tyrone Power won the lead role and provided a stilted portrayal, complete with unconvincing accent, of the fateful matador in Hollywood's version of *Blood and Sand* (1941). A movie based on Isabel Allende's popular book *The House of the Spirits* was heavily criticized because the main characters in the story, which focused on the history of a Chilean family, were all played by non-Latino actors (Ebert 1994).

As the U.S. demographic landscape has changed, so has the marketing strategy of the movie industry. A recent report of the Motion Picture Association of America (MPAA) found that Latino moviegoers represented 24 percent of the total in 2007, despite declining numbers of moviegoers among the general public (MPAA 2007). The report stated that Latinos were responsible for buying 297 million tickets compared to 150 million for African Americans and 115 million for all other ethnicities combined.

The study further found that Latinos, who represented almost 33 percent of the Anglo moviegoers in 2007, purchased 10.8 tickets per person, a rate almost 75 percent higher than the average of 7.9 tickets per person for the overall market. Commenting on shifts in the movie industry, Tito Alvarez of Hispanic Media Marketing said, "This . . . is about more than Spanish-speaking movies; the impact of attendance of Hispanics at movie theaters across the country affects the profitability potential of all mainstream blockbusters" (MPAA 2007).

Population changes and the burgeoning Latino market have led media managers to take care not to offend their newfound audience. Recognition of the potential of their dollars has prompted media executives to pay attention to the perceived sensitivities of this audience—and to attempt to avoid the stereotypes of the past. For example, the National Latino Media Council, a coalition of 16 of the nation's largest Latino advocacy organizations, stated that the level of diversity in employment at the major television networks improved by the end of 2009. The NLMC's *9th Annual Media Report* noted incremental progress in the hiring of Latinos, both in front of and behind the camera, at the four major networks: ABC, CBS, NBC, and Fox.

The NLMC gave ABC and Fox the highest marks, saying they offered shows with central Latino characters that feature Latino actors in prime time shows, such as America Ferrera in *Ugly Betty*, Eva Longoria Parker in *Desperate Housewives*, and Carlos Bernard on Fox's *24*. CBS was commended for featuring Latino actors in prominent regular roles such as Michael Irby in *The Unit*, Eva La Rue and Adam Rodriguez in *CSI: Miami*, and Enrique Murciano and Roselyn Sanchez in *Without a Trace*. In these roles, Latinos are presented as intelligent and in leadership roles, often with no overt reference to their heritage, as if to acknowledge their natural place in the national ethnic mosaic. Change is coming, but slowly.

Persistent Problems in the Press

Although media stereotyping of Latinos is most visible in the entertainment industry, the news media are not without fault. News coverage in the 1960s and beyond led to a stereotype that left most of the mainstream United States confused over the status and quality of life of Mexican Americans. In its quest to identify leaders and to rely upon them as quick and easy sources of information, the press painted a picture of Latino life in which Cesar Chávez and his United Farm Workers Union symbolized the Chicano

Migrant grape pickers who work from field to field in northern Mexico and California take a break. (Courtesy of Tomás Castelazo.)

Civil Rights movement and framed an understanding of the broader Latino population as well.

Little wonder, then, that many in the United States believed at that time that Latinos were a rural phenomenon. On the contrary, more than 90 percent of Latinos live in cities and suburbs, and while problems persist in rural areas where migrants experience some of the worst living and working conditions with chronic health problems and little access to a formal education, the old, stereotypical images of the Mexican *bracero*, or a seasonal hired hand who is ignorant, unsophisticated, crude, and unkempt, comprise the predominant media message. Early in the twenty-first century, media researchers Clint Wilson, Lena Chao, and Felix Gutierrez (2003) found that reporting on people of color in Anglo U.S. news media was characterized by five distorted patterns:

1. Omission from newscasts,
2. Representation as a threat,

3. Source of confrontation and social disturbance,
4. Stereotypical news selection with distorted emphasis on violence and illegality, or
5. Inclusion in truly multiracial coverage.

The first four biased patterns of coverage had been practiced so consistently by the news media that they became established policy, according to the research (Wilson, Chao, and Gutierrez 2003, 116–117). As of 2003, journalists and editors had grudgingly begun to adopt the fifth pattern.

For decades, the mainstream press has struggled with its historical practice of stereotypical coverage (or complete omission) of the Latino community. Gutierrez (1978) said the mainstream news media discovered the community during the turbulent mid-1960s, when news organizations began to wake up to the existence of what the press termed "the invisible minority." During this period, journalists seemingly rushed to cover this newfound group with simplistic generalizations and facile headlines that relied more upon the biases of the Anglo reporters, editors, and publishers than upon reality. For example, Gutierrez (1978) cited a *Time* magazine reporter who rode through East Los Angeles in 1967 writing about "tawdry taco joints and rollicking *cantinas*," "the reek of cheap wine," and "lurid hotrods." "Such simplistic approaches," wrote Gutierrez, "glossed over the reality of Chicano life in the United States and played on the preconceptions and stereotypes of those controlling the media and their predominantly Anglo audience" (1978, 1).

In addition, media accounts of Latino immigration tend to be one-sided, giving extensive coverage to the political debate while inadequately portraying the individuals, many of whom have come in pursuit of the "American dream," as did millions of immigrants before them from nations throughout the world. In that sense, most Latino immigrants are no different from any previous immigrants; they've come to pursue a better life for themselves and their families.

In maintaining the negative image of Mexican immigrants, however, the mainstream press persists in using the doubly pejorative term "illegal alien" to describe people who come into the United States and are considered burdens on the system (Carter, Thomas, and Ross 2010). Latino civic organizations have asked for a change in newspaper and TV newsroom policies and encouraged media to replace the term "illegal alien" with alternative terms such as "illegal immigrant" or "undocumented worker," but change has been slow to be accepted by news managers. Time did little to change that approach. Recently, news items focused predominately on crime in the barrio, ignoring some of the more positive activity in the Mexican-American community.

The second stereotypical image of Latinos that remains prevalent in the media is that of the urban punk—the gangbanger. Ethnic media groups, such as the National Association of Hispanic Journalists (NAHJ), have strongly recommended that news organizations use such terms more selectively and consider the damage they cause. To be sure, crime rates are high in the impoverished barrios and ghettos in the United States, and much of this crime is caused by illicit drugs and trafficking. But drugs are not solely the plague of the inner cities; they are also a fact of life in Anglo suburbia. Much is written about drug traffickers, but little is said about the drug consumer. The insatiable U.S. appetite for drugs enables the illegal drug trade.

In response, Latinos have expressed dissatisfaction with the stereotypical news coverage. In 1990, for example, the Hispanic Link news service conducted a national survey of leaders of Latino organizations, with 79 percent of those surveyed believing local newspapers had failed to improve coverage of Latinos (Rodriguez 1990). Elsa Nunez-Wormack, then chair of New Jersey's Hispanic Association of Higher Education, expressed the consensus when she said, "There's a lot going on in our communities, but we only see the bad—the stereotypes" (quoted in Rodriguez 1990, 1–2).

Recently, cable news programs have become a major source of public images and information about immigrants. Renewed fear and paranoia about the latest wave of Latino immigration fueled by one-sided, histrionic commentary by such national media figures as Lou Dobbs of CNN prompted NAHJ to publicly applaud his 2009 departure from CNN (NAHJ 2009).

Traditional print media also continued to struggle, owing in large part to the virtual absence of Latinos from the newsroom. As newspapers flailed to maintain their economic viability and amid flagging readership and tumbling advertising revenues, the American Society of Newspaper Editors (ASNE) documented losses in newsroom employment that disproportionately impacted journalists of color. In 2009, ASNE reported that "minority" personnel in the nation's newspapers constituted only 13.4 percent of the total, down from the previous year and equal to the percentage back in 2005. Latinos constituted only 4.47 percent of newspaper personnel in

2009, roughly equal to the percentage in 2006 and 2008, despite dramatic growth in the Latino population (ASNE 2009).

With such low numbers of employees, it is not surprising that U.S. newspapers have not fared well in the eyes of the Latino community in portraying the realities of life, issues, and concerns. The press presents them as reluctant Americans who are inappropriately loyal to their Spanish language and fails to portray those who are hardworking with jobs no one else wants. Emphases on illiteracy and school dropout rates, without perspective, sociological context, or analysis, fuel the stereotype of Latinos as less intelligent than Anglos. News solely focused on crime creates an image of Latino neighborhoods and barrios as hotbeds of violence and illegal activity.

Concluding Comments

In many respects, the "gangbanger" has become the *bandito* of the new age, awakening slumbering stereotypes of dangerous, violence-prone Latino men. At the same time, the historic image of the community inhabited by docile, singing *braceros* sweating in the fields beneath the sun and sombrero-clad men constantly on siesta persists as a subtext to stories in which today's immigrants are broadly presented as unable to help themselves and dependent upon Anglo generosity.

Despite the arrival of new Latino faces on television and movie screens and the growth of Latino-owned and -managed media, today's news and entertainment media fail to consistently present them as whole people within a complex and multifaceted community. They fail to focus on the good work done by Latino community organizations. Their achievements give way to more visually dynamic media accounts of gang members, complete with their signature attire of baggy, low-slung pants, oversized shirts, and tattoos (for more about the stereotypes associated with tattoos, see chapter 18).

Despite the difficulties of the mainstream press to adapt to the changing national demographic landscape, Latino publications seemed to portend a brighter future. Kirk Whisler in his 2009 report for *Hispanic Link* noted that a total of "834 Hispanic newspapers, 556 Hispanic magazines and another 526 journals, annuals, yellow-page directories and newsletters [keep] this nation's ever-growing Latino population, now approaching 50 million, informed." With some exceptions, the previous year's $1.4 billion in revenue from Latino publications signaled an emergent and successful cultural press, with Latino newspapers reaching a circulation of 17.8 million and magazines achieving a combined circulation of 31.6 million (Whisler 2009). Whisler concluded in his report,

> Today Hispanic newspapers serve all but four of the country's 50 states and almost 200 markets nationwide. This provides far better coverage than any other media serving the Hispanic community (2009).

Latino publications also reported growth in the emerging online market. In 2009, 443 newspapers and 311 magazines maintained websites, the majority of which are updated at least weekly (Whisler 2009). Millions of people turn to these sites for more balanced news and entertainment because these sources are more attuned to the realities of Latino life in the United States. Although bad news is reported, it is balanced by the good things that happen in communities with stories that cover fashion, holidays and customs, recipes, and home life. These media offer more stories about trends in music and literature, an added focus on celebrities and their lives, and stories and advertisements in bilingual formats about products and services of particular interest to Latinos.

In 2003, the U.S. Census Bureau announced that Latinos had overtaken the African-American population as the nation's largest minority group. Yet their representation in news and entertainment media remains far below that, both in number and in the variety of characters or positions they represent. Today it is vital that the news and entertainment media more accurately reflect the realities and the broad spectrum of the large and growing Latino population in the United States rather than rely on the practices and stereotypes of the past. Progress is being made, but it is slow, and there remains a long way to go.

Notes

1. See http://www.youtube.com/watch?v=GadFKMPh8GY (accessed March 19, 2010).

2. See http://www.youtube.com/watch?v=h4vDcx2V0PA (accessed March 19, 2010).

3. See http://www.youtube.com/watch?v=EQhu1s-gsRg (accessed March 19, 2010).

Sources

American Society of Newspaper Editors (ASNE). 2009. Annual employment survey: Percent and number of newsroom employees by group. April 16.

Berg, Charles Ramirez. 2002. *Latino images in film: Stereotypes, subversion, and resistance.* Austin: University of Texas Press.

Bureau of the Census. 2009. Facts for features: Hispanic heritage month 2009. July 15. http://www.census.gov/Press-Release/www/releases/archives/facts_for_ features_special_editions/013984.html (accessed March 18, 2010).

Carter, Diane, Ryan Thomas, and Susan Dente Ross. 2020. You are not a friend: Media conflict in times of peace. *Journalism Studies.*

Cengage. N.d. Hispanic heritage: Edward Olmos. *Gale Cengage Learning.* http://www.gale.cengage.com/free_resources/chh/bio/olmos_e.htm (accessed March 18, 2010).

Ebert, Roger. 1994. Review: *The House of the Spirits. Chicago Sun Times,* April 1. http://rogerebert.suntimes.com/apps/pbcs.dll/article?AID=/19940401/REVIEWS/404010302/1023 (accessed March 18, 2010).

Gutierrez, Felix. 1978. Through Anglo eyes: Chicanos as portrayed in the news media. Paper presented at the Association for Education in Journalism 61st annual conference, Seattle, WA, August 13–16.

HearUsNow.org. N.d. Hear us now, communities: Latino. http://www.hearusnow.org/other/8/latino/ (accessed March 18, 2010).

Jessica Alba: Biography. 2008. *People,* April. http://www.people.com/people/jessica_alba/biography (accessed March 18, 2010).

Motion Picture Association of America (MPAA). 2007. Movie attendance study 2007: Ethnicity. http://www.mpaa.org/MovieAttendanceStudy.pdf (accessed March 18, 2010).

National Association of Hispanic Journalists. 2009. NAHJ welcomes Dobb's departure from CNN. November 20. http://www.nahj.org/2009/11/dobbsdeparture/ (accessed March 18, 2010).

National Latino Media Council (NLMC). 2009. Diversity report cards: 9th annual media report. December 4. http://www.nalip.org/nalip/documents/NLMC_Diversity_Reportcard_2009.pdf (accessed March 18, 2010).

Rodriguez, Roberto. 1990. Daily papers misread Latinos, say leaders. *Hispanic Link Weekly Report,* April 9.

Whisler, Kirk. 2009. Print is dead? Hispanic publications defy trend, tell a different story. News Report. *Hispanic Link.* May 24. http://news.newamericamedia.org/news/view_article.html?article_id=a61d85293886b3ff8cd812b79d1f8dab (accessed March 18, 2010).

Wilson, Clint C., II, Felix Gutierrez, and Lena Chao. 2003. *Racism, sexism and the media: The rise of class communication in multicultural America.* Thousand Oaks, CA: Sage.

Chapter 23

Drawing Dehumanization: Exterminating the Enemy in Editorial Cartoons

Erin Steuter and Deborah Wills

Good cartoons . . . hit you primitively and emotionally. . . . A cartoon cannot say, "on the other hand," and it cannot defend itself. It is a frontal assault, a slam dunk, a cluster bomb.

Doug Marlette (1992, 10)

On September 4, 2007, an editorial cartoon by Pulitzer Prize–winning cartoonist Michael Ramirez appeared in the *Columbus* (Ohio) *Dispatch* and in the more than 400 other newspapers in which Ramirez's work is syndicated. The cartoon portrayed a map of the Middle East with its center, the country of Iran, replaced by a huge sewer grate. In case the reader misses the reference, the word "Iran" is superimposed on the grating in bold capital letters; beneath it, in smaller letters and much more faintly, is the word "Extremism." Out of the sewer comes a swarm of cockroaches that cover the grate and spread across the adjoining countries of Iraq, Pakistan, Afghanistan, Turkey, and Saudi Arabia. The image was striking: some commentators compared it to depictions both of Jews in

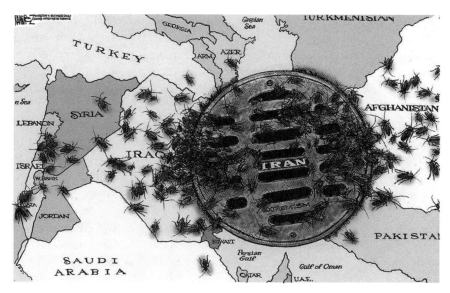

Editorial cartoon by Michael Ramirez depicting Iran as a large drain. (Courtesy of Michael Ramirez and Creators Syndicate, Inc.)

pre-Holocaust Germany and Rwandan Tutsis before the 1994 genocide. "It is very sad," said Ali Sheikholeskami, executive director of the Islamic Cultural Center of Northern California, "that American media has come down to such a level and that there is no outcry of the American public against these types of cartoons or this type of dehumanization of an entire nation" (quoted in Memarian 2007b).

Those who objected to Ramirez's cartoon argued that the cockroach image invited an exterminationist response and offered a dangerous metaphorical model in an already highly charged political situation. For many Iranians, it was "a visualization of a new propaganda war that echoes the way a large part of the U.S. media backed the invasion of Iraq in 2003" (Memarian 2007a).

Such political and historical resonances raise key questions about the ways in which political cartoons may reflect, reproduce, reinvigorate, or even introduce dehumanizing images of those we see as racial or cultural enemies. Of particular interest are the ways in which such dehumanizing images, especially those representing the enemy as animals, vermin, or insects, reinforce larger assumptions about the indistinguishable "sameness" of our enemies. These pictures eradicate differences of belief and action and conflate individual leaders or policies with entire nations or ethnic groups. Using such images as its focus, this chapter explores why certain dehumanizing images dominate many political cartoons that create suggestive patterns of representation that link the enemy to an animal.

The following analysis of depictions of Arabs and Muslims in political cartoons is based on principles fundamental to semiotic analysis: that images and objects signify or mean things that go beyond their immediate literal meaning, and that this extended or figurative meaning is based on and can infinitely expand the relationship of the object or image to the larger systems of meaning (cultural, economic, textual, and so on) that provide their context. This is to say that political cartoons belong to broader systems of communications within a society and culture and derive their meanings from the specific images used and the codes and conventions of cartooning. However, these meanings are also derived from viewers' own understanding of surrounding political issues, journalistic coverage, pre-existing assumptions, and so on.

In this way, then, political cartoons provide signs that the viewer understands and decodes within a system of meaning that is colored by personal knowledge and experience. Following the methodology proposed by Terry Warburton (1998), we first provide "initial descriptions" of the cartoons we examine, then we discuss their "immediate connotation" or apparent meaning, and then the larger "systemic connotation" derived from their connection to the broader network of meanings is exposed (257). By analyzing the patterned quality to repeated visual tropes, such as "Arabs as Rats" or "Muslims as Insects," we are also able to identify recurrent narrative threads woven through and interconnecting these images such that the "visual depiction *begins* as a common basis for the construction of meaning" (Warburton 1998, 258, emphasis added).

Cartoons in Context

Editorial cartoons offer one of the most provocative examples of the way negative images of the enemy and the Other permeate our consciousness. Political cartoons are intriguingly situated at the intersection of popular and political culture, speaking to aficionados of both and comprising a hybrid of the two. Timely and topical, they are meant to elaborate and comment upon current events, and usually they articulate a specific political message from a particular ideological perspective. Through their use of humor, they may "speak the unspoken, explicitly connecting with implicit assumptions of their readers in ways that generate powerful responses" (Gottschalk and Greenberg 2008, 9). At the same time, they are allied to other graphic forms, such as newspaper comics or "funny pages," and they draw upon some of the visual codes and shorthand techniques common in these other forms. As with satire and stand-up comedy, political cartoons often bring together the strange bedfellows of humor and outrage. Similar to newspaper headlines, they also reach a wider audience than do full-text news articles. In fact, they are often the most widely read feature of the editorial section (Caswell 2004, 13).

Lucy Shelton Caswell (2004) observes that editorial cartoons have a complex function. They both reflect and mold the opinions of their readers. While good cartoonists may be "driven by a sense of moral duty" to support what they believe to be right or oppose what they believe to be wrong, they must take care not to alienate newspaper management or readers irrevocably (14). Although the cartoonist traditionally has a certain license to forcefully articulate his or her political opinions, views which "reflect and contribute to" the formation of political attitudes (Bouvier 2001, 91), the effectiveness of the cartoon is limited by readers' knowledge of the issues and contexts surrounding it. This means that the cartoonist "must gauge the community's familiarity with the topic of the day and choose images to express her or his opinion succinctly and appropriately" (Caswell 2004, 16).

Editorial cartoons are, therefore, complex in their workings and effects. Although North American journalistic tradition treats editorial cartoons not as mere illustrations but as persuasive communications with the rhetorical force of editorials or op-ed columns, they are also the product of the "seemingly incongruous partnership of capitalism and freedom of expression" (Caswell 2004, 14). The cartoon therefore has a tripartite role as a "culture-creating, culture-maintaining and culture-identifying artifact" (DeSousa and Medhurst 1982, 84). The economy of the cartoon form ensures that the artist has a limited space in which to make his or her point. While, as several scholars have noted, this intensifies the immediate impact of the cartoon (Caswell 2004, 18), it also limits the cartoonists' control of the message, since it is the reader who must decode the cartoon's visual metaphors within an economical, sometimes cryptic, frame. For both readers and scholars of cartoons, therefore, the meanings of political cartoons require that their "metaphors must always be studied within their sociopolitical context" (El Refaie 2003, 76).

Although early theorists of cognitive metaphor like George Lakoff and Mark Johnson (1980) postulated that metaphors are shaped by our physical experience as infants and are therefore universal to all humans, others building on their work have since argued for a greater specificity of interpretation. Recent scholars suggest that the connection of metaphors to thought cannot be considered as entirely universal but must be examined within specific social, cultural, and political contexts because readers are likely to bring "their own experiences and assumptions" to the process of interpreting visual metaphors (El Refaie 2003, 78). This individuality of interpretation, however, is counterbalanced by the recognition that dominant tropes are broadly shared and their figurative meaning is understood across a given community. Thus, for example, although an idiosyncratic interpretation of an image may still exist or be facilitated by a cartoonist (such as the snake being represented as benign, as it might be for botanists or owners of pet reptiles), the shared, long-standing, communal understanding of the snake as representing something evil, deceptive, and deadly will inevitably dominate any reading of the metaphor.

Since such contexts are often multifaceted and complex and can differ widely across and between different communities of readers, both the visual representations of political cartoons and the contexts from which

Cartoon showing snake, representing monopolies involving senators, with tail wrapped around dome of the U.S. Capitol, facing personification of "Liberty" and "Puck" asking Uncle Sam, "What are you going to do about it?" (Courtesy of the Library of Congress.)

they derive their meanings deserve attention. While a cartoon's visual metaphors are perhaps its most powerful strategies (Gombrich, quoted in El Refaie 2003, 75), they are also its most volatile. Metaphors themselves are often complex in their workings and, as such, can be interpreted uniquely or idiosyncratically by individual readers. However, given interpretations can also come to dominate how a certain visual metaphor is understood. Some recent scholars argue that "conventionality," that is, the way in which certain common metaphors are lodged or entrenched in our systems of thought, is by itself an elusive concept. The connection between metaphors and how we interpret them is dynamic rather than static and, therefore, "cannot be determined once and for all but depends on the specific discourse concept" (El Refaie 2003, 82). In other words, while there is always the possibility that individual readers will assign highly unique or idiosyncratic meanings to a certain visual symbol, within the

IVE HAD A DEAL OF TROUBLE, BUT THIS REPAYS ME FOR IT!"

Uncle Sam is represented as a baby eagle hatched from a "Centennial" egg under a large eagle that says, "I've had a deal of trouble, but this repays me for it!" in this wood engraving that was originally published in *Harper's Weekly* in 1876. (Courtesy of the Library of Congress.)

broader social and cultural contexts that make up an "interpretive community," certain readings or understandings will come to dominate (Fish 1980, 14).

Even the cartoonist's clear intention does not always control how his or her image will be interpreted. Symbolic images of the United States as an eagle, for example, are a popular shorthand in political cartoons and have been used in ways that support, question, or critique the war in Iraq. Even in cartoons intended to critique, however, the strong cultural associations of the eagle with virtues like strength, nobility, or fierce individuality metaphorically frame the symbolic bird in a positive way.

As viewers, we may become entangled in familiar symbolism to the extent that we cannot completely distance ourselves from it. Dennis Mumby and Carole Spitzack (1983) call this effect "metaphoric entrapment." In metaphoric entrapment, a concept is understood so thoroughly and consistently in terms of a particular metaphor that it doesn't appear to make sense in any other terms. Our thinking about something (e.g., the war or the enemy) "becomes so tied up with a particular metaphoric structure that alternative ways of viewing the concept are obscured or appear to make less sense" (Mumby and Spitzack 1983, 164).

The Enemy as Vermin

Images of the enemy as bestial, animalistic, or otherwise less than human proliferate in editorial cartoons. Human–animal fusion is a common feature of cartoon's visual shorthand. One cartoon by Gary Varvel (2004) shows an image of a Saddam-headed rat trapped in a box, huddled out of the beam of an infantryman's flashlight.[1] Jeff Parker's (2002) "Foxy Saddam" depicts British Prime Minister Tony Blair contemplating a solution to the controversy over a ban on fox hunting by positioning a picture of Saddam's head on a fox's body. Daryl Cagle's (2006) "Saddam Skin Rug" portrays George W. Bush posed in a big-game hunter's pith helmet on a bearskin rug; the head of the bear is depicted as the head of Saddam Hussein.

The practice of merging two distinct visual images, one human and one not, into a single image within which the component parts can still be detected is a common trope (El Refaie 2003, 77). In "Saddam Skin Rug," then, Saddam's head is still clearly discernable as a human head, while the attached body is still clearly that of an animal. Technically, the clear presence of both visual elements in the fused form makes it difficult to misunderstand or misidentify the cartoon's component figures. Visually, however, the merged image of human and beast solidifies and confirms the debased, mutated, monstrous Otherness of the hybrid figure to such an extent that we may not recognize its humanity even in its pain, death, and defeat. The very monstrosity of this hybrid suggests that it is right and natural that the subject *should* be the hunter's prey.

As with any system of metaphors that collaborate to supply a consistent visual vocabulary, one of the key effects of this human–animal fusion is that such visual metaphors come to be considered "relatively 'natural' and unremarkable" (El Rafaie 2003, 81). When certain metaphorical patterns come to dominate the cultural imagination by depicting the enemy in such consistent and recognizable ways (by regularly emphasizing, for example, their perceived monstrosity, unnaturalness, or debased natures), it becomes easier and more habitual to simply absorb and accept the idea that our enemies or "opposites" are simply fundamentally different from us, and different in a way that is alien and unsettling.

Another example of the visual hunt metaphor is found in Mark Streeter's (2004) depiction of a giant, plumed, heroic-looking eagle descending with talons spread to grasp a tiny creature labeled Saddam that is popping its head out of the ground. The caption reads "Eagle Captures Chicken in Rat Hole." The pictorial lessening of the enemy into inhuman insignificance that simultaneously dehumanizes and transforms into something odious (i.e., vermin) is a thread that can be identified in several cartoons: in the *Los Angeles Times*, a Michael Ramirez (2003) cartoon shows a huge hand in a sleeve decorated with American stars clutching a tiny, bewhiskered rat labeled "Saddam" over the caption "Gotcha!" In Rod Emmerson's (2004) "A Weapon of Mass Humiliation," a rat with the face of Saddam sighs in resignation as Uncle Sam's arm, with its identifying stars-and-stripes sleeve, reaches out a gloved hand to fastidiously pluck it up by the tail. In Allen Lauzon Falcon's (2003) "Saddam Rat Caught," we find another depiction of Uncle Sam's gloved hand, in the familiar stars-and-stripes sleeve, holding between thumb and forefinger a bedraggled-looking "Saddam Rat," pictured with a scaly tail snaking out from beneath a patched, filthy robe.

The rat image, in these cartoons, works on two levels. It is trivial, perhaps ridiculous: The "Saddam Rat," in its comically threadbare robe and scraggly beard, looks distinctly silly dangling from the oversized fingers of Uncle Sam's gloved hand. On another level, even a comically rendered rat invokes strong cultural associations: Rats are, in many countries, seen as a particularly loathsome and dangerous type of vermin that is associated with pollution, infestation, pestilence, disease, and contagion. The metaphor of the enemy as a slightly ridiculous, trivialized pest that is nevertheless abhorrent and potentially dangerous is also present in Jeff Parker's (2005) cartoon that shows an imperious but irritated British lion, draped in the Union Jack, directing an annoyed glance at a black rat labeled "terrorism" that chomps on the lion's tail.

In the "America's hand" cartoons, however, we see something not present in the English version, that is, the provocative suggestion of precision, cleanliness, and fastidiousness. Like the "man of the house" whose job is to protect the wife and children and pluck and dispose of a rodent, the symbolic U.S. hand does not turn away from the dirty job that must be done but performs it with neatness and precision, to protect those who, like U.S. women and children, may need paternal protection but may be too squeamish or weak to undertake the necessary act of eradication themselves. In these images, the task is portrayed as necessary and almost surgical. In fact, in Emmerson and Lauzon's cartoons, the rolled cuffs of Uncle Sam's white gloves visually suggest a doctor's gloves, donned for serious and surgically tidy medical tasks performed by an expert. In each of the "America's hand" cartoons, we see no messiness, no blood, no civilian deaths, only the singular and easily identified pestilent enemy dangling midair. The scale, scope, and damage of the war are completely unrepresented in this image of paternal protection.

The paternal hand metaphor, with its implicit promise that we are "in good hands," also suggests a clean, quick, almost sterile precision to the act of eliminating the enemy. It incorporates some of what George Lakoff (2003) observes at work in the "Nation as a Person" metaphor, in which a country's leader represents and stands in for all of its people. Lakoff (2003) notes that this metaphor hides the fact that

> the 3,000 bombs to be dropped in the first two days [of the war on Iraq] will not be dropped on that one person. They will kill many thousands of the people hidden by the metaphor, people that according to the metaphor we are not going to war against.

This ability of visual metaphor to obscure individual detail and mask the personal behind the symbolic is one of its potentially most dangerous properties. Sam Keen (1991), a pioneer in analyzing propagandistic representations of the enemy, makes this point succinctly. He argues that nations deliberately avoid thinking individually about the enemy, since this allows them to be harsher or more brutally comprehensive in waging war. Keen observes that

> we systematically blur distinctions and insist that the enemy remain faceless, because we are able to perpetuate the horror of war, to be the authors of unthinkable suffering only when we are blind ourselves to what we are doing. (1991, 24)

Representing the enemy as rats or vermin effectively renders them faceless and less than human, but it also goes one step further by emphasizing their "mass nature." Rats are most horrifying and dangerous when they appear in a multitude. Unlike humans who bear children and establish homes, rats breed and nest. As they breed, they reproduce and create multitudes with swarms that threaten to spill over; pollute our safe, human homes; and raise instinctive fears and primal impulses to destroy the source of the threatening incursions.

Plagues of Insects

Hiding a nation's citizens behind a metaphor that obscures both their humanity and their individuality is also a key function of insect metaphors, especially metaphors of swarms. Comparisons that associate the enemy with the indiscriminate (the enemy attacks blindly because of its inherently destructive nature) and the interchangeable (all members of the enemy are identical in nature, motivation, and intent) appear in editorial cartoons as in other forms of media. In Cameron Cardow's (2006) cartoon from the *Ottawa Citizen*, terrorists are drawn as realistic-looking cockroaches crawling over the surface of the Canadian flag. The caption reads, "Terrorists. Even the best homes get them." The enemy is portrayed as a corrupter who enters and despoils the sacred space of the home and who brings filth, disease, and spoilage in its wake. In Cardow's cartoon, the elaborate visual detail of the roaches evokes a shudder. Their flat bodies and sweeping antenna seem to desecrate the flag they crawl upon. The grotesqueries of the depiction seem to demand a response of eradication or extermination.

This implied message about the intrusion of threatening swarms and the need to eradicate or exterminate them generates anxiety in Canadians who may have felt safe in their presumption that terrorism is something that happens elsewhere. The cartoon delivers a jarring message of vulnerability: Your home, too, is prey to these threatening, inhuman invasions. On an intellectual level, the cartoon plays with the idea of the domestic and the political; on an emotional level, it strikes viscerally. By verbally and visually conflating "nation" with "home" in the cartoon's juxtaposition of the flag with its reference to "the best homes," alarm is elevated to paranoia. The word "home" calls up all that is closest and dearest to us, and it makes the threat appear not only political but also deeply personal. In this way, the cartoon's internal logic is not far from historical propaganda images of the enemy as invader and defiler. The insects that crawl over the flag recall images from the Nazi film *Der Ewige Jude* (*The Eternal Jew*) (1940) that portrays Jews as rats who crawl across a map of Europe. Both of these visual metaphors are linked in their reliance on overt national symbols (flag, map) being grotesquely overrun by swarming tides of filthy, disease-carrying invaders, and by the powerful, visceral reaction such a visual staging of desecration invokes.

A similar linking of the enemy to a swarming, invading mass is made in Daryl Cagle's (2001) cartoon "Dead or Alive" in which George W. Bush, dressed in a cowboy costume with a sheriff's star, fires his six-shooters into a teeming swarm of cockroaches, under a "WANTED: Dead or Alive" poster of a single, huge roach. There is a significant visual tension in the cartoon between the single "criminal" roach shown in the poster and the massed, teeming swarm into which Sheriff Bush fires. It is clearly impossible for either Bush or the viewer to identify the individual "wanted" cockroach among the horde. All merge into a single, inseparable identity. While Bush's use of pistols to kill cockroaches is offered as a kind of comic overkill, viewers may find themselves identifying with Bush's stance, since we, like him, cannot be expected to differentiate between individual bugs in an advancing tide. Within this conceptual frame, the indistinguishability that extends to encompass every human enemy prompts the viewer to conclude that there are no innocent insects.

Hierarchy of Humans

The visual messages imply that enemies attack what is most sacred. They come at us, our families, our homes, and the cleanliness, purity, and comfortable safety of our nation. As Sam Keen (1991) reminds us, the "lower down in the animal phyla" enemy metaphors descend, "the greater sanction is given to the soldier to become a mere exterminator" (16). Over time, many nations have used similar insect metaphors to debase "domestic" enemies, that is, those whom dominant groups perceive as a threat within the borders or boundaries of the national home. This message is reflected in the vermin metaphors that are regularly applied to immigrant groups, especially when increases in immigration begin to be perceived as a threat to security. In *Brown Tide Rising*, Otto Santa Ana (2002) documents how media discourse on immigration typically uses "overtly racist and dehumanizing" terms. Animal images provide the dominant metaphor for immigrants, with secondary metaphors of the hunt which support and reinforce it. Illegal immigrants are described as "hunted down," "baited," "lured," and "ferreted out." News reports frequently talk about the "hordes" "pouring" across the border instead of employing more accurate and neutral descriptions such as "people walking across."

Santa Ana argues that far from being mere figures of speech, such metaphors produce and support negative public perceptions of the Latino community. He reveals how metaphorical language repeatedly publicly portrays them as invaders, burdens, parasites, diseases, animals, and weeds (2002, 83). (For related discussion, see Ramón Chávez's chapter 22.) Just as common language choices feed into larger, dehumanizing metaphoric frames, so the common visual images of editorial cartoons support larger ways of thinking about the enemy as inhuman.

Countering Stereotypes

Editorial cartoons are important to examine because of the way they encapsulate and communicate assumptions and positions. Editorial cartoons are extremely influential and convey information in a compressed or truncated way that often replaces fuller accounts and reinforces shorthand notions of others, such as stereotypes. Many people get their news more from such cartoons than from full-text articles. Audience studies "consistently show that editorial cartoons enjoy higher readerships than editorials" (Hussman cited in Plante, 2004, 12).

John Temple, editor of Denver's *Rocky Mountain News*, observed, "There's something about a cartoon that distills so much into a small space" (cited in Plante 2004, 13). Similarly, *New York Times* editor Ethan Bromer noted, "Cartoons suck the air out of editorial pages because they are the one thing many people glom onto. In other words, they get in the way of people reading the page more closely" (quoted in Gottschalk and Greenberg 2008, 9).

Recognizing this powerful and potentially injurious influence, a few cartoonists are working to supplement, critically address, or undermine some of the dominant, dehumanizing patterns found in many North American

editorial cartoons. These cartoonists employ some of the same visual metaphors commonly found in more mainstream editorial cartoons in order
to expose the racism of these images and their familiarity and persistence
in our public discourse. They may also invert or turn these images on their
heads in order to invite readers to rethink them, or they may mobilize
such images to comment critically on government policy on the war on
terror. In doing so, they suggest ways to reframe the way more dominant
cartoon images frame the enemy as rodent, vermin, or otherwise less than
human.

In one such thought-provoking cartoon by Mike Lester (2003), we see a
stylized version of Uncle Sam in the foreground wearing a uniform labeled
"Sam's Pest Control" and holding a canister of poison. In the other hand,
he proudly dangles a rat. Around him is a decimated home. Lamps are
smashed, furniture is overturned amid piles of rubble, and only a few walls
remain standing. Behind one broken wall we glimpse a tank, and through
a ragged hole in the roof we see the tower of a mosque. In the middle of
this wreckage stands an Arab family. The family is visually coded as Arabic
through familiar signifiers such as the father's beard and the mother's robe
and head covering. The tank in the street is a clear shorthand suggesting
this scene is set in a military zone. Within the home, mother and son gaze
in blank shock at the ruin. The father, a pained smile on his face, stammers,
as Sam proudly proffers the rat, "Thanks. . . . I think."

This cartoon is remarkable for the way it turns the pest metaphor back
on itself, clearly implying that the wanton destruction caused by the hunt
for a single enemy rat is dangerously disproportionate. Equally remarkably,
the cartoon paints both the result of the hunt and the Arab family in pointedly
human terms—the humanity of the pictured Iraqis is emphasized by their
domestic setting and family grouping, an image that is radically different
from the undifferentiated, aggressive swarms through which they are often
depicted. The human costs of the war in Iraq are thus poignantly evoked,
as symbolized in the small but central detail of a family photograph in the
cartoon home that has been knocked carelessly aside by the exterminator's
violence.

Cartoons such as Lester's oppose dehumanizing conventions by offering
strong visual alternatives. Jean Plantu, who draws for Paris's *Le Monde*,
created "Cartooning for Peace," an international association of cartoonists
promoting civil rights. Such initiatives encourage cartoonists from different
countries to communicate and become part of a larger public conversation
on the potency of the image. UN Secretary-General Kofi Annan supported

this initiative, calling for cartoonists across the globe to acknowledge the "big responsibility" that comes with their position:

> We need to engage cartoonists in the discussion. They can help us to think more clearly about their work, and how we react to it. And perhaps we can help them to think about how they can use their influence, not to reinforce stereotypes or inflame passions, but to promote peace and understanding. (EuropaWorld 2006)

The images that make up the metaphors of editorial cartoons are important because of the way they participate in larger systems. Metaphor offers us a unique insight into our ideas and assumptions, at once reflecting and shaping the spectrum of our values. The role of metaphor and the discourses it sustains are so fundamental that, as E. L. Doctorow (1977) has argued, "The development of civilizations is essentially a progression of metaphors" (233).

Like metaphors based in language, metaphors based in visual messages matter. In their framing of events and identities, they offer a way to understand our world and to act within it. With this power to generate and shape action, metaphors are a potent force. Our cultural lexicon of dehumanizing metaphors is remarkably enduring. Not only has it colonized the discussion of the war on terror, but also it has permeated our public conversations about other denigrated or marginalized groups. However, as the work of some cartoonists shows, editorial cartoons can also invite readers to think critically about the images that circulate through cartoons.

Note

1. Many of the contemporary cartoon examples discussed in this chapter can be found in two publications by the authors of this chapter; see Steuter and Wills (2008, 2009).

Sources

Bouvier, Virginia. 2001. Imaging a nation: U.S. political cartoons and the war of 1898. In *Whose war? The War of 1898 and the battles to define the nation*, ed. Virginia Marie Bouvier. Westport, CT: Praeger.

Caswell, Lucy Shelton. 2004. Drawing swords: War in American editorial cartoons. *American Journalism* 21 (2): 13–45.

DeSousa, Michael, and Martin Medhurst. 1982. Political cartoons and American culture: Significant symbols of campaign 1980. *Studies in Visual Communication* 8 (1).

Doctorow, Edgar Lawrence. 1977. False documents. *American Review* 29: 231–232.

El Refaie, Elizabeth. 2003. Understanding visual metaphor: The example of newspaper cartoons. *Visual Communication* 2 (1): 75–95.

EuropaWorld. 2006. Annan backs French idea of cartoons for peace. *EuropaWorld*, October 20. http://www.europaworld.org/week282/annanbacks201006.html (accessed March 19, 2010).

Fish, Stanley. 1980. *Is there a text in this class? The authority of interpretive communities*. Cambridge, MA: Harvard University Press.

Gottschalk, Peter, and Gabriel Greenberg. 2008. *Islamophobia: Making Muslims the enemy*. New York: Rowman & Littlefield.

Keen, Sam. 1991. *Faces of the enemy: Reflections of the hostile imagination*. New York: Harper Collins.

Lakoff, George. 2003. Metaphor and war, again. *AlterNet*, March 18. http://www.alternet.org/story/15414/ (accessed March 19, 2010).

Lakoff, George, and Mark Johnson. 1980. *Metaphors we live by*. Chicago: University of Chicago Press.

Marlette, Doug. 1992. Journalism's wild man. *American Journalism Review*, January–February. http://www.ajr.org/Article.asp?id=1444 (accessed March 19, 2010).

Memarian, Omid. 2007a. Iran says cockroach cartoon crosses the line. *Human Rights Tribune*, September 24. http://www.humanrights-geneva.info/Iran-says-Cockroach-Cartoon,2255 (accessed August 31, 2009).

Memarian, Omid. 2007b. US cartoon no joke to Iranians. *Asia Times*, September 20.

Mumby, D. K., and C. Spitzack. 1983. Ideology and television news: A metaphoric analysis of political stories. *Central States Speech Journal* 34: 162–171.

Plante, Bruce. 2004. What publishers think about editorial cartoons. *Nieman Reports*, December 22, 11–13.

Santa Ana, Otto. 2002. *Brown tide rising*. Austin: University of Texas Press.

Steuter, Erin, and Deborah Wills. 2008. Infestation and eradication: Political cartoons and exterminationist rhetoric in the war on terror. *Global Media Journal: Mediterranean Edition* 3 (1). http://74.125.155.132/search?q=cache%3AW1dhVrcME0AJ%3Aglobalmedia.emu.edu.tr%2Fspring2008%2Fissues%2F2.%2520Political%2520cartoons%2520and%2520exterminationist%2520rhetoric.pdf+%22Cameron+Cardow%22+%22canada+buggy+flag%22&hl=en&gl=us (accessed March 19, 2010).

Steuter, Erin, and Deborah Wills. 2009. *At war with metaphor: Media, propaganda, and racism in the war of terror*. Lanham, MD: Lexington.

Warburton, Terry. 1998. Cartoons and teachers: Mediated visual images as data. In *Image-based research: A sourcebook for qualitative researchers*, ed. Jon Prosser, pp. 252–262. London: Routledge.

Chapter 24

Gulf Arabs: From Caricatures to Image Managers

Nancy Beth Jackson

Until the second half of the twentieth century, nobody paid much attention to the Arab nomads on the northeastern tip of the Arabian Peninsula along the Arabian or Persian Gulf. The Bedouins, or Bedu, lived a life of subsistence in one of the harshest environments on earth. Since before recorded history, they herded camels across the sands or traveled to the sea to fish, trade, and look for pearls. With virtually no natural resources, they relied on oasis-grown dates for nourishment while they traded pearls with their neighbors in India for bare necessities.

"Arab" is a broad term that goes beyond religion, skin color, nationality, or politics. According to the Old Testament, the Arabs are descendants of Ishmael, the son of Abraham and Hagar, an Egyptian slave. Abraham banished Hagar and her son to the desert with bread and an animal skin filled with water after his long-barren wife Sarah gave birth to Isaac. The biblical tale of illegitimacy and outcasts helped establish early stereotypes of Arabs. Until the twentieth century, the Bible was the main source of information about Arabs and the Middle East for many Americans.

Advancing out of Moorish Spain, Arab horsemen were repulsed by Charles Martel at the Battle of Tours in southwestern France in 721, a battle often cited as a turning point in European history. Conflict between the two cultures continued to shape geography and history. Arabs and the

Published around 1905, this photograph shows a portrait of a Bedouin man holding a sheathed dagger. (Courtesy of the Library of Congress.)

West developed in what amounted to parallel universes, with jihads and crusades defining their relationship instead of diplomacy.

Representing the West were the British, who staked out the region as a sphere of influence without thinking it worthy of being a colony. They called the sparsely populated area "the pirate coast" following several centuries of harassment along the vital trade routes to India, the British Empire's "jewel in the crown." Using sea raids by the powerful Al Qawasim tribe of Ras Al Khaimah as an excuse, the British mounted a decisive expedition in the early nineteenth century. Attacking from both land and sea, the British destroyed the Al Qawasim fleet, a victory that led to a series of treaties with Bedu tribesmen along the coast. In 1853, the British signed treaties with hereditary sheikdoms or emirates along the coast, leading to a protectorate called the Trucial States in what is now the United Arab Emirates.

Taken around 1927, the picture shows Sheik Hammad es Sànea, head of the Tarabin tribe near the city of Beersheba in what is now Israel. (Courtesy of the Library of Congress.)

Other treaties during the century added neighboring Bahrain, Kuwait, and Qatar as British protectorates, effectively making the Gulf a British lake.

For the British, the region was little more than a refueling station, first for ships and later for airplanes. No infrastructure such as schools, hospitals, or roads was put in place. The first newspaper in the Trucial States did not appear until 1927, when several issues of a two-page sheet, a compilation from Arabic newspapers in Iraq and Kuwait, passed hand to hand among the few literate inhabitants of the emirate of Sharjah. Postage stamps and currency were recycled from British India. A handful of merchants along the coast participated in a larger world, but most of the Bedouin continued to live much as they always had, secluded from the world, roaming the vast sand desert from the Rub' al Khali or "Empty Quarter" in the southern third of the peninsula to the shores of the Gulf. In his history of Abu Dhabi, Mohammed Al-Fahim (1995) quotes a late nineteenth-century traveler as saying, "The inhabitants walk around with a piece of cloth around their waist, naked from the waist up with no shoes and nothing to cover their heads, armed with a spear, a sword or an antiquated gun" (25). The period after World War II saw revolutionary changes in the rest of the world but not among the Bedouin of the Gulf region. They remained poor and isolated. The term "Gulf Arab" became a popular, and often derogatory, designation for Arabs of the Arabian Peninsula only after immense oil resources transformed the desert from Saudi Arabia to Oman a few generations ago.

Sir Wilfred Thesiger (2008), a British explorer who lived among the Bedouins in the Empty Quarter from 1945 to 1950, did much to romanticize the desert dwellers. He found dignity, generosity, hospitality, courage, and other noble qualities in the traditional Bedu life. In *Arabian Sands* (Thesiger 2008), he wrote that he had embarked on his journey "with a belief in my own racial superiority, but in their tents I felt like an uncouth, inarticulate barbarian, an intruder from a shoddy and materialistic world" (38). Living among the tribes, he learned "how welcoming are the Arabs and how generous their hospitality" (38). He would later mourn the advent of so-called modernity (9).

Thesiger's "noble savage" of the desert differs greatly from negative media stereotypes of Arabs, a people who originated in the Arabian Peninsula. "Probably no ethnic or religious group has been so constantly and massively disparaged in the media as the Arab over the past decades," journalist David Lamb first wrote in 1987, a generation before 9/11. "Being an Arab is a liability everywhere but in the Arab homelands, for virtually everywhere else the Arab is stereotyped in negative terms" (1987/2002, 131). Reporting on a study of public opinion that applied adjectives like "barbaric and cruel," "treacherous," "warlike," and "rich," Lamb concluded that "the West sees the Arab as being a millionaire, a terrorist, a camel herder or a refugee, but not as a human being" (2002, 131).

Greater understanding has not come with globalism and new communication technologies. Lamb (2002) reported,

> To a large extent, the Arabs are misjudged in the West—and caricatured in a manner once reserved for blacks and other minorities—for the simple reason that they *are* different. Their language, dress, prayers, behavior and thoughts don't fit into any neat pattern easily grasped by Westerners. Yet in little more than three decades, moving from illiteracy to video in a single step, they have become an important new global force. (xvi)

Nevertheless, the violent Arab stereotype is perpetuated in Hollywood, where they are usually cast as villains, as Jack G. Shaheen (2001) pointed out in *Reel Bad Arabs*. In one of many examples portrayed in *Robin Hood*,

Prince of Thieves (1991), the movie opens with Crusaders being tortured in the most barbaric ways within a dungeon under a mosque in Jerusalem.

Origins of a Stereotype

In 1867, Mark Twain popularized and recast ancient Arab stereotypes into an American mold when he set off as a journalist on a paddle-steamer cruise of the Mediterranean. His newspaper dispatches, rare reportage from that part of the world in the nineteenth century, received broader circulation when published in book form in 1869 as *The Innocents Abroad* (1869/2002). The immensely popular book established Twain as a major U.S. writer. Parodying William Cowper Prime, a contemporary travel writer who sentimentalized Bedouin life, Twain introduced his readers to an Arab world of filth, confusion, and violence. He compared one guide to a land-dwelling pirate: "A tall Arab, as swarthy as an Indian . . . sunbeams glinted from a formidable battery of old brass-mounted horse-pistols and the gilded hilts of blood-thirsty knives" (1869/2002, 386–387). Traveling in what was then Palestine, he described "the country [as] infested with fierce Bedouins whose sole happiness, in this life, is to cut and stab and mangle and murder unoffending Christians" (387). At every turn, Twain takes literary pot shots at the Bedouins. Even after admiring the "firm lips, unquailing eyes and kingly stateliness of bearing" of some Bedouin herdsmen and comparing them favorably to "Joseph and his brethren," Twain added he was sure they would sell off their younger brothers if they had a chance because "they have the manners, the customs, the occupation and the loose principles of the ancient stock" (359).

Poking fun at Prime's dramatic and romantic accounts of desert warriors and their steeds, Twain recounted meeting "half a dozen Digger Indians (Bedouins) . . . cavorting around on old crow-bait horses" (1869/2002, 411). He wrote,

At last, here were the "wild, free sons of the desert," speeding over the plain like the wind, on their beautiful Arabian mares we had read so much about and longed so much to see! Here were the "picturesque costumes!" This was the "gallant spectacle!" Tatterdemalion vagrants—cheap braggadocio— "Arabian mares" spined and necked like the ichthyosaurus in the museum, and humped and cornered like a dromedary! To glance at the genuine son of the desert is to take the romance out of him forever—to behold his steed is to long in charity to strip his harness off and let him fall to pieces! (411)

Despite Twain's descriptions, the earliest motion pictures featured Prime's romanticized son of the desert who dominates the silent screen in the person of Rudolph Valentino, the "Latin Lover" cast as Hollywood's Sheik of Araby. His portrayal of a Bedouin chieftain helped make him the cinema's first male sex symbol as he menaced and then romanced fair-haired beauties until the damsels melted into his well-muscled arms. Valentino's Sheik, more commonly spelled "sheikh" today and pronounced "shake" instead of "sheek," was no tattered vagrant on a "crow-bait" horse. He was a dashing prince of the desert wearing elegant robes, living in an opulent tent, and served by a French valet who had been with him since his school days in Paris.

The genesis of *The Sheik* (1921) was a best-selling romance novel written by a British farmer's wife. A sequel was the basis for *Son of the Sheik* (1926), Valentino's last film.[1] A genre of sultry desert romances and films in which Arabs carried off unwilling beauties followed. These romances continue in the twenty-first century in the form of Harlequin novels. Amazon.com maintains a "Sheikhs and Desert Love" site that contains "a collection of romantic novels and all things sheikh," featuring titles like *Captive of the Desert King, Captive of the Harem, Amber and the Sheikh*, and *Desert Prince, Bride of Innocence*. In this genre, the male protagonist is a stereotypical "desert prince." The slender heroine with long flowing hair usually is from an English-speaking nation. In *Desert Prince, Bride of Innocence*, she is a nanny.

The earlier portrayals of the desert Arab were exotic and erotic for the times, but they were also menacing. A title card in *The Son of the Sheik* has him ordering his captive to obey him. On another card, he proclaims, "An eye for an eye—a hate for a hate—that is the law of my father!" Valentino's smoldering eyes and a soundtrack with minor key melodies and eerie organ swells set the mood, signifying danger. Yet *The Sheik* also inspired "The Sheik of Araby," a bouncy Tin Pan Alley hit that became a jazz standard. The lyrics are far less menacing than the films, suggesting only that the sheik will creep into someone's tent at night. One version declares, "I'm a cad," suggesting the purpose is a sexual dalliance rather than something more malevolent. The tune is so pervasive that today it is available as a mobile ringtone.

The Arabic word "sheikh" literally means "elder," often with the connotation of being a Muslim scholar. In many places in the Middle East, including the Gulf, it is a title awarded to important men, particularly those of royal lineage. Yet the prevalent image in Western novels, films, and song

Rudolph Valentino, who starred in *The Son of the Sheik* (1926), is shown in profile holding a pipe. (Courtesy of the Library of Congress.)

has little to do with elders or scholars. As a 2008 National Public Radio segment, "Valentino's Sheik: An 'Other' Made to Swoon Over," noted, "*The Sheik* was less concerned with authenticity than with perpetrating a fantasy of sexual extremes; in doing so, it promoted stereotypes of the Middle East as a decadent, primitive culture" (Ulaby 2008).

From Danger to Rich and Crass

The screen image of the desert Arab fared little better in the mid-twentieth century with the 1962 release of *Lawrence of Arabia*, the epic blockbuster starring Peter O'Toole as Lawrence and Omar Sharif, born an Egyptian Catholic, as his Bedouin "noble companion in battle and adversity," Sherif Ali. According to Jack Shaheen (1989), who has written extensively about

Arab screen images, the movie introduced some respect for Islam and the Bedouins and some new and more realistic images, such as the Arab as victim. "At times the strength of character of the Bedu, the nomads of Arabia, surfaces: they are admired for their ability to 'cross 60 miles of desert in a single day,'" Shaheen observed. Yet from the first scene with Ali, Lawrence's Tonto, the Bedouins are portrayed as violent, volatile, and dangerous, contrary to Bedouin traditions of hospitality to strangers. The most damaging scenes come after the conquest of Damascus, when the courageous tribal warriors bicker on how to provide the city with basic services like telephone, water, and hospitals. The stereotype conveyed is that "the Arabs cannot function in organized society" (Shaheen 1989).

Because Gulf Arabs were off the beaten track until the mid-twentieth century, they were also isolated from popular culture stereotypes. However, the discovery of incredibly rich oil and natural gas resources in Saudi Arabia and along the Gulf changed all that. The Valentino variety of dashing sheikhs gave way to caricatures of overweight and overbearing Gulf Arabs, so flush with their sudden wealth that even their fellow Arabs developed negative stereotypes about "the Gulfies" or "Oil Sheikhs." During the oil crisis of 1973–1974, Western editorial cartoonists tapped the distinctive dress, prominent features, and facial hair of the Gulf Arabs for inspiration. One in 1973 by the German cartoonist Fritz Behrendt shows a toothy, big-nosed "oil sheikh" holding up the leaders of the United States, Britain, France, and Germany with the nozzle of an oil pump.

Like the "ugly Americans," an epithet that originated with the 1958 novel of the same name by William Lederer and Eugene Burdick (1958/1999), Gulf Arab tourists acquired a reputation of being boorish, arrogant, and rude, particularly in Cairo and London where many vacation, often congregating in specific neighborhoods or luxury hotels. In just a few decades, the desert Arabs, whom Wilfred Thesiger and others had seen as noble and untainted, became stereotyped as the most crass of the nouveau riche, an image that continues today in both old and new media.

Until the 1970s, Beirut was the vacation spot of choice for many newly rich Gulf Arabs. They began summering in Cairo during the Lebanese Civil War and soon became a major force in the tourism economy. According to dominant images and storylines, they came not to see the pyramids but for more contemporary pleasures like belly dancers, discos, casinos, and other libertine activities forbidden at home. In a 1992 *New York Times* article headlined "Arab Favorite for Nice Times (and Naughty Ones)," William E. Schmidt wrote that the Arab tourists came to "let their hair down and indulge in the Arab equivalent of what the British call a 'dirty weekend,'" filling the front tables in bawdy night clubs where they had been known "to string $100 bills into necklaces as favors for their favorite belly dancers."

By the end of the 1990s, when Lisa L. Wynn (2007) worked on her doctoral dissertation concerned with travelers to Egypt, she reported that "the arrival of Gulf tourists in the summer changes not only the visual but also the moral landscape of Cairo." Wynn found

> a widespread image among Egyptians of Gulf Arabs as nomadic Bedouins without history or civilization, the nouveaux riches of the Middle East who lord their wealth over the rest of the Arab world but who do not actually know how to behave in a manner that suits such socioeconomic status. (2007, 162)

Gulf Arabs were seen as sex-crazed and overbearing but a necessary evil because of their spending power, particularly as their influx into Egypt continued. In May 2008, ArabianBusiness.com reported that the number of Gulf Arab tourists visiting Egypt reached 1.9 million in 2007 and brought in revenues of $2.2 billion (T. Malik).

A similar negative image developed in London, where "throngs from the Gulf" offended British sensibilities by flaunting their wealth and disregarding local laws and customs, according to Nesrine Malik (2008), writing in *The Guardian*. Stereotypes were reinforced as women in burqas, carrying oversized designer bags and often trailed by their maids, engaged in marathon shopping excursions to Harrods and Selfridges to buy luxury items available at home but with the cachet of being purchased abroad. She noted, "The ostentatious flamboyance of the Gulf tourist is at odds with the more reserved and understated British attitudes towards dress and transportation."

Today, the web makes it easier to spread such images. For example, in August 2008, various blogs reported that a sheikh from Qatar had spent about $45,000 flying his Lamborghini to London for an oil change. The web also gives wider and more immediate dissemination to negative news and images about Gulf Arabs, such as *The Times* (London) article in July 2008 headlined "15 'Slaves' of Emir's Widow Freed from Captivity in Luxury Brussels Hotel" (Charter 2008) or a video originally aired on ABC Television and then widely circulated in which a member of the Abu Dhabi royal family was shown torturing a man he believed had cheated him in business. The sheikh was later acquitted in UAE courts.

Stories, including those with no basis in fact, that once were limited to one country now travel the world in a click of the mouse. Snopes.com routinely debunks urban myths about Gulf Arabs, including one circulated first by email in 2005. The message shared a slide show of what was purported to be the palatial home of Sheikh Zayed bin Sultan Al Nahyan, founder of the United Arab Republic and ruler of Abu Dhabi. The accompanying text read, "Amazing what $2.55 a gallon gas can buy, isn't it?. . . As you get ready to fill your car or van or truck up with gas, remember you helped BUY this house and car." Snopes reported that the photos were indeed for real, but the description was inaccurate. The Emirates Palace is actually a palatial hotel in Abu Dhabi.

Counterimages

Using new technologies and media planning, Gulf Arabs have begun to respond to the abundance of negative coverage by creating and manipulating their own images. First it was Dubai positioning itself as an international business hub that would rival New York, London, and Hong Kong. The emirate seemingly set out to create projects for the *Guinness World Records*, such as the world's tallest building and the world's richest horse race. Dubai built artificial islands that could be seen from space and the Middle East's first indoor ski slope, only reinforcing stereotypes of Gulf Arab excess. To Westerners, the message often came across that the emirate had more money than taste. While Dubai sought to be seen as a shining city in the desert, the image backfired after the world's financial crisis in 2009. Suddenly, Arab wealth became a mirage. International journalists equated Dubai to a sand castle in print and in web videos, slideshows, and blogs.

Dubai's more financially powerful sister emirate, Abu Dhabi, and other Gulf states have attempted to construct and manipulate images by building cultural capital drawn from Bedouin traditions or purchased from abroad. Government officials sponsor international film festivals, open world-class museums, and host professional sporting events. Despite the best intentions, these cultural events were nevertheless perceived as lavish and excessive. As Larry Rohter (2009) wrote in the *New York Times*,

> Today they are swimming in oil and natural-gas wealth. That has encouraged a burst of lavish investment in everything related to culture and entertainment: museums like the Guggenheim and Louvre in Abu Dhabi, film

academies, branches of American and European universities, even Formula 1 automobile races.

Nowhere has this effort to reshape their world image been more ambitious than in the United Arab Emirates (UAE), particularly Abu Dhabi, the federation's capital. *Fortune* magazine (Gimbel 2007) called it the world's richest city and the new Xanadu, the lavish summer capital of Kublai Khan portrayed in Orson Welles's classic *Citizen Kane* (1941). Abu Dhabi set out to become the world's premier cultural destination and embraced a romanticized desert Arab heritage. Officials chose to launch a campaign to present a carefully massaged image of the emirate as a sophisticated international city. No wonder that in 2008 the *International Herald Tribune* headlined its story describing the activities of the government's investment firm headed by the Tufts University–educated Khaldoon al-Mubarak and considered the largest in the world: "With Little Bluster, Abu Dhabi Makes Investment Noise" (Thomas 2008). The news report described al-Mubarak dressed in a traditional *kandoora* at home, but, when representing the emirate aboard, he wore a Western "designer stubble and perfectly tailored blue suit . . . a figure of suave aplomb."

Abu Dhabi invested heavily to create a year-round cultural and entertainment center on par with Paris and New York. For example, massive development was launched to transform two sandy islands, Saadiyat and Yas, minutes from the center of the city. On Saadiyat Island, international architects Jean Nouvel and Frank Gehry were commissioned to design versions of the Louvre and Guggenheim museums. Gary Player, the South African championship golfer, planned the course at the Saadiyat Beach Golf Club with its clubhouse designed by Gehry. On Yas Island, a $36 billion development project hosted its first Formula One Grand Prix race in 2009 and included plans for a Ferrari theme park which promised—in Dubai-like superlatives—the world's fastest rollercoaster.

To make sure everyone who lived in the capital communicated the same message, the government established an Office of the Brand of Abu Dhabi in 2007. In addition to promoting international images, Abu Dhabi stressed an idealized representation of Emirati (or Bedouin) heritage with camel races, Arabian stallions, falcons soaring in desert skies, and noble nomadic hospitality. Although Edward Said (1979) argued against romanticized images by Westerners in *Orientalism*, Abu Dhabi and the UAE now promote such representations not only to attract tourists but also to create and solidify a national identity in a country founded less than 40 years ago.

Conclusion

It is too soon to tell whether the orchestrated and well-financed efforts to replace negative stereotypes of Gulf Arabs with a sophisticated international image will succeed. Branding experts would say yes, but stereotypes cannot be managed like a public relations campaign. Embedded and long-term stereotypes are often unforgiving because they are engrained in the subconscious and inscribed in the culture over generations, especially when given new life with media gone global. One of the more striking aspects about the Gulf Arabs is the speed with which their nomadic society was transformed in part through the importation of technologies and experts who rapidly tapped the region's energy resources.

Yet, as the natural wealth because of a lucky geology becomes depleted, government officials like those in Abu Dhabi look to culture as a way to diversify their economic base and reframe their global image. As they have learned, however, culture may not be as easily imported and adapted as oil technologies. Importing cultural icons may succeed only in reinforcing the nouveau riche stereotype of the "oil sheiks," who once again are imagined as the greedy consumers of international culture in the same way they craved designer handbags and fancy cars.

Note

1. See http://www.youtube.com/watch?v=7OAlbfZRCvY (accessed March 20, 2010).

Sources

Al-Fahim, Mohammed. 1995. *From rags to riches: A story of Abu Dhabi.* London: London Centre of Arab Studies.

Behrendt, Fritz. 1973. Cartoon on oil crisis. *European Navigator.* http://www.ena .lu/cartoon-behrendt-oil-crisis-1973-021100143.html (accessed December 26, 2009).

Charter, David. 2008. 15 'slaves' of emir's widow freed from captivity in luxury Brussels hotel. *The*[London] *Times.* July 2.

Gimbel, Barney. 2007. The richest city in the world. *Fortune,* March 12. http://money .cnn.com/magazines/fortune/fortune_archive/2007/03/19/8402357/index .htm (accessed December 26, 2009).

Lamb, David. [1987] 2002. *The Arabs.* New York: Vintage.

Lederer, William J., and Eugene L. Burdick. [1958] 1999. *The ugly American*. New York: Norton.

Malik, Nesrine. 2008. The gulf between us. *The Guardian*, August 11. http://www.guardian.co.uk/commentisfree/2008/aug/11/london.middleeast (accessed December 4, 2009).

Malik, Talal. 2008. UAE invests $4bn in Egypt tourism sector. Arabianbusiness.com, May 8. http://www.arabianbusiness.com/518815-uae-invests-4bn-in-egypt-tourism-sector (accessed September 2, 2009).

Rohter, Larry. 2009. Mixing oil and Hollywood: Tribeca festival expand to the Persian Gulf. *New York Times*, October 23. http://www.nytimes.com/2009/10/24/movies/24tribeca.html?_r=1&scp=1&sq=Larry Rohter Mixing Oil and Hollywood&st=cse (accessed October 24, 2009).

Said, Edward. 1979. *Orientalism*. New York: Vintage.

Schmidt, William E. 1992. Cairo journal: Arab favorite for nice times (and naughty ones). *New York Times*, September 9. http://www.nytimes.com/1992/09/09/world/cairo-journal-arab-favorite-for-nice-times-and-naughty-ones.html?scp=4&sq=Cairo Journal William Schmidt&st=cse (accessed August 31, 2009).

Shaheen, Jack. 1989. Lawrence of Arabia: Memorable for what it is, regrettable for what it might have been. *Washington Report on Middle East Affairs*, November. http://www.washington-report.org/backissues/1189/8911015.html (accessed December 26, 2009).

Shaheen, Jack. 2001. *Reel bad Arabs: How Hollywood vilifies a people*. Brooklyn: Olive Branch Press.

Thesiger, Wilfred. 2008. *Arabian sands*. London: Penguin Classics.

Thomas, Landon, Jr. 2008. With little bluster Abu Dhabi takes the stage. *International Herald Tribune*, October, 29, p. I.

Twain, Mark. [1869] 2002. *The innocents abroad*. New York: Penguin Classics.

Ulaby, Neda. 2008. Valentino's sheik: An "other" made to swoon over. National Public Radio, February 4. http://www.npr.org/templates/story/story.php?storyId=18602260 (accessed September 2, 2009).

Wynn, Lisa L. 2007. *Pyramids and night clubs*. Austin: University of Texas Press.

Chapter 25

Beyond the Crisis Narrative: Muslim Voices in the Web Era

Marguerite Moritz

I consider it part of my responsibility as President of the United States to fight against negative stereotypes of Islam wherever they appear.

Barack Hussein Obama, Cairo, June 4, 2009

Less than six months into his presidency, Barack Obama gave a major international address that called for "a new beginning between the United States and Muslims around the world" (Obama 2009). His complex, detailed speech engaged major themes that included nuclear proliferation, international economic linkages, the rights of women, religious freedom, the threat of terrorism, and the intractable Israeli–Palestinian conflict.

For students of media, it was particularly noteworthy that in this high-visibility setting with so many issues under consideration, Obama also chose to comment upon the use of stereotypes and implicitly acknowledged the negative portrayals of Islam that have been commonplace in main-stream Western media for decades.

The speech generated worldwide attention and was regarded by some as a turning point in U.S.–Middle East relations.[1] However, just as racism did not end in the United States with the election of an African American to the White House, mediated representations of Muslims did not take a sudden turn because of the president's promise. Nonetheless, the effort to put this topic on the political agenda comes at an opportune time. The

U.S. President Barack Obama speaks at Cairo University on June 4, 2009. (Official White House Photo by Chuck Kennedy.)

rapid, widespread change in the creation, distribution, and consumption of media texts we can witness during the digital era offers genuine possibilities for more diverse and more nuanced representations in which Islam is no longer routinely linked with extremism, exoticism, and repression. In a globalized, digitized age, as channels proliferate, so do opportunities for more voices to tell their own stories, create their own images, and reflect their own diverse cultural and religious identities.

The Islamic Religion

Islam, along with Christianity and Judaism, is one of the world's major monotheistic religions. Founded in the seventh century, its holy book is the Qur'an, its sacred prophet is Muhammad, and its God is Allah. Structurally, Islam does not recognize a central or single religious authority.

According to a 2009 Pew Research Center report (Miller 2009), 23 percent of the global population, or 1.57 billion people, are followers of Islam, with its numbers continuing to grow. Not all Muslims are Arab. They live on every continent, while a 60 percent majority live in Asia. Another 20 percent reside in the Middle East and North African countries, where they comprise up to 95 percent of the total population. This is one reason why Arabs and Islam are often conflated.

Estimates of the Muslim population in the United States vary widely. *U.S. News and World Report* (Headden 2008) puts the number at more than 5 million, while the Pew Report (Miller 2009) estimates it to be 2.5 million people, or less than 1 percent of the total U.S. population. Regardless, Islam is one of the fastest growing religions in the United States, with many African-American followers.

Islam in U.S. Media

Because of the long-standing global dominance of Western media, the images, news reports, and life stories of non-Western people and societies have been shaped in Hollywood, New York, and London. Accounts of major international events—the 9/11 attacks, the bombing of Afghanistan, and the invasion of Iraq—have been dominated by Western journalists whose reporting is circulated across global media networks. Story selections are not neutral but heavily favor events that have strong narrative elements (such as heroes and villains) and graphic imagery. These are what people watch and remember. Often called the first rough draft of history, journalism shapes both our initial perceptions of events and our collective memories of them (see, e.g., Edy 1999).

With respect to Islam, when Muslims have not been rendered silent, they typically have been represented as threatening religious fanatics. For decades, critics have charged Western media with heavy reliance on damaging, inaccurate, and sensational stereotypes in their representations of Islam. In his seminal work on this topic, Edward Said (1979) used the term "Orientalism" to capture the ways in which Muslims have been constructed as the exotic, extremist, violent, intolerant Other (see also Said 1981).

Depictions in U.S. motion pictures are considered particularly damaging because of the enormous international popularity of the U.S. cinema. When Jack Shaheen (2001) examined more than 900 American films going back to the earliest days of the cinema, he found that in the vast majority of cases, Hollywood had "used repetition as a teaching tool, tutoring movie audiences by repeating over and over, in film after film, insidious images of the Arab people" (1). The "systematic, pervasive, and unapologetic degradation and dehumanization" extend beyond action films and thrillers (1). In 1992, for example, the Disney animated film *Aladdin*—a financial blockbuster with earnings in excess of $217 million ($342 billion

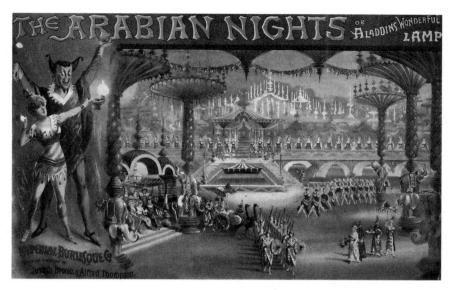

This lithograph shows a poster that advertises a production of "Aladdin's Wonderful Lamp" from 1888. (Courtesy of the Library of Congress.)

in 2010 dollars)—included a song with the following lyrics: "They cut off your ears if they don't like your face. It's barbaric but hey, it is home." The American-Arab Anti-discrimination Committee (Wingfield and Karahan 1995) issued vocal protests, and noted that the lead characters or heroes of the fantasy were given light skin, "Anglicized features and Anglo-American accents," while the other characters were "dark-skinned, swarthy and villainous-cruel palace guards or greedy merchants with Arabic accents and grotesque facial features."

Shifting Media Constructions and Players

Whether in news, literature, film, or the arts, narratives are constructions (Bruner 1991). As such, they give material form to events and experiences. Media professionals shape narratives through their selection of subjects, through their use of language and images, and through repetition, placement, juxtaposition, and volume. These constructs embellish stories with actors, experts, or witnesses as well as with techniques such as music tracks, montages, slow motion effects, computer-generated images, and so on (Tuchman 1980). Professional codes and practices, competition, technologies, audience demographics, and ratings all come into play as narratives are processed and produced to create compelling tales. All stories, however, have a point of view, a perspective, a bias.

As Robert Entman (1993) points out in his discussion of framing, media are continually directing readers and viewers *toward* certain aspects of culture and society that they consider most important and away from others: "To frame is to select some aspects of a perceived reality and make them more salient" than others (52). Not only what the media choose to present but also how they choose to present it comprise an important part of the framing function that media organizations carry out. Susan Ross (2003) writes that media frames are most powerful when they describe

> people, places or issues about which we have no direct information. Media frames tend to be most influential when they provide a means for us to interpret and understand the unknown. The frames we encounter in media provide a template for our vision of the foreign, the marginal, the other. (32–33)

In a critical look at political messages, Kathleen Hall Jamieson and Karlyn Kohr (2001) similarly find that the media are "pervasive and forceful persuaders with the ability to shape our perceptions and to influence our beliefs and attitudes" (122). Framing thus helps explain how media depictions influence audience perceptions.

Contemporary narratives draw on existing stereotypes to simplify and focus their messages. In the case of Islam, those stereotypes include veils, harems, suicide bombers, and religious extremists (Shaheen 2001). Media narratives frame Islam as a threat because such a tactic keeps U.S. media on the patriotic side of the debate and on the side of power. Anti-Arab and anti-Islam images and texts resonate with U.S. audiences because that frame not only fits neatly into established stereotypes but also provides an easy way to reduce complex issues into simplified stories of good guys versus bad. Entertainment and news narratives draw on the same cultural mythologies, and hence it is no accident that fictional depictions of Islam have a great deal in common with stories ripped from the headlines. It is precisely this monolithic view created in the West that emerging Muslim voices hope to challenge.

Indeed, new voices, narratives, and images are finding their way into the media. The rapid development and global spread of communication technologies in the web era have opened the means of production and distribution to a vast array of people. As media scholar Nabil Echchaibi (2010) noted when addressing an international conference on Islam and the media,

> You can't talk about Islam today without talking about media. Even 80-year-old religious leaders have websites and blogs. . . . In fact, clerical authority can be established on the Web or on TV alone, without a connection to a traditional mosque.

A native Moroccan, Echchaibi is one of a growing number of scholars who study the use of both conventional and social media among Muslims. For him, today's cultural production by "Muslims in diaspora and Muslims in the Middle East is very rich" and is one of the main ways audiences can experience "the Muslim story behind the crisis story" (2010). Blogs, discussion groups, websites, and social-networking channels provide a space for Muslim perspectives and a link to communities where Muslims are not only critiquing media but also producing media, as the following examples illustrate.

Little Mosque on the Prairie

Even before it went on the air, the Canadian television show *Little Mosque on the Prairie* was something of a media sensation.[2] Critics and audience members alike wondered if a program could or should portray Islam through the lens of comedy. But when the show premiered in January, 2007, it was an immediate hit and one of the highest-rated programs the Canadian Broadcasting Corporation (CBC) had launched in years (Doyle 2007). Hailed for its amusing depictions of ordinary Muslims who lived in a small Saskatchewan community and caught up in everyday dilemmas, the show never sought to be political, according to its creator, Zarqa Nawaz.

Nawaz, the child of Pakistani parents who immigrated to Canada when she was five, grew up and went to school in Toronto with the intention of becoming a doctor. When medical school plans failed to materialize, she went to work for the CBC as a researcher and eventually studied film production. Her first effort, *BBQ Muslim* (1996), was a short comedy about two Toronto suburbanites who become terrorist suspects when their gas barbeque explodes during a cookout.

Despite technical flaws, the film won a spot in the prestigious Toronto Film Festival precisely because she was taking on a subject no one else was willing to touch and she did it with humor. Nawaz said the film "got in and people were laughing. I was amazed and I wanted to prove it wasn't an accident" (2010). She then came out with *Death Threat* (1998), in which an aspiring Muslim writer issues a fatwa on herself to attract publicity. Other films followed, all with the focus on comedy. In 2005, the National Film Board of Canada commissioned Nawaz to do a documentary, which resulted in the critically acclaimed *Me and the Mosque* (2005). Nawaz, who claims to be the only Muslim comedy writer in Canada, returned to comedy in 2007 with *Little Mosque*.

The show's concept is largely autobiographical. The setting is a fictional town in the province where Nawaz lives with her family:

> It's a small city, so there is only one mosque, and all ethnic groups go to it. I developed the characters, like the feminist who wears a hajib, from people I know, all with different ideologies. I never meant for it to be edgy. It's a slice of life on the prairie. (2010)

Tensions and comedy emerge from religious, gender, and generational issues: Can Muslim kids go trick or treating? Can Muslim women wear bathing suits in front of the male swimming instructor if he's gay? Is it wrong to haggle over price if you're buying a prayer rug? As Nawaz said, "Nobody has done a comedy about Muslims before, so they are not sure how to take it. Some non-Muslims wonder, 'Are we allowed to laugh?'"

The premiere episode drew more than 2 million viewers, a major ratings achievement for any show produced in Canada, where audiences gravitate heavily toward American programs (Doyle 2007). After much critical acclaim and media attention, the show was picked up for international syndication in France, Switzerland, Finland, Turkey, Israel, and the United Arab Emirates. By the time it entered its fifth season in 2010, it was distributed in 60 countries. In the United States, the Fox cable network bought the rights to the story line with the intention of creating an American version of the show but ultimately decided against going forward with the project. Nawaz says U.S. television executives believed that their audiences were not ready for any show that plays with the topic of Muslims. "There is too much Islamophobia in the U.S. for that. In Canada, the show can exist because the environment is different" (2010).

One of those differences is the economic structure of the Canadian broadcasting system. While today's globalized media share many common features that cross national borders, important differences remain. National policies and practices can be highly influential in shaping programming content. The U.S. broadcasting system has been commercially based since its earliest days. Canadian television, on the other hand, follows a public service model with a commitment to multiculturalism, diversity, and inclusiveness (see, e.g., Hogarth 2002). Writing in Toronto's *Globe and Mail*, television critic John Doyle (2007) noted that the "mere existence [of *Little Mosque*] is a grand-slam assertion that Canadian TV is different and that the best of Canadian TV amounts to a rejection of the hegemony of U.S. network TV" (R1).

The 99

While *Little Mosque* deliberately looks at issues of faith and religious practice in daily life, *The 99*, a superhero comic book series, has no overt discussions of Islam.[3] Characters neither pray nor read the Qur'an. Creator Naif Al-Mutawa says he chose to focus the series on "storytelling, shared values, dialogue, social action and religious pluralism," hoping to attract children of all faiths (2010a).

His first comic book appeared in the Middle East in 2006. *Forbes* (Eaves and Noer 2008) named *The 99* one of the top 20 pop culture trends circulating globally, called the series "a phenomenon in the Arab world. . . . [R]egional sales of the Muslim comic book were second only to *Superman*." In 2007, the series began publication in the United States. Since then, producers have introduced a line of after-school products, an animated television show, and a theme park in Kuwait with four or five other projects in production.

When Al-Mutawa got the idea for a comic book series and founded the Teshkeel Media Group in 2004, he recalled that he "didn't want another fifth-world production" (2010a). He set out instead to secure sufficient financing to afford top artists in the field. The result, he says, has made *The 99* "a cultural icon in the market." Born in Kuwait, Al-Mutawa received both an MBA and a doctorate (in clinical psychology) from Columbia University. He worked with victims of torture for a decade and considers himself a social entrepreneur and a businessman on a social justice mission.

In an open letter to his five young sons that was posted on the BBC's website (2010a), Al-Mutawa wrote about his motivations:

> I needed to find a way to take back Islam from its hostage takers. . . .
> I uncapped my pen to create a concept that could be popular in the East

and the West. I would go back to the very sources from which others took violent and hateful messages and offer messages of tolerance and peace in their place.

The superheroes of the series are ordinary boys and girls who come to possess one of 99 stones, each imbued with a magical power. To overcome the many obstacles in their paths, they must work together with at least three others who also possess the stones. The gems trace their origins to the 13th century, when invaders destroyed the city of Baghdad and its magnificent Dar al-Hikma library. Its books from every religion and culture were thrown into the Tigris and seemingly destroyed. But, according to the comics, caretakers placed 99 stones in the river, where they soaked up the collected wisdom of the ages before finding their way to 99 countries around the globe. Based on the 99 names or attributes of Allah as written in the Qur'an, the stones embody universal values such as wisdom, strength, and compassion. Since its introduction, *The 99* reportedly sells more than a million comics a year and is published in a variety of languages.

Conclusion

Media representation is both textual and visual. Because we live in a highly visual culture, images play an increasingly powerful role in shaping our beliefs and values. In addition, pictures operate differently from written texts, which rely upon linear, sequential argumentation. Images, on the other hand, are emotional. They are associative, nonsequential, and perceived as believable. Images also persist in our memory much more powerfully than do written texts alone.

Our collective image of Islam in the West comes in large part from the persistent media focus on the crisis narrative. News, by definition, is about unusual, extraordinary, and sensational events that are highlighted in headlines and underscored with graphic images. Through repetition and consistent representation, news makes the unusual seem normal and the extraordinary seem ordinary. The heroes and villains of entertainment television and film are similarly created to be dramatic. At the same time, they resonate with cultural biases of the audience. Fiction builds on our preconceptions and often exaggerates them. In both fiction and factual portrayals, the summary message is that Islam equals extremism.

The 9/11 attacks gave rise to discussions around the globe about how to define and represent Islam in ways that go beyond the crisis story. One lesson that should have been learned since 9/11 is that Muslims are not one homogeneous group. No single profile can capture the contemporary Muslim experience. No single authority figure speaks for all Islam. However, it is consistently those who speak with the most sensational rhetoric who are most likely to be portrayed in the media.

Because of the rapid growth of Islam in the West, media practices that open up space for negotiation and cultural [ex]change need to be identified and supported. While no single program, image, or narrative can counteract stereotypes that have been circulated over centuries, a diversity of representations begins a process of change in which public discourse opens up alternative views. As communication moves ever faster, the institutional authority asserted by mainstream Western media is increasingly open to challenge and reconfiguration. A new generation of culturally savvy Muslims artists has seized the opportunity to expand the images of Islam beyond those that have become so dominant and damaging in all media forms.

A group of Iranian young adults enjoy the day outside the village of Masouleh in northern Iran, about 120 miles northwest of Tehran, 2007. (Courtesy of Ahmad Motalaei.)

Notes

1. See http://news.bbc.co.uk/2/hi/8083171.stm (accessed March 21, 2010).
2. See http://www.youtube.com/watch?v=_I4YrgGHCXE (accessed March 21, 2010).
3. See http://www.the99.org (accessed March 21, 2010).

Sources

Al-Mutawa, Naif. 2010a. Public address. January 8, University of Colorado, Boulder.

Al-Mutawa, Naif. 2010b. Why I based superheroes on Islam. BBC.com, July 2. http://news.bbc.co.uk/2/hi/middle_east/8127699.stm (accessed January 31, 2010).

Bruner, Jerome S. 1991. The narrative construction of reality. *Critical Inquiry* 18 (1): 1–21.

Doyle, John. 2007. *Little Mosque on the Prairie* serves interests of the whole public. *Globe and Mail*, January 9, R1. http://www.fundamentalistfilms.com/_projects/littlemosque/jan0907e.php (accessed Feb. 8, 2010).

Eaves, Elisabeth, and Michael Noer, eds. 2008. In pictures: 20 trends sweeping the globe: Swash-buckle with *The 99*. *Forbes*, January 9. http://www.forbes.com/2008/01/09/culture-global-internet-forbeslife-globalpop08-cx_ee_pop_land.html (accessed January 31, 2010).

Echchaibi, Nabil. 2010. Public address at the Islam & the Media Conference. January 10, University of Colorado, Boulder.

Edy, Jill A. 1999. Journalistic uses of collective memory. *Journal of Communication* 49: 71–85.

Entman, Robert M. 1993. Framing: Toward clarification of a fractured paradigm. *Journal of Communication*, 43.

Headden, Susan. 2008. Understanding Islam. *U.S. News & World Report*, April 7.

Hogarth, David. 2002. *Documentary television in Canada*. Quebec City: McGill-Queen's University Press.

Jamieson, Kathleen Hall, and Karlyn Kohr. 2001. *The interplay of influence: News, advertising, politics, and the mass media*, 5th ed. Belmont, CA: Wadsworth.

Miller, Tracy, ed. 2009. Mapping the global Muslim population: A report on the size and distribution of the world's Muslim population. Pew Research Center. http://pewforum.org/docs/?DocID=450 (accessed January 31, 2010).

Nawaz, Zarqa. 2010. Public address at the Islam & the Media Conference. University of Colorado, Boulder, January 9.

Obama, Barack. 2009. Text: Obama's speech in Cairo. *New York Times*, June 4. http://www.nytimes.com/2009/06/04/us/politics/04obama.text.html (accessed March 21, 2010).

Ross, Susan D. 2003. Unconscious, ubiquitous frames. In *Images that Injure: Pictorial Stereotypes in the Media*, 2nd ed., ed. Paul Lester Martin and Susan Dente Ross, pp. 29–34. Westport, CT: Praeger.

Said, Edward W. 1979. *Orientalism*. New York: Pantheon.

Said, Edward W. 1981. *Covering Islam: How the media and the experts determine how we see the rest of the world*. New York: Pantheon.

Shaheen, Jack G. 2001. *Reel bad Arabs: How Hollywood vilifies a people*. Brooklyn: Olive Branch Press.

Tuchman, Gaye. 1980. *Making news: A study in the construction of reality*. New York: Free Press.

Wingfield, Marvin, and Bushra Karaman. 1995. Arab stereotypes and American educators. American Arab Anti Discrimination Committee. http://www .adc.org/index.php?id=283&no_cache=1&sword_list[]=arab&sword_ list[]=stereotypes&sword_list[]=american&sword_list[]=educators (accessed January 31, 2010).

PART VI

Images of Inside, Outside, and Other

Paul Martin Lester

It is probably no surprise by those who know me and others who wish they didn't that my favorite category of animals, vegetables and minerals—nouns and concepts—is the often denigrated and dismissed "miscellaneous." I have no idea why components of this catchall are so often belittled. After all, the miscellaneous typeface is responsible for some of the most creative and specialized uses of this fundamental component of graphic design, while the category that pertains to informational graphics includes court-room sketches, television schedules, calendars, icons, logos, flowcharts, time lines and illustrations. And although I caution and discount students who cite their parents or friends, Wikipedia (the footnote sources are okay, but not Wiki directly) and dictionaries, I confidently break one of my con-ventions by quoting good old Noah and his definition of miscellaneous:

> Consisting of diverse things or members, having various traits [and] dealing with or interested in diverse subjects. (Merriam-Webster 2010)

Now really, how perfect is miscellaneous as a category for a book that advocates diversity in people, thoughts, actions and presentations?

Imagine after Hurricane Katrina in 2005, the residents of the flooded zones in New Orleans had nowhere else to go. A sprawling blue-tarped temporary city would necessarily bloom amid the ruins, compounding America's shame. Such is the reality of Haitian people after the devastating 7.0 earthquake of 2010. Manoucheka Celeste reminds us that pictures of people from the impoverished nation about 700 miles southeast of Miami were a staple of news reports long before the recent disaster. Unfortunately, they contribute to a body of visual messages that stereotype all immigrants to this country.

Perhaps you have noticed by now that many of the contributors are members of the cultural group that is the subject of a chapter. The selection of these talented and thoughtful individuals was, of course, no coincidence—who is more qualified to speak of images that injure *and* heal than those who live with their representations every day? Diane Carter is a mother of two adopted children and writes about the selling of the service by various agencies through their website pictures. As often is the case, economic influences underlie motivations that cause unethical image selections.

Since work began on the first edition of *Images that Injure*, I have tried to find someone to write about media stereotypes of the future—imagined inequities based on cultural groups that have yet to be invented. Previously everyone I asked turned me down. However, one thing I know about Lawrence Mullen—he is fearless. Even though I introduced him to the strange, futuristic networked world of Second Life, he immersed himself into the avatar-based communities far more than I had the time for and came away not only with classes for his graduate students about and taught within the software program, but also through interviews and research developed a deep understanding of what motivates us all whether in second or real life. Anyone at all curious about the mysterious worlds and characters that can be found on a computer in a matter of clicks should read his chapter.

The honor of the last chapter that details stereotypical messages in the media goes to Melvin D. Slater. It so happens that our preface author and mentor to many, Everette E. Dennis has a special interest in political cartoons. For an article in *Journalism Quarterly* he wrote that the most powerful among them are "scorching indictments of people and issues" (1974). Slater not only confirms that assessment but also illuminates how the field often purposely stereotypes politicians for less than honorable reasons. Given the deep divisions made public by the 2008 presidential campaign and the election of Barack Obama, cartoons are a necessary and worthy area of study and are made more comprehensible by Slater's analysis.

Sources

Dennis, Everette E. 1974. The regeneration of political cartooning. *Journalism Quarterly*, Winter: 664–69.

Miscellaneous. 2010. Merriam-Webster's online dictionary, http://www.merriam-webster.com/netdict/miscellaneous (accessed March 31, 2010).

Chapter 26

Minding the Borders: Images of Haitian Immigrants in the United States

Manoucheka Celeste

The camera offers a close-up on a woman's feet, one of which is out of focus while the details of the other are sharp. The bright orange nail polish and yellow sandals call attention to her dark chocolate skin. She wears a black monitor around her ankle. Her entire body is cut out of the frame. Although the view of the words on the monitor is obstructed by the chair leg, readers can see "property of . . . incorporated. . . . 1-(888)-809-5990 REWARD." The article begins with the story of a woman waiting to hear about her deportation back to Haiti. The photograph's caption leaves the woman without a last name and identifies her solely as "Evelyn, a Haitian immigrant."[1]

If we are to believe, as Nederveen Pieterse (1992, x) writes, that "[e]very picture tells a story: visual imagery too has a narrative character and structure," then what story does this image tell about this woman and about "Haitian immigrants"? What story does it tell about immigrants in general? In this specific case, it appears that although the woman has made it to "the land of the free," she is by no means free. She is in technological shackles, without a full name and without a home. Without a face, she is objectified. She appears to not belong. The image provides so little information about

Evelyn, a Haitian immigrant, wears a permanent tracking device while she awaits a decision from Immigration and Customs Enforcement officials on whether she will be deported back to Haiti or allowed to stay with her five-year-old daughter, who was born in the United States. (Courtesy of Sandra C. Roa and the New York Times Institute.)

her that it is difficult to imagine who she is beyond the description of her as a Haitian immigrant who awaits deportation. This picture is symbolic of the immigration experience of many, including Haitians.

Despite the Statue of Liberty's request to "Give me, your tired, your poor, Your huddled masses yearning to breathe free," choices are made about who is (and is not) eligible and desired as a citizen of the United States. As borders are increasingly monitored, and despite the seemingly fluid movement that globalization promised, representations of immigrants serve to inform public opinion and policy makers about who belongs inside a nation's borders. Images potentially influence decisions regarding who

Published in Frank Leslie's *Illustrated Newspaper* in 1886, this wood engraving shows the reconstructing of the Statue of Liberty on Bedloe's Island. (Courtesy of the Library of Congress.)

is allowed to enter this country and the likelihood for immigrants to be accepted into their new home.

This generic "Haitian immigrant" is employed here to discuss current and historical photographs of Haitian immigrants in the mainstream press to argue that the visual is political. This chapter focuses on Haitian immigration because of Haiti's history with the United States and the status of these immigrants once they reach the border.

Regardless of the immigration policy of the United States, Haitians are a visible part of the public debate in U.S. media for and against immigration, with images used to support arguments. What do the overtones of the pictures suggest? In the story of immigration, who gets to be heroic and brave? Who is criminalized or demonized? What are some implications of these images as a whole on areas such as policy and law, and what do these images of immigrants tell about what it means to be "American"? How do Haitian immigrants actually live in the United States in light of the Statue of Liberty's symbolic welcoming?

Ultimately, this chapter will conclude with more questions than answers, but its goal is to open up a space to discuss the role played in the immigration discourse by mainstream images of Haitians and to consider some of their real-life consequences. Informed theoretically and methodologically by cultural studies, this chapter presents a visual analysis of select photographs from searches of the Associated Press Images database and google.com culled from the last decade of press coverage. Tropes are identified as an aid for the close readings of photographs.

The media's role in shaping the way we see the world is a key consideration. As Stuart Hall (2003) writes, media are a part of the dominant means of ideological production as "[t]hey produce representations of the social world, images, descriptions, explanations, frames" (90). Hall adds that media construct definitions of race and the meaning it carries. Media also inform us of who belongs in our society through immigration discourse that inscribes immigrant status—some are welcomed, and others are turned away.

The History You Cannot Leave Behind

In a song that catches many of the nuances and historical contestations of immigration, "Hollywood Meet Bollywood," Haitian-born hip hop artist Wyclef Jean says, "Marco Polo was an immigrant, Columbus was an immigrant, even America was named after immigrants" (Duplessis et al. 2007). He continues, "Immigration knocking at my door. I don't know what they're knocking for. It's so hard to live, an illegal immigrant."

One of the dominant culture's immigration stories centers on their discovery of the Americas in which they situate themselves as "natives" and all others as newcomers who must assimilate in order to become American (with some exceptions such as African Americans, who remain foreign). What Columbus, pilgrims, and the like "discovered" were inhabited spaces. Yet the story of discovery and "civilizing the continent" presents ideal narratives of immigration as Western discovery of paradise and conquest of foreign lands deemed backward and exotic, such as the Caribbean (Buck 1993; Friedman 1992; Sandoval 2000). U.S.-produced television shows, such as *House Hunters International*, the reality television show in which Westerners often search for idyllic alternatives to their frenzied lives, chronicle these adventures as entertainment.

As Chela Sandoval (2000) writes, Western colonial exploration opened up other world geopolitical regions, making available vastly different languages, cultures, and riches for Western consumption (6). Wilson Valentín-Escobar (2000) calls this rediscovery of sorts the "Columbus effect" and says it is necessarily followed by a process of appropriation. Discussing the mainstream music industry's proclaimed discovery of Cuba's Buena Vista Social Club, Maria Elena Cepeda (2001) says this effect resonates in discourse through the dominant culture's telling of the history of the United States and other colonized places. "History, culture, identity—in essence *being* itself—commences at the moment of discovery" (71).

In the song mentioned above, Jean calls attention to the way people in the United States imagine immigration and its realities. As he notes, it is "hard to live," particularly in a nation where citizenship on many levels determines the amount of humanity with which one is treated and where, despite one's status, an immigrant is often represented as "illegal" and always foreign. We are reminded that not all citizens are treated equally (Schiller and Fouron 2001). Immigrants, regardless of their citizenship status, are often portrayed as burdens on the U.S. treasury who take advantage of social services. Catherine Squires (2007) writes that immigrants "have been demonized periodically in public campaigns for punitive policies (such as California's Prop 209 and attempts to create English-only amendments) and in media representations" (150). Part of the immigrants' daily struggle plays out publicly with mainstream media representing various immigrant groups as outsiders or Other.

Yet the particular story of Haitian immigration is incomplete without mention of the Haitian republic's rocky relationship with the U.S. government. Following a slave revolt, Haiti was established in 1804 as the first noncontinental African republic and the second independent nation in the Western Hemisphere. While the direct impact of Haiti's revolution on other slave revolts at the time is debated, the revolution undoubtedly transmitted discomfort to slaveholders in the United States who wanted to keep African-American people as property (Dash 1988; Geggus 2001).

The U.S. government did not recognize Haiti's independence until 1862, 37 years after Haiti's former colonizer, France, had done so.

Since then, the U.S. military has occupied Haiti twice and today maintains a considerable military, economic, cultural, and political presence in the country. With its share of dictators, some backed by the U.S. government, Haiti has experienced regular economic and political collapse along with mounting environmental problems. Haitians began migrating to the United States in the 1800s, but the migration from the late 1900s until recent times consists primarily of environmental, political, and economic refugees. For generations, Haiti's upper and middle classes also migrated to attend universities or pursue other ventures.

The January, 2010, earthquake exponentially magnified the fragility of the country's infrastructure and strained resources. The role of the Haitian government in the immediate post-quake response was reported to be inadequate. Many Haitians sought refuge abroad after immigration was allowed on a temporary basis (Dwyer and Davis 2010). Despite the diversity of Haitians who have moved to the United States, it is the large migrations of poor Haitians, particularly after political disturbances, that have come to typify this group for the U.S. media.

Malissia Lennox (1993) argues that the history of Haitian-U.S. relations informs immigration policy that discriminates amongst refugees. In 1992, an executive order from President George H. W. Bush mandated "the complete exclusion of Haitian refugees from the United States without a determination of their claims for political asylum." The order resulted in 98 percent rejection of Haitian asylum claims (Lennox 1993, 688). Despite a promise to change the policy, President Bill Clinton said, according to one of his assistants, that his goal was "to keep Haitians in Haiti" (Lennox 1993, 688).

Race in the United States critically shapes how Haitians are pictured, particularly regarding immigration. The long history of the marginalization, discrimination, abuse, and murder of African-American people in the United States is well documented, and notions of "blackness" are homogenized in the popular imagination, blurring or erasing vast cultural and ethnic diversity into a single image. Georges Fouron, a Haitian, and others (Schiller and Fouron 2001) identified the shock for immigrants who found themselves at the bottom of the racial hierarchy once they arrived in the United States. Fouron described examples of racism that occurred throughout his migration experience. However, he was able to follow the idealized immigration script and obtain an education, secure employment, and provide for his family. Nonetheless, he remained among those discriminated against by law enforcement officials because of the color of their skin (American Civil Liberties Union 2010).

Despite this lived reality, the myth of the "American dream" (Gray 1995; Jhally and Lewis 1992) continues to be celebrated in the United States even though many of the people who built the country and continue to labor in it do not benefit from the uplift ideology. The dream, as reward for their own labor, remains a distant mirage for many. The myth holds up the few who are successful as proof that the dream is possible while safeguarding the structures of inequality, injustice, and oppression (Gray 1991) despite social and structural challenges, and it suggests that failure to achieve the dream is an individual failure. This ideology largely ignores the social and structural barriers that exist for people of color or poverty in the United States and the unresolved issue of race that work together to construct a specific and deeply entrenched image of the Haitian immigrant.

Good Immigrant, Bad Immigrant: The Power of the American Dream to Confer Legitimacy

All images of Haitian immigrants are not negative. Instead, polarized images distinguish between those who are desirable and undesirable. Negative images emphasize failure to conform to the imagined "good immigrant" model. In general, undesirable citizens are photographed in undifferentiated groups and framed as nuisances or disturbances of social order. In contrast, individual "good immigrants" are shown as hardworking and successful through personal effort.

Images of those furthest from the mythological "American success story" tend to erase individual identity. These immigrants are photographed from a distance in large groups in which individual faces or characteristics are difficult to make out. They generally are in the process of immigrating and, in recent years, tend to be shown in or near boats. The "boat people" are shown in tattered clothing and as disheveled and disoriented. In some images, law enforcement officers are present, signaling immigrants as a threat and/ or a drain on resources. Although Haitians of various backgrounds have been moving to the United States for more than 200 years, since the media introduction of the "boat people" phenomenon in the 1980s (Boswell 1982; Miller 1984), images link Haitian immigrants to this negative concept that evokes notions of being "fresh off the boat" and "wet behind the ears," which highlight the burdens of strangeness, newness, and naïveté.

Another set of images of Haitians en masse presents them protesting, usually against U.S. immigration policy. These visuals are strikingly similarly to dominant representations of Mexicans and Mexican Americans, who also are often presented protesting anti-immigration policies (see chapter 22 for discussion of images of Mexican Americans). Damon DiCicco and others (in press) argue that protest groups are often shown in the news as a problem and a threat and that "coverage depicting protests as bothersome has become increasingly prevalent" (15).

However, Haitians are shown as a nuisance or a threat even when they are not in a sizeable group. One representative picture on MSNBC's website (Diaz 2004) captures this perfectly. Pictured in "Little Haiti," an area in south Florida with the largest concentration of Haitians in the country, an Anglo male police officer stands between two men shouting, according to the caption, about ousted Haitian President Jean Bertrand Aristide. Since the officer is the only face we see, the viewer's eyes are drawn to him. Although the article focuses on Haiti and its people, the only person who is fully seen and recognizable is an Anglo man in a uniform. He symbolically represents the law, or the good force that combats evil. Following Jean Kilbourne's (2003) analysis, this image reinforces a racial hierarchy by framing who is important and powerful, and who is not. The Haitians are not fully embodied, which suggests that they have little agency and lack the ability to shape their own reality.

On the other end of the spectrum, images that focus on the individuality of immigrants generally represent those immigrants as desirable. Such immigrants stand alone. They are photographed away from friends and family and are outside their communities. These model citizens are often embodied as students or young and upwardly mobile people who come to represent the possibilities or uphold the tenets of the American dream. In one example, Edner Paul is described as excelling in school and college bound.[2] The headline reads, "New to the US, he blazed a path: MIT-bound math quiz is latest triumph for O'Bryant." Paul is pictured in school, seated passively and relaxed on a bench in front of a row of dark beige lockers. Both hands hold his green backpack on his lap. Although he is not directly in front of the camera, he is centered. He smiles shyly. The neatly dressed teenager is portrayed as a well-mannered student and an ideal citizen. He is removed from anything that could mark him as Haitian, including his home. The narrative of this image celebrates his individual achievement as it erases such markers as race, ethnicity, and history within the "melting pot" of the United States.

This photograph represents a genre of images in which individuals *personify* the possibility of success for immigrants in the United States. The images and accompanying text contrast who they have become today with their historic lack of opportunity in Haiti. Ultimately, success is a testament to the United States and the ideal of individualism.

From such a portrait, Herman Gray (1995) writes that "we walk away with a sense that society is fine, there's no problem, you just have to work hard, you have to have the same values, have the right kind of desires and aspirations, and it'll be alright" (137). What is missing, however, from the "before and after" nature of photographs of successful Haitians—and, by extension, potentially all immigrants—is everything that happens in between. What obstacles do immigrants encounter in the United States once they arrive? What opportunities did the people in these individualized success stories benefit from? How and why do these opportunities, which are often unique, elude others?

Regulating Borders through Transnational Representations: The Story "Over There"

In early 2009, *Miami Herald* photographer Patrick Farrell won a Pulitzer Prize, the most prestigious award in journalism, for his images of Haiti after hurricanes in 2008 in which four storms hit the country in as many weeks.[3] The newspaper's director of photography, Luis Rios, said, "It is exceptional documentary photography with a purpose—to chronicle the misery and heartache of the Haitian people" (quoted in Viglucci 2009). Among Farrell's pictures in this photo series, one image captures 11 dead, mostly naked children lined up in the street, with the lower parts of other people's bodies shown standing over the children. Another picture shows women giving birth in a clinic, their naked bellies in full sight as they lie prone on the tables. The only fully clothed woman whose face can be seen clearly walks out of the clinic to make room for another to take her table. While childbirth in the United States is seen as private but celebratory, these Haitian women have lost their privacy and instead are framed as a burden on an under-resourced clinic and nation who foil international attempts to "rescue" them. Because viewers are not privy to any other aspect of these women's lives, it is easy to ask, "Why are they having babies?" These images fuel Western desires to control the fertility of the "Other," which has played out around the world, including in sterilization programs in Puerto Rico (Briggs 1998).

Farrell's images are hailed in the *Miami Herald* article for capturing the devastation, heartache, and deep mourning for the many people who lost their family members, homes, and livelihoods. And the Pulitzer Prize duly celebrates Farrell's artistry. Yet we must stop to assess not only the damage and injury he captures but also the damage and injury of his work for the newspaper. We must acknowledge that—because of the ethnocentric nature of media (Gans 1979) and U.S. society at large—the photographs would never be acceptable if they were of Anglo Americans or Europeans, particularly because such images would challenge the West's "superiority" (Said 1978, 6).

Despite photographers' best intentions, the history of photography of marginalized people lacks empathy. Photographs tend to adopt what Edward Said (1978) calls a strategy of "flexible positional superiority, which puts the Westerner in a whole series of possible relationships . . . without ever losing him the relative upper hand" (7). In this tradition, Farrell's photographs focus on bodies, not on people or their humanity. They shock because they force viewers to look, but they do not capture a sense of kinship or connection or the impact of human loss. They frame Haitians for the Western gaze, allowing the Westerner to view the suffering of the "Other" for pleasure from a safe distance. They transform the tragedy of the "Other" into a commodity for Westerners to consume, reinforcing Western dominance.

Most Haitians do not see or read the *Miami Herald* and will never see how their tragedy was recorded and portrayed to readers. Yet the power of such dehumanizing images is magnified by the media's repeatedly selective and fleeting interest in the coverage of distant human suffering. As Rose-Marie Chierici (1996) writes, "[T]he countries' turmoil . . . catches our attention for a while but then blends into the daily fare of more violence elsewhere, other famines, mass migrations and political strife to which we have become accustomed" (407).

The media's temporary interest in Haiti is emblematic of the struggle to analyze news coverage that simultaneously harms and benefits by stereotyping victims while at the same time publicizing relief efforts (see chapter 22 for a related discussion concerned with the Jerry Lewis MDA telethon). The photographed people, then, become components of a public relations campaign. While they struggle to cope and return to some normalcy in their daily lives, the pictures become crass commodities.

Conclusion

To critique the content and the comments on Farrell's images and his award serves to illuminate the limitations of the usefulness of such photographs as they frame Haiti as a lawless, unlivable disaster area. While attempting to show Haitians' humanity, such crisis coverage of Haiti, and particularly this celebrated photo series, strips them of that same humanity and dignity by showing them in ways most U.S. citizens would not be shown. These images mark Haitians as a huddled mass that is not welcomed. Farrell's photographs present Haitians as "people out there" (Lutz and Collins 1998) who are "dispossessed," homeless, cast out of their own homes, and not among "us." They are distant and, as such, non-threatening.

Such images do not encourage a desire to welcome Haitians, or others in similar plights, who may need to make the United States their home. Instead, they serve to regulate their migration. The 2010 earthquake

Local residents stand amid destroyed buildings in Jacmel, Haiti, a seaport town about 20 miles southwest of Port-au-Prince after an earthquake struck the region January 12, 2010. (Source: U.S. Air Force photo by Master Sgt. Jeremy Lock.)

propelled Haiti back into the media spotlight for weeks with the number and extreme content of graphic images increasing in daily news reports. Once again, pictures of the Haitian dead, dying, or injured were a staple of the daily catastrophe reporting. Through the Western gaze, Haiti again was made the ultimate symbol of Otherness, with the entire country shown as "dispossessed" and peopled by an undesirable "huddled mass."

As long as victims of violence and natural disasters are not shown in their full humanity, the immigration discourse will repeat itself. This is the catastrophe within the disaster.

Notes

1. See http://www.nytimes-institute.com/miami09/2009/01/09/for-haitian-immigrants-hurricanes-complicate-deportation-cases/ (accessed March 22, 2010).

2. See http://www.boston.com/news/education/k_12/articles/2009/06/07/blazing_a_path_for_fellow_students_to_follow_math_wiz_bound_for_mit_leaped_obstacles_on_way_from_haiti_at_top_of_class_haitian_beats_path_to_mit_still_blazing_a_path/ (accessed March 22, 2010).

3. Seehttp://www.miamiherald.com/2009/04/20/1008735/a-people-in-despair-haitis-year.html (accessed March 22, 2010).

Sources

American Civil Liberties Union. 2010. ACLU lawsuits against the Maryland State Police, racial justice/racial profiling: Driving while Black in Maryland. February 2. http://www.aclu.org/racial-justice/driving-while-black-maryland (accessed February 4, 2010).

Boswell, Thomas. 1982. The new Haitian diaspora: Florida's most recent residents. *Caribbean Review* 11 (1): 18–21.

Briggs, Laura. 1998. Discourses of forced sterilization in Puerto Rico: The problem with the speaking Subaltern. *Differences* 10: 30–65.

Buck, Elizabeth. 1993. *Paradise remade: The Politics of culture and history in Hawai'i*. Philadelphia: Temple University Press.

Cepeda, Maria Elena. 2001. Columbus effect(s): Chronology and crossover in the Latin(o) music "boom." *Discourse: Berkeley Journal for Theoretical Studies in Media and Culture* 23: 63–81.

Chierici, Rose-Marie. 1996. Lifting the veil of anonymity: A Haitian refugee's tale. *Identities* 2 (4): 407–417.

Dash, J. Michael. 1988. *Haiti and the United States: National stereotypes and the literary imagination*. Houndmills, UK: Macmillan Press.

Diaz, Alan. 2004. Concerns for homeland in Miami's "Little Haiti." *Photograph Miami: MSNBC.*

DiCicco, Damon T. In press. The public nuisance paradigm: Changes in mass media coverage of political protest since the 1960s. *Journalism and Mass Communication Quarterly.*

Duplessis, Jerry, Lamont Coleman, Devon Golder, Mohamad Abdel Wahad, and Wyclef Jean. 2007. Hollywood meet Bollywood. Los Angeles: EMI Music Publishing and Sony/ATV Music Publishing.

Dwyer, Devin, and Teddy Davis. 2010. Obama grants Haitians illegally in U.S. "protected status" for 18 months. ABC News. http://abcnews.go.com/Politics/ HaitiEarthquake/haiti-earthquake-illegal-haitians-protected-status-quake/ story?id=9570995 (accessed March 22, 2010).

Friedman, Jonathan. 1992. Myth, history, and political identity. *Cultural Anthropology* 7 (2): 194–210.

Gans, Herbert J. 1979. *Deciding what's news: A study of* CBS Evening News, NBC Nightly News, Newsweek *and* Time. New York: Random House.

Geggus, David Patrick. 2001. *The impact of the Haitian revolution in the Atlantic world, the Carolina Lowcountry and the Atlantic world.* Columbia: University of South Carolina Press.

Gray, Herman. 1991. *Color Adjustment.* San Francisco: Newsreel.

Gray, Herman. 1995. *Watching race: Television and the struggle for "Blackness."* Minneapolis: University of Minnesota Press.

Hall, Stuart. 2003. The whites of their eyes: Racist ideologies in the media. In *Gender, race and class in the media*, ed. Gail Dines and Jean Humez, pp. 89–93. Thousand Oaks, CA: Sage.

Jhally, Sut, and Justin Lewis. 1992. *Enlightened racism: The Cosby Show, audiences, and the myth of the American dream*, Cultural Studies. Boulder, CO: Westview Press.

Kilbourne, Jean. 2003. The more you subtract, the more you add: Cutting girls down to size. In *Gender, race, and class in media*, ed. Gail Dines and Jean M. Humez, pp. 258–267. Thousand Oaks, CA: Sage.

Lennox, Malissia. 1993. Refugees, racism, and reparations: A critique of the United States' Haitian immigration policy, *Stanford Law Review* 45 (3): 687–724.

Lutz, Catherine A., and Jane L. Collins. 1998. *Reading* National Geographic. Chicago: University of Chicago Press.

Said, Edward. 1978. *Orientalism, Western conceptions of the Orient.* New York: Pantheon.

Sandoval, Chela. 2000. *Methodologies of the oppressed.* Minneapolis: University of Minnesota Press.

Schiller, Nina Glick, and Georges Eugene Fouron. 2001. *Georges woke up laughing: Long-distance nationalism and the search for home.* Durham, NC: Duke University Press.

Squires, Catherine R. 2007. *Dispatches from the color line: The press and multiracial America*, SUNY Series on Negotiating Identity. Albany: State University of New York Press.

Valentín-Escobar, Wilson. 2000. Marketing memory/marketing authenticity in Buena Vista Social Club Recordings. Paper presented at the LASA Congress, Miami, FL. March 16.

Viglucci, Andres. 2009. *Miami Herald* photographer Patrick Farrell wins Pulitzer for Haiti images. *Miami Herald.* April 20. http://www.maimiherald.com/209/04/20/10008884/miami-herald-photographer-patrick.html (accessed Jan. 4, 2011).

Chapter 27

Exotic Babies for Sale

Diane Carter

Media scholars tend to agree that visual messages are more than benign window dressing for news, entertainment, and advertising messages. They play an important role in a type of "ideological abuse" (Barthes 1972, 11) that occurs whenever media outlets present potentially damaging social practices as normal, acceptable, or even desirable. Scholars have demonstrated the various ways in which media images reflect and support the interests of social elites at the expense of less powerful cultural groups (Gamson et al. 1992). But what happens when the images are produced to promote the interests of society's *weakest* members? What harm could there be, for example, in using images of third world children to encourage U.S. citizens to adopt orphaned infants and children from foreign countries?

Intercountry adoption,[1] a social practice in which an individual or a couple legally adopts one or more children from outside their home country, has become increasingly common in the United States during the past two decades (Evan B. Donaldson Adoption Institute n.d.). While the social turmoil triggered by national and international conflict during and after World War II compelled some U.S. families to adopt foreign orphans after 1945, the number of foreign-born children adopted by U.S. parents skyrocketed in the 1990s (U.S. Department of State n.d.). Although the rate of intercountry adoptions has slowed since 2004, when a record 22,884 visas were issued to immigrant adoptive children, U.S. families continue to adopt between 15,000 and 20,000 foreign children each year (U.S. Department of State n.d.).

While intercountry adoption is characterized by advocates as a compassionate act of charity in which orphaned children from undeveloped countries receive love, care, and "the advantage of a permanent home" (Convention on the Protection of Children n.d., overview), critical adoption scholars (e.g., Cartwright 2005; Dorow 2006; Hübinette 2006; Park Nelson 2006; Quiroz 2007a, 2007b) contend that the children of third world women are commodified in the political economy of intercountry adoption to produce orphans for Anglo adoptive parents. Prospective parents, on the other hand, tend to conceptualize adoption in much more pragmatic terms, primarily as a means of starting or adding to their family (Park Nelson 2006). Individuals who become interested in intercountry adoption often begin their search for adoption advice and information on the web, where prospective parents can easily find information on intercountry adoption agencies (DellaCava, Phillips, and Engel 2004).

Scholars in a wide variety of fields recognize that the web has become "a key site for the articulation of social issues" (Mautner 2005, 809). Although the sheer volume of adoption content on the web has made it difficult for researchers to critically examine the massive body of intercountry adoption content, a few researchers, most notably Pamela Ann Quiroz (2007a, 2007b), have begun to study web-based adoption content. This chapter features an expansion of Quiroz's work, discusses how intercountry adoption agency website images construct foreign orphans, and explains how these constructions reproduce the marketplace mentality (Dorow 2006) that has become a hallmark of intercountry adoption.

Intercountry Adoption in the Mass Media

Increased media coverage of intercountry adoption has paralleled the rise in intercountry adoptions over the past decade. The practice has become particularly visible in broadcast entertainment programming, with adoption story lines that appear with increased regularity on television dramas, sitcoms, talk shows, and newsmagazine programs (Waggenspack n.d.). Cable television networks first began to produce adoption-specific programming in 2002, when the Hallmark Channel aired its first adoption series, *Adoption: Real Families, Real Stories*. The hour-long reality television and documentary format featured adoptive parents, adoption industry professionals, birthparents, and sometimes the adoptees themselves talking about their experiences with adoption. A significant number of these programs featured families whose children had been adopted outside the United States. In 2004, Discovery Health introduced *Adoption Stories*, a 30-minute reality series that won the network a Daytime Emmy award.[2] Both programs appealed to viewers who hoped to gain access to insider perspectives and images that would otherwise have been unavailable except through direct contact with an adoptive family.

Although intercountry adoption has also become increasingly visible in mainstream print media, with coverage in such diverse publications as *Time* (Webley 2009), *National Geographic* (Sperry 2008), the *Washington Post* (Givhan 2009), and *The Economist* ("Saviours or Kidnappers?" 2010), by far the most explosive growth in adoption content has occurred on the web. The web is a popular tool among prospective parents, who use it to search for information; to communicate with adoption agency personnel, home study providers, and other professionals; to connect with other adoptive parents; and to share photos and information with friends and family (DellaCava, Phillips, and Engel 2004). Individuals and couples who become interested in adoption often begin their search for advice and information on the web.

Dark Undercurrents

Although adoption proponents characterize intercountry adoption as a compassionate act, critics caution that increasingly stringent national and international regulations governing adoption practices have failed to eliminate a dark undercurrent of greed, oppression, and prejudice that lurks just beneath the surface, spurring repeated charges of child abduction, trafficking, and exploitation similar to those leveled against a group of Baptist church members detained in Haiti after they attempted to remove 33 children from the country following a devastating earthquake in January, 2010 (Thompson 2010). If these critics are correct, then intercountry adoption may not only transform thousands of children into commodities but also place millions of children in mortal danger.

While modern intercountry adoption began with efforts to rescue children from the effects of international conflict beginning with World War II and continuing through the Korean and Vietnam wars (Evan B. Donaldson Adoption Institute n.d.), in the past two decades the emphasis has shifted to meeting parents' desires to adopt children with "racial flexibility, good health, young age [and] distanced birth mothers" (Dorow 2006, 61). Significantly, Anglo parents, who represent 92 percent of all U.S. parents who adopt children from outside the country (Vandivere, Malm, and Radel 2009, 13), overwhelmingly prefer to adopt Anglo or light-skinned children—if they can afford them, that is.

In a study of U.S. domestic adoption agency websites, Quiroz found that children are "categorized, labeled, described *and priced* along racial lines" (Quiroz 2007a, 50, emphasis added). This practice of categorizing children according to skin color is replicated on a grand scale in the international arena, as adoption fees in countries that offer light-skinned children for adoption tend to be higher than in countries in which available children are expected to be non-Anglo (U.S. Department of State n.d.). Images of children on adoption agency websites support and reflect this racial preference in subtle yet potentially devastating ways.

At the same time, while the news media occasionally report on negative outcomes such as disrupted adoptions that arise when adoptive families find themselves unable to cope with the effects of a child's early emotional or physical deprivation and neglect, intercountry adoption agency websites continue to support the notion that intercountry adoption is a win–win proposition for orphaned children and adoptive parents alike. Although international laws prevent most adoption agencies from posting photos of waiting children on their websites, agencies are not prohibited from using other types of images in marketing appeals. These website images generally can be categorized into four types: images of race, images of poverty, images of families, and images of the exotic "Other." In the following sections, I will briefly discuss the messages that each type of picture conveys to prospective parents and other online viewers.

Color-Blind Images of Race

The first category of images consists of stock photographs of babies and children. These images often comprise mixed-race groupings of children or are presented in slide shows in which pictures of children appear in succession. For example, the home page of Villa Hope Adoption Agency, an intercountry adoption agency that facilitates adoptions from China, Latin America, Russia, Ukraine, and Vietnam, features a slide show consisting of three photos. The first photograph is a black-and-white image of hands: Three light-skinned adult hands cup a pair of dark-skinned children's hands, which, in turn, cradle a cardboard cutout of a house.[3] The second photograph is a color image of four girls jumping as if for joy. All of the girls appear to be between 5 and 10 years of age, and all are dressed in blue jeans and colorful T-shirts; three of the girls have dark skin, and the fourth is Anglo. The third photo is a candid snapshot of an apparently Latina girl standing before an indistinguishable background.

Children in this type of image appear to be happy, healthy, and well fed, but, beyond this, the pictures offer limited visual information. These stock photographs tend to promote positive thoughts about babies and children, and they also take a colorblind approach to racial difference. Notably, two of the three photos in the Villa Hope slide show feature children with dark skin, although one would not expect that Chinese, Russian, Ukrainian, or Vietnamese children would be likely to have skin of the same hue as the children pictured in the slideshow photos.

While such an approach appears to challenge social barriers against interracial adoption, race remains a problematic issue in both domestic and intercountry adoption. In the United States, adoption has historically been linked to racial discrimination as the practice of removing children from one home and placing them in another was used to control a variety of groups, including African slaves (Hübinette 2006); Native-American children, who were removed from their biological families and placed in boarding schools, where they were forced to renounce their native language and traditions (White Hawk 2006, 296); and Catholic and Jewish children of Italian, Polish, and Irish descent, who were taken from their homes in poor immigrant neighborhoods and placed on orphan trains to serve as inexpensive labor for Protestant farmers (Kahan 2006). Citing the historical ties between adoption and discrimination and concerns that transracial adoption prevented African-American children from developing healthy cultural identities (Barry 2006, 62), the National Association of Black Social Workers sought and won legislation that in 1974 mandated race matching in adoption. Native-American tribes gained similar protections in 1978 with the passage of the Indian Child Welfare Act (White Hawk 2006). Both laws have since been weakened with the passage of the Multi-Ethnic Placement Act of 1994 and the Inter-Ethnic Placement Act of 1996, which "prohibit denying or delaying adoption placement based on race" (Quiroz 2007a, 3).

Although race is no longer a legal impediment to transracial adoption, it remains a significant factor in intercountry adoption, as many parents pay sizeable premiums to adopt Anglo or light-skinned children from Asia and Eastern Europe. According to *Adoptive Families Magazine Online*, parents who wish to adopt a child from these regions must be prepared to spend $25,000 to $30,000 or more in fees and travel expenses for each child they plan to adopt (Waggenspack n.d.). In contrast, parents who adopt children of color from Ethiopia spend a few thousand dollars in fees, plus a bit more for travel expenses, to complete their adoptions. Images that gloss over racial

Anglo- and African-American dolls are left alone in a sink at a Head Start children's center in New York City, 2009. (Courtesy of Paul Martin Lester.)

difference allow viewers to continue to choose light- and Anglo-skinned children while outwardly embracing the colorblind notion that racial difference is insignificant.

Images of Poverty

The second category of images presents highly stereotyped depictions of destitute third world children. In one such image, found on the home page of the Americans for International Aid and Adoption website, an Asian girl, perhaps 2 or 3 years of age, looks sadly through a window.[4] The girl's hair appears uncombed; blue paint is peeling from the wooden window frame. Another agency, All God's Children International, modified its home page after the January, 2010, earthquake in Haiti to include a link to a page entitled "Haiti's Unbelievable Tragedy." This page features several news photographs of Haitian children, some crying, others resting in the arms of Anglo rescue workers or staring vacantly into the distance.[5]

The children are dirty, and their clothing is torn and covered with plaster dust. (See chapter 26 for more extensive discussion of images of Haitians.) Some children appear to be injured. In the largest photo, a large gauze dressing is taped to one boy's filthy head.

Images such as these that portray children in the state of desperate need that is often associated with deep poverty, disease, natural disasters, or political upheaval and violence can be divided into two basic categories. In the first category, children appear in groups, pressing together, often reaching their hands out toward the camera lens as if to grasp a morsel of food. The photographed children are not displayed as unique individuals but rather are a huddled mass that symbolizes abject poverty and absolute need. They are visible but unknown, pictured yet faceless, and visually undifferentiated from one another and from the hordes of poverty-stricken children they represent. Children in the second category of photos sit or stand alone. Often, these children seem to stare through the camera lens directly into the eyes of the viewer, as if personally seeking contact and pleading for help. These images provide viewers with an emotionally safe distance from which to imagine how they might feel should they decide to "rescue" such a child (Hübinette 2006, 144).

Whether photographed in groups or alone, children in these images are almost always dressed in threadbare or ill-fitting clothing. Many are barefoot; most are unkempt. Children appear in crowded orphanage settings, walking along unpaved roads or inner-city sidewalks, or rummaging atop garbage dumps, often without a single adult in sight. By constructing unaccompanied children as destitute orphans, these images create a powerful sense of urgency and need that may be particularly appealing to prospective parents who seek to justify why they wish to adopt a child from a foreign country when some 123,000 children await adoption in the U.S. foster care system (U.S. Department of Health and Human Services 2009). Although none of the children in these images of poverty are available for adoption, and although some may not even be orphans, the demand that these images helps to generate for needy yet "salvageable" foreign children may have devastating effects on women, infants, and children in the United States and abroad who continue to bear the brunt of discriminatory social, economic, or military policies.

Images of Families

The third and largest category of adoption website images includes photos of children whose adoptions have been finalized. Many adoption agency websites feature "welcome home" photos on their home pages. Others collect photos from adoptive families and present them in slide shows or on specially designated family "photo album" web pages. Some of these photos appear to have been staged by professional photographers in studio settings. Others are snapshots of (invariably happy) children interacting with their new parents, siblings, or other members of their adoptive families. In contrast to the images of poverty described in the previous section, children in these photographs are squeaky clean and well groomed, and, in most cases, they are also smiling broadly as if to suggest that the act of adoption is all that is needed to overcome the myriad of social problems that orphan thousands upon thousands of children each year.

These happy family images manage negative information by excluding it. Carefully staged post-adoption family portraits discount the significant challenges that adoptive families and children often face, particularly in the days and weeks immediately after the family returns to the home country. Parents and children may struggle to overcome difficulties brought on by language barriers, jet lag, unfamiliar food, and cultural expectations governing such basic activities as eating, toileting, and bathing. Children must begin to trust the new adults in their lives, although they may also be grieving the loss of birth or foster family relationships and familiar surroundings. At the same time, adoptive parents must negotiate the integration of a new family member into the existing family structure.

Post-adoption photos not only reinforce the notion that adoptees, once home, conform easily to their new families, but also reinforce the notion that adoptees "fit" easily into a foreign society and culture. The home pages of European Children Adoption Services, Harrah's Adoption International Mission, and Wasatch International Adoptions, for example, feature photos of children seated casually in front of large American flags.[6] Many agencies include similar images in their websites that reinforce the notion that children can easily slip the bonds of their birth countries and assimilate seamlessly into U.S. culture.

Orphaned Children as the Exotic Other

The fourth category of images found on adoption agency websites explicitly links children to a particular country or culture of origin. Kim Park Nelson (2006) has argued that orphaned children serve as "authentic objects of culture" in intercountry adoption, appealing to those whose desire to adopt is commingled with a desire to travel to exotic places and "consume" exotic goods, including, in this case, the children of another country. In this sense, children represent but one of the "ample opportunities to shop for authentic, exotic merchandise while there" in an exotic locale (Park Nelson 2006, 94). Indeed, Park Nelson (2006) notes that parents sometimes explain their choice of national origin for their adoptive child by expressing a strong interest in the cultural enrichment they expect to gain by importing a child from a particular country into their home (93). Thus, parents who adopt infants from Russia may see their children as exemplars of Russian culture and cherish their children's so-called Russian-ness long after the children have fully assimilated into U.S. society. In similar fashion, Tobias Hübinette (2006) has attributed the relative popularity of Asian children to the expectation that Asian children are a nearly ideal addition to the perfect U.S. family. They are believed to be "docile and submissive, clever, hardworking, kind, quiet and undemanding, besides being cute, childlike and petite" (145).

In his influential works on Orientalism, Edward Said (1978; 1994) argued that Western notions of individual and social superiority are embedded in beliefs about cultural differences between East and West. Orientalist beliefs are constructed in social discourses and images that reflect and reproduce Western power, hegemony, and colonial aspirations of dominance. Feminist scholar Usamah Ansari (2008) also points out that "Orientalist imaginations are gendered" (51). She argues that third world women, in particular, are trapped in discourses that objectify their bodies while simultaneously depicting them as "inherently victimized and in need of help" (51).

The imagined differences between East and West also render orphaned children as ideal objects for consumption, particularly since their perceived difference is represented as an attractive quality (Dorow 2006). Adoption agency website images mirror and reinforce Orientalist attitudes and beliefs. Photographs of children wearing traditional ethnic costumes or standing near iconic cultural artifacts encourage website visitors to celebrate and embrace stereotyped notions of cultural difference. New Beginnings Family and Children's Services Inc., for example, features a photo on its China adoption page of six toddlers: All wear colorful Chinese pajama-style costumes and are seated in a row on a red velvet sofa under the watchful eye of a smiling caretaker.[7] In this photo, the babies are once again virtually indistinguishable from one another. One cannot be sure whether they are boys or girls. They wear bright, colorful clothing featuring Mandarin collars. The display reminds one of a set of baby dolls lined up in a store window. While these children might, in fact, be orphans, they are not alone. Instead, they are closely supervised by a woman who stands behind the sofa with a cheery smile that contrasts sharply with her severe hairdo and somber black suit.

Children are sometimes posed in website photographs in ways that reinforce damaging racial and ethnic stereotypes. Images of Asian girls hugging stuffed animals or being held or kissed by Anglo males, presumably their adoptive fathers, call to mind problematic notions of Western dominance that construct Asian women as passive yet highly sexualized subjects of colonialist male chauvinism in film and television programming (Sun 2003). Similarly, when children from a single racial group are dressed in nearly identical clothing in group photographs, the images reinforce a notion that all members of an ethnic group are alike. Stereotyped racist and sexist images such as these allow website visitors to envision the bodies of orphaned foreign children as strange and exciting yet controllable cultural consumables—in short, as ideal objects for consumption.

Image versus Reality

One point on which adoption advocates and critics agree is the fact that for each orphan who is adopted, thousands more have no statistical chance of ever being selected. The reasons for this difference are twofold. First, the sheer number of orphaned children has overwhelmed national and international child welfare structures. According to the United Nations Children's Fund (2005), as many as 143 million orphaned children live in Africa, Asia, and Latin America alone. Second, the vast majority of orphaned children are considered unadoptable for a number of reasons. In many cases, children are simply too old. According to the Child Welfare League of America (2007), U.S. families overwhelmingly prefer to adopt infants and children under the age of 5, yet more than half of the world's orphans are adolescents, and another 47 million between the ages of 6 and 11 are unlikely to be chosen because of low demand for school-aged children. Likewise, children in the U.S. foster system and abroad who suffer from physical or mental disabilities or diseases such as HIV/AIDS are much less likely to be selected for adoption than healthy children.

Even more disturbing is the increased evidence that the large sums of money that typically change hands in intercountry adoption have created incentives for individuals to attempt to profit at the expense of orphaned children. David Smolin (2006) likens intercountry adoption to money laundering, arguing that the system creates powerful inducements for child abduction and other crimes. Although adoption facilitators allegedly work to ensure that each adoption is in "the best interests of the child" (Convention on the Protection of Children 1993), some U.S. parents have learned too late that they had become unwitting partners in adoption scams. The Department of Homeland Security announced one such crime in February 2009, when four U.S. adoption agency workers pled guilty to fraud. Officials found the workers had facilitated the adoptions of 37 Samoan children by telling prospective parents that they had been abandoned, while telling birth parents that the adoptions would not be permanent ("Defendants Sentenced" 2009; Tribolet, Whitcraft, and Michels 2009).

Conclusion

As these examples demonstrate, many of the photographs in intercountry adoption websites normalize a harmful perspective of Western superiority in which light-skinned infants and young healthy children are constructed as desirable objects, available for sale to the highest bidder. Photos that play on notions of Oriental difference, exploit images of third world poverty and distress, deny the role of race in intercountry adoption, and create unreasonable expectations of post-adoption experiences reinforce a political economy in which orphaned foreign children are commodified for the pleasure of Anglo adoptive parents in the United States and other Western countries. These images play an important role in the reproduction of discriminatory social practices, and in the justification and normalization of the purchase of non-American children. It is incumbent upon both adoption agency staff and website visitors to critically consider how seemingly innocuous images of orphaned children reinforce discriminatory social practices, perpetuate inequalities, and sustain hurtful stereotypes.

Notes

1. Although the practice of adopting a child from a foreign country is referred to by many names, including "international adoption" and "transcountry adoption," signatories to the Hague Convention on the Protection of Children and Co-Operation in Respect of Intercountry Adoption, an international treaty between the United States and 54 other countries, use the term "intercountry adoption" (Convention on the Protection of Children 1993).

2. See "Adoption Stories," http://health.discovery.com/tv-schedules/series .html?paid=62.11094.103674.25099.x (accessed March 23, 2010).

3. See Villa Hope Adoption, http://www.villahope.org/ (accessed March 1, 2010).

4. See Americans for International Aid & Adoption, http://www.aiaaadopt.org/ (accessed March 23, 2010).

5. See All God's Children International, http://www.allgodschildren.org/ (accessed March 1, 2010).

6. See Wasatch International Adoptions, http://www.wiaa.org/ (accessed March 23, 2010).

7. See New Beginning China Adoption, http://new-beginnings.org/china_adoptionion.php (accessed March 1, 2010).

Sources

Ansari, Usamah. 2008. "Should I go and pull her burqa off?" Feminist compulsions, insider consent, and a return to Kandahar. *Critical Studies in Media Communication*, 48–57.

Barthes, Roland. 1972. *Mythologies*. New York: Hill and Wang.

Cartwright, Lisa. 2005. Images of "waiting children": Spectatorship and pity in the representation of the global social orphan in the 1990s. In *Cultures of transnational adoption*, ed. Toby Alice Volkman, pp. 185–212. Durham, NC: Duke University Press.

Child Welfare League of America. 2007. International adoption: Trends and issues. http://ndas.cwla.org/include/pdf/InterntlAdoption_FINAL_IB.pdf (accessed March 1, 2010).

Convention on the Protection of Children and Co-Operation in Respect of Intercountry Adoption. 1993. Hague Conference on Private International Law. http://hcch.e-vision.nl/index_en.php?act=conventions.pdf&cid=69 (accessed February 28, 2010).

Defendants sentenced in Samoan adoption scam. 2009. *Immigrations and Customs Enforcement*, February 25. http://www.ice.gov/pi/nr/0902/090225saltlakecity.htm (accessed March 1, 2010).

DellaCava, Frances A., Norman Kolko Phillips, and Madeline H. Engel. 2004. Adoption in the U.S.: The emergence of a social movement. *Journal of Sociology & Social Welfare* 31 (4): 141–160.

Dorow, Sarah. 2006. *Transnational adoption: A cultural economy of race, gender, and kinship*. New York: New York University Press.

Evan B. Donaldson Adoption Institute. N.d. International adoption facts. http://www.adoptioninstitute.org/FactOverview/international.html (accessed March 1, 2010).

Gamson, William A., David Croteau, W. Hoynes, and T. Sasson. 1992. Media images and the social construction of reality, *Annual Review of Sociology* 18 (August): 373–393.

Givhan, Robin. 2009. Celebrity Adoptions: Mom & Doubt. *Washington Post*, April 5. http://www.washingtonpost.com/wp-dyn/content/article/2009/04/02/AR2009040204294.html (accessed March 1, 2010).

Hübinette, Tobias. 2006. From orphan trains to babylifts: Colonial trafficking, empire building, and social engineering. In *Outsiders within: Writing on transracial adoption*, ed. Julia Chinyere Oparah and Sun Yung Shin Jane Jeong Trenka, pp. 139–150. Cambridge, MA: South End Press.

Kahan, Michelle. 2006. "Put up" on platforms: A history of twentieth century adoption policy in the United States. *Journal of Sociology & Social Welfare* 33 (3): 51–72.

Mautner, Gerlinde. 2005. Time to get wired: Using web-based corpora in critical discourse analysis. *Discourse & Society,* 16: 809–828.

Park Nelson, Kim. 2006. Shopping for children in the international marketplace. In *Outsiders Within: Writing on Transracial Adoption*, ed. Julia Chinyere Oparah and Sun Yung Shin Jane Jeong Trenka, pp. 139–150. Cambridge, MA: South End Press.

Quiroz, Pamela Ann. 2007a. *Adoption in a color-blind society*. New York: Rowman & Littlefield.

Quiroz, Pamela Ann. 2007b. Colorblind individualism, adoption, and public policy. *Journal of Sociology & Social Welfare* 34 (2): 57–68.

Said, Edward. 1994. *Culture and Imperialism*. New York: Random.

Said, Edward. 1978. *Orientalism, Western conceptions of the Orient*. New York: Pantheon.

Saviours or kidnappers? International adoption 2010. 2010. *The Economist*, February 4.

Smith, Stacy Jenel. N.d. "Adoption fever" among celebrities: Good or bad? *Netscape Celebrity*. http://webcenters.netscape.compuserve.com/celebrity/becksmith.jsp?p=bsf_celebadoption (accessed March 1, 2010).

Smolin, David M. 2006. Child laundering: How the intercountry adoption system legitimizes and incentivizes the practices of buying, trafficking, kidnapping, and stealing children. *Wayne Law Review* 52: 113–200.

Sperry, Shelley. 2008. The politics of adoption. *National Geographic*, February 11. http://ngm.nationalgeographic.com/geopedia/The_Politics_of_Adoption (accessed March 1, 2010).

Sun, Chyng Feng. 2003. Ling Woo in historical context: The new face of Asian American stereotypes on television, In *Gender, race, and class in media: A text-reader*, ed. Gail Dines and Jean M. Humez, pp. 656–664. Thousand Oaks, CA: Sage.

Thompson, Ginger. 2010. Case stokes Haiti's fear for children, and itself. *New York Times*, February 1.

Tribolet, Beth, Teri Whitcraft, and Scott Michels. 2009. Four sentenced in scheme to 'adopt' Samoan kids. *ABC News*, February 26. http://abcnews.go.com/TheLaw/story?id=6958072&page=1 (accessed February 28, 2010).

United Nations Children's Fund. 2005. *State of the world's children 2006: Excluded and invisible.* N.d. http://www.unicef.org/sowc06/pdfs/sowc06_fullreport .pdf (accessed March 3, 2010).

U.S. Department of Health and Human Services. 2009. Trends in foster care and adoption. http://www.acf.hhs.gov/programs/cb/stats_research/afcars/trends .htm (accessed March 1, 2010).

U.S. Department of State. N.d. Country information. http://adoption.state.gov/ countryinformation.html (accessed February 28, 2010).

Vandivere, Sharon, Karin Malm, and Laura Radel. 2009. *Adoption USA: A chartbook based on the 2007 national survey of adoptive parents.* Washington, DC: U.S. Department of Health and Human Service's Office of the Assistant Secretary for Planning and Evaluation.

Volkman, Toby Alice. 2006. Embodying Chinese culture: Transnational adoption in North America. In *Cultures of transnational adoption,* ed. Toby Alice Volkman, pp. 81–116. Durham, NC: Duke University Press.

Waggenspack, Beth. N.d. Four myths about adoption. *Adoptive Families Magazine Online.* http://adoptivefamilies.com/articles.php?aid=608 (accessed February 28, 2010).

Webley, Kayla. 2009. Why Americans are adopting fewer kids from China. *Time,* April 28.

White Hawk, Sandra. 2006. Generation after generation we are coming home. In *Outsiders within: Writing on transracial adoption,* ed. Julia Chinyere Oparah and Sun Yung Shin Jane Jeong Trenka, pp. 291–302. Cambridge, MA: South End Press.

Chapter 28

Virtual World Stereotypes

Lawrence Mullen

[H]umans have always been virtual.

Tom Boellstorff (2008, 33)

From the realistic experience of a flight simulator to the fantasy worlds of multi-user online games, a virtual world is a computer-generated environment viewed either on a screen (such as a computer monitor) or with a head-mounted, goggle-like display. Today's virtual worlds serve many purposes. They can teach, entertain, and help users to escape reality. They can also enhance understanding and experiences in the real world.

Virtual worlds are simulated, computer-based environments in which users can interact with other people and objects via an avatar. As Lon Safko and David Brake (2009) tell us,

> In addition to being a fun, entertaining way to pass time, virtual worlds give you the opportunity to browse new and unexplored domains, visualize and participate in imaginary communities and do business in a virtual marketplace with real customers and colleagues. (305)

The above is a general definition of the virtual world concept. In the context of this chapter about stereotypes, it is important to remember that each virtual world, the way it is constructed, the nature of the participants, and their attitudes, needs, and beliefs brought into the world—all these variables and more determine the nature of stereotypes within any

Most of the 2,000-year-old drawings on the wall of the Montana Pictograph Cave State Park 13 miles south of Billings remain symbolically mysterious. (Courtesy of Paul Martin Lester.)

particular virtual environment. As Tom Boellstorff (2008) explains, "There are many ways to tell the history [of virtual worlds]" (32) and many ways to define the concept.

Having started with a modern definition, we could trace the concept of virtual worlds back to the prehistoric cave drawings of some 10,000 to 20,000 years ago (see Boellstorff 2008; Heim 1995; Rheingold 1991). Created from the minds and memories of our early ancestors, these pictures of animals and hunting scenes were made for ritualistic purposes and created a type of virtual reality upon the cave walls.

Worlds of Stereotypes

Such imagery also hints at the idea of stereotypes as mere shades of what is the truth. The origins of photography could also be seen as another starting place for a discussion of stereotypes in virtual worlds because photographs allow ideas, thoughts, stories, and beliefs to be displaced in time and space. Photographic images also have the ability to shape opinions and form "pictures in our heads," as Walter Lippmann (1922) put it. These pictures are, however, quite limited. As Lippmann noted,

> Man is no Aristotelian god contemplating all existence at one glance. He is the creature of an evolution, who can just about span a sufficient portion of reality to manage his survival, and snatch what on the scale of time are but a few moments of insight and happiness. (1922, 18)

Our incomplete images of reality lead to stereotypes, which we use to simplify our complex world and help us understand people and groups of people, sometimes positively, sometimes negatively. Additionally, stereotypes are often culturally defined: "In the great blooming, buzzing confusion of the outer world, we pick out what our culture has already defined for us, and we tend to perceive that which we have picked out in the form stereotyped for us by our culture" (Lippmann 1922, 55). In other words, our culture, in a sense, prepackages stereotypes for us. In general, then, stereotypes can be defined as widely (culturally) held oversimplified images or ideas of types of people.

Likewise, many virtual worlds come with prepackaged stereotypes in the form of characters, or avatars, developed by the makers of the game or social network. For example, in the virtual world of Farmville, one's character (a farmer) has a limited number of choices for the look of his or her avatar and no choices of clothing. Every farmer avatar exclusively wears overalls, a shirt, and shoes.[1] Second Life, another virtual world, also has a prepackaged set of avatars to choose from, but it allows a player an almost unlimited number of choices for developing one's representation in the virtual world. This flexibility of Second Life's avatar construction is important to the ways in which stereotypes are created.

The Evolution of Virtual Worlds

For now, however, this chapter begins its exploration of virtual world stereotypes in the 1970s, where we find the early development of networked, computer-based virtual worlds. Computer graphics were primitive in the 1970s. Virtual worlds were primarily text-based with the visual nuances of virtual environments left to the imagination. Players of these multiuser dungeons, or MUDs as they were called, would verbally describe the environment, the actions of their character, and the situations they were in. As communities arose from these text-based worlds, stereotypes soon followed because, as Benedict Anderson (1991) recognized, the concepts of boundaries, membership, and non-membership, as well as an us-versus-them mentality, are implicit to the concept of community. One is either part of a community or an outsider. From such boundaries arise concepts such as alienation, segregation, discrimination, and the kinds of injurious stereotypical images that are the focus of this edited volume.

The earliest multiplayer online game using simple graphics was Maze War, which came out in 1974. In this first-person shooter game, one in which a user is in control of a weapon, players wander a maze and appear as eyeballs to other players. Shooting other players gives you points, while getting shot loses points (Library of Congress 2009). Throughout the 1980s and 1990s, the visual aspects of computer-generated virtual worlds became more complex with greater detail and a tendency toward greater visual realism. Today, more powerful computers, especially those made specifically for gaming purposes, as well as improved graphics cards are making realistic, high-resolution images the norm. It is this "realness" of the image that is important for understanding the significance of stereotypes in virtual worlds.

Second Life

This chapter focuses primarily on the stereotypes in the virtual world of Second Life, which, as of this writing, is one of the more popular multi-user online games.[2] Developed by a San Francisco–based company called Linden Labs, Second Life is a virtual world that many use for social networking. After a beta testing period, Second Life went public on June 23, 2003. As a visual extension of the early MUDs, Second Life users, or "residents" as Linden Lab labels them, engage in various activities, including entertainment, romance, hobbies, graphic design, photography, and commerce.

Many users have virtual families and are members of interest groups and communities of all types. A sophisticated virtual world, Second Life draws a broad range of participants from around the world (including many universities, news agencies, and representatives from various science, health, and governmental entities). Indeed, a large, diverse, international population engages with this environment. Since its inception, the popularity of Second Life has skyrocketed. In fact, Second Life is the largest virtual world without a gaming foundation (Safko and Brake 2009, 305). In an interview, Mark Kingdon, the CEO of Linden Labs, said that Second Life notes more than 1.2 million log-ins every 30 days while its servers contain more than 2 billion user-created items (Safko and Brake 2009, 305).

Stereotypes and the Avatar

An avatar is the computer image of oneself, that is, the visual representation one takes on in the virtual setting. In the computer gaming world, the term was first introduced in 1985 with Ultima IV.[3] Taken from the Sanskrit word "avatara," the term is associated with a Hindu myth of gods taking on human form to mix and mingle with humanity. As such, there is the sense of "stepping down" from the divine to a lower spiritual plane of mortal beings. This sense of the avatar suggests the way computer users take an avatar form to occupy a bodily presence in the cyberspace world over which they exert a great deal of control.

In other media, the manifestation of the human form in cyberspace could be seen in the 1982 movie *Tron*. In this film, a computer hacker (Jeff Bridges) is transported inside his computer. Though not an avatar in the true sense of the word, the manifestation of a bodily presence in cyberspace is evident in this movie and its sequel, *Tron Legacy* (2010).[4] The 1980s cyberpunk literature is also replete with the concept of the avatar. Vernor Vinge's (1981) short story "True Names" is arguably the starting point of the cyberpunk genre.[5] A mathematician and computer scientist, Vinge foresaw several aspects of virtual worlds, including the concept of griefing—the act of harassing other people in the virtual environment—and questions about people with disabilities. *Snow Crash*, Neal Stephenson's (1992) classic cyberpunk novel, defines the concept of the avatar as something used by people to communicate with each other in virtual reality. The virtual world, or "Metaverse" as Stephenson calls it, is "a moving illustration drawn by [the] computer according to specifications coming down the fiber-optic cable" (1992, 33):

> The people are pieces of software called avatars. . . . Your avatar can look any way you want it to, up to the limitations of your equipment. If you're ugly, you can make your avatar beautiful. If you've just gotten out of bed, your avatar can still be wearing beautiful clothes and professionally applied makeup. You can look like a gorilla or a dragon or a giant talking penis in the Metaverse. (33–34)

Here we find avatar protocol addressed, but Stephenson also explored questions of inequality in the virtual space. For example, if you do not own a house in the Metaverse, you are considered "a peon." And there are some people with greater sophistication in the Metaverse than others, and this sense of sophistication is primarily manifested through the look of the avatar having a sense of realism and an appreciation for detail. A key stereotypical concept is thus defined for the virtual world through the concept of sophistication that is manifested in a variety of ways. One way is with the stereotype of the "noob," or newbie, a beginning player who lacks sophistication. An experienced player can almost always detect a noob by the way he or she looks or acts.

Starting as a newbie, the beginning Second Life player is given a choice of 12 avatars: five male (one with dark skin), six female (one with dark skin), and one androgynous elf-like character. Once "in-world," the player can manipulate the avatar in a variety of ways. Changing the avatar's appearance is something that many people spend a fair amount of time and money on. The player can recreate the avatar by changing its height, body mass, head size, various facial characteristics, hands, feet, distance between its eyes, and more. Over 100 aspects of your avatar can be manipulated. But rather than spend the time making these alterations, a player can spend money purchasing avatar shapes, skins, hairstyles, eyes, teeth, eyelashes, and more that are made by other players and sold at any of the variety of virtual stores and shopping malls in Second Life. From basic human characteristics of race, gender, or body type to exotic, alternative, nonhuman forms, the opportunities to create a stereotypical or non-stereotypical avatar seem almost limitless.

In fact, what may be most interesting here is that, unlike many of the chapters in this book in which stereotypical images are produced and fixed in time by media sources, the avatars and their associated stereotypes in this virtual world are created by the users of the medium.[6] For example, how tall or short the avatar is, as well as its hair color, are features that are fully controlled by the person behind the avatar. And just as in real life, a tall avatar has the advantage over short avatars in terms of authority, power, and control in a virtual situation. Most avatars in Second Life are quite tall by reality standards. As for hair color, female avatars are more varied than men, wearing blonde, red, black, and brunette colors as well as pink, purple, and various mixed-color styles. Fewer men then woman are blonde in Second Life, where men primarily use darker colors for their avatar hairstyles. Few men have gray hair, and fewer still are bald.

Blonde hair, which is more frequent among female avatars, is associated with a lack of intelligence, and red hair with mystery and uniqueness. In a

On Second Life, "Dr. Les" is a silver-headed professor of communications, an avatar of a silver-headed professor of communications in real life. (Courtesy of Paul Martin Lester.)

general sense, then, the same stereotypes for hair are applied in the virtual world as in real life. At least one person reported that in the virtual setting, blonde hair is also used "to get the things she wants faster," which might in fact be a real-life stereotype of the color as well.

Like many of the physical characteristics of avatars, these attributes are easily manipulated and changed. The users of Second Life create the stereotypical images, not some outside agency over which they have no control, and although the avatars are cartoon-like in appearance, they have realistic qualities including movement, color, and general human or non-human appearance.

Avatars are, as Dennis Waskul (2009) states, "remarkably life-like in appearance, mobility and the ways in which they subtly move" (4). An avatar in Second Life (and in many other online games) is controlled with the computer keyboard or with the mouse pointer using heads-up displays (HUDs) shown on the computer screen. Pointing and clicking on arrows and other parts of the HUD (or using the arrows or other keys on your keyboard) make the avatar walk, fly, run, and generally move within the virtual environment. More complex motion is achieved with animations and pose balls.[7]

Virtual Stereotypes Matter

Why should we care about avatar stereotypes in the virtual world? One reason on the surface level of consideration is the massive number of people involved with virtual worlds. Estimates suggest that 80 percent of all internet users will be in non-gaming-oriented virtual worlds by 2011 (Daniel 2008). Beyond the huge numbers of people involved, however, are several more subtle reasons for seeking to understand stereotypes in virtual worlds. The three-dimensional graphics, textures, interplay of light and shadow, and stereophonic sound in the virtual world of Second Life convey a sense of realism that can result in immersion—of physical embodiment—associated with your avatar. From increased heart rate to romantic heartbreak, the immersive nature of the virtual world can cause feelings and real bodily reactions for a user.

Several Second Life users have reported that their experiences in the virtual world have affected how they deal with their actual lives physically and psychologically. Fundamental considerations such as the clothes one wears can be altered by the way one dresses his or her avatar in the virtual setting. In extreme cases, one's experience in the virtual world has caused family problems leading to divorce. More optimistically, one's self-esteem in the real world can be enhanced with improved communication skills or with greater understanding of interpersonal relationships due to the ways one communicates and interacts in the virtual realm.

The immersion experienced in virtual worlds is, indeed, different from immersion in other media (Dovey and Kennedy 2006): "The challenges, thrills and threats are experienced and produced through *intimate* mental, emotional and physical engagement by the player with the game and with the game technology" (104, emphasis added). Such immersion can lead to altered states of consciousness in which the player is totally absorbed in an activity. A strong attachment to one's avatar is often the result as one immerses oneself more deeply into the virtual world and the drama it can provide. And as more time, personal effort, and financial resources are spent in virtual worlds, a narcissistic attachment to one's virtual representation can occur.

Many in Second Life claim that their avatar "is me" and that there is "no difference between the real me and who I am in Second Life." Indeed, a strong connection with one's avatar shepherds a sense of presence that "the user feels corporeally connected to the virtual world" (Ryan 2001, 14). In this regard, Maurice Merleau-Ponty's (1962) claim of the embodied nature of consciousness is also important for our understanding of avatars in virtual worlds. For Merleau-Ponty, feelings and perceptions are embodied and not solely mental states. This idea helps to explain that those represented as avatars in the virtual environment are embodied subjects. Consequently, virtual stereotypes can and do have real, actual world meanings and consequences. They are important because they define the way users understand themselves and others not only within the virtual world but also in their actual lives. It is with this understanding of the effects of virtual world living that a few stereotypical forms that exist in Second Life can be examined.

Stereotypes in Second Life

Stereotypes are facts of life, and there's no escaping them in virtual worlds. In fact, virtual worlds suffer from a kind of stereotyped "original sin." In other words, the people using them are stereotyped from the outset as computer geeks who are "lonely, lazy, depressed, addicted, using shared fantasies to kill one another and to kill time" (Guest 2007, 26). This stereotype of the solitary computer game player fails, however, to take into account collaborative play and social contexts that surround and support game playing, especially the kind of social networks that exist in Second Life (see Newman 2004, 145–162). The solitary gamer stereotype persists and follows one into the virtual setting, where one finds more stereotypes— many of which are taken straight from real-world daily lives and implanted into the virtual setting. These include racial and ethnic stereotypes, sex and sexual orientation stereotypes, and stereotypes of body size, age, and disability, among others.

It is important to understand that virtual worlds create images that stereotype at times and at other times create new, alternative ways of looking at race, sex, and other aspects of identity. For example, sexuality in Second Life is both stereotypical and extremely complex and creatively constructed. Male and female avatars in this virtual setting are highly idealized: muscular, thin, young, and very often scantily clad. But variations of sexuality run the gamut from conservative/traditional to taboo alternative forms that include escorts, sex workers, she-males, pony girls, and fem-boys all engaged in various sexual acts, some of which involve extreme and dangerous activities and paraphilia. Criminalized forms of sexual behavior have also found their way into virtual worlds, with adults playing child avatars and engaging in acts of avatar pedophilia.

Perhaps not surprisingly, young (child) and old avatars are rare in the virtual world of Second Life, although there are many reasons for choosing to portray oneself as either a child or an elderly avatar. Alternately aged avatars are, for example, often used to satisfy taboo or fetishized forms of sexual experience, as mentioned above. Obese avatars are rarer than young or old avatars. Two arguments for the creation of overweight and otherwise socially scorned avatars are to instill more realism into the virtual setting or simply to respond to a sense of exhaustion from overexposure to idealized beauty in the computer world.

An overweight avatar takes a breather on Second Life. (Courtesy of Paul Martin Lester.)

Avatars of clear race or ethnicity are also less prominent than Anglo avatars. Many Afro female avatars take on a distinctive stereotyped shape with pronounced hips and thick buttocks. Afro male avatars are often sighted wearing excessive jewelry (or bling) and stereotypical "Black urban" clothing. Their dance clubs cater to specific musical tastes by playing hip-hip, rap, R&B, house, and similar forms of music stereotyped to this racial category (for more about race and ethnicity in cyberspace, see Nakamura 2002; Kolko, Nakamura, and Rodman 2000). Asian avatars in Second Life are multidimensional and can be traditional geishas, *anime* characters with large eyes and doll-like features, samurai sword fighters, and avatars that resemble gaming characters such as Sonic the Hedgehog. They, along with Brazilian, German, Italian, and other ethnic groups, can often be found sprinkled across the virtual landscape, but they tend to self-segregate into groups to enable themselves more easily to speak their native languages with each other as they interact socially.

Paraplegic and other avatars with physical disabilities are also found in the virtual world of Second Life. Rather than have a physically abled avatar

An Afro woman as seen on Second Life. (Courtesy of Paul Martin Lester.)

"Kim" uses a wheelchair on Second Life. (Courtesy of Paul Martin Lester.)

with the ability to walk and move about unaided, some with disabilities often desire to maintain a link to reality and the physical condition they understand best.

Thus, their avatars use wheelchairs, or attach prosthetic arms or legs. Like African Americans in Second Life, they also have their own groups and virtual dance clubs. There are, however, many with disabilities who use the virtual setting to (virtually) live in a non-disabled way, giving their avatar the ability to walk, dance, and otherwise be fully abled. Interestingly, some females with disabilities are stereotyped as fetishized objects and are solicited for sexual experiences. Moreover, when they do venture away from the circle of people with disabilities to go to virtual dance clubs with able-bodied avatars, some are unwilling to dance with them or engage in casual conversation and often shun them. One person with disabilities reported that she was so disgusted by the way others treated her in the virtual setting that she eventually stopped using Second Life.

Besides these implanted stereotypical forms from the real world, there are stereotypes that are specific to the virtual realm. Some would argue, however, that to separate reality from virtual reality is an exercise in futility (e.g., Waskul 2009). It makes little sense, they would say, to draw firm lines between the actual and the virtual. Indeed, people bring many of the ideas, feelings, and things they are familiar with into the virtual world, as demonstrated above, but there are differences. There are, for example, two stereotypical identities that originate primarily from cyberspace. These include newbies and griefers. Animal avatars constitute a third virtual-world stereotype that, although one can draw clear lines between this and real-world identities, is different enough from their real-world counterparts to warrant discussion as virtual world stereotypes.

Newbies

Everyone, no matter in which virtual world, is a newbie at some point, but the stereotypical newbie in a virtual world has a variety of visual characteristics that define her. These include unrealistic-looking hair and skin, stiff movements, and basic clothing. Newbies may ask a lot of questions and not know how to engage certain elements within the virtual setting. True newbies are awkward, unknowledgeable, and unsophisticated.

Griefers

Griefers are people whose primary goals are to irritate and harass others. They engage in pranks and other annoyances within the virtual world. Unlike newbies, they don't have particular physical characteristics that define them, so just about any type or style of avatar can be a griefer. Griefers will, however, use visual tactics to cause disruption. For example, there are griefers who have used images of flying penises to disrupt Second Life activities. Griefers are "the bad boys and girls" of the virtual realm, refusing to play or interact in socially accepted ways or in ways dictated by the virtual world's rules of engagement or play. Though there is generally a negative connotation to this stereotype, there are some who see them in a more positive light—as those who make the virtual world "more interesting." Griefers are stereotypically characterized as criminals in the virtual setting and when discovered are usually banned by land, shop, and club owners. Those who persist in griefing activities can face more severe sanctions, such as having their account deleted by Linden Labs.

Animal Avatars

A variety of animal avatars are found in the virtual world of Second Life. Some avatars take on pure animal forms and role-play as pets or other animal characters in the virtual setting. "Furries" are another animal avatar form and are arguably the most vilified avatar character. Furries are anthropomorphic animals with human personalities and characteristics. They communicate using human language, have human facial characteristics, walk on two legs, and are covered in fur yet wear clothes. Stereotyped as excessively sexually active, they are often accused of odd, bizarre, and taboo behaviors.

Another animal form is the neko. "Neko" is a term taken from the Japanese for cat, or, more specifically, catgirl. However, in Second Life, one can find both male and female forms of these avatars. Neko avatars

Animal-like avatars are called "Furries" on Second Life. (Courtesy of Paul Martin Lester.)

are more human-like than furries, wearing only a cat's tail and ears while the rest of the avatar remains human in form and function.

Many users have the opinion that there is an aura of instability or strangeness, or a general sense that something must be wrong, with someone who would choose to represent herself as a furry or neko. The reality is that some people playing as animal avatars have had trauma in their lives at some level that may influence them psychologically. Some identify with a particular animal form, claiming that it represents them better than a human form. Others, however, simply choose to be a furry or neko for the fun and entertainment of it.

Conclusion

As virtual worlds continue to grow and become mainstream components of our media-rich visual environment, understanding how users influence them and, in turn, are influenced by them will be important. Stereotypes— how they are constructed, nurtured, altered, and redefined in virtual settings—occupy one small piece of the social milieu in virtual worlds. With the early development of these environments, there is substantial borrowing from real-world experiences as stereotypes are adapted from the real world and implanted into the virtual. But the internet and virtual worlds within it also redefine how individuals think and interact with others. They create their own virtual culture with unique phenomena, language, and associated jargon. This new milieu offers new opportunities to observe and challenge stereotypes and images that injure. This chapter takes a small step to try to understand these emergent social landscapes complete with their problems and their promises.

Notes

1. Developed by Zynga, Farmville is one of the more popular Facebook applications in which you grow and harvest crops, collect products from farm animals and fruit trees, and basically care for a farm. By sending gifts, leaving notes, and fertilizing their crops, there is also some limited social interaction in Farmville with neighbors and their farms.

2. Although Second Life has some game-like elements, it is primarily a social environment in which users are not there to "win" anything or "level up" but rather to socialize. Thus, I hesitate to categorize Second Life as a game in the traditional sense. There are many other virtual worlds that act more like social networks than games. These include Open Sim, Sociolotron, SimCity, Wonderland, Kaneva,

there.com, Active Worlds, Prototerra, Twinity, World of Warcraft, and Croquet, to name a few.

3. Ultima IV: Quest of the Avatar is considered one of the most important role-playing games in the history of the genre (see http://www.gamespot.com/pc/rpg/ultima4/player_review.html?id=486231). The goal of the game was to become "the Avatar." In later versions of the game, the avatar became the computer user's visual, on-screen persona with a customizable appearance.

4. See *Tron Legacy*, http://www.youtube.com/watch?v=a1IpPpB3iWI accessed March 23, 2010).

5. See "Editorial Reviews," http://www.amazon.com/True-Names-Opening-Cyberspace-Frontier/dp/0312862075.

6. Second Life's website states, "Second Life is a 3D virtual world created by its Residents (people like you) that's bursting with entertainment, experiences, and opportunity. The Second Life Grid provides the platform where the Second Life world resides and offers the tools for business, educators, nonprofits, and entrepreneurs to develop a virtual presence" (from http://lindenlab.com).

7. A pose ball is an object found in the virtual world of Second Life that poses or animates your avatar when touched or sat on. Most are spherical, but any object can be made into a pose ball. So, rather than making your avatar sit by touching a pose ball floating above a chair, you instead click on the chair itself. Although there are many kinds, some of the more popular pose balls are ones that animate the avatar into sexual poses or movements between two avatars (for which two or more pose balls are used—usually, stereotypically pink for female and blue for male).

Sources

Anderson, Benedict. 1991. *Imagined communities*. New York: Verso.

Boellstorff, Tom. 2008. *Coming of age in* Second Life: *An anthropologist explores the virtually human*. Princeton, NJ: University of Princeton Press.

Daniel, John. 2008. The self set free. *Encyclopedia Britannica*. http://www.britannica.com/bps/additionalcontent/18/35694514/The-self-set-free (accessed March 23, 2010).

Dovey, Jon, and Helen W. Kennedy. 2006. *Game cultures: Computer games as new media*. New York: Open University Press.

Guest, Tim. 2007. *Second Lives: A journey through virtual worlds*. New York: Random House.

Heim, Michael. 1995. The design of virtual reality. In *Cyberspace/cyberbodies/cyberpunk: Cultures of technological embodiment*, ed. Mike Featherstone and Roger Burrows, pp. 65–77. London: Sage.

Kolko, Beth E., Lisa Nakamura, and Gilbert B. Rodman, eds. 2000. *Race in cyberspace*. New York: Routledge.

Library of Congress. 2009. The sound of the noising machine. *National Game Registry*, March 17. http://thenoisingmachine.wordpress.com/2009/03/17/national-game-registry-1974-maze-war/ (accessed Feb. 5, 2010).

Lippmann, Walter. 1922. *Public opinion*. New York: Harcourt, Brace.

Merleau-Ponty, Maurice. 1962. *Phenomenology of perception*, trans. Colin Smith. New York: Humanities Press.

Nakamura, Lisa. 2002. *Cybertypes: Race, ethnicity, and identity on the Internet*. New York: Routledge.

Newman, James. 2004. *Videogames*. London: Routledge.

Rheingold, Howard. 1991. *Virtual reality*. New York: Summit.

Ryan, Marie-Laure. 2001. *Narrative as virtual world: Immersion and interactivity in literature and electronic media*. Baltimore: Johns Hopkins University Press.

Safko, Lon, and David K. Brake. 2009. *The social media bible: Tactics, tools & strategies for business success*. Hoboken, NJ: John Wiley.

Stephenson, Neal. 1992. *Snow crash*. New York: Bantam.

Vinge, Vernor. 1981. *True names*. http://www.facstaff.bucknell.edu/rickard/TRUE-NAMES.pdf (accessed October 28, 2009).

Waskul, Dennis. 2009. Now the orgy is over. Unpublished

Chapter 29

Editorial Cartoons and Stereotypes of Politicians

Melvin D. Slater

During the 2008 presidential campaign, two cartoons on the covers of national magazines caused a media stir. The July issue of *The New Yorker* featured a cartoon drawn by Barry Blitt. It showed the Obamas in the Oval Office with Michelle in terrorist garb toting an automatic rifle while the future president was dressed as a Muslim. A framed portrait of Al Qaeda leader Osama bin Laden hangs on a wall, while the American flag burns in the fireplace. The two give each other a "fist jab," and their sly smirks indicate their successful takeover of the country.[1] Two months later, *Vanity Fair* returned the favor in a parody penned by Tim Bower in which Cindy and John McCain greet each other similarly in the presidential office. Here, Cindy holds several bottles of prescription medicine, John is supported by a rolling walker, and President George W. Bush's portrait hangs on a wall with the U.S. Constitution in flames.[2]

These cartoons illustrate the contentious nature of U.S. politics during the campaign as political cartoonists used their skills to join in the national discussion in the most diverse presidential campaign in the nation's history. Image makers participated in political discourse by providing pictures to entertain and inform the voting public.

During the 2008 U.S. presidential campaign, Senators Joseph Biden, Barack Obama, and McCain, and Governor Sarah Palin, like others before them, worked with their staffs to manage the images they disseminated of themselves to the voting public. Concurrently, cartoonists played up the contrast between the candidates in print and web publications. As often happens, sometimes the images themselves were the news. This chapter highlights the multiplicity of images, stereotypes, and engrained narratives evoked by cartoons of politicians. This analysis demonstrates how these images, and their embedded meanings, compound and conflict with each other. As such, this exploration helps illustrate why individuals rely on quick categorizations (schemata) to decode the constant flood of images and construct meaning.

My review of nearly 700 photographs and political cartoons published about the campaign in five major metropolitan daily newspapers, two news magazines, and *Rolling Stone* immediately before and after the November 4 election concentrated on the images of Obama, Biden, McCain, and Palin.[3] To interpret the images, I relied primarily on schema theory, which suggests that viewers manage complex visual messages and come to understand them by making quick categorizations based on one or more dominant characteristics (Fiske and Taylor 1991). Unfortunately, the dominant schemata of race, gender, age, and physical attractiveness are often tied to prejudices and discrimination.

Overall, the images of politicians during the waning weeks of the campaign demonstrated a striking pattern, with the candidates in similar poses, at similar locations, and sharing common gestures. Most of the photographs served as illustrations, providing visual emphasis to the text of an article. In general, the political cartoons relied more heavily and obviously on stereotypes and exaggerations to portray important and complex issues related to the campaign, often in comical ways.

History of Cartoons in Politics

Political cartoons first arrived on the American political scene when Benjamin Franklin placed a cartoon in the May 9, 1754, edition of the *Pennsylvania Gazette* urging the colonies to "Join, or Die" (Hess and Kaplan 1968). Generally, leaders of the American Revolution were spared the satire of cartoonists in the spirit of goodwill and cohesion as the new nation moved ahead on a path of unity, so George Washington and John Adams received reverent treatment. However, Thomas Jefferson was handed a heavy dose of graphic criticism from cartoonists (Katz 2004).

With the invention in 1828 of lithography, the use and distribution of political cartoons rose sharply. As a consequence, "[F]or much of the

"JOIN, or DIE" is attributed to Benjamin Franklin and originally appeared during the French and Indian War (1754–1763). It was reintroduced to unite the colonies at the start of the Revolutionary War. (Courtesy of the Library of Congress.)

nineteenth century, political cartoons wielded tremendous influence in presidential races because they, along with more-respectful hand-drawn portraits, were the only candidate pictures voters had" (Gilgoff 2008). By the 1900s, political cartoons were as much a part of the political landscape as the politicians themselves, wielding a high level of influence on public opinion. One demonstration of the impact of political cartoons arises from a 1950 cartoon by Herbert Block (pen name Herblock) that satirized the Republican Party platform and introduced the term "McCarthyism" (Lamb 2004), which became a part of U.S. culture, capturing the essence of Cold War hysteria.

Unlike news photographers, whose work may help politicians shape their own images or occasionally capture them in awkward moments, cartoonists craft their own reality. Their work depends upon cutting through conventions and surface appearances, using stereotypes, exaggeration, and distortion of physical attributes to help establish quick visual cues to pointed

The PRAIRIE DOG sickened at the sting of the HORNET — or a Diplomatic Puppet exhibiting his Deceptions!

In this cartoon from 1804 by James Akins, Thomas Jefferson, pictured as a scrawny dog, is stung by the French dictator, Napoleon Bonaparte, as a hornet, and coughs up $2 million in gold coins, the price of a secret deal to purchase West Florida, while a French diplomat dances with glee. (Courtesy of the Library of Congress.)

and often sharply critical commentaries. In the words of Joan Connors (2005), political cartoons constitute a

> unique form of media message; they offer voters an opinion on the campaign or candidates encapsulated typically in a single image. However, for those images to be comprehended and appreciated, cartoonists make reference to other events or images to allow readers to receive and digest the message quickly. (479)

Stereotypes of Politicians

In the "glad-to-see-you" stereotype, we see photographs of a politician waving, shaking hands, or giving a thumbs-up sign to the "common people." The candidate is portrayed as athletic or an outdoor person. In media images, politicians throw balls, pitch horseshoes, fish, hunt, jog, and play

"YOU MEAN I'M SUPPOSED TO STAND ON THAT?"

Conservative Republican senators push a reluctant GOP elephant to a shaky pedestal created by Communist hunter Senator Joseph McCarthy in this political cartoon drawn by Herbert Block, 1950. (Courtesy of the Library of Congress.)

basketball in order to tap into the nation's obsession with sports and to convey energy, strength, and a competitive spirit. The politicians can also appear as the head of a family. Shown with a child and/or a spouse, they are cast in a glow of reflected innocence and project a concern for education and the future. When candidates are shown with their family members, they demonstrate "family values." In addition, the politician's spouse must also play a stereotypical role for the watchful eye of the photographer or editorial cartoonist.

Female politicians can also be seen as sex objects, mothers, subservient helpers, children, and iron maidens (Carlin and Winfrey 2009). Most female politicians are discussed in terms of their physical attractiveness, hairstyles, and fashion sense rather than their position on issues. They can be presented as moms, emphasizing the maternal influence and caregiver aspect with regard to their own children and grandchildren but also deeply in touch with family issues that include health care and education. They sometimes are portrayed as weak, dependent, or childish individuals who need protection by and from males. The opposite, the strong woman, is presented as somewhat unfeminine and yet capable of handling tough situations.

Age was a factor in the 2008 presidential campaign as questions about John McCain's health and mental capacity were reported. Age discrimination and other age-related societal concerns were publicized in the media, and ageist stereotypes were perpetuated by media images. Stereotypes of older members of society (Roscigno et al. 2007) extended to politicians and represented aging candidates as slow (witted), unorganized, less responsive, and inflexible. (See relevant discussion of ageism in chapter 17.)

Race received special attention in the 2008 presidential campaign with the introduction of representations of Obama as an African American candidate, although he is biracial (his father is black and his mother is white). (For a discussion of race and the related concept of "hypo-descent," see chapter 9.) Stereotypes of African Americans developed since slavery that present and portray them as unintelligent, emotionally unstable, overassertive, and happy-go-lucky (Rhinehart 1963) continue in the media despite severe and ongoing criticism of their harm to society. (For related analysis, see chapter 8 on images of African Americans in the news.)

The Candidates in 2008

During the 2008 presidential campaign, Senator Hillary Rodham Clinton and Governor Sarah Palin became as well-known as their male counterparts, with the media devoting as much attention to their clothing and hairstyles as to their political positions on key national issues. The media presented fewer images of Clinton during the campaign than following the election, when interest about her possible role in the Obama administration increased. The majority of the photographs of her in newspapers and magazines portrayed her as a positive leader with the opportunity and abilities to land a key cabinet position. She was often shown in cordial and supportive positions alongside Obama or vice presidential candidate Joe Biden in which she appeared as a mainstream participant in the future political leadership of the United States. Images that emphasized routine aspects of her political involvement suggested that Clinton could be elevated above limited stereotypical gender roles to be taken seriously in U.S. politics on a level similar to that of men.

Images of Palin, who was relatively unknown in national politics, exhibited more variety than those of the other candidates during the campaign.[4] Her addition to the 2008 campaign provided cartoonists the opportunity to portray her unique rise to the presidential campaign, her gubernatorial record, and her family life. Slightly fewer than 90 percent of the reviewed cartoons that featured Palin employed exaggeration, bias, or extreme depictions of the Alaska governor to caricature her role. Many of the cartoons focused attention on Palin's family and specifically on her pregnant daughter. Palin was portrayed in a *Washington Post* cartoon as a gun-toting beauty with a baby in tow, and in the *Charlotte Observer* as a wide-eyed "hockey-mom-in-chief," "a female woman of not-male persuasion," and feisty, with an image of Palin kicking Obama in the shin above a caption in which McCain asks, "Who says I made a bad choice for my sidekick?"

Images of John McCain captured aspects of him as an older candidate, emphasizing his actual gray hair, slightly bent posture, and wrinkles.[5] Political cartoons overwhelmingly portrayed McCain negatively. A closer look at the cartoons of McCain show that many reflected stereotypes related to his age. In one *Dayton Daily News* cartoon, for example, an excited Palin waves to Alaska delegates while standing in front of and upstaging McCain. One delegate turns to another and says, "Great ticket! Who's the old guy?"

The media presented images of Obama less frequently than McCain prior to the election, but the number of Obama images increased following the election as media focused in on the president-elect.[6] More than half of the political cartoons studied here employed familiar, extremely negative, racist caricature exaggerations. These political cartoons often portrayed Obama as incompetent. For example, one representative post-election cartoon in the *Charlotte Observer* used a metaphor of Obama struggling to walk a larger than normal dog to convey the idea that he was not capable of handling the big job of running the country.

Use of Political Images

Political cartoonists play a role in political discourse by providing the voting public with images of candidates during campaigns and as they perform their official duties. Once out of bounds, the private lives of politicians today are more public, with access to personal images proliferating in traditional media and the internet. While the publication of such images generates debate, many argue that virtually all representations of politicians help to inform, monitor, and protest or dissent their candidacies and policies. Images of politicians campaigning, meeting with constituents, conducting the public business, and interacting with their families all contribute to the overall flow of information to the voting public about a particular public official.

Political photographers and cartoonists also monitor the actions of politicians as part of the watchdog function of media. Images are used, as in the case of whether Obama wore a flag pin on his suit lapel, to address the patriotism, values, and character of politicians. Cartoonists create images of politicians to parody and criticize their positions. The cartoons of the Obamas and McCains in the Oval Office are examples of work that make popular viewpoints visual.

Conclusion

For more than a century, politicians have understood that visual messages can be used to influence the voting public. Although politicians and their staffs work to insure that access is provided "only to those events that they wish to publicize" (Schlagheck 1994), many of the proliferating media images are outside of their control. Populist stereotypes, the glad-to-see-you politician, and the politician as robust athlete, father figure, or parent help politicians present themselves in a positive manner. In contrast, the prevalence of gender, race, and age stereotypes in images of politicians generally highlights negative characteristics or places politicians in negative situations that can damage a political campaign or undermine public support for an issue.

When, as in the 2008 U.S. election, the president is an African American, race is added to the stereotypical mix. A February 2009 *New York Post* cartoon by Sean Delonas portrayed a policeman shooting a chimpanzee with the caption "They'll have to find someone else to write the next stimulus bill."[7] The drawing sent shockwaves across the nation. Many interpreted the cartoon as a reference to the economic stimulus bill signed by President Barack Obama. Others said it was a far too familiar and hateful depiction of race. The cartoon is but one extreme example of the images used against politicians that rely heavily on "exaggeration and distortion" (Abraham 2009, 153) to "elicit controversy" (Rall 2009).

The controversial cartoon in the *New York Post* that compared President Obama to a violent chimpanzee shot by police is made into another one that presumes a KKK connection. (Courtesy of Carlos Latuff.)

The 2008 presidential campaign provided an opportunity to examine political images seen in the U.S. media by voters and other observers of the U.S. political scene. The diversity of candidates placed issues of gender, race, and age in the forefront. While some images challenged prevailing stereotypes, many portrayals of politicians relied heavily on time-honored, static, and easily decoded symbols. While overtly harsh images were in the minority, political cartoons took personal potshots at the candidates in ways that did not contribute to reasoned debate about the candidates and important public issues. Although the impact of cartoons on voter selection is not fully known (Adler et al. 1980), public and media criticism can encourage image makers and their editors to limit the use of negative stereotypical political images that unfairly injure the candidates and harm political debate and decision making.

Notes

1. See *The New Yorker* Obama cover at http://gothamist.com/2008/07/14/new_yorker_obama_cover_ironic_or_of.php (accessed March 23, 2010).

2. See the *Vanity Fair New Yorker* parody at http://www.buzzfeed.com/jonah/vanity-fair-new-yorker-parody (accessed March 23, 2010).

3. One hundred and seventy-two cartoons published during the six weeks between September 1 and November 21, 2008, in the *Wall Street Journal*, the *Washington Post*, the *New York Times*, the *Atlanta Journal Constitution*, the *Charlotte Observer*, *Time*, *U.S. News & World Report*, and *Rolling Stone*, were used for this chapter.

4. See Sarah Palin cartoons at http://politicalhumor.about.com/od/sarahpalin/ig/Sarah-Palin-Cartoons/ (accessed March 23, 2010).

5. See John McCain cartoons at http://politicalhumor.about.com/od/johnmccain/ig/John-McCain-Cartoons/ (accessed March 23, 2010).

6. See Barack Obama cartoons at http://politicalhumor.about.com/od/barackobama/ig/Barack-Obama-Cartoons/ (accessed March 23, 2010).

7. See the *New York Post* cartoonist under fire at http://thinkprogress.org/2009/02/18/nypost-chimp/ (accessed March 23, 2010).

Sources

Abraham, Linus. 2009. Effectiveness of cartoons as a uniquely visual medium for orienting social issues, *Journalism Communication Monographs* 11 (2): 117–165.

Adler, Jerry, Jane Whitmore, Phyllis Malamud, William D. Marbach, and Nancy Stadtman. 1980. The finer art of politics, *Newsweek*, October 13, 74.

Carlin, Diana B., and Kelly L. Winfrey. 2009. Have you come a long way, baby? Hillary Clinton, Sarah Palin, and sexism in 2008 campaign coverage, *Communication Studies* 60 (4): 326–343.

Connors, Joan L. 2005. Visual representations of the 2004 presidential campaign political cartoons and popular culture references, *American Behavioral Scientist* 49 (3): 479–487.

Fiske, Susan T., and Shelley E. Taylor. 1991. *Social cognition*. New York: McGraw-Hill.

Gilgoff, Dan. 2008. Picture power. *U.S. News & World Report*, March 10, 38–40.

Hess, Stephen, and Milton Kaplan. 1968. *The ungentlemanly art*. New York: MacMillan.

Katz, Harry. 2004. An historic look at political cartoons, *Nieman Reports*, 44–46.

Lamb, Chris. 2004. *Drawn to extremes: The use and abuse of editorial cartoons*. New York: Columbia University Press.

Rall, Ted. 2009. Dwindling cartoonists still connect with readers. *American Editor*, Spring, 16.

Rhinehart, James W. 1963. The meaning of stereotypes. *Theory into Practice* 2 (3): 136–143.

Roscigno, Vincent J., Sherry Mong, Reginald Byron, and Griff Tester. 2007. Age discrimination, social closure and employment, *Social Forces* 86 (1): 313–334.

Savage, Charlie. 2009. Accused 9/11 mastermind to face civilian trial in N.Y. *The New York Times*, Nov. 13, http://www.nytimes.com/2009/11/14/us/14terror.html (accessed Feb. 19, 2011).

Schlagheck, Carol. 1994. Enough is enough, say columnists, *News Photographer*, September, 57.

Conclusion: Ethics in a New Key

Clifford Christians

In Susanne Langer's (1957) striking book *Philosophy in a New Key*, symbolization is used to understand the human mind. Symbolic thought sets up a new theory of the arts and gives coherence to our piecemeal struggles with issues of life and consciousness. In parallel terms, this third edition of *Images That Injure* opens a new veranda on media ethics. Symbolic transformation, this distinctive activity of the human species, comes into its own here as image making. In these provocative chapters, the cases, reflections, and analysis enable us to do media ethics from a fresh perspective.

For a decade or more, academics and professionals have been working together on a second generation of communication ethics. Instead of the traditional approach called "rationalist individualism," the goal now is a media ethics that is transnational, gender inclusive, and cross-cultural. Rather than a Western-style ethics that is monocultural and gendered male, our challenge has been a revolution in all three areas. Internationalizing the field and the major contributions of feminist ethics have made major impacts to date. But the multicultural dimension remains underdeveloped. This volume opens new pathways into it. It exemplifies multicultural ethics at its best. It establishes the ethics of harm in the most comprehensive manner to date. For the wider context of media ethics, its impact is indelible as well. Let me elaborate what I mean.

Mainstream Ethics

There are two problems in ethics that need to be overcome for multiculturalism to flourish: formal rules and ethical models built on the abstracted self. These chapters generally avoid those two liabilities. For the most part, the moral claims that are made about images that injure do not appeal to formal principles or individuated choice. However, both issues are deeply entrenched in media ethics as a whole and warrant a systematic review so that the promise of this pathbreaking book will be fulfilled.

Alasdair MacIntyre's *After Virtue* (2007) establishes ethical formalism in terms of Western intellectual history. What he calls the "Enlightenment Project" for ethics was born at the time when science introduced the laws of physics to explain nature. Philosophers constructed principles to explain human behavior and basically agreed that morality must be justified in terms of rational standards. Immanuel Kant and others in the Enlightenment Project were committed to constructing an ethics that moves from premises about human nature "to conclusions about the authority of moral rules and precepts" (MacIntyre 2007, 52).

Consistent with the ethical rationalism that has been the prevailing paradigm in philosophical ethics, communication ethics has presumed that rationality marks all legitimate claims about moral obligations. The general trend in formalist morality entails an ethical rationalism that requires autonomous moral agents to apply rules consistently and self-consciously to every choice. Rational processes create basic norms that everyone must follow and against which all failures in moral duty can be measured.

Mainstream media ethics also presumes the disembedded self and is a premier reason that multiculturalism has not received adequate attention to date. At the centerpiece of traditional media ethics is the autonomous self, a theory of human nature presumed to be unproblematic. As the physical sciences suggested to the Enlightenment mind, if the atom is the fundamental building block of all matter, are discrete individuals the essential unit of society? The astrophysical worldview of the seventeenth-century Age of Science provided an analogue for humans as irreducible, self-sufficient entities. Consider, for example, the radically individualistic character of René Descartes's classic phrase, *cogito ergo sum*. In his *Meditations Concerning First Philosophy* (1641/1998), Descartes sought an absolute proof that "I" exists. Whether one dreams of appearances or negotiating the real world, one's own mind is necessary. Therefore, Descartes concluded that an individual's thinking capacity is indubitable, even if one used the most strenuous tests of skepticism and doubted everything.

But John Locke's (1689/2003) conception of government as the consent of sovereign individuals most forcefully shaped the ethical thinking that has dominated the ethics of the Occident. In Lockean terms, the self is an independent mental substance having no specified relation whatsoever with other mental substances in which the individual and society stand in natural opposition. The mainstream view disembeds the self and operates by procedures. Sociologically speaking, a fierce independence from external controls and an insistence on rights are firmly etched into our traditional approach to morality.

Dialogic Ethics

The editors and contributors for this book think about "images that injure" in a different way. Rather than uncritically assuming formalism or individualism, they reflect a dialogical ethics instead. And because they are not trapped in the limitations of the mainstream view, they are able to make substantial progress in the morality of representation. The book is not merely important in itself as a manual on visual messages or as a textbook that teaches diversity in a provocative format. In order to understand this book's long-term significance, its role in and support of dialogic communication ethics need to be highlighted.

A shorthand version of multiculturalism and ethics argues that a dialogical model ought to be substituted for monologic transmission between discrete individuals. For an ethics of diversity to be legitimate intellectually and possible practically, dialogic social philosophy is the only foundation. A dialogic paradigm is a decisive alternative to rationalism and individualism and a fruitful framework for ethics in an age of globalization and multiculturalism. The social bondedness of dialogic theory enables us to start over intellectually. In so doing, it establishes a credible ethics to understand the images of diversity and to act on them virtuously.

According to the dialogic perspective, *Homo sapiens* is the one living species constituted by language. Therefore, humans are fundamentally cultural beings. As creators, distributors, and users of culture, humans live in a world of their own making. Rather than one-dimensional definitions of the human species as *Homo faber, Homo economicus*, or *Animale rationale*, our cultural character verifies both our dialogic composition as a species and the relationship of human beings to mediated language.

In traditional epistemology, all acts are monologic, though actions may be coordinated with others. However, when the lingual interpretation of our experience and ourselves constitutes who we are, human action is dialogic. Our experience is then understood largely in terms of rhythm with other non-individuated actors. Humans are dialogic agents within a language community. Therefore, all moral matters must be seen in communal terms. A self exists only within webs of communication, and all self-understanding implicitly or explicitly acknowledges the social origin of all concepts of the good life and so of us.

The dialogic tradition of social thought, represented primarily by Mikhail Bakhtin, Martin Buber, and Emmanuel Levinas, constitutes a productive approach to the relationship between ethics and sociality. For Buber (1965), restoring the dialogic ought to be the primary aim of humankind (209–224). He speaks prophetically that only as I-Thouness prospers will the I-It modality recede (Buber 1958). Levinas's interaction between the self and the other makes diversity normative. Multiculturalism in his theory is not only a political strategy but also a public philosophy (1981). As the Russian linguist Bakhtin argues correctly in *The Dialogical Imagination* (1983), only oral language represents a dependable source of opposition and struggle. Therefore, as this book demonstrates, social groups defined by ethnicity, sexuality, illness, age, religion, and so on can be locations of activism and not just centers of contemplation or protest.

This tradition enables us to endorse dialogue as the most appropriate framework for the ethics of representation. Buber's (1958) theory of communication makes the dialogic relation primal in his famous aphorism "In the beginning is the relation" (69). He intends that ontologically as a category of being. This irreducible anthropological phenomenon cannot be decomposed into simpler elements without destroying it. There are not three components—sender, message, and receiver—to be dismembered for scientific analysis. The reciprocal bond is an organic whole forming an interpretive unit centered in the human psyche. All the variables are conjugal relationships, and isolating them is academia's version of Humpty Dumpty. Communication rests in our spirit, in our interpretive capacity— not in the mind, cogito, or intellectus. The commonplace phrase "We're with you in spirit" is actually a powerful truth; the oneness of our species is born along the stream of consciousness. I resonate at the center of being with the moral imagination of others. Our human bond is an ethical commitment rooted in value-saturated symbols.

Buber, Levinas, and Bakhtin categorically reject all dualisms between self and culture. And Paulo Freire (1973) adds to their dialectical unity with this symmetrical summary: "I cannot exist without a not-I; in turn the not-I depends on that existence. ... There is no longer an 'I think' but 'we think'" (137). In Freire's terms, it is our ontological vocation as creative subjects to live meaningfully within the world while transforming it. Freire (1970) presumes an explicit anthropology, conceiving of humans as existing not only in everyday reality but also through symbols separating from it in their consciousness (69). Humans are able to adopt postures ranging from a nearly undifferentiated spontaneous response to a critical attitude that entails a conscious process of intervention. As with the dialogic tradition generally, Freire declares that we have understood reality when we have gotten inside the self-in-relation. He presumes a symbolic paradigm with the distinctively human as the meaningful center.

Critique of Mainstream Ethics

Dialogic ethics contradicts the metaphysical foundations on which the Western canon is based. Social constructions replace formal law systems. Contextual values become the centerpiece instead of ethical prescriptions. In the dialogic model, morality is rooted in everyday experience and has multiple levels of complexity. From the dialogic perspective, a formalist ethics of procedures fails to recognize that as lingual beings, humans forget and remember, struggle with the past and hope for the future, listen and speak, and show remorse and make excuses. In Nel Noddings's (1984) terms, an ethic that concentrates on arranging principles hierarchically and that derives conclusions logically is "peripheral to or even alien to, many problems of moral action. ... Moral decisions are, after all, made in real situations; they are qualitatively different from the solution of geometry problems" (2–3). In dialogic ethics, moral experience is formed in terms of its origins, present concerns, and outcomes. Rational calculation and impartial reflection are replaced by an understanding of the good that is nurtured in community.

An insistence on rational principles alone does not lead to a unified moral system. When the Enlightenment's common beliefs and values began to disintegrate with secularism and industrialism, the modernist project proved to be unsustainable. Of necessity, individuals must make choices but do so in moral confusion. To Alasdair MacIntyre (2007), for instance, our fragmented society has no conception of the common good and no way to persuade one another about what it may be. Therefore, the teaching, acquisition, and exercise of morality can occur only if we construct "local forms of community within which civility and the intellectual and moral life can be sustained through the new dark ages which are already upon us" (263).

Communication theorist and educator James Carey (1987) put this critique in terms of journalism. He argued that to treat ethics as a formal system is to exclude from discussion the *rationale* for and *embedded inequalities* of the press. Journalism ethics as a system of rules is a "purely negative enterprise." It is preoccupied with gifts, junkets, conflicts of interest, sensationalism, and unattributed sources, while accepting as a given "the entire structure of professional life" (6). "The ethics of journalism often seems to be a cover, a means of avoiding the deeper questions of journalism as a practice in order to concentrate on a few problems in which there is general agreement" (Carey 1987, 6). Rules may stifle practices that damage the press's credibility or are patently unfair. "But none of this will solve the real problems of journalism. In fact, those problems cannot be solved; they can only be dissolved into a new set of practices, a new way of conceiving what journalism is and how one ought to go about it" (Carey 1987, 16).

This book validates the critique of formalism *and* individualism. In its application to journalism, advertising, and entertainment, the dialogic perspective generates a deep struggle over the media's character and mission. It doesn't accept the traditional rationale as a given. The general overview of part I insists, in effect, that formal prescriptions and the liberal self be exorcised and replaced by the dialogic instead. The chapters as a whole demonstrate how a moral life develops through community formation and not in the obscure sanctums of isolated individuals. Moral values are situated in the social context rather than anchored by theoretical abstractions.

Narrative

Dialogic ethics puts a premium on narrative. It emphasizes narrative so that it guarantees that ethical models are not formalist and individualistic. It advocates a new perspective on moral philosophy in which dialogic ethics points to narrative as the way humans make life meaningful. Humans are storytelling animals. The mainstream, modernist tradition neglects the concrete, in particular our common social and emotional experience. But narratives lived out in a historical context are what contribute most to moral action.[1]

Narrative is the mode of communication specifically suited to virtue. In MacIntyre's (2007) perspective, the human capacity to narrate enables us to understand how character unfolds. Narrative specifies both continuity and starting anew. Human character does not develop by itself without context. Character presupposes a story, without which it would be simply unintelligible. MacIntyre wants to avoid the randomness he associates with modern subjectivity and believes this can be achieved in part by stressing the close relation between character, narrative, and accountability. "It is because we live out narratives, and because we understand our own lives in terms of the narratives that we live out, that the form of narrative is appropriate for understanding the actions of others" (MacIntyre 2007, 212).[2]

The shift from formal principles to story, from individuals to community formation, illustrates how dialogic ethics can be put to work. Stories are symbolic frameworks that organize human experience. Through stories, we constitute ways of living in common. In Walter Fisher's (1987) terms, we are narrative beings who exhibit "an inherent awareness of *narrative probability*, what constitutes a coherent story, and [a] constant habit of testing *narrative fidelity*, whether or not the stories they experience ring true with the stories they know to be true in their lives" (5, emphasis in original). Humans pursue this narrative logic rather than merely recount episodes and action. Stories that exhibit the attributes of coherence and fidelity inspire us to join with others who share them. Stories also become public discourse when they are driven by good reasons. They make sense collectively and form the warrant for communal decision making.

Carey (1987) argued that news is a narrative genre akin to storytelling.[3] He proposed that journalism be understood not as an outgrowth of science and the Enlightenment but as an extension of poetry, the humanities, and political utopianism. For Carey,

[J]ournalism only makes sense in relation to the public and public life. Therefore, the fundamental ethical problem in journalism is to reconstitute the public, by nurturing its narratives. Journalism ought to be conceived less on the model of information and more on the model of a conversation. ...

All journalism can do is preside over and within the conversation of our culture: to stimulate it and organize it, to keep it moving and to leave a record of it so that other conversations—art, science, religion—might have something off which they can feed. The public will begin to reawaken when they are addressed as a conversational partner and are encouraged to join the talk rather than sit passively as spectators before a discussion conducted by journalists and experts. (1987, 17)

As this book illustrates, stories are told to communicate to one another about who we are, what we care about, and our aspirations. Storytelling transforms our identity as persons into a shared, public reality. Thus parts II to VI correctly put image making in the narrative mode. The stories of Lenape Native Americans, various Cinderella characterizations, images in music videos, those with breast cancer, Jewish youth, Haitian immigrants, and persons with disabilities activate our conscience and galvanize public discourse.

Symbolism and Morality

The dialogic ethics that drives this book not only highlights narrative but also makes symbols come into their own. It verifies with Susanne Langer the commitment to symbolization that we need for ethics "in a new key." In a dialogic theory of communication, persons are displayed, made accessible, nurtured, and integrated into social units through symbol, myth, and metaphor. Words are concrete forms of life. Their meaning derives from an interpretive, historical context that humans themselves supply. Our constitutive relations as humans are symbolic, and therefore stereotypes cut into our deepest being.

What cell is to biology, symbol is for communication. Cultures are interconnections of symbolic forms, those fundamental units of meaning expressed in words, gestures, and images. Realities called "cultures" are inherited and built from symbols that shape our action, identity, thoughts, and sentiment. Communication, therefore, is the creative process that builds and reaffirms through symbols. Culture signifies the constructions that result.

Human behavior, in this vision, is symbolic action—action signifying something, as do phonation in speech, pigment in paintings, and notes in music. Our world is an intricate series of accrued inference and implication. A twitch of the eye is more than a contracting eyelid; it may actually be a mischievous wink, or it can indicate a conspiracy. News reading thus becomes a dramatic act. Readers and viewers face not pure information but a drama. Competing forces are portrayed nudging one another into patriotism, class antagonisms, resentments, or support. Speak the verbal symbol "death," and listeners will provide their own range of understanding that indicates the cessation of brain waves or heartbeat, a disembodied soul meeting its maker, or separation from a human community.

Humans stitch together views of the world to orient themselves and provide social cohesion. We take pieces of cloth and demand that flags be respected as our national emblem. Many Christians believe that bread signifies Jesus's body, and words such as "redskins," "cripples," and "freaks" dehumanize persons. Although not identical to that which they symbolize, symbols participate in their meaning and power. They share the significance of the signifier. In addition, they illuminate their referents so that they are transparent. They permit us to express levels of reality that otherwise remain hidden. Symbols open up the human spirit, where our worldviews are inscribed.

A symbolic theory of communication recognizes human creativity as this species' distinctive feature. Creative beings not only exist in a vast museum but also are their own curators. Concepts are not isolated from their representations. The social and individual dimensions of language are a unified whole. The symbolic approach to communication ransoms us from Locke's unproductive question "How can disembodied and isolated minds engage one another?" (1689/2003). Through the social nature of language, we integrate the message with communal formation. Carey (1988) calls it the ritual view in which ceremonies define the meaning and purpose of celebratory events and not merely exchange information. In this book's effort to grapple with ethics while shifting us from print to the visual, we finally feel at home theoretically. From a dialogic perspective that privileges symbolization, multiculturalism is not a supercilious pursuit.

The interactive, dialogic model sees social and political entities as multiple spaces for constructing everyday life. The reciprocal voices of the dialogic self are situated and articulated within the decisive contexts of gender, race, class, religion, and so on. Starting over intellectually is no magic wand that eliminates our struggles over racism and the internet, hate speech, stereotypes in the media, and the politics of multiculturalism generally. The point is that this book shows the kind of conceptual clarity at the foundational level that is necessary for moving us forward productively over the long term.

When symbolic theory revolves around a dialogic axis, the application to stereotypical mediated images is obvious. Though the world of technological images is our linguistic home and not something alien or frivolous, we can simultaneously nurture personal arenas in dialogic terms. Alongside a critique of mediated structures that transforms them vigorously, human beings can create oppositional symbolic worlds interpersonally within subcultures and neighborhoods. Creating and nurturing symbolic worlds that heal are never automatic anywhere, but in the free spaces, grassroots symbol making is likely to be participatory. Examples of locally produced symbolic worlds that heal exist all over the globe. This book helps expand their numbers.

Conclusion

Media ethics that develops itself in and through dialogic theory is the most sophisticated normative model at present. It embodies the commitments of narrative and symbolism, while it benefits from the breadth and range of dialogic social philosophy. The dialogic perspective enables us to engage one another about our mutual responsibilities toward multiculturalism. In working on stereotypes in the media, we are not simply open to the other's perspective. We should actively listen and contribute with a view to uncovering truths about the moral life that motivate us to action. When we give reasons for our acts, they "point to feelings, needs, impressions and a sense of personal ideals" rather than to "principles and their applications" (Noddings 1984, 3). Consistent with dialogic ethics, this book does not treat morality as an impersonal action-guiding code for individuals but rather as a shared process of discovery and interpretation in which we continually and thoughtfully adjust our positions in light of what others have said and done.

Visual messages form an organic whole with our deepest humanness, and their vitality or oppression inevitably conditions our wellbeing. For media ethics, symbolic theory lays a new foundation on which to build in a visual age, and this book is a prototype of what to construct.

Notes

1. Widely considered the most influential theological ethicist at present, Stanley Hauerwas trades on the same insight that stories constitute a community's moral framework. For Hauerwas, the axis of ethics is not formal rules of proper procedure, but stories of substantive morality grounded in appropriate forms of community. Moral power is inseparably connected to a body of language we inherit. Our lingual legacy moves us toward a moral horizon, and thereby holds the whims of autonomous individuals at bay (see, e.g., his classic *A Community of Character*; Hauerwas 1981).

2. The narrative turn has its roots in John Dewey's pragmatism also. For Dewey's *Human Nature and Conduct* (1930), the task of ethics is understanding

those problem situations where we distinguish good conduct from bad. Conflict and a tangle of incompatible impulses prompt us to ask the question, "What is good?" These are the clues we need for a conception of values that is not grounded in rationalism. Goodness and badness are not objective properties of things themselves, nor do they merely express subjective attitudes. Rather, value judgments say something we believe is true about the world. Thus Dewey's contextualism challenged both metaphysics and emotivism as possible homes for values. He did not seek an ultimate normative standard, but investigated the social conditions under which we consider our assertions warranted. For Dewey, interpretation that arises within dialogue was the only appropriate method for morality, rather than pure reason or divine revelation.

3. Carey taught a seminar at Columbia University to "sensitize students to ethical and political considerations that underlie . . . contemporary journalism." Its first week centered on stories and asked, "What is the relation between journalism and other expressive arts—fiction, history, etc.?" This unit—titled "Why Write? Why Tell Stories?"—assigned Robert Coles's *The Call of Stories: Teaching and the Moral Imagination* (1989).

Sources

Bakhtin, Mikhail M. 1983. *The dialogical imagination: Four essays*, trans. C. Emerson and M. Holquist. Austin: University of Texas Press.

Buber, Martin. 1958. *I and thou*, 2nd ed., trans. R. G. Smith. New York: Scribner's.

Buber, Martin. 1965. *Between man and man*, trans. W. Kaufmann. New York: Macmillan.

Carey, James W. 1987. Journalists just leave: The ethics of an anomalous profession. In *Ethics and the media*, ed. Maile-Gene Sagen, pp. 5–19. Iowa City: Iowa Humanities Board.

Carey, James W. 1988. *Communication as culture*. Boston: Unwin Hyman.

Coles, Robert. 1989. *The call of stories: Teaching and the moral imagination*. Orlando, FL: Houghton Mifflin.

Descartes, René. [1641] 1998. *Meditations and other metaphysical writings*, trans. D. M. Clarke. London: Penguin.

Dewey, John. 1930. *Human nature and conduct*. New York: Modern Library.

Fisher, Walter R. 1987. *Human communication as narration: Toward a philosophy of reason, value, and action*. Columbia: University of South Carolina Press.

Freire, Paolo. 1970. *Pedagogy of the oppressed*. New York: Seabury.

Freire, Paolo. 1973. *Education for critical consciousness*. New York: Seabury.

Hauerwas, Stanley. 1981. *A community of character*. Notre Dame, IN: University of Notre Dame.

Langer, Susanne K. 1957. *Philosophy in a new key: A study of the symbolism of reason, rite, and art*, 3rd ed. Cambridge, MA: Harvard University Press.

Levinas, Emmanuel. 1981. *Ethics and infinity*, trans. R. A. Cohen. Pittsburgh, PA: Duquesne University Press.

Locke, John. 1689/2003. *Two treatises on government*. New Haven, CT: Yale University Press.

MacIntyre, Alasdair. 2007. *After virtue: A study in moral theory*. Notre Dame, IN: University of Notre Dame Press.

Noddings, Nel. 1984. *Caring: A feminine approach to ethics and moral education*. Berkeley: University of California Press.

Afterword

We must not see any *person as an abstraction. Instead, we must see in every person a universe with its own secrets, with its own treasures, with its own sources of anguish, and with some measure of triumph.*

Elie Wiesel

This word cloud created at wordle.net shows the top 150 most used terms of the approximately 140,000 in this book and highlights the main themes—images, media, news, people, and so on. (Courtesy of Paul Martin Lester.)

Sources

Wiesel, Elie. 1992. Foreword. In George J. Annas and Michael A. Grodin, *The Nazi doctors and the Nuremberg code: Human rights in human experimentation* (p. ix). New York: Oxford University Press.

Wordle.net (accessed March 31, 2010).

Glossary

Agency   Within the context of rhetoric, the capacity of an individual to act to express one's own identity, to communicate effectively with others or as a component of political action intended to advance certain objectives or achieve particular results.

Archetype   A pattern that emerges from active mental processing that helps reconcile and explain complex and often contradictory characteristics of the human psyche.

Commodification   The act of treating someone or a group of people as a thing that can be bought and sold, valuable only for its usefulness to the owner. *See* Objectification.

Construct   A real or imagined concept.

Construction   *See* Social Construction.

Dialogic   Related to discussion among individuals.

Discourse   A connection of utterances or texts. The formal body of speech and writings on a topic.

Frame   The discursive context used to interpret and understand texts. The repeated and common use of cultural presumptions and presuppositions to encode and decode language.

Genre   A category of artistic expression identified by similarities in form, style, approach or topic.

Griefing   In a multi-person gamer, or virtual world, to engage in harassing, disturbing, and annoying other players rather than to pursue the game's objective.

Hegemony   Dominance through acquiescence of those being overpowered.

Heteronormative   Related to the support of opposite gender pairings as the sole normal human sexual choice.

Heuristic   An aid to learning or understanding. Experience-based skills that help solve problems. Self-educating mental techniques that improve performance and assist understanding.

Icon and Iconic images   A representative symbol of something. A well-known linguistic sign that directly or figuratively represents or stands in for the thing it signifies.

Individuation   In Jungian psychology, the open-ended process of maturing to become wholly oneself. Psychological integration of the conscious and the unconscious.

Lexicon   The meaningful symbols or figurative vocabulary of a person, group or field of knowledge.

Locus   The perceived position or place of something abstract.

Marginalization   Social oppression and exclusion of entire groups of people from the core functioning of society.

Media   Environments of communication, both internal and external to individuals, that encompass the body's brain and nervous system, clothing and possessions, gestures and handwriting, architecture and art, as well as all forms of mass media, such as television, publications, film and the internet.

Mediatype   Any stereotype that is repeatedly constructed, enacted, and disseminated via television, film, radio, internet, smartphones, and other forms of communication.

Meme   Through analogy to genetic inheritance, an idea or cultural practice that replicates through repetition and imitation and may evolve through the mutation of misunderstanding or produce new variants through combination with other ideas or practices.

Metaphor   A figure of speech that applies a word or phrase to an act or thing to which it does not *literally* apply. A symbolic representation or description of something or someone.

Miscegenation   Reproduction by and the offspring of couples of different races.

Objectification   The act of degrading a human being to the status of a mere object. *See* Commodification.

Other[ness]   The construction of boundaries to identify something as different, or other, within the process of defining and constituting the self. The use of the oppositional other to delineate, segregate, exclude, subordinate, or oppress as a mechanism of power. That which is not the same as oneself or one's own group and can therefore be objectified, demonized, or dehumanized.

Postmodernism   A genre of art that rejects the overly optimistic stance of modernism for ironic, self-referencing principles and practices.

Rhetor   Originally, an orator; figuratively, the means by which an idea or concept is effectively or persuasively communicated to leave a strong, lasting impression.

Schema(ta)   A mental construct of some aspect of the world. A mental model that aids information interpretation and processing by relying on rapid determination of what is common among a group or set. A mental framework that organizes information about a specific theme or topic to assist assimilating and understanding new ideas and information.

Semiotic   Describing the nature, use and interpretation of signs and symbols in text and talk.

Simulacra   The image or representation of someone or something, usually unsatisfactory, partial or negative.

Social Construction   A communication-based theory that suggests that humans understand reality less through our direct personal experience of it and more through our mental composite of ideas, images, texts and, finally experiences. The mental assemblage through which one views and understands reality.

Symbol   A sign that represents or stands for something else.

Symbolization   The use of symbols to covey meaning.

Trope   A conventional or established idea or phrase. A figurative or metaphoric use of a word or expression.

Index

About the Contributors

HELENA BILANDZIC, Ph.D., is a professor of media and communication at the Zeppelin University, Friedrichshafen, Germany. Her current research interests include narrative processing and persuasion, cultivation, media use, and methodology. She has also taught at universities in Munich, Erfurt, Ilmenau, Berlin, and Hamburg. She is vice chair of the Audience and Reception Studies Division of ECREA and associate editor of *Communications: The European Journal of Communication.*

JAMES W. BROWN has photographed and written about the Lenape, or Delaware, Native Americans for the last decade, with a focus on efforts to pass along a nearly lost culture to younger people of the tribe. He first became aware of the Delawares when he was inducted into the Order of the Arrow, the Boy Scouts of America national honorary society. His work on the Lenape has taken him from Arizona to Ohio, with the majority effort in Oklahoma and Indiana. Since 1982, Brown has directed the Indiana University School of Journalism at Indiana University–Purdue University Indianapolis. He is a full professor and a 2009 inductee into the Indiana Journalism Hall of Fame.

RICK BUSSELLE, Ph.D., is an associate professor in the Murrow College of Communication at Washington State University. His research focuses on narrative processing, cultivation, and the social construction of reality surrounding issues of crime, race, and poverty.

DIANE CARTER is an adjunct faculty member in the Department of Psychology and Communication Studies at the University of Idaho and a Ph.D. candidate at the Edward R. Murrow College of Communication at Washington State University. Her dissertation examines how systematic distortions in communication in and about the intercountry adoption system mask problematic social and global inequities and reproduce capitalist ideology at the expense of disadvantaged children in the United States and abroad. She is an adoptive mother of two children from Russia.

MANOUCHEKA CELESTE is a doctoral candidate in communication at the University of Washington (UW). She studies transnational media representations of race, class, gender, and citizenship. She focuses on the Caribbean, including Haiti, Latin America, and the United States, with a particular focus on gendered and racialized representations in popular culture, including Haitian artist Wyclef Jean and Beyoncé Knowles. She is interested in the relationship between (re)presentation and material realities. She cofounded the Women of Color Collective at UW and the Dialoguing Difference Conference. Prior to attending UW, Manoucheka earned a B.S. in journalism and an M.A. in mass communication from the University of Florida, where she was inducted into the university's Hall of Fame. She thanks her advisors Jerry Baldasty, Michelle Habell-Pallan, Susan Harewood, Habiba Ibrahim, and Ralina L. Joseph for their unwavering support and Drs. Joseph and Harewood for their extensive feedback with this particular project.

RAMÓN (RAY) CHÁVEZ is the director of the Oklahoma Institute for Diversity in Journalism at the Gaylord College, University of Oklahoma. He is a founding member and former board member of the National Association of Hispanic Journalists and is a member of the Native American Journalists Association.

CLIFFORD CHRISTIANS is a research professor of communications at the University of Illinois–Urbana, where he is also a professor of media and cinema studies and a professor of journalism. He has been a visiting scholar in ethics at Princeton, Oxford, and the University of Chicago. His latest books, which he has coedited or coauthored, are *Media Ethics: Cases and Moral Reasoning* (8th ed.); *Normative Theories of the Media*; *Handbook of Mass Media Ethics*; *Ethical Communication: Moral Stances in Human Dialogue*; and *Key Concepts in Critical Cultural Studies*.

J. B. COLSON earned a B.F.A. in photography from Ohio University. After doing news and documentary photography in Central America as a U.S. Army Signal Corps photographer, he completed graduate studies in documentary film at University of California, Los Angeles. He made nontheatrical films in the Detroit area before teaching at the University of Texas, where he inaugurated an accredited program in photojournalism. For more than 20 years, he headed it with students at the bachelor's, master's, and Ph.D. levels. In the 1980s, he worked in Mexico with Professor Jean Meyer and the Colegio de Michoacán documenting village life, and he produced work he displayed in seven one-man exhibitions. He currently teaches a seminar on the criticism of photography. His essays include the introduction to the book *Russell Lee Photographs*.

AMANDA DECKER is a master's candidate in journalism and media studies at the University of South Florida, St. Petersburg. She holds a bachelor's degree from the State University of New York at Binghamton, where she studied philosophy, politics, and law. Her research interests include communication and cultural studies.

EVERETTE E. DENNIS is the Felix E. Larkin Distinguished Professor in the Fordham Graduate School of Business at Lincoln Center, New York City, where he directs the Center for Communication. He is author and coauthor of many books, including *Understanding Media in the Digital Age* (Allyn & Bacon 2010). Formerly, he was founding director of the Media Studies Center at Columbia University and founding president of the American Academy in Berlin.

AUDRA R. DIERS, Ph.D., is an assistant professor in public relations at Marist College. She specializes in crisis response and strategic communication. While most of her work focuses on the relationships between crises, organizations, and stakeholders, she is also interested in applying these concepts to issues of social justice in both national and international contexts. From 1998 to 1999, she studied and worked with the Lesbian Gay Bisexual and Transgendered Association at the University of Wyoming both before and after Matthew Shepard's murder.

BONNIE L. DREWNIANY is an associate professor at the University of South Carolina, where she teaches creative strategy in advertising, advertising campaigns, and a seminar on Super Bowl commercials. She is coauthor of *Creative Strategy in Advertising* (with A. Jerome Jewler).

DENI ELLIOTT is the Eleanor Poynter Jamison Professor of Media Ethics and Press Policy at the University of South Florida, St. Petersburg. She is graduate director in the Department of Journalism and Media Studies and serves as the university's ombudsperson. Elliott also serves as the ethics officer for the Metropolitan Water District of Southern California. Elliott has published books, chapters, and articles for scholarly, trade, and lay audiences in several areas of practical ethics.

WILLARD F. ENTEMAN is professor of philosophy, emeritus, at Rhode Island College. Previously, he was provost and professor of philosophy at Union College in New York as well as president and professor of philosophy at Bowdoin College in Maine. He has taught on a visiting basis at a number of universities as well as at the Poynter Institute in Florida. His books include *The Problem of Free Will* and *Managerialism: The Emergence of a New Ideology*. He has written numerous articles on philosophical topics and on higher education. He is currently working in an area he calls "found philosophy," which means examining philosophical approaches taken by people not normally considered part of hardcore philosophy. For example, he is working on the philosophic assumptions in Native-American stories and on the metaphysical assumptions of the legal status of the corporation. He would be glad to hear from people who would like to follow up on topics addressed in his chapter. The easiest way to reach him is through email at wenteman@gmail.com, which he monitors regularly.

LUCY A. GANJE is professor of art/graphic design at the University of North Dakota, where she founded the Native Media Center and teaches a course on American Indian art.

KATHERINE L. HATFIELD-EDSTROM, Ph.D., is an assistant professor of communication studies at Creighton University. She specializes in areas of rhetoric and public culture, visual and political communication, and argumentation and public address. As a critical scholar, she is interested in the communicative nature of the visual. Her research has involved topics as varied as HIV/AIDS, terrorism, iconicity, public service campaigns, and health. She is the secretary of the National Communication Association's Visual Communication division. She happily resides in Omaha, Nebraska, and is a member of the Creighton Community.

DINA IBRAHIM teaches radio and television production courses. Her research interests are in analyzing the post-9/11 visual framing of U.S. television news representations of Muslims as well as the psychological impact of television depictions on Jewish and Muslim audiences in the United States and the Middle East. She has reported for the BBC World Service Radio in London; CNN in Atlanta and Cairo; NPR in Austin, Texas; and United Press International in Cairo.

NANCY BETH JACKSON, Ph.D., has written extensively for the *New York Times* and the *International Herald Tribune* and authored a history of the International Junior League. She directed the Penney-Missouri Awards Program and the Bloomberg College Editors' Leadership Workshop. She also taught at Columbia University, the University of Missouri, the American University of Paris, the American University of Cairo, and Zayed University in Abu Dhabi.

LEE JOLLIFFE is a woman who became interested in men's rights and roles when her then-husband stayed home with their child while she became an associate professor of journalism. She teaches visual communication, media design, writing, and honors courses at Drake University. Author of more than 80 research papers and articles and more than 200 magazine articles and newspaper columns, she is now embarked on a historical novel set in the first-century Mediterranean region.

PAUL MARTIN LESTER is a professor of communications at California State University, Fullerton. He is the author of *Visual Communication: Images with Messages* (5th ed.); *On Floods and Photo Ops: How Herbert Hoover and George W. Bush Exploited Catastrophes*; and *Photojournalism: An Ethical Approach*. He is also the editor of the *Visual Communication Quarterly*. He is proud to report that he is a product of three of his professors who also contributed to this edition: Jim Brown, J. B. Colson, and Ev Dennis.

DEBRA L. MERSKIN is an associate professor in the School of Journalism and Communication at the University of Oregon. She teaches courses about the representation of race, gender, and class. Her research has appeared in numerous journals, including *The Howard Journal of Communication, American Behavioral Scientist, Sex Roles*, and *Mass Communication & Society*. She currently is completing a book on the psychological and cultural underpinnings of gender, race, and class stereotypes in U.S. media and serves as coeditor, with Mary-Lou Galician, of *Critical Readings on Sex, Love, Romance in the Media: Media Literacy Applications*.

MARGUERITE MORITZ is professor and UNESCO Chair in International Journalism Education at the University of Colorado. Her research looks at professional codes and practices in contemporary news and entertainment media. She examines the creation and use of still and video images in the digital era; the representations of women, gays, and other marginalized groups; and the impact of crisis reporting on journalists and their subjects. Her doctorate is from the Department of Radio, Television and Film at Northwestern University.

LAWRENCE MULLEN, Ph.D., is professor of media studies in the Hank Greenspun School of Journalism and Media Studies at the University of Nevada, Las Vegas. His interest in virtual worlds springs from his work in visual studies, and he has published works on the visual representation of the president of the United States, the history of visual literacy, and the techniques of visual data collection, to name a few.

JACK A. NELSON is emeritus professor of communication at Brigham Young University. His book *The Disabled, the Media, and the Information Age* (1994) became a standard in disability studies. His chapter "Virtual Reality: A Brave New World for Those with Disabilities" (1994) probes into the future that still may be unfolding for those with serious handicaps. Nelson has published and presented widely in the disability movement. He has been a paraplegic since the age of 18 and uses a wheelchair, from which he still hunts and fishes. He has worked on newspapers and magazines. In addition to disability, he has specialized in the frontier press and the press of Latin America. He has traveled widely in Central America doing research on the emerging press there.

JULIANNE H. NEWTON is associate dean for undergraduate affairs and professor of visual communication in the University of Oregon School of Journalism and Communication. She is author of *The Burden of Visual Truth: The Role of Photojournalism in Mediating Reality*, and coauthor (with Rick Williams) of *Visual Communication: Integrating Media, Art and Science*, which won the 2009 Marshall McLuhan Award for Outstanding Book in Media Ecology. Her publications span scholarly, professional, and public forums, and her documentary photographs have been exhibited internationally.

PAULA M. POINDEXTER has worked as a newspaper manager and executive at the *Los Angeles Times* and as a reporter and producer at KPRC-TV, the

NBC-affiliate TV station in Houston. Her research and teaching primarily focus on diversity in news coverage, the audience for news, and research methods and ethics. Poindexter's most recent book is *Women, Men, and News: Divided and Disconnected in the News Media Landscape*. Poindexter, who earned her Ph.D. from Syracuse University, is currently the graduate advisor in the School of Journalism at the University of Texas at Austin. An associate professor of journalism, she was interviewed by CNN about her research in diversity in news as part of the *Black in America* documentary. In 2009, Poindexter received AEJMC's inaugural Lionel C. Barrow Jr. Award for Distinguished Achievement in Diversity Research and Education.

HENRY PUENTE is an assistant professor of communications at California State University, Fullerton. He specializes in the marketing and distribution of U.S. Latino films. Prior to becoming an academic, Puente worked in the entertainment industry for several years and has held various positions in broadcasting, film, and special events programming.

KATHY BRITTAIN RICHARDSON is a professor of communication at Berry College. She has a B.A. in communication and religion/philosophy from Shorter College, and an M.A. in journalism and Ph.D. in mass communication from the Grady College of Journalism and Mass Communication at the University of Georgia. She is a coauthor of *Media Ethics: Cases and Moral Reasoning* and *Applied Public Relations: Cases in Stakeholder Management*. She serves as editor of *Journalism & Communication Monographs*. She has published journal articles and book chapters addressing media ethics, music videos, product placement, visual imagery, communication pedagogy, and student press regulation.

SUSAN DENTE ROSS is professor of English at Washington State University and founding director of Paxim, a research consortium on peace communication. She is a Fulbright Fellow and Sr. Scholar and has held research and distinguished faculty fellowships at Eastern Mediterranean University, Netanya College, the University of the Aegean, the University of Calgary, and UNESCO. She has published widely on the roles of the law and of the media in advancing social equity, justice, and peace.

CHEMA SALINAS is a doctoral student in communication studies at Arizona State University. His background in music as a performer and sound engineer grounds his work in rhetoric and performance studies. The rhetorical properties and cultural implications of music and other forms of artistic expression (which include the creation and maintenance of counterpublics around musical genres as well as the visual expression of tattoos and other body modifications) constitute the core of his interest. Having several large and obvious tattoos, he has felt firsthand the painful stigmatizations to which modified bodies are commonly subjected.

PAULA MARIE SENIORS, an assistant professor in Africana studies and sociology at Virginia Tech, won the Letitia Woods Brown Memorial Prize from the Association of Black Women Historians for her book, *Beyond "Lift Every Voice and Sing": The Culture of Uplift, Identity, and Politics in Black Musical Theater* (2009). She also has published "Transforming the *Carmen* Narrative: The Case of *Carmen the Hip Hopera*," in *Message in the Music: Hip Hop, History, and Pedagogy*; "Jack Johnson, Paul Robeson and the Hyper Masculine African American Übermensch," in *Harlem Renaissance: Politics, Arts, Letters*; "Cole and Johnson's *The Red Moon* (1908–1910): Reimagining African American and Native American Female Education at Hampton Institute," in *The Journal of African American History*; "Red, Black, and Yellow, Conquest, Slavery, and Indispensable Labor: Teaching and Learning American History through a Multicultural Curriculum," in *The Black History Bulletin*; and "Ada Overton Walker, Abbie Mitchell and the Gibson Girl: Reconstructing African American Womanhood," in *The International Journal of Africana Studies*.

GWEN SHARP received her Ph.D. from the University of Wisconsin–Madison and is an assistant professor of sociology at Nevada State College. She teaches in the areas of gender, race and ethnicity, sexuality, and pop culture. Her research addresses the sociology of agriculture, qualitative methods, American Indian land rights, gender and the body, and pedagogical techniques. Her current research looks at representations of gender and reproduction in biology textbooks and the cultural bases for the continued dominance of family farmers in the U.S. beef industry. She coedits the website Sociological Images (www.contexts.org/socimages).

MELVIN D. SLATER is a military retiree who served as a graphic artist and a communications officer in the U.S Army Signal Corps. He has worked as a broadcast journalist and public affairs specialist for the U.S. Army, as a web producer for the *Augusta Chronicle*, and as a production assistant for

WJBF News Channel 6 in Augusta, Georgia. His research interests include mass media effects on public discourse and media ethics. He holds a B.A. in telecommunications and an M.S.A. in corporate communications, and is currently working toward a Ph.D. in mass communication at the University of South Carolina.

ERIN STEUTER is professor of sociology at Mount Allison University, where she specializes in examining the ideological representations of the news. Recipient of multiple awards for her teaching and research, her published works have appeared in *Political Communication and Persuasion, Canadian Journal of Communication, Journal of American and Comparative Cultures*, and other noted academic journals. She and Deborah Wills are coauthors of *At War with Metaphor: Media Propaganda and Racism in the War on Terror* (2008).

LISA WADE is an assistant professor of sociology at Occidental College. After earning an M.A. in human sexuality from New York University, she turned to sociology and earned her M.S. and Ph.D. from the University of Wisconsin–Madison. Her research addresses the relationship between social inequality and the body, especially as sexuality becomes a marker of difference. Her primary research project examines how contests between social actors (e.g., journalists, activists, doctors, and politicians) over the meaning of genital-cutting practices (in the United States and elsewhere) reveal the body as socially constructed in ways that reproduce or challenge hierarchies in both abstract and concrete ways. She coedits the website Sociological Images (www.contexts.org/socimages).

RICK WILLIAMS is dean of the Division of the Arts at Lane Community College and executive director of ArtsWork for Education. His publications include theoretical and practical explorations of the use of arts and visual communication to enhance creativity, intelligence, problem solving, decisionmaking, and performance. He is author and photographer of the visual ethnographic book *Working Hands*, and coauthor (with Julianne Newton) of *Visual Communication: Integrating Media, Art and Science*, which won the 2009 Marshall McLuhan Award for Outstanding Book in Media Ecology.

DEBORAH WILLS is associate professor of English at Mount Allison University. She has received awards for her teaching and her writing. Her research areas include disability and illness in poetry, eschatology, science fiction and cyberpunk, magic realism, and violence in literature and film. Her research is published in *Reconstruction: Studies in Contemporary Culture*; the *Journal of War and Culture Studies*; and other noted academic journals. She and Erin Steuter are coauthors of *At War with Metaphor: Media Propaganda and Racism in the War on Terror* (2008).

MICHELLE A. WOLF teaches media and social issues, media research, media literacy, and pedagogy courses and conducts qualitative research on media representations of disenfranchised groups. She is especially interested in the range and diversity of mass-mediated images of and stories about marginalized and often powerless communities, and the exclusion of certain cultural groups from these representations. Professor Wolf has been active in media literacy efforts and issues surrounding electronic media representations since the 1970s.